JOAN OF ARC IN THE ENGLISH

IMAGINATION, 1429–1829

# JOAN OF ARC IN THE ENGLISH IMAGINATION, 1429–1829

GAIL ORGELFINGER

THE PENNSYLVANIA STATE UNIVERSITY PRESS | UNIVERSITY PARK, PENNSYLVANIA

Library of Congress Cataloging-in-Publication Data

Names: Orgelfinger, Gail Margaret, 1951– author.
Title: Joan of Arc in the English imagination, 1429–1829 / Gail Orgelfinger.
Description: University Park, Pennsylvania : The Pennsylvania State University Press, [2019] | Includes bibliographical references and index.
Summary: "Explores representations of Joan of Arc in English culture from 1429 until the early nineteenth century, examining the factors that shaped retellings of her military successes and execution"—Provided by publisher.
Identifiers: LCCN 2018044814 | ISBN 9780271082189 (cloth : alk. paper)
Subjects: LCSH: Joan, of Arc, Saint, 1412–1431—In literature. | English Literature—History and criticism.
Classification: LCC PR153.J63 O74 2019 | DDC 820.9/351—dc23
LC record available at https://lccn.loc.gov /2018044814

Copyright © 2019 Gail Orgelfinger
All rights reserved
Printed in the United States of America
Published by
The Pennsylvania State University Press,
University Park, PA 16802-1003

The Pennsylvania State University Press is a member of the Association of University Presses.

It is the policy of The Pennsylvania State University Press to use acid-free paper. Publications on uncoated stock satisfy the minimum requirements of American National Standard for Information Sciences—Permanence of Paper for Printed Library Material, ANSI Z39.48–1992.

For my sister, another redoubtable Joan,
and in memory of my mother.

CONTENTS

List of Illustrations | ix
Acknowledgments | xi
A Note on the Text | xiii

Introduction: "Those Cursed Breeches" | 1

1. "We Have Burned a Saint": Joan of Arc and the English in France | 13

2. "The Martiall Maide": Joan of Arc and the French in England | 36

3. "Penthesilea Did It. Why Not She?": An English Virago | 63

4. "A Pievish Painted Puzel": Joan of Arc and Mary Queen of Scots in *1 Henry VI* | 94

5. "Tom Paine in Petticoats": Domesticating Joan of Arc | 127

Afterword: "Is That Meant to Be Me?" | 161

Notes | 165
Bibliography | 191
Index | 221

ILLUSTRATIONS

MAP
1. The Geography of Joan of Arc's Youth. Map © Ellen Heo | 25

FIGURES
1. Statue of Sancta Joanna de Arc, Winchester Cathedral. Photo © Dr. John Crook | 2
2. Thomas Fuller, *The Profane State*, 1642. Photo: Library of Congress | 69
3. Frontispiece to *1 Henry VI*, ed. Nicholas Rowe, 1709. Photo: Folger Shakespeare Library | 117
4. Frontispiece to *1 Henry VI*, ed. Nicholas Rowe, 1714. Photo: Folger Shakespeare Library | 118
5. W. N. Gardiner, *La Pucelle d'Orleans*, Harding's Shakespeare, 1793. Photo: Folger Shakespeare Library | 120
6. "Mrs. Baddeley in the Character of Joan la Pucelle," 1776. Photo: Folger Shakespeare Library | 121
7. "Miss Stuart as Joan la Pucelle," 1776. Photo: Folger Shakespeare Library | 121
8. William Hamilton, "Joan of Arc and the Furies," 1795. Photo: Folger Shakespeare Library | 122
9. Charles Turner Warren, "King Henry VI, Part I," 1806. Photo: Folger Shakespeare Library | 122
10. Alan R. Branston, "Then take my soul," 1810. Photo: Folger Shakespeare Library | 123
11. Henry Fuseli, "Enter Fiends," 1805. Photo: Folger Shakespeare Library | 123
12. John Thurston, "Break thou in pieces!," 1826. Photo: Folger Shakespeare Library | 124
13. Joan of Arc donning armor. Photo: Folger Shakespeare Library | 128
14. John Opie, "Joan of Arc Declaring Her Mission," 1806. Photo: Folger Shakespeare Library | 146
15. John Thurston, "Joan of Arc in Prison," from Hume, *History of England*, 1803. Photo: University of Maryland, Baltimore County | 146
16. Leicester Cathedral East Window. Photo: Leicester Cathedral Chapter | 162
17. Leicester Cathedral, detail: Joan of Arc. Photo: Will Johnston Photography | 163

ACKNOWLEDGMENTS

My interest in Joan of Arc was initially piqued when I included excerpts from her trial testimony in a course titled The Literature of Chivalry. My students were fascinated by the words of a young woman around their own age whose life turned into legend. I became fascinated as well, and designed another course, Images of Joan of Arc. Because I taught in the English department, we focused on English and American texts about the Maid, and in the course of exploring this literature, I discovered a great deal of variety in English approaches to rewriting her story. My first debt of gratitude, then, goes to the many students at the University of Maryland, Baltimore County—English majors and nonmajors alike—who contributed their own questions and imaginations to our study of the Maid in England.

This book focuses on times gone by, but I could never have accomplished the research without the ongoing revolution in electronic resources. While I also consulted traditional monographs and articles, even microfilm, the generosity of some of the great world libraries and the efforts of individuals enabled me to read manuscripts and early printed books online in their original forms. Access to many of them was provided through the library system of the University of Maryland. Even in the twenty-first century, however, human beings remain essential for the exchange of ideas and for help and support with research. The reference and interlibrary loan staffs at the Albert Kuhn Library at UMBC were dogged and tireless in tracking down sources whenever I asked, and they succeeded every single time. Special thanks to Robin Moskal and Lidia Schechter of UMBC, as well as Paul Espinosa, Curator, George Peabody Library, Johns Hopkins University; Michael Zeliff at the McKeldin Library, University of Maryland, College Park; Catherine Maguire at the Maryland Law Library, Annapolis; and Abbie Weinberg of the Folger Shakespeare Library, Washington, D.C.

The English Department and Dresher Center for the Humanities at UMBC offered opportunities for me to speak about my early ideas and receive feedback. Funding provided by my department as well as by the College of Arts, Humanities, and Social Sciences enabled me to travel to present a number of papers exploring preliminary ideas for this book. Thanks especially to Dean Emeritus John Jeffries, and English Department Chairs Jessica Berman, Christopher Corbett, and Orianne Smith. My colleagues in the English and History departments, the Honors College, and the Medieval and Early Modern Studies Minor program—notably Raphael Falco, Thomas Field, James Grubb, Preminda Jacob, Susan McDonough, Kate McKinley, Michele Osherow, Anna Shields, and Simon Stacey—also offered much support and advice.

The International Joan of Arc Society, most of all its founder, Bonnie Wheeler, encouraged my work for over a decade. Other members of the society—and those who participated in its yearly sessions at the International Medieval Congress at Western Michigan University—warmly supported my efforts, and gave honest and valuable feedback: Jeremy Adams (who, sadly, died as I was completing the manuscript), Ann Astell, Stephanie Coker, Kelly DeVries, Nora Heimann, Nadia Margolis, Jane Marie Pinzino, Craig Taylor, Larissa J. Taylor, and especially Deborah Fraioli.

Throughout the long decade of thought and writing, Robin Farabaugh was a steadfast friend and excellent sounding board. Katherine Zapantis Keller and Amy Froide read the entire manuscript and gave me many fine suggestions. The anonymous reviewers for Penn State University Press helped me make this a better book than I could have accomplished on my own. Working with the Press has been a thoroughly rewarding experience, and I owe special gratitude to my editor Eleanor Goodman, who patiently listened to yearly updates and provided both frank and empathetic support.

Thanks are not adequate for my chief sustainer, supporter, and patient listener, Chuck Hanna, my husband and partner these forty years and more.

A NOTE ON THE TEXT

During the first session of her trial, Joan was asked her name and surname, and she answered, "Where she was born she was called Jeannette, and in France, Jeanne; and she knew nothing of her surname." She did not use her father's or mother's informal surnames, Darc and Romée.[1] She signed (or dictated) her letters "Jeanne la Pucelle," or simply "La Pucelle." In Craig Taylor's words, this epithet "celebrated Joan's youth and virginity, and in the process constructed a different, empowering identity for her, to stand against the more familiar roles of wife, mother or widow."[2] She did not call herself "The Maid of Orleans." Thus, in a book about English perceptions of the Maid, I shall use the English version of her name, Joan, unless quoting directly from a French or Latin source or referring to a fictional character.

In general, I have silently expanded contractions in both Latin and English texts. Otherwise, except for replacing /þ/ with /th/, /vv/ with /w/ and substituting /j/ for /i/, /u/ for /v/, and vice versa for readability, I have retained original spellings.

Unless otherwise indicated, all translations are my own.

# INTRODUCTION

## *"Those Cursed Breeches"*

> Fatal to England, Fortunate to France;
> Of th'one I curb'd the surly Arrogance;
> And with my Lance the tott'ring Throne sustain'd
> Of th'other Realm, whose Freedome I regain'd.
>     The smoakie Ordures of the burning Pile
>     Could not my spotless Innocence defile;
>     And my opprobrious Death more mischief brought
>     To those that caus'd it, then my Arm that fought.
> —Pierre Le Moyne, "Sonnet," *The Gallery of Heroick Women*, 1652

Standing tall in golden armor and gazing heavenward past the point of her raised sword, the statue of Sancta Joanna de Arc in the retrochoir of Winchester Cathedral (see fig.1) seems oblivious to the nearby tomb of Cardinal Henry Beaufort, bishop of Winchester, who reportedly wept at the sight of her execution yet ordered her ashes to be thrown into the river Seine.[1] The young peasant girl had persuaded the dauphin, nobility, and ecclesiastics of France during a time of crisis in 1429 that God had mandated her mission to raise the siege of Orléans and crown Charles VII king. Barely a year after her triumphs, she was captured and sold to the English, who tried her on charges of heresy and, after months of interrogation, burned her alive in the marketplace of Rouen.

FIGURE 1   Statue of Sancta Joanna de Arc, Winchester Cathedral.

Five hundred years later, a fundraising appeal for the Winchester memorial, dedicated in 1923, explains it as "a slight act of reparation, and as an earnest that we in England join in the admiration and reverence for her with the great nation which in her days was our gallant enemy, but which has now become our trusted friend and heroic ally."[2] Coming just five years after the end of World War I, and three years after Joan's canonization by the Catholic Church, this acknowledgment would seem to place a period on a centuries-long evolution of English opinion.

The story of Joan of Arc has been told and retold in England for six hundred years, beginning in her own lifetime. It is in some sense a tidy narrative, charting the conversion of English sentiment from demonization to devotion—in the words of James Darmesteter, "witch, heroine, saint in turn." The London chronicle of 1429 called her a "wycche." In the seventeenth century, the churchman Thomas Fuller only half-humorously suggested that God alone could know "whether Saint, Witch, Man, Maid or Whore."[3] In the twentieth century, more than one English World War I memorial featured her image. And so it is, in essence, true that Joan's story changes in tandem with English changes of heart—from official denunciation to sheepish remorse, focusing on the national characteristic of magnanimity, to assimilation. But that is not the whole picture.

The idea for this book arose out of a research experiment that actually had nothing directly to do with Joan of Arc. Over a decade ago, I was exploring the newly launched Internet Library of Early Journals to evaluate its usefulness for a writing assignment. To test its search and browse capabilities, I chose *The Gentleman's Magazine* and entered "Joan of Arc." An article dated May 7, 1737, appeared, and I was dumbstruck at its tone. Here is a brief excerpt: "The French blame the English, for having on Pretext of Witchcraft unjustly burned Joan of Arc, whose sole Crime was the having very successfully served her King and Country, the English now agree, that their Fore-Fathers did amiss in acting so contrary to the Laws of Equity, and what is termed Bonne Guerre." However, the essay continues, the English "would have spared Joan's Life, but they insisted on her laying aside those cursed Breeches, of which she was so obstinately fond."[4] In reality, Joan had agreed to wear women's clothing to save her life when threatened with immolation in late May 1431. Days later, she was once more clad in men's garb because, she was reported to have said, she "preferred" it, and to her it was "more lawful and appropriate to keep men's clothing when she was among men than women's clothing."[5] But her English guards had apparently removed her woman's dress overnight, leaving her with a choice between keeping her word or guarding her modesty. The priest Jean Massieu, an usher at Joan's trial, later testified that "at length, compelled by a call of nature, she took the male clothing, for there was no other clothing to be had from her guards that day."[6] Guillaume Manchon, a notary, recalled that when asked, Joan had declared that she acted to defend her chastity against the threats of her jailers.[7] However, *The Gentleman's Magazine* explained Joan's "relapse" otherwise: "The Holy Heroine, at length finding that she absolutely must resolve to die, or return to wearing Petticoats, determined on the latter. But the Mischief of all was, that she put on the Petticoat without advising with *S. Catherine*, who, on returning to make her a Visit in Prison, was very angry at finding her dressed like a Woman." Although the author acknowledges a trustworthy French source, the parliamentarian Etienne Pasquier's *Les Recherches de la France* (1560), the diction—"petticoats" and "cursed breeches"—instantly undercuts any serious consideration of the relationship between Joan's male apparel and her execution. And its tone foreshadows Samuel Taylor Coleridge's famous critique of the Maid in Robert Southey's 1796 epic poem, *Joan of Arc*, as "a Tom Paine in petticoats."[8]

Aside from tone, however, the *Gentleman's Magazine* article also demonstrates a propensity for English writers to "translate" their French or Latin sources on Joan of Arc rather freely. Pasquier was one of the earliest writers to consult the transcripts of both of the Maid's trials: her 1431 condemnation and the hearing that nullified her conviction in 1456. He updated and revised his *Recherches de la France* throughout his lifetime. It was frequently reprinted, including in 1723, shortly before the *Gentleman's Magazine* article.[9] The English writer seems to have read Pasquier's chapter on Joan rather carefully. He acknowledges an English breach of chivalric honor. After Joan's capture at Compiègne in May 1430, Pasquier writes, the English, "abandoning the usual procedure observed for prisoners of war, resolved to put her on trial."[10] Pasquier twice affirms that Joan resumed her male garments "by the express commandment of the saints" and "by the counsel she had during the night." But as for Saint Catherine's horror at her *jupons*, Pasquier has nothing to say.

With that article as a starting point, I began to examine not only what English writers had to say about the career and execution of Joan of Arc but also the context in which they wrote and the genres they chose. The Joan who appeared in early chronicles during the turmoil of the fifteenth century was a one-dimensional "witch," and that identity was exploited in demonologies well into the nineteenth century. Consider that her English antagonists, chiefly John, Duke of Bedford, Regent of France for Henry VI (and Cardinal Beaufort's half nephew) had every reason to vilify the Maid and, through her, the king she had set up in contravention of the 1420 Treaty of Troyes, which declared the heir of Henry V monarch of both England and France.[11] Bedford publicly referred to her as "disciple and limb of the fiend."[12] Indeed, most famously in the case of the main sources for *1 Henry VI*—Edward Hall's and Raphael Holinshed's histories of England—Bedford's vituperation prevailed over Joan's vindication in 1456, even as excerpts from the trial transcripts emerged in print. To his narrative of Joan's career and execution printed in 1548, Hall adds a vehement peroration on her unwomanly behavior, including the matter of her dress: "Where was her womanlie behavior, when she cladde her self in mannes clothing, and was conversant with every lozell, gevyng occasion to all men to judge, and speake evill of her, and her doynges."[13] He was writing in the 1540s, just when the literary form of the *querelle des femmes* or "woman question" was about to explode into virulent political and social commentary in England. Yet Thomas Heywood placed Joan of Arc among praiseworthy *English* viragos in his 1624 history of women. In the aftermath of the Revolution, at the turn of the nineteenth century, she was more often selectively domesticated. By the mid-eighteenth century, historians had transformed her into a deluded, if virtuous, enthusiast.

While some late medieval and early modern English writers disparaged, ignored, displaced, or reassigned Joan's successes, not a few others acknowledged Joan's victories and praised her as a "virago"—in short, they displayed the variety and complexity of response still orbiting around this compelling yet mysterious figure. When examining the historiographical and critical heritage of Joan in England, I also discovered that considerations of Joan's afterlife in the English consciousness, both in the context of the Hundred Years' War and otherwise, have too often been based almost exclusively on evaluative criteria of the simplest kind: Was the writer "for" or "against" the Maid? Was she represented as a "saint" or a "witch"? Can one identify at what point the English were "converted" to writing a "proper" (i.e., adulatory) history of the Maid? But no serious examination of the myriad portrayals of Joan of Arc in English culture up to now has sought to understand and account for the complexity of Joan of Arc's afterlife.

Two nineteenth-century scholars undertook to answer those questions: James Darmesteter in his "Jeanne d'Arc jugée par les Anglais" in 1883 and Pierre Lanéry d'Arc in his monumental annotated bibliography, *Le Livre d'or de Jeanne d'Arc* in 1894. Each exemplifies the tireless encyclopedic impulses of nineteenth-century scholarship, whose thoroughness recommends their continuing value. Indeed, I make no pretense of having read *every* English work Lanéry catalogs. A renowned scholar of Iranian philology and a Jew, Darmesteter was a fervent French patriot. According to Gaston Paris's posthumous tribute, he associated the political emancipation of French Jews by the Revolution with his devotion to Joan of Arc, whom, in Paris's words, he regarded "an angel of fraternal harmony."[14] Darmesteter was also a knowledgeable critic and admirer of English literature. It is not surprising, then, that he would seek to demonstrate English progress toward "true" appreciation of Joan of Arc. But his attempt is sometimes strained, especially when he concludes that Joan Puzel's invocation of spirits in act 5 of *1 Henry VI* is done for "love of country," and thus "the earliest rehabilitation of Joan of Arc in English literature is due to the master hand of Shakespeare."[15] He firmly asserts, "The posthumous fortunes of Joan of Arc in England may be divided into three characteristic periods—Witch, Heroine, Saint in turn. She traversed two hundred years of wrathful insult, then a century of human justice, until, with the advent of 1793, she touches the final state of adoration, the apotheosis.... Nowhere in Europe has the heavenly character of Joan been more exquisitely felt, more amply proclaimed, than by the sons of those who scouted [scorned] her and burned her at the stake."[16] It was in 1793 that Robert Southey undertook his epic *Joan of Arc*, completing the first version by the autumn of that year.[17] Indeed, Darmesteter pinpoints the revolution in English opinion "from the day when an English poet could, with impunity and even with success, adopt as the heroine of an epic poem the accursed and loathsome sorceress of by-gone ages," with the result that "a whole past of international hate was for evermore eclipsed."[18]

The "success" of Southey's poem, especially his choice of Joan as an epic heroine, was questioned, but he *is* most often invoked as "the first English writer on Jeanne in whose work we see any noticeable advance towards a more sympathetic treatment of the heroine," in the words of one of her modern biographers, W. S. Scott. Perceptively, Scott adds, "it must be admitted that it was not so much an admiration of the person of the Maid as his youthful enthusiasm for the doctrines of the French Revolution which inspired him to write his long epic poem *Joan of Arc*."[19] To this day, some historians hold that the English regarded Joan as Bedford's "hateful witch, the foul limb of the fiend" until Southey's time. Karen Sullivan, in her survey of nineteenth-century English biographers of Joan, observes, "When English opinion changes at the end of the 18th century, it is against that anti-Johannic tradition that the authors defined themselves."[20] As recently as 2007, Malcolm Vale, who cogently summarizes Joan's role in "the construction and reconstruction of national histories in Europe," subscribes to the commonplace: "From a fundamentally hostile stance, as taken up from the sixteenth century onwards, English opinion began to change dramatically at the end of the eighteenth century."[21] Even Ardis Butterfield's nuanced view of "the gradual construction of belief and its closely matching counterpart of accusation," or "the process of public assent" about Joan, is still loosely organized under a rubric of three "phases"—"from heretic, to innocent believer, and in due course, saint."[22] This study demonstrates the simultaneity of such English opinions about Joan of Arc.

In fact, elements of Darmesteter's formula can be traced to the mid-seventeenth century, albeit with an entirely different purpose, in Thomas Fuller's sketch of Joan in *The Profane State* (1642), whence Darmesteter no doubt found it:

> Here lies *Joan of Arc*, the which
> Some count saint, and some count witch;
> Some count man, and something more;
> Some count maid, and some a whore.

Fuller's doggerel echoes through the centuries, even in contemporary scholarship. For example, Marina Warner's *Joan of Arc: Image of Female Heroism* is organized according to similar epithets—including "Harlot," "Heretic," "Ideal Androgyne," "Saint or Prophet." And Anke Bernau adopts Fuller's verse for the title of her fine study "'Saint, Witch, Man, Maid or Whore?': Joan of Arc and Writing History."

Nor could the bibliographer Lanéry d'Arc resist passing judgment on a given writer's attitude toward the Maid and, by implication, toward France. He often goes beyond description to evaluation. Of the Joan described in Robert Fabyan's *New Chronicles of England* (1516), he writes "he understood her only on the basis of national bias on the one hand, and on the other, by French narratives, that, in exalting the heroine, incensed English chauvinism."[23] Lanéry nominates William Guthrie, author of *A General History of England* (1744), as the first English historian who "who had a sense of the real Joan," proclaiming, of course, his own conviction of who the "real Joan" was.[24] Guthrie had indeed praised Joan, at least in this work, while maintaining a steadfastly skeptical view of divine inspiration, but Lanéry chose just one adulatory passage to highlight, translating it into French. Here is what Guthrie had written, despite his disclaimer that "very possibly, there was nothing in what she had revealed" to Charles that could convince him of her authenticity: "Had

Joan been an imposter, or capable of entering into any collusion of this kind, I am of the opinion that she never could have performed the great actions, or effected the mighty designs she had in hand. Nothing but enthusiasm, which is a sincere, warm, disinterested operation of mind, could have supported her in this; the least proposal of collusion must have damped its fervour; the least consciousness of deceit must have extinguished its properties."[25] Lanéry's example betrays one of the pitfalls of seeking a moment when English attitudes changed. Because Guthrie was a Scot, and Scotland was traditionally a French ally, we should expect him to be generally sympathetic to Joan. In his *General History of England* (1744), he was. Yet, in his *General History of the World* (1766), Guthrie began his mostly appreciative account with the bald statement that "the whole of her appearance and conduct was the contrivance of *Charles* and his courtiers," a theory launched in the mid-sixteenth century by the French historian Guillaume du Bellay.[26] The complexity of English (or British) responses to Joan of Arc has almost always been overlooked and underestimated.

Attempts to "rehabilitate" the English by identifying the earliest advocate for Joan did not end with the nineteenth century. Writing in celebration of Joan's beatification in 1909, Herbert Thurston proposed, "All honour be to John Rastell, the brother-in-law of Blessed Thomas More, and himself a confessor of the Faith, who in his brief notice of the events of 1429–30, speaks of the great success achieved by the Pucelle, but refrains from all opprobrious epithets. The passage, though its sympathy is only negative, deserves to be quoted as the first sign of a wish on the part of Englishmen to do justice to their great adversary."[27] Rastell's *Pastyme of People* (1529), however, merely follows and indeed heavily edits his source, Fabyan's *New Chronicles*. Thurston does not question Darmesteter's "stages," but he does recognize that the availability of translations from French sources influenced English writers such as the seventeenth-century cartographer John Speed to write "some sort of apology" for Joan's execution.[28] At the same time, however, some English redactors ignored King Alfred's ancient formula for translation: "sometimes word for word, and sometimes sense for sense." Sixteenth-century English translators of Cornelius Agrippa and Matteo Bandello added material to reformulate the story of Joan and markedly changed its "sense." Thus, the image of Joan was deliberately manipulated to suit an English bias. In the early nineteenth century, an abridged English translation of a skeptical French study of Joan occasioned scathing reviews for its sketchy scholarship.

Thurston does acknowledge, if only tangentially, the significance of politics and religion in English accounts of the Maid. For example, in his assessment of John Lingard, an English Catholic who wrote in the early nineteenth century, he observes, "It seems not improbable that the Catholic historian was unconsciously influenced in his presentment of the character [of Joan] by the sense that any too ready acceptance of a miraculous element in her career would at once be pounced upon by unfriendly Protestant critics and taken as evidence of the writer's superstition and consequent untrustworthiness in all matters in which Catholic feeling could be evoked."[29] In his 1819 *History of England*, Lingard praised Joan's Catholic piety but concluded, "An impartial observer would have pitied and respected the mental delusion with which she was afflicted."[30]

Like Thurston, Charles Wayland Lightbody, in the epilogue to *The Judgements of Joan* (1961), sees a religious divide in English opinion about Joan: Reformation-era Protestants identified her with the Catholic Church and the monarchy of France (and, as I shall argue, specifically with the controversy over Mary Queen of Scots), whereas "later generations of Protestants . . . accepted as valid . . . the view . . . that she was a heretic" and thus "a forerunner of the later Protestant movement."[31] Enlightenment historians, however, do not view her that way. For many writers, it seems almost impossible to resist the temptation to determine a turning point from misprision to praise—if misprision is to be defined as French Catholicism and praise as English Protestantism. But, in fact, neither historians nor literary historians have attempted a broad view of Joan's legacy to England that analyzes the contexts in which writers position themselves to grapple with the narrative of her sentence and execution. Nor have the exigencies of genre been part of the discussion. These are the goals of my study.

I am far from the first to consider the afterlife of the Maid in English letters, but I am the first to analyze her historiography systematically in its political and social contexts. Darmesteter's essay was followed in 1891 by Marie Dronsart's article and Félix Rabbe's monograph, both titled "Jeanne d'Arc en Angleterre."[32] The former argues that the French Revolution and John Wesley's Methodism precipitated a long-awaited English epiphany about Joan. Until the late eighteenth century, according to Dronsart, the English determinedly falsified the historical record out of pride and self-interest. She vigorously chides English writers, including Shakespeare, for relying on English sources rather than French ones for inspiration. But English writers did not, in fact, ignore the work of their Gallic counterparts, as Fabyan's *New Chronicles* is the first to demonstrate. To be sure, some French writers, unlike Darmesteter, have conveyed a traditionally French Anglophobia. P.-H. Dunand, for example, concluded in 1903, "The Joan of Arc of the legend created by the English is nothing more than a banal visionary, a false prophetess and an adventurer."[33]

A number of studies have discussed the avatars of Joan invented by selected British writers, but these generally have focused on the nineteenth and twentieth centuries.[34] Ingvald Raknem's *Joan of Arc in History, Legend and Literature* (1971) surveys the best-known French, English, German, and American accounts of the Maid from the trial transcripts through Jean Anouilh's *L'Alouette* (1952). But he does not consider very much historical material and skips the seventeenth century completely. Gerd Krumeich focuses on historical and political literature of the nineteenth and early twentieth centuries in his *Jeanne d'Arc in der Geschichte* (1989). Despite its promising title, John Lamond's *Joan of Arc and England* (1927) is a memoir by a soldier who served during World War I in Calais, where he was much affected by witnessing a *fête* in her honor. Although he mentions George Bernard Shaw's *St. Joan* and follows the playwright in seeing Joan as both Catholic and proto-Protestant, he focuses only on her lifetime and rehabilitation. John Flower fulfills the intention to "illustrate the process whereby a certain figure became iconic" and to "provide a descriptive context for the *display* of material."[35] As such, his *Joan of Arc: Icon of Modern Culture* (2008) offers a rich collection of nearly 150 images. Ann Astell offers a sophisticated reading of authorial self-projections in literary treatments of Joan in the nineteenth and twentieth centuries in *Joan of Arc and Sacrificial Authorship* (2003).

Given the countless appearances Joan of Arc in English *belles lettres*, I circumscribed my own inquiry by chronology and deliberate omission. The years 1429 to about 1829 range from the earliest English references to Joan during her lifetime to the novelist Sir Walter Scott's history for children, *Tales of a Grandfather*. Once the French historian Jules Michelet published his account of Joan of Arc, essentially a canonization, in volume 5 of his *Histoire de France* (1841), the floodgates opened in both Great Britain and France, and new considerations of her poured into print, reanimating, in some cases, the nations' ancient frictions.[36] For example, at the same time Thomas De Quincey warmly praises Joan, he castigates "the bitter and unfair spirit in which M. Michelet writes against England."[37] The proliferation of Johannic literature in the nineteenth century and after has already been sufficiently considered. Nor did I wish to recreate a categorical survey of allusions to Joan in English letters over four centuries. Rather, I have preferred for the most part to concentrate on representative works that were widely read and thus disseminated particular images of Joan in English opinion. Thus, for example, while I consider Joan's reputation as a witch in demonologies and her inclusion in collections of worthy women, much of my attention in chapter 3 is on Thomas Fuller's conclusion in *The Profane State* (1642) that Joan should not have been executed, but rather made "the Laundresse to the English, who was the Leader to the French Army."[38]

Chapter 1 provides a contextual framework. The chapter asks, "What did Joan of Arc know about the English and how and when did she know it?" Rather than retelling in detail the history of Anglo-French relations and the role of Joan in the Hundred Years' War, a topic well covered by historians, I consider geography to talk about how news of the war, awareness of diplomatic relations, and royalist propaganda reached Domrémy in Lorraine, Joan's birthplace, in surprising abundance. I do this in order to reconstruct, inasmuch as is possible, Joan's own opinion of the English. Thus, I also analyze the diction she chooses to refer to the English in her letters, and how she was later reported to have spoken with or about her enemies during her military career and at her condemnation trial.

In chapter 2, I reverse the first question by reexamining what early English chroniclers and historians wrote about Joan, including the earliest document of exculpation, a letter drafted by John, Duke of Bedford, regent for Henry VI in France, to be sent across Europe in the young king's name. By issuing that epistolary manifesto in June 1431, England was defending its role in executing the Maid, and that *apologia* appears, if often disguised, in strong statements of English character. These statements appear not only within historical narratives but also in the context of the *ethos* that underlies such works' nationalistic prologues and prefaces. Because the actuality of a woman warrior was so unusual, I briefly examine how early chronicles of English history wrote about English viragos such as Ælfleda of Mercia (d. 918) and Empress Maud (d. 1167) as possible models for their treatment of Joan.[39] Such royal women were married and bore children, so the chroniclers had to accommodate the conundrum of the reproductive potential of a female in battle. Later, they had to confront the importance of Joan's virginity to her charismatic leadership. This context explains the sudden accusation by the *Brut* chronicle in the late fifteenth century that Joan pled her belly to delay her execution, with its implied defense of a time-honored English legal process. The chapter culminates in discussions of John Speed's account of Joan in his 1611 *Historie of Great Britain*, important for incorporating both English and French sources, and Richard Baker's 1643 *Chronicle of the Kings of England*, an anachronistic but very popular attempt at a comprehensive chronicle.[40]

The English "Joan" was not confined to historical texts. The early modern period witnessed the increasing containment of the Maid to collections of famous or heroic women, bound up as that genre was with social and religious debates about women in society. In chapter 3, I examine the principles of selection and association imposed on the figure of Joan as a witch in demonologies and as a woman warrior or virago. She is included in the first printed English demonology, Francis Coxe's *Short Treatise declaringe the detestable wickednesse of magicall sciences* (1561), and she reappears nearly three hundred years later in Sir Walter Scott's *Letters on Demonology* (1830) as a falsely accused "innocent, high-minded, and perhaps amiable enthusiast."[41] In his 1624 survey of woman's history, the *Gynaikeion* (or "woman's room," referring to the domestic spaces reserved for woman), Thomas Heywood associates Joan with "English Viragos" rather than witches. Yet in his later *Life of Merlin*, a history of England, he presents her as a sorceress.

Joan of Arc was also associated with political anxieties surrounding the final years of Elizabeth I, particularly those expressed in the figure of Joan Puzel in *1 Henry VI*. While not dismissing the fine work scholars have done to show how that character embodies anxieties about the Queen of England, in chapter 4, I argue that the life and death of Mary Queen of Scots reverberate even more strongly in Joan Puzel. At the same time, the changeling figure of Joan in that play—prophetess, warrior, witch—reproduces avatars of the Maid already present in sixteenth-century English letters. Even after the restoration of the monarchy in 1660 brought women actors to the London stage, *1 Henry VI* was produced only once, so that the figure of Joan Puzel becomes, for over a century, two dimensional—the subject of textual commentary or engravings that begin to suggest the Romantic era's nervousness about "those cursed Breeches, of which she was so obstinately fond."

Although the matter of Joan's attire was a continuing topic of debate beginning in her own lifetime, her domestic femininity becomes a major focus in the late eighteenth century and Romantic era, as shown in chapter 5. In his *History of England* (1762), David Hume retells a fifteenth-century account of Joan's reported desire to return to Domrémy after Charles VII's coronation. By popularizing that one small detail from the nullification trial, Hume provided an opening for writers, including some women, to indict Joan herself for eschewing her own instinct to return to a gender-defined role. Despite the participation of some English women writers in the discourses of Revolution, others seek to realign Joan's achievement with socially gender-appropriate aspirations.

CHAPTER 1

## "WE HAVE BURNED A SAINT"

*Joan of Arc and the English in France*

Truly that is a good woman. If only she were English!

At the end of May 1431, a young Frenchwoman condemned for apostasy, heresy, idolatry, and dressing in men's garments was burned alive in the marketplace of Rouen under the aegis of English civil authorities. The English king, whose claim to the throne of France Joan of Arc had so fiercely resisted, was residing in the town as preparations were made for his coronation in Paris.[1] No witness reports that he attended the execution. No evidence survives of his reaction to the extinguishing of a demonic foe. What Henry VI heard or saw, whether the smoke wafted to his quarters, will never be known. He was not yet ten years old. The French king, his uncle, had traveled widely that spring but by May 30 had returned to his château at Chinon, where he had first encountered this young woman on a mission to save his kingdom.[2] Charles VII remained silent on the entire matter of Joan of Arc until 1450, when he initiated an inquiry into the legality of her trial after the French recaptured Rouen. At that time, the testimony of surviving witnesses to the execution of the Maid of Orléans conveyed an authentic sense of its emotional impact on all present, not least some Englishmen.

The capture of the "wycche" was already being chronicled in London, and her inspiration of the French transmuted into idolatry for a false "goddesse" in whom they put their faith.[3] Since English superstition was proverbial, the Rouennais were not surprised that they ascribed the Maid's success to malign supernatural influences.[4] Guillaume de la Chambre, a Master of Arts and Medicine, recalled that while many in the marketplace wept, "several Englishmen laughed."[5] Yet Jean Massieu (a curé and deputy clerk for Jean d'Estivet, the promoter at Joan's trial), who had escorted Joan to and from her cell, remembered, "Then the judges who were present and even several Englishmen were provoked to great tears and crying, and in fact, wept most bitterly.... Some even said that she had been a good woman."[6] He added that when Joan asked for a cross to comfort her at the stake, it was an Englishman who fashioned one out of a stick of wood for her.

That was a spontaneous gesture of simple humanity. Afterward, Pierre Cusquel, an ordinary citizen of Rouen remembered, "Jean Tressart, secretary to the King of England, returning from the site of Joan's punishment, anxious and lamenting, bewailed what he had seen there, saying in effect, 'We are all lost, for a holy person has been burned.'"[7] Tressart was likely a lay administrator acting as liaison between the governments in England and France. One "Jean Testart" was among several persons reimbursed through King Henry VI's Norman chancery in Paris on December 26, 1431.[8] It is important to establish that such a person existed, so as to mitigate somewhat the suspicion of *ex post facto* inventions for self-justification. Beyond remorse, the effect of the execution was life changing for one English soldier, who had hated Joan exceedingly, according to Friar Isambart de la Pierre. Was this perhaps one of her prison guards, even one who had been instrumental in substituting male clothing for the dress she had agreed to wear after her abjuration? He had, the friar recalled, admitted that he had added faggots to the pyre, but was later "rendered thunderstruck, in a sort of daze," at the sight of Joan's suffering. Once recovered, he confessed to a Dominican friar "that he had grievously erred, and that he repented what he had done against the said Joan, whom he considered a good woman."[9] Perhaps the most intriguing memory of the day is that of Jean Tiphane, a member of the medical faculty of the University of Paris, who treated Joan's illness while she was in prison. Tiphane maintained that he had attended the trial only "out of fear of the English." And then he recalled overhearing a "great English lord whose name he did not recollect" say, "Truly that is a good woman. If only she were English!"[10]

These memories, even if flawed by advancing age and the lapse of decades, suggest that even in her lifetime Joan had elicited contradictory emotions from the English and their allies. At her military pinnacle, she was an object of fear—both military and spiritual. Indeed, two English military orders issued in 1430—addressing the desertion of English soldiers in France and the refusal of English soldiers to go to France—are often ascribed to dread of the Maid, although her name does not appear in either, and the second was issued when she was already a prisoner.[11] Jean Dunois, the so-called Bastard of Orléans, recalled that on May 7, 1429, as soon as Joan appeared in that city with her banner, the English trembled with fear, while the king's soldiers took heart.[12] The chronicler Enguerrand de Monstrelet, firmly attached to the Anglo-Burgundian alliance, noted that by mid-June, when the French army was attacking English-held Beaugency, "by the renown of that Maid... most of their men were completely astonished and terror-stricken."[13] He had heard that the English were "more afraid of her than of a hundred troops," testified Pierre Miget, also a promoter at Joan's trial.[14] Jean Fabri, an Augustinian monk, went so far as to say that they "proceeded against her from the hate they had for her, and that they feared her greatly."[15] Yet something about her genuine piety and her suffering touched the essential humanity of some English bystanders at her execution, even as others laughed.

Nor were the English alone in expressing conflicting views of the Maid. Carefully questioned on her spirituality by French ecclesiastics at Poitiers in 1429 after she had announced her mission to the dauphin at Chinon, she was found to have "no evil... in her, only goodness, humility, virginity, devotion, honesty and simplicity."[16] She was hailed as the fulfillment of sanctioned prophecy "for, more than 500 years ago, Merlin, the Sybil and Bede foresaw her coming, [and] entered her in their writings as someone who would put an end to France's troubles," the poet Christine de Pizan triumphantly wrote.[17] Significantly, in the Middle Ages, prophecy had an important political dimension, especially in France. Vincent Challet and Ian Forrest describe the prophetic voice as frequently that "of a poor and humble woman who comes from the margins of the kingdom and makes her way to Paris or to London to speak to the king and deliver a message from God."[18] At the same time, the potential that such a prophecy could be false raised the specter of heresy. And so, while one French theologian who scrutinized the credibility of Joan's divine mission concluded that "this Pucelle... does not go beyond the instructions and inspirations that she attributes to God,"[19] another responded that she was a heretic, a fornicator, a liar, and an idolater.[20] On this one point, at least, the cross-Channel antagonists were in accord: Neither English nor French could fathom the Maid.

In the remainder of this chapter, I hope to indicate how Joan of Arc herself fathomed the English, a question her interrogators probed, and one that, because of her diction, led to hasty conclusions in the past. First, I examine how a young girl living beyond the borders of "France" could have received both military and diplomatic news. Second, I reexamine Joan's recorded words—dictated, transcribed, translated, and recalled after the lapse of many years. Derisive judgments about her king's enemies appear rarely in Joan's own statements, even as childhood impressions were replaced by direct experience and, eventually, adversarial confrontations. Of Joan of Arc's actual knowledge of and encounters with the English after her departure from Vaucouleurs in February 1429, yet before she was remanded to their custody at the end of 1430 for the remainder of her life, we have some, but tantalizingly little, information. Before she undertook her journey to Chinon to meet the dauphin, what did Joan of Arc, or any resident along the River Meuse and its tributaries, really know about the English or England at a time when their direct sufferings came at the hands of Burgundians? And how did they come to this knowledge?

I had originally written "the hated English," but on reflection, I realized that in her early years, Joan never expressed personal opprobrium toward the enemies of her king even when provoked. Only twice was she even reported—retrospectively—to have used the epithet *godon* (usually glossed as "goddam") to refer to them. Historians' assumptions that after a Burgundian raid on Domrémy in 1428, Joan developed a "hatred" for the English are plausible, to be sure, but unsupported, except by the English or English sympathizers themselves.[21] During her trial, she was even asked if God hated the English. She did not reply directly, only that she knew nothing of God's love or hate for the English, nor of what he would do about their souls.[22] Nevertheless, article 52 of the original seventy indictments read to her on March 28, 1431, states that her fall (or leap) from the tower of Beaurevoir, where she was initially imprisoned, was motivated by "hate and contempt" for the English.[23] She had testified that her act was partly out of a desire to save herself and partly out of a desire to save certain people in need.[24] Naturally, declarations devaluing her mission from one inspired by God to one inspired by personal revenge would reduce her overall credibility before a hostile audience. Yet, as Xavier Hélary summarizes the case, "if Joan showed no specific hatred towards the English, she was perfectly sure of two things: the French and the English are different, and the English must return to their own land and quit the realm of France."[25]

Indeed, while the English were the initial aggressors in the Hundred Years' War, based on Edward III's claim of direct descent from Philip IV through his mother, France had as much (or as little) reason to argue that it should rule its island neighbor.[26] England's hopes for the success of its efforts to claim the throne of France arguably had peaked in 1415 with its victory at the battle of Agincourt. Henry V moved swiftly to translate the psychological as well as the military victory into concrete form. Rather than claiming the Gallic crown outright, as his great-grandfather had done, he negotiated the Treaty of Troyes, signed in 1420. This document stipulated that any offspring of the proposed union between Henry and the French king Charles VI's daughter, Catherine of Valois, would be monarch of both England and France upon the deaths of the present kings.[27] In effect, this agreement disinherited the French dauphin Charles who, since 1418, had acted as regent for his father (Charles VI suffered increasingly severe episodes of insanity). Both he and Duke John of Burgundy, even as they parleyed with each other, were attempting to negotiate a truce with the English.[28] In due course, on December 6, 1421, Catherine gave birth to a son, the future Henry VI. Just nine months later, however, at the age of thirty-five, his father died and the infant became king of England by right of succession. With the death of his French grandfather in October 1422, he was proclaimed king of France in accordance with the treaty, with John of Lancaster, Duke of Bedford, the late king's brother, assuming the regency.[29] The infant's French uncle, the dauphin Charles, however, claimed the throne and was recognized as king in some regions of France, holding court at Mehun-sur-Yèvre, near Bourges, which had been the nominal seat of government since 1419, when Charles had fled Paris after being implicated in the assassination of Duke John.[30]

Seven years before the dauphin decamped, around 1412, Jacques, sometimes called Darc, a well-established farmer in Domrémy, a town near Neufchâteau in Lorraine, and his wife, Isabelle, called Romée, had a daughter, whom they named Jehanne, or Jeannette.[31] Despite a fifteenth-century letter stating that her date of birth was the feast of the Epiphany, January 6, this date is not otherwise supported.[32] Joan herself could only approximate her age. Asked during her trial, she said she thought she was nineteen, and contemporary accounts do not contradict her.[33] "From about the age of 13," she testified, "she had a revelation of our Lord from a voice that advised her to govern herself. And that first time, she was very frightened. And she said that the voice came around midday, in summer, she being in the garden of her father, on a day in June, and she said that the said voice came from the right side, towards the church. And she said that the said voice was hardly ever without a light, which was always on the side of the said voice."[34] Other voices later manifested themselves, and at first instructed her to "conduct herself well, to go to church often." But later she was counseled that "it was necessary that she should come into France" so "that she would raise the siege before Orléans."[35] This, as a result of dogged stubbornness, native intelligence, some ineffable charisma, and mixed support from the French army, she did in May 1429, much to the dismay of the English. Allies of Duke Philip of Burgundy, a natural foe of the dauphin who was implicated in the murder of his father in 1419, fortuitously captured the Maid outside besieged Compiègne in 1430 and sold her to the English by the end of that year.[36]

Joan's understanding that from her home she would have to travel "into France" reminds us to pay heed to late medieval perspectives on geographical, political, and regnal communities as well as how these are labeled. How are we to understand what "France" or "French," "England" or "English" connoted to Joan of Arc? A letter defending her execution circulated to the prelates and nobles of France in 1431 over the signature of the young King Henry speaks of the necessity of safeguarding "our lordship and our loyal and obedient people," with no mention of "England."[37] In his charge to the commission tasked with reviewing Joan's trial and its outcome in 1450, King Charles VII mentions "our ancient enemies and adversaries, the English" in the first sentence.[38] Preferring collective eponyms over modern national labels—"English" and "French," as opposed to "England" and "France"—suggests that Joan herself intuited such semantic differences. From her own testimony, it is clear that her allegiance was to the king first, and that an idea of "France" was tied to the monarchy, not primarily to a territory. Her letter of March 22, 1429, to the English occupying Orléans demanding that they "surrender to the Maid" refers throughout to "France" as the kingdom (*royaume*) rightfully held by Charles VII. She threatens that if Bedford and the English army do not obey her, they shall witness "such a great battle cry as has not been heard in France for a thousand years."[39] In her letters and trial testimony, moreover, Joan seldom refers to "England," as if to deny sovereignty to her enemy. The March letter is addressed to the "King of England." Another letter sent to the English in Orléans, recalled a quarter of a century later by her confessor, Jean Pasquerel, addresses "you men of England" and again refers to the "realm" of France.[40]

Otherwise, throughout her trial, she refers to "the English," even once to the "King of the English," reserving her use of "England" almost exclusively to the physical territory. On March 12, 1431, for example, she expresses her desire to go to "England" (*Angleterre*) to rescue Charles, Duke of Orléans, imprisoned since Agincourt, just as she had testified her voices told her she must go to "France."[41] While these distinctions may be deliberate, they must be viewed with some caution, for much of the testimony from both the original and nullification trials was recorded in indirect discourse, and in Latin, from French speakers. Just as Latin distinguishes *anglia*, the country, from *anglicus*, its people, so also French distinguishes *Angleterre* from *les anglais*. Joan was also asked if Saint Margaret—named during the trial as one of her voices— spoke to her in English. She replied, "Why should she speak English when she is not on the side of the English?"[42] Such distinctions also bore on the region in which Joan of Arc was born. The poet and diplomat Alain Chartier wrote in his *Epistola de puella* (1429), possibly addressed to the duke of Milan: "If you asked about her nation [*nacionem*], she belongs to the kingdom; if [you asked] about her homeland [*patriam*], [she belongs] to the city of Vaucouleurs, that is to say by the river Meuse."[43] Tellingly, he does not name "France."

Yet although northern France, including Domrémy, was mostly under the control of English or pro-English forces,[44] it was not the English but their allies, the Burgundians, who harried the territory around Lorraine during Joan's childhood, and her direct experience with them was limited. At her trial, she testified that it was "out of fear of the Burgundians" that "she went to Neufchâteau with a woman named la Rousse, where she stayed for about fifteen days" in 1428.[45] She also recalled "that she only knew one Burgundian, whose head she would have wished to be cut off, that is, if this had pleased God."[46] Herein lies an example of Joan's often overlooked sense of humor, for Gerardin d'Epinal, that very "Burgundian" (probably in reference to his politics, but possibly to his place of birth) not only testified to her womanly domesticity and spiritual qualities at the hearings to nullify her conviction, but also remembered that, addressing him as *compère* (friend) she told him before leaving the town that "if you weren't Burgundian, I'd tell you something." This suggests that she saw him first as a fellow townsman and only second as a partisan.[47] Nevertheless, she had no doubt that Burgundians as well as English were the enemy, for her voices told her so, as she testified on February 24, 1431: "from the time that she understood that the voices were for the king of France, she had never loved the Burgundians." Moreover, her voices also told her that the Burgundians "would have war, if they did not do what they must."[48] Article 10 of her condemnation represents somewhat accurately what she said but chooses diction that suggests more than Joan herself did: "And she knows this [about the Burgundians] through the revelations [per revelacionem] of Saints Katherine and Margaret who often spoke to her in French and not English, because they were not of their party. And, once she knew by revelation [per revelacionem] that the voices were for the prince [discussed] above, she did not love the Burgundians."[49] The repetition of *per revelacionem* in the context of ecclesiastical indictments suggests that the phrase is used to impugn Joan's testimony, not endorse it. Where Joan uses *voix*, or "voice," the scribe uses *revelacionem*. The doctrine of revelation is complex, and Joan herself insisted on circumspection about what she herself called in French *revelacions*, which she seems to distinguish from the voices that conveyed them. At the start of her trial, Joan preemptively refused to talk about certain revelations: "But of the revelations made to her by God, [these] she had never told or revealed save to Charles whom she said was her king, and if one were to cut off her head, she would not reveal them, because she knew by these visions that they should be kept secret."[50]

If Joan had encountered only one Burgundian in her youth, it seems unlikely she had ever knowingly laid eyes on an Englishman. All the historians of the Hundred Years' War I have consulted state emphatically, in Edouard Perroy's words, that "the English had never penetrated" Lorraine, despite their presence throughout Champagne.[51] Although the area where Joan grew up is conveniently referred to as "Lorraine," its political geography during her lifetime reflected—and was affected by—the complexity of shifting alliances among the three great powers fighting for dominance to the west, as well as the involvement of the Holy Roman Empire, whose boundary with "France" lay just east of the River Meuse. In part because of the wealth and power of the duke, relations among Burgundy, England, and France at the turn of the fifteenth century were extraordinarily problematic, as their alliances shifted for political reasons and because of family quarrels whose roots were firmly fixed around lingering notions of feudal loyalties.[52] The imperial bishopric of Toul, where Joan defended herself against breach of promise in 1428,[53] was an active locus for jurisdictional control between the emperor and Duke Charles II of Lorraine.

The lands to the north of Domrémy belonged to the manor of Vaucouleurs, technically part of English-occupied Champagne, yet a lone outpost of support for the dauphin, locally administered by Robert de Baudricourt. To the southwest lay the Duchy of Burgundy, which during most of Joan of Arc's lifetime allied with England against the crown, and to the southeast lay the Comté of Burgundy. Domrémy itself owed one part of its allegiance to the crown directly and another part indirectly, through the duke of Bar. Areas to the west of the River Meuse, the so-called *Barrois mouvant*, were held by the duke of Bar as the king's vassal.[54] In Alain Girardot's words, "In effect, Lorraine was the crossroads of all disputes: the war between the French and English, the Valois feud, the schism between Church and [Holy Roman] Empire, and the contention between the houses of France and Burgundy."[55] However, from the English victory at Agincourt in 1415 until the siege of Orléans in 1429, there was no real fighting near the Meuse, although at one point, Edward III's army had come within fifty miles of the river, as far east as Châlons. According to Anne Curry, the "greatest extent of English control before 1429" did extend all the way to the river, including Domrémy.[56] To be sure, "control" on a map does not suggest occupation or garrisoning, but

English garrisons had been established in Nogent-le-roi and Montigny-le-roi in Bassigny, one of the districts of the Barrois, before 1426.[57] Moreover, the Bassigny region was apparently being severely harassed by the English, for in 1423, Duke Charles of Lorraine felt it necessary to write to the duke of Bedford, complaining about depredations in the area carried out during the captaincy of one Dicon Amors (or Digon Amore).[58] After the English rout of the French at Verneuil in 1424, Curry notes, "the frontier garrisons to the south and east [were] much reduced in size."[59] Overall, while Lorraine was certainly a crossroads for conflict, during Joan of Arc's childhood it would seem no English forces spent any length of time there, if they crossed into the area at all.

However, since Joan's parents both apparently had family connections in Champagne, it is worth considering whether she might have learned to misprize the English on personal, not merely political, grounds. It has been suggested that Jacques Darc was born in Ceffonds, a little over fifty miles west of Domrémy, around 1380,[60] a time when brigandage was again increasing.[61] The English had pillaged Révigny in Champagne (about thirty miles from Ceffonds) three times in 1360.[62] Although we do not know when Jacques migrated east, he must have heard stories of the English depredations in the previous generation. The chronicle attributed to Jean de Venette, for example, describes a raid in eastern France in 1365 led by "the Archpriest" Sir Arnold de Cervole:

> As they passed through the county of Champagne, they rapidly despoiled its merchants and other inhabitants of horses, money, goods, furnishings, and food whenever opportunity offered, in the unfortified country villages, along the roads, in the houses, or in the fields. Then when they had added unto themselves other companies of robbers like themselves, they entered the duchy of Bar, which but a short time before had been called a county, thence to the duchy of Lorraine and finally betook themselves, unopposed, to the district round Verdun and beyond as far as Metz, a very rich city, everywhere plundering and devastating.[63]

A contemporary of de Venette, Hugo de Montgeron, a parish priest, described English depredations in and around Sens, northeast of Orléans, in 1358 more graphically. He detailed how they seized food and possessions, extracted ransoms, and for those who could not pay, burned houses and inflicted death, imprisonment and other punishments: "whippings, wounds, hunger, and want beyond belief."[64] Throughout his narrative, de Venette emphasizes the suffering of the peasants at the hands of not only robbers and pillagers but the nobles as well; many contemporary witnesses echo him. Having examined many such accounts to ascertain the extent of the devastation, Clifford J. Rogers concludes that "the consistency and the sheer volume of the narrative and archival records on the subject show that the destruction was unquestionably both widespread and severe."[65] Indeed, as late as 1423, English forces overcame the village of Sainte-Ménehould, some sixty miles north of Ceffonds.[66] Even though de Venette describes conditions before Jacques Darc was born, such horrors would not have vanished out of collective memories. Joan's father might well have conveyed such stories as he had heard to his own children.

It has also been suggested that Joan traveled west into the Burgundian-held area around Sermaize in Champagne, a town over fifty miles from Domrémy. The argument for a familial relationship between Domrémy and Sermaize is this: Isabelle Vouthon (or Romée), born near Domrémy in Vouthon, had two brothers, Jean and Henri Vouthon, living in Sermaize.

A family cousin testified in 1476 that he had visited his relatives in Domrémy, and they and their children returned the visits.[67] Such a journey would surely have increased Joan's chances of encountering outposts or outriders of the English in Champagne, for it was an area known to be inhabited by soldiers or looters.[68] Notably, as Anne Curry points out, Henry V had a "policy of conquest . . . in the enforcing of Anglo-Burgundian rule in Champagne and Brie."[69] Indeed, Sermaize, which is believed to have been loyal to the dauphin, itself came under attack. In April 1423, Jean, Comte de Salm, appointed governor-general of the duchies of Lorraine and Bar the previous year, besieged and overtook the town.[70] Two years later, Charles Aimond writes, while the Cardinal of Bar was staying at Varennes, "a messenger from the lord of Louppy came to warn that the 'English had set fire to Revigny and the area of Chaumont.'"[71] Louppy, Revigny, and Chaumont lay within the comté de Champagne, the latter only thirty-one miles from Neufchâteau. Sermaize lies only five and a half miles from Revigny; Louppy is less than ten miles distant. To enter that area in the 1420s, one surely took the risk of encountering pro-English troops.

Just as Lorraine was "the crossroads of all disputes," it was also "the natural outlet for vagabonds, bands of English and Burgundians, [and] 'German' pillagers" from about 1380 until 1430.[72] But what, where, and under whose direction, if any, were these *bandes anglaises*? Were they comprised of actual Englishmen—deserters, mercenaries, or nonmilitary vagabonds? Did they rove through the borderlands in the early fifteenth century as they had in the mid-fourteenth?[73] Nicholas Wright cautions that by the early fifteenth century, "brigand" had come to denote not only "armed bands" of discharged soldiers who made their living by robbing passersby, but also peasants "who, in the process of arming themselves in their own defence, had been led into a similar existence."[74] Despite such danger, some historians have found it plausible that not only would the whole family from Domrémy travel a convoluted route to visit their relatives but that when the parents were unable to leave home, they would mount Joan's brother on a borrowed horse, with his sister riding behind him.[75] Even if we could establish with certainty that the family from Domrémy visited the family in Sermaize, and even if we accepted that inhabitants familiar with the route would know how best to attempt to skirt English or mercenary patrols, a large question remains: Would loving parents allow two children, even if one were a teenaged boy, Joan's older brother Jean, to travel alone along a circuitous route, so far into enemy-held territory? It seems highly unlikely. Champagne, Lorraine, and Bar were in a volatile state at this time, and Joan must have been well aware of the proximity of her king's enemies even if she did not encounter them.

In such an unstable area, what was the extent and accuracy of the information Joan and other residents along the Meuse received about both regional and more widespread conflicts? Most Johannic scholarship focuses on how news *of* Joan was disseminated, but more important for analyzing her early knowledge of the English is how news came *to* Joan.[76] Domrémy itself was not a backwater; it was, in fact, sited on a major thoroughfare, along which merchants, pilgrims, and other travelers passed, bringing their gossip and news.[77] It is a commonplace that there were sophisticated networks of communication throughout Europe and beyond in the late Middle Ages—of papal and royal embassies, of couriers facilitating merchants' negotiations and trades, of official pronouncements, of rumors. It is also a commonplace that news traveled in the mouths of mendicant friars, who, as Hervé Martin writes, "didn't much concern themselves with political borders,"[78] an important point especially on the eastern frontier.

The work of Julien Briand, based on municipal records chiefly from Champagne, offers provocative evidence that prelates and mendicant friars actively cooperated with urban authorities, who, in Briand's words, "meddled directly with the content of their sermons."[79] Furthermore, they exploited feast-day processions to disseminate official information, even propaganda, in the public reading of letters and other official documents. He suggests that from the archbishop of Reims, Regnault of Chartres himself, down to parish priests, ecclesiastics were recruited by municipal authorities to spread information that went far beyond the spiritual to encompass municipal and regnal politics. A pious and royalist young girl would certainly have responded to public preaching by mendicant friars, although such sermons as survive—many out of or based on manuals—focus more generally on the glory of the French monarchy than on specific political events.[80] While it would be unwise to extrapolate wholesale Briand's findings to Lorraine, we know that in Neufchâteau, Joan confessed to Franciscan friars, also ardent royalists.[81] Given her natural piety, it would be surprising had she not attended public sermons there and elsewhere. Given her staunch support for her king, it would be equally surprising had such sermons not reinforced the message of her voices.

Tidings of the war itself would have passed into and out of Vaucouleurs from couriers farther afield. It's doubtless that Joan learned that way about the devastating defeat of French and Scottish forces at Verneuil in 1424[82] as well as about other military news. Bertrand de Poulengy, an experienced fighter and later one of Joan's companions on her journey to the dauphin at Chinon, reported visiting her family several times, no doubt discussing what he knew of the war and matters in France.[83] By early 1429, Joan knew a fair bit about regnal marriage politics, as well. Jean de Metz (also called de Nouillonpont), another of her early companions, recalled that when he first met her in Vaucouleurs she declared, "there is no one on earth, be he king or duke, or King of Scotland's daughter, or anyone else, who can restore the kingdom of France . . . except through me."[84] She was referring accurately to the embassy Charles VII had sent to Scotland in late 1427 or early 1428 to negotiate the betrothal of his son Louis, then five years old, to Margaret of Scotland, then four. James I of Scotland ratified the agreement in letters patent dated July 19, 1428; Charles ratified it at the end of October.[85] If Joan had heard about this agreement by early 1429, there seems little question that the inhabitants along the Meuse were well and promptly informed.

Nor did the news have to come to them. Despite the threat of encountering Burgundians or brigands on the road, Joan, her family, and her friends seem not to have been deterred from traveling within Lorraine—visiting friends and relations, journeying to holy sites, and indeed fleeing from hostile forces (map 1). Even if we discount visits to Sermaize, it is unlikely that in her youth Joan left Domrémy "only twice," referring to her escape to Neufchâteau and her first appeal to Robert de Baudricourt in Vaucouleurs.[86] As a child, Joan sometimes made her confession close to home at Greux.[87] Just to the northeast of Domrémy lay Maxey-sur-Meuse, where children loyal to the dauphin or the Anglo-Burgundians fought their mock battles.[88] Bertrand de Poulengy remembered that she had gone to the chapel of Notre Dame de Bermont, a few miles from Domrémy.[89] In the early seventeenth century, a letter from

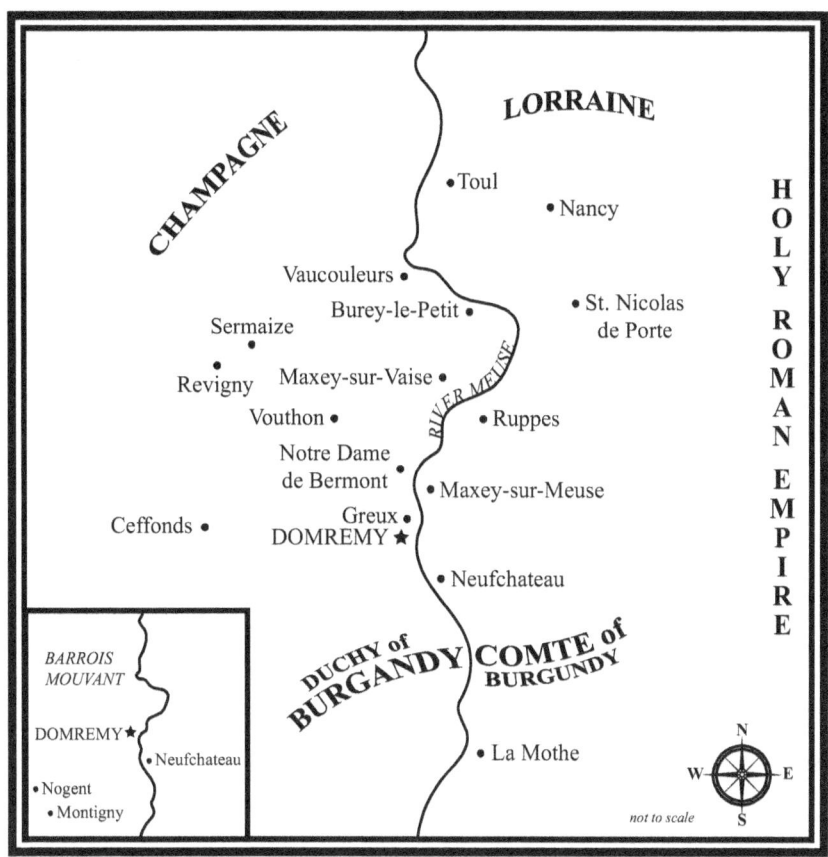

MAP 1   The Geography of Joan of Arc's Youth.

Jean Hordal, who claimed descent from Joan's brother Pierre, to Charles du Lys, another supposed great-nephew, mentions several other places the Maid had frequented: "Rup, Neufchâteau, and la Motte."[90] Ruppes is a town approximately five miles east-northeast of Domrémy. It might have drawn Joan because of its Romanesque church, with its twelfth-century baptismal fonts, or the chapels dedicated to Saint Catherine and the Virgin Mary in the chateau.[91] One of Joan's godmothers, Jeanette Thiesselin, was from Neufchâteau,[92] so Joan might have visited the town voluntarily, and not just as a one-time refugee. Her family, it seems, also had some connection with the ruined city of La Mothe-en-Bassigny, south of Neufchâteau, which had been established as a fortification in the mid-thirteenth century by the duke of Bar. Husson Lemaistre, a brazier in Rouen who hailed from Viville near La Mothe, "three leagues from Domrémy," said he had knowledge of Joan's mother and father, although he never saw Joan.[93] Little is known of the fortified town of La Mothe, but Thiebaut de Bar founded the church *L'Annunciation de Notre Dame* there in the thirteenth century.[94] That the investigators into Joan and her family's reputations thought it important to include testimony from two men from La Mothe speaks to some association of the Maid with that town, even if we cannot be sure what it was.

What we do know for certain is that in 1428, Joan of Arc traveled farther afield than she had previously in order to advance her mission: north to Vaucouleurs, south to Neufchâteau, possibly northeast to Toul, north again to Maxey-sur-Vaise, Burey-le-Petit, and Vaucouleurs, and east to Nancy and St. Nicolas de Port.[95] One Geoffroy de Foug testified he had seen her in Maxey-sur-Vaise north of Domrémy, on the road to Vaucouleurs.[96] Her relative Durand Laxart recalled her staying with him and his wife at Burey-le-Petit.[97] Joan's first journey to Vaucouleurs was in May 1428, around the feast of the Ascension, according to Bertrand de Poulengy.[98] It is not clear when she answered the legal summons against her at Toul, over twenty miles from home. Her father might well have attempted to arrange a marriage for her upon her return from Vaucouleurs, fearing for her virtue and reputation. Again, we do not know when precisely he had his dreams of her going off with soldiers, although she testified that it was when she was still with her father and mother and she thought it was more than two years after she heard her voices, but before she visited Vaucouleurs.[99]

In July 1428, Joan and her fellow citizens fled Domrémy when the forces of Anthony of Vergy, the Burgundian governor of Champagne, invaded the area, compelling them to take refuge south in Neufchâteau.[100] As a refugee, Joan apparently helped out at an inn where any number of travelers or messengers might have brought tales of the enemies of France, either directly or via the Empire, for Neufchâteau was a major crossroads along both the north-south and east-west corridors. By the turn of the fifteenth century, however, the cloth trade from England no longer followed that route. Where better could a curious young woman, one who had experienced increasing divine insistence that she undertake her mission to save France, integrate inspiration with information? She was able months later to chastise the ailing Duke Charles of Lorraine about his adultery, a circumstance apparently well known in Neufchâteau.[101]

At the end of December that same year, Joan went back to her relatives in Burey-le-Petit, ostensibly to assist with the impending birth of their child, and again petitioned Robert de Baudricourt in Vaucouleurs. At this time, she answered the summons of Duke Charles to visit him in Nancy. Because of the dangers on the road, she was sent under a protective escort to travel those twenty-three or so miles. She also took advantage of her proximity to visit St. Nicolas de Port, home of a relic of St. Nicholas, the patron saint of Lorraine. Both Toul and Neufchâteau were important trading and pilgrimage routes, and even though Joan spent little time in either, while there, she had ample opportunity to hear reports and gossip about the English.[102] Yet such stories, even gossip, however much they convey localized loyalties, do not seek to change minds, although they might evoke anger or incite other emotional responses.

Testimony during the trial to nullify Joan's conviction suggests how close the English were to the northwestern borders of Lorraine, a likelier venue for Joan's sighting any of her king's enemies. Both Jean de Metz and Bertrand de Poulengy, Joan's companions on her journey to meet the dauphin, stated that they traveled at night to avoid enemy troops. Jean said that on their way to Chinon, "for fear of the English and the Burgundians, who were everywhere along the way, we sometimes proceeded at night."[103] Bertrand stated the same: "And in setting forth on the first day, we were afraid because of the Burgundian and the English soldiers who at that time were in control, and so we traveled by night."[104] It is not impossible that, even in avoiding those patrols, Joan did set eyes on English troops from a distance. However, despite Mark Twain's invention of a nocturnal encounter between Joan and a Burgundian scouting party seeking the "pestilent limb of Satan,"[105] we cannot know if she glimpsed English soldiers or brigands on that journey. Once Joan reached Chinon, and especially after her mission was validated at Poitiers, she must have been inundated with stories about the English: the suffering in Orléans caused by the siege; the continued imprisonment in England of Charles, its duke; the duc d'Alençon's capture after Verneuil; the military leader Etienne de Vignolles's (La Hire's) missions to Orléans.[106] Even if Joan were under the political tutelage of Yolande d'Aragon, the dauphin's mother-in-law, who, as Larissa Taylor asserts, "opposed . . . what she saw as the pro-Burgundian politics of Charles VII's counselors,"[107] we cannot know whether Joan met Yolande's messengers. I have found no evidence that any English envoys or heralds visited Chinon or Poitiers in the spring of 1429, when Joan might have at least cast eyes on one.[108]

Not until Joan actually entered Orléans do we have any concrete evidence—despite some intriguing possibilities—of her exchanging as much as a glance with an Englishman. In keeping with her "Letter to the English," sent from Blois in April 1429, calling on the English to leave France or suffer dire consequences, she now took the opportunity to threaten them in person.[109] A citizen of the city recalled that "two or three times she went to call upon the English to go back to their country, and that the king of heaven commanded it of them."[110] Whatever she knew and had heard about the English beforehand, Joan was certainly not prepared for the vicious personal insults she first encountered on April 30, 1429. According to her page, Louis de Coutes, she was already in an irascible mood that day, impatient to fight and frustrated by Dunois's refusal to engage the English immediately.[111] It is not too difficult to imagine that the sight of the English defending their "boulevard" infuriated her further.[112] Louis's account makes clear that Joan herself initiated the ensuing shouting match: "Joan went to the bulwark that the King's men held facing the English bulwark, and from there she addressed the English opposite, telling them in God's name to retire, otherwise she would drive them away. And one called the Bastard of Granville answered Joan most abusively, asking whether she expected them to surrender to a woman, and calling the French who were with Joan 'unbelieving pimps' [maquereaulx mescréans]."[113] In such encounters, sexually charged insults were the norm. Despite these and other insults to her chastity, Joan did not reply in kind, demonstrating no personal hatred of the English.

For example, that same evening, according to the *Journal du siège d'Orléans*, following a message from Joan and threats from Dunois, two French heralds captured by the English were released. However, the *Journal* reports that they were charged to relay to Joan this counterthreat: "that they would burn her and put her to the fire, and that she was nothing but a 'ribaude,' and as such she should go back to minding the cows."[114] While *ribaude* is usually translated as "whore," in his *Dictionnaire de l'ancien langue française*, Godefroy provides examples that it also connoted a soldier who plundered, a *pillard*—a neat double insult for the virgin commander in the king's army.[115] The *Journal* notes that she was very angry to hear this, and toward evening, she approached the English-held Tourelles, in DeVries's words, "a fortified gate, with two flanking towers and a drawbridge separating it from the Loire bank."[116] From the bridge, Joan again demanded that they yield in the name of God. Captain William Glasdale, who had taken over the defense of Orléans after the death of the Earl of Salisbury the previous fall, "responded villainously, insulting her and calling her cowherd, as before, shouting that they would have her burned if they could."[117] French has no equivalent for "cowherd" and the English "coward" and French *couard* are close homonyms, so they might well sound alike to a French ear. The English besiegers probably had only rudimentary French. Angrily, Joan replied that he lied, the Orléans citizen's narrative adding that she told Glasdale he would die without his Lord, that is, unshriven.[118] There were apparently many witnesses to this exchange. Dunois recalled that it was Glasdale himself who spoke to the Maid most unjustly and with great dishonor and contempt.[119] Undaunted, on the following day, May 1, according to the *Journal du Siège*, she addressed some Englishmen near the Croix Morin in the same terms as she had the previous evening and received back "as villainous words as they had spoken at the Tourelles."[120]

On May 5, her confessor Jean Pasquerel recalled, Joan wrote another letter to the English: "You, men of England, who have no right whatsoever in this kingdom of France, the King of Heaven warns you and sends you word through me, Joan the Maid, to abandon your fortifications and to return to your own country, or else I will make such an assault that will be remembered forever. And I write to you for the third and last time; I will not write again."[121] Under her signature, she added, "I would have sent you my letter in a more appropriate fashion; but you are holding prisoner my messengers, or in French, *héraulx*; you have detained my herald Guyenne. If you send him back to me, I will return several of your men, taken in the fort of St. Loup, for not all of them were killed." The confrontational way she transmitted the demand was by arrow flight. By now, it cannot have surprised her that "when they had [read it], [the English] began to shout, 'Here's news from the Armagnacs' whore!'" Even so, "when she heard this, Joan began to sigh and weep copious tears, calling upon the King of Heaven's aid."[122]

Two days later, the French army determined finally to reestablish control over the bridge guarded by the Tourelles. At some point during the day, Joan was wounded by an arrow, but not seriously enough to prevent her returning to energize the king's troops. The chaplain Pasquerel reported that she again called on Glasdale to yield, at which point the bridge collapsed and Glasdale drowned. His narrative clearly suggests cause and effect: "[Joan cried] Classidas, Classidas, yield, yield thee to the King of Heaven. You called me 'whore'; I have great pity for your soul and the souls of your people. Whereupon Glasdale, armed from head to foot, fell into the river Loire and drowned. And Joan, moved by pity, began to weep strongly for the soul of Glasdale and the others who were there drowned in great numbers."[123] During the nullification hearings, only Pasquerel quotes Joan accusing Glasdale himself of calling her "whore." However, another anonymous fifteenth-century account of the siege suggests that it was known that one English captain did slander her in this way: "It was said that she had told an English captain that he must abandon the siege along with his company, or misfortune and shame would come to all; whereupon he defamed her greatly with words such as ribald and whore."[124]

Just as certain Englishmen were to weep at the sight of her execution, so Joan wept at the sight of Glasdale and other armed soldiers drowning in the Loire without the opportunity to shrive themselves—and this despite their hurtful calumny of her. Indeed, throughout the siege, Joan seems to have separated individual suffering from the necessity of defeating the enemy of France—by violence, if they did not accede to her commands to surrender. The citizen of Orléans noted, "The said Joan the Maid took in good patience the insults that the said English said and did."[125] Still, these calumnies did not turn her defiance to hatred or her innate compassion to enmity. Pasquerel and others later spoke not only of her tears for William Glasdale but also of her distress for any soldier, be he French or English, who might die unconfessed. On May 4, after an attack on the boulevard of St. Loup, Pasquerel recalled, Joan "lamented much" that so many English had been killed "without confession."[126] According to Louis de Coutes, once, when an English prisoner appearing near death was brought near Joan, she dismounted, held his head while he confessed, and consoled him to the best of her ability.[127]

Joan of Arc's forbearance was tested by more than insulting words. She came to know the English all too well from the time she was taken outside of Compiègne on May 23, 1430, until her death. We might well expect her to have flung words of defiance at the duke of Burgundy when he visited her after her capture. But of this encounter, the chronicler Monstrelet coyly reports only that "the Duke went to see her in the lodge where she was and spoke some words to her which I do not well remember, although I was present."[128] In his 1459 *Oratione* on the duke before Pope Pius II, Jean Jouffroy, bishop of Arras, claims that "Philip drew back from her and disdained to look her in the face," saying nothing.[129] Jules Quicherat offered a reconciliation of the two accounts by stating that the duke was showing his contempt for Joan by evincing no particular curiosity about her or speaking any word of consequence—thereby imprinting none on Monstrelet's memory.[130] A second encounter took place at Noyon on June 6, when Philip brought his new wife, Isabella of Portugal, to see Joan, reportedly at the Duchess's request. No record of their conversation exists.[131] In his letter to Henry VI on May 23, Philip reports Joan's capture, referring to her twice only as "she that thei calle the Pucelle."[132]

Unlike his English allies at Orléans, Duke Philip did not call Joan insulting names. As we have seen, she herself "began to sigh and weep copious tears" when English soldiers called her "the Armagnacs' whore." Yet at some point, although she had not exchanged profanities with Glasdale, she had learned or permitted herself to use the epithet "godon," which is usually taken to be at least mildly profane, but may not have been regarded so by Joan herself.

She famously abhorred swearing. A woman who had known her in her youth testified that Joan never swore; so did Jean de Metz.[133] Joan was especially offended to hear the Lord's name taken in vain and upbraided La Hire as well as the duc d'Alençon for their blasphemies.[134] In fact, according to a widow in Orléans, the Maid actually collared a "great lord" in the street and admonished him for his cursing and blasphemy.[135] So not only it is not surprising that Joan's use of the epithet *godon* is reported only twice, the word itself might not have been considered blasphemous. The first, a passing remark, occurs in the later deposition of Colette Milet, who said she went to see the Maid in the home of Jacques le Bouchier at Orléans. There, she says, he offered Joan a shad to eat, but Joan replied, "Keep it until this evening, for I will bring you a *godon* tonight." Moreover, Colette testified not only to Joan's modest demeanor, but also to her modest conversation.[136] Raoul de Gaucourt, the king's chief officer or bailiff of Orléans, agreed: "Only good words ever came out of her mouth, to edify and give good advice."[137] These examples suggest that someone, either Colette or the scribe, saw no contradiction between Joan's modest speech and her use of *godon*.

Later on, Joan again used the word to refer the English, but this time in the presence of some of her captors. Imprisoned in Rouen, surrounded by Englishmen—guards, prosecutors, and even noblemen such as the Earl of Warwick, Richard Beauchamp—there can be no doubt Joan feared and despised them and had reason to do so. English sympathizers surrounded her during both the public and the private questioning. Jean Massieu recalled that Joan had five English guards "of the most wretched estate" on twenty-four-hour watch, and that Anne, Duchess of Bedford, wielded her influence to protect the Maid from assault during her incarceration.[138] The patience Joan had shown in the face of insults at Orléans was sorely tested in prison. Indeed, at least once she was reported to have exchanged "rude words," with Jean d'Estivet, although only his insult of her is recorded.[139] After her death, however, a hostile writer claimed that Joan had said "Shit! Shit!" to a herald, impugning her memory by suggesting she was hypocritical in her attitude toward transgressive speech.[140]

On May 13, 1431, John of Luxembourg, who had custody of Joan for several months after her capture at Compiègne, visited Joan in her cell. Several other English nobles accompanied him. According to the later testimony of Aimon de Macy, a Burgundian knight also present, John mocked Joan with an offer to ransom her. Joan was furious, and responded, "I know very well that the English will have my death, believing that after my death they will win the kingdom of France; but, if there were 100,000 more godons than there are at present, they should not have the kingdom."[141] The transcript carefully glosses "godons" as "gallice," or "French." What did Joan mean or think she was saying this time?

Philologists and historians seem to agree only that *godon* was relatively new-minted in the fifteenth century and that it was used disparagingly. Although most often associated with the English, later on the term was used more generally.[142] One fifteenth-century lyric applied the word specifically to Henry VI, the "little Goddon King" (*petit roy Godon*).[143] In some cases, the word was associated with English drunkenness by analogy with "godale," or "good ale."[144] In others, it evoked English gluttony.[145] An early seventeenth-century English-French lexicon glosses *godon* as "a filthie glutton, or swiller."[146] Many examples survive to demonstrate that it was a popular coinage in its time. It was certainly derogatory, but was it considered a profanity?

In his *Dictionnaire historique*, compiled in the eighteenth century, Saint Palaye defined *goddon* as "surnom des Anglois" (nickname for the English), deriving it from "goddamn."[147] In his edition of Joan of Arc's trial documents, Jules Quicherat cautiously glossed it as "a popular fifteenth century expression for the English."[148] Godefroy had conceived of a more specific etymology: "an insulting term directed at the English because of their national oath 'god damn.'"[149] However, none of the surviving fifteenth-century examples contextually relates the epithet to the English "goddamn." Indeed, the sole instance of the term in the *Oxford English Dictionary* before the seventeenth century cites only de Macy's testimony, defining "goddon" merely as "an Englishman." Otherwise, "goddamn" is not recorded as an English profanity until 1640.[150] It seems likely, then, that in using a commonplace and fairly innocuous term of insult for the English, Joan's diction was consistent with her lifetime abhorrence of profanity. She was, of course, finally accused of more serious crimes of language: blasphemy and heresy.[151]

Not a month after Joan's execution, letters in Latin and French over the signature of King Henry VI went out to European leaders describing her trial and arguing that the English motivation was devoid of self-interest, and a legitimate response to an imminent danger.[152] The missive lays bare the English view of Joan just after her death. Carefully rehearsing the status of the English as God's true people obedient to the ecclesiastical authority that required that the Maid be remanded for trial, the letter expresses England's pious judicial intention toward the "false prophetess" (the appellation "prophetess" is echoed in the two earliest versions of the London chronicle mentioning Joan, for the year 1431).[153] After summarizing the twelve articles that condemned Joan and rejoicing in God's "great mercy and clemency" for allowing her to be captured, the letter launches a defense of the execution, emphasizing Joan as both religiously and politically schismatic. First, she was "notorious and defamed for crimes of treason against God," and thus turned over to ecclesiastical judgment "as is right." The implication is that the Holy Mother Church would also protect her from any vengeance or punishment by secular authorities. Such retribution would be reasonably lawful (*raisonnablement licite*) because of the "the great harms and inconveniences, horrible homicides and detestable cruelties and other innumerable evils that she committed against our lordship and loyal, obedient people."[154]

Although the letter focuses on Joan's crimes against religion, it is clear that the legitimacy of Henry VI's secular realm in France and possibly in England was also at issue in Joan's trial and vindicated by God and man in her conviction. Only three decades earlier, Henry's grandfather had usurped his cousin Richard II's throne. The Lancastrians *were* legitimately descended from kings, but Henry IV was neither Richard's heir presumptive nor heir apparent. The letter is, moreover, unquestionably in the voice of John Bedford, in whom Joan had inspired what was apparently personal loathing.[155] When he spoke or wrote in his own behalf, not the king's, his antipathy is clear. True, she had publicly questioned his status as regent of France in her letter of March 22, 1429, addressing "you, Duke of Bedford, *who call yourself* Regent of the Kingdom of France" (emphasis added).[156] She had taken it upon herself to force the lifting of the siege of Orléans, reanimating French morale. She had led the dauphin Charles to a public coronation in Reims, flouting the duke's dedication to maintaining the legacy of his brother and king, Henry V. In August 1429, scant weeks after the coronation on July 17 and with the humiliating rout of the English forces at Patay a month earlier still rankling, the regent challenged the French king to single combat and wrote to "Charles de Valois, who used to call yourself Dauphin de Vienne and now without grounds call yourself king." Among the grievances to be resolved by this encounter that Bedford notes was the fact that Charles's legitimacy was suspect because he was supported by "superstitious and damned persons, such as a disorderly and discredited woman, wearing the clothing of a man and of dissolute conduct."[157]

The duke expressed the full extent of his frustration with Joan's temerity—perhaps displacing his fury at the Earl of Salisbury's independent decision to lay siege to Orléans and his continuing disagreements on policy with Humphrey, Duke of Gloucester—in his testimony to Henry VI's Privy Council in 1434, when he submitted articles defending his conduct of the wars in France in the early years of the king's reign.[158] After asserting his desire to reassert his loyalty and "discharge of myself as toward eny defaute or blame" that "myght to the hurt of my name or fame," the duke rehearses his many victories in France after the death of Henry V. I quote at length to show the context in which his antipathy toward Joan of Arc resurfaces:

> Everything there prospered for you until the time of the siege of Orléans, undertaken by God knows whose advice. At which time after the misfortune that befell my cousin Salisbury (whom God absolve), it seems by the hand of God, a great blow fell upon your people who were assembled there in great numbers, caused in great part as I believe by a lack of steadfast belief and unlawful fear they had in a disciple and limb of the fiend called the Pucelle who used false enchantments and sorcery, the which stroke and discomfiture not only greatly lessened the number of your people there but also caused the courage of the rest to decline exceedingly, and encouraged your adversaries and enemies to assemble forthwith in great numbers, to which several of your great cities and towns . . . yielded themselves without resistance or waiting for help.[159]

Bedford then describes how efficiently he regrouped the English forces and initiated a series of moves to recover from this disaster.[160] The duke's witness is both personal and disingenuous. During the fifteenth century, momentum was building toward the era of concerted witch-hunting, suggesting that his choice of language—"disciple and limb of the fiend"—was politically canny. Moreover, he and his audience knew full well whose advice had directed the Earl of Salisbury's army toward Orléans, even after Bedford had advised they be mustered toward Angers: the duke of Gloucester.[161]

Defiant words were part of Joan's stock in trade, but profane or personally insulting ones were not—not when news of French losses reached Domrémy, not when she was publicly defamed as a whore, not when she stood dying before an immense crowd including many English. During her youth, a great deal of accurate and timely information about the conduct of the war, about major battles and diplomatic relations made its way regularly throughout the areas loyal to the crown. Some of this probably included deliberate propaganda, strategically circulated in border areas and in places where travelers holding sundry loyalties might converge. At least as early as 1424, with reports about the French loss at Verneuil, the Maid's heavenly inspiration was informed by facts and intensified by propaganda disseminated in sermons. A pious and passionate adolescent who seems to have traveled widely and freely, even amid the dangers posed by her geographical situation, would likely have been drawn to preaching and processions that advanced the cause of the dauphin as the rightful king. She was in places and circumstances in which she might well have learned a great deal about the paunchy, profane English, and just possibly in her youth glimpsed one or more insular soldiers or noncombatants. Nevertheless, in spite of the burning of Domrémy, of insult, injury, and abuse, Joan of Arc did not indulge in a personal hatred for those she casually referred to as *godons*—until they proved to her in the marketplace of Rouen that they "were all lost" and deserved to be damned by her God.

CHAPTER 2

"THE MARTIALL MAIDE"

*Joan of Arc and the French in England*

> It is not to be doubted but that the magnanimity of the English would have spared her, had they not found it necessary to deface the opinion which the French, even with superstition, had conceived of her.
> —John Speed, *Historie of Great Britaine* (1611)

An English traveler to Orléans in 1622 witnessed a "procession 'twixt Military and Ecclesiastic for the Maid of Orleans, which is perform'd every year very solemnly; her Statue stands upon the Bridge, and her Clothes are preserv'd to this day, which a young Man wore in the Procession." James Howell, future historiographer to Charles II, adds that after the English were "driven to Normandy," one "Anne de Arque" was "taken Prisoner, and the English had a fair revenge upon her, for by an Arrest of the Parliament of Rouen she was burnt for a Witch."[1] In April 1644, another traveler described that same statue (later destroyed) of the medieval city's liberator: "At one of the extreames of the bridge are strong toures; and about the middle neere one side, the statue of the Virgin Mary, or Pieta, with a Christo Morto in her lap, as big as the lif; At one side of the Crosse kneeles Charles the vii[th] arm'd, and at the other Jane d'Arc the famous Pucele arm'd also like a Cavalier with boots & spurs, her hayre dischevel'd as the Virago who deliver'd the Towne from our Countrymen, what time they beseig'd it: The valiant Creature being afterward burnt at Rouen for a Witch."[2] Five years later, in the spring of 1649, yet another young Englishman visited Orléans in his turn and reported, "In honor of [the Maid of Orléans] they make yearely a generall procession the eight of May, which is the day shee raised the seege of the english, where all the orders of the towne doth assist, which goes as farre as the bridge where there is a Masse said."[3] The 1644 tourist, diarist John Evelyn, while identifying with "our Countrymen," praises Joan of Arc without apparent irony as a "virago"—simply, a warrior woman—and "valiant," as Gabriel Harvey had written of her in his 1584 *Commonplace Book*.[4] The later tourist, Robert Montagu, Lord Mandeville, can so distance himself from any defensive chauvinism as to refer to his ancestors as "the English." Two hundred years after her death, two hundred years after she raised the English siege of Orléans and established Charles VII on his throne, the statue of Joan of Arc embodies neither shame nor threat to the descendants of those Englishmen who had called her "witch," "whore," and "limb of the fiend."[5]

Such nonchalance is not new or unusual among English redactors of the events that led eventually to the relinquishment of their nation's last foothold on the Continent. The earliest chronicles denominate Joan of Arc as a witch. Some later historians impugn her virginity. Others seem deliberately to displace her from the scenes of her greatest triumphs in their accounts of the Hundred Years' War or the reign of Henry VI. Still others transfer her successes to her male counterparts. Not a few ignore her completely, as does William Martyn in his 1615 *Historie and Lives of Twentie Kings of England*. Martyn gives all credit for the lifting of the siege of Orléans to Jean, duc d'Alençon, and all credit to the dauphin Charles himself for recovering Reims so that he could be crowned there.[6] Yet by the turn of the seventeenth century, English writers, sometimes indignantly, sometimes wryly, generally acknowledge their ancestors' culpability for Joan's death. As Malcolm Vale puts it, "British national histories—not normally discussed in this context—have tended to be remarkably accepting of the view that it was as a result of English coercion, pressure and threat that Joan was condemned and put to death."[7] Indeed, the histories often repeat the arguments in Bedford's letter to Europe, justifying the execution and arguing for the legality of the sentence, or asserting that Joan herself drove the English, proud of their native magnanimity, to their limit. In essence, the publication of John Speed's *Historie of Great Britaine* in 1611, with its extensive use of a recent French history and a prologue that boasts of an internationally favorable view of Great Britain, marks a point when Joan's story is definitively integrated into the larger narrative of English history by most historians. Speed is the first to move English opinion in a new direction: acknowledge the possibility of one's ancestors' error, but turn the ultimate blame back on the Maid herself. The execution of

Joan of Arc, carried out by the civil—that is, English—authorities in Rouen on May 30, 1431, handed down to the island nation an unsettling legacy: the distasteful reputation of having burnt not an apostate, idolater, and relapsed heretic but, as the king of England's secretary Jean Tressart had lamented, "a holy person."[8] From the fifteenth through the seventeenth centuries, English writers had to accommodate not only this conundrum but also the increasing number of printed French texts that began to incorporate information from the manuscripts of Joan's trials. In this chapter, I explore how the English approached the uneasy marriage of conflicting national points of view.

Given the focus on domestic affairs in England during the fifteenth century amid the upheaval of the struggle between Lancastrians and Yorkists during the so-called Wars of the Roses commencing in 1455, it is not surprising that most English chronicles of the time pay little or no mind to Joan of Arc. Nor was she mentioned in official documents, except those drafted by the duke of Bedford: the 1431 letter to Europe and his articles of defense before the Privy Council in 1434. Not until after her conviction for heresy was nullified in 1456, coincident with the struggle between Lancastrian Henry VI and Yorkist claimants to the throne, did the English begin to intuit the need to construct their own history of Joan of Arc. Thus, the story of Joan of Arc told by the London chronicle, dating from the beginning of the fifteenth century, is made to fit into a narrative highlighting the dangers of domestic upheaval.[9] The invention of a new calumny, Joan's claim to be pregnant to avoid execution as printed in William Caxton's *Cronycles of England* in 1480, was a direct response to a post–Lancastrian England.

Early in the fifteenth century, while the English king was still in his minority and the war with France was ongoing despite Joan of Arc's efforts, the chroniclers recorded rather little about the Maid—likely all they knew. Even though they portray her as a witch and associate her capture with young Henry's arrival in France in 1430, they reflect none of the antipathy of Bedford or of her pro-English judges. As W. T. Waugh pointed out long ago, most emphasize the capture of the Maid with little attention to any of her battles and none to her role in Charles's coronation. They offer no account of her trial or execution.[10] Some historians of the Hundred Years' War such as Edouard Perroy found the chroniclers' indifference rather strange, for "if Joan's feats of arms had created in the ranks of the English soldiers such dismay as legend would have been quick to exaggerate, fugitives and deserters would have communicated it to their fellow-countrymen." Perroy adds, "Moreover, if Bedford had staged the trial at Rouen in order to bolster up his tottering rule, he would not have failed to circulate its result widely in England. But nothing like this is to be found in the English chronicles, whose aridity, brevity, and inexactitude prove that there was little or no interest in England in the adventure which posterity turned into a wonderful epic."[11] That very brevity and inexactitude attest that in the decades between Joan's death and the nullification proceedings, what was important to English writers was potential and actual civil upheaval, soon to be realized in Jack Sharpe's uprising against ecclesiastical wealth and property in 1432 and Jack Cade's 1450 rebellion against perceived abuses of power and mounting national debt, as well as in the struggle for the crown.[12]

The London chronicle's emphasis on the dangers of domestic disorder accords with concerns evident in the original articles of indictment at Joan's trial, which represented her actions as an affront to conventions of class and gender as well as to political and ecclesiastical authority. Article 66, for example, read to her on March 28, 1431, itemizes her divergence from such norms: "Some of these matters depart from divine, evangelical, canon, and civil law, and are contrary to decrees approved in general councils."[13] Both in the articles and in the London chronicle, Joan is associated with political and religious rebellion; the latter overlook the potential narrative drama and didactic value of her military achievements, trial, and execution. This might seem surprising, for, as Mary-Rose McLaren notes, the chroniclers often narrate the course of major battles, not merely for their intrinsic interest, but "to discuss implicitly the qualities of kingship."[14] Thus, for Chris Given-Wilson, they suggest a contemporary "sense of being English," which "meant above all supporting the nation at war, whether it be with France and Scotland, England's traditional enemies, or further afield."[15] While the story of Joan's execution might have illustrated the appropriate punishment for rebellion (under the guise of heresy), the reminder might just as easily have evoked the debacles at Orléans and Patay and the disturbing achievement of the coronation of Charles VII.

Just over half of the surviving manuscripts of the London chronicle—fifteen out of twenty-three manuscripts—even mention Joan of Arc. In her study of the fifteenth-century chronicles, Mary-Rose McLaren identifies four distinct versions, distributed among two groups dating from before and two dating from after the Nullification.[16] The first and earliest version describes the English capture of a "wycche," whom the Armagnacs (the supporters of Charles VII), it reports, considered "as a prophetesse and a goddesse."[17] The narrative juxtaposes the arrival of the newly crowned Henry VI in France with Joan's capture, clearly inviting the reader to connect cause and effect.

The second version provides further details: "[On] the xxiij day off May ayenst nyht, byfore the toune off Compayne ther was a woman takyn y-armed in the ffeld with many other worthy capyteyns, the whiche was called Pucell de Dieux, a false witche, ffor thurh her power the dolphyn and alle oure adversariis trusted hooly to have conquerd ayen all ffraunce, and never to have hadde the wors in place that she hadde ben Inne, ffor they helden hire amongest hem ffor a prophetesse and a worthy goddesse."[18] This second version anticipates Martyn's 1615 *Historie* by crediting the "duke of Lanson" [Alençon] with the victory at Orléans. This is the earliest English example of the displacement of Joan from the scenes of her greatest triumphs, but it would not be the last. The chronicle makes clear that the young king had left his insular realm in reliable hands, because it then takes up the duke of Gloucester's defeat of Jack Sharpe's rebellion back in England. It showcases the importance of the monarch's presence in that part of France still held by the English and associates him favorably with the forces of godliness and good order that removed Joan from the field of battle and reduced her influence over the dauphin. Another manuscript version of this text rearranges the order in which it reports Henry's landing at Calais on St. George's Day (April 23) and Joan's capture (May 30), in effect transforming his arrival into a triumphal entry.[19] McLaren suggests that such rearrangements were made deliberately in order to bring attention to "causation and significance."[20] Yet another recension, dating from after the nullification, restores the chronology, suggesting no connection.[21] As we shall see, after the nullification Joan's English reputation was radically altered.

These early city chronicles also deal circumspectly with Joan's attire, a matter that was later to dominate English considerations of her, one that had been an integral part of the Rouen indictments and was emphasized in Henry's letter to Europe. She is a "woman" and armed, but not armed *like*, or dressed *as*, a man.[22] The chroniclers make no direct connection between such transgressive behavior and their denomination of Joan as a witch. Yet they did demonstrate their interest in witchcraft trials, notably that of Eleanor Cobham, Duchess of Gloucester, in 1440.[23] Significantly, a version of the chronicle possibly dating from *after* the nullification refers to the capture and execution of "Pusylle" but does not name her as witch or sorceress. Rather, by reporting her death after its account of the beheadings of Jack Sharpe and his followers—including a woman—the chronicle implies, according to McLaren, that it was "simply one of a collection of deaths for heresy and rebellion."[24] Warnings of the consequences of rebellion against divine order had, of course, immediate echoes in the England of the 1460s. From those circumstances emerged a new way to denigrate Joan of Arc.

By the late 1450s, England had lost all the territory it had claimed or conquered in France save Calais, effectively ending the Hundred Years' War.

Henry VI experienced his first mental breakdown in 1453 and did not reassume his duties for over a year.[25] He was forced into exile in 1461, the same year Charles VII died, removing from power both the uncle and nephew whose fates the Treaty of Troyes had sought to determine. Coincidentally, their respective fathers, Henry V and Charles VI, had died within weeks of each other in 1422. Both the new king of France, Louis XI, and Charles the Bold, who became duke of Burgundy in 1467, had a stake in the outcome of England's internal power struggle. Duke Charles supported the Yorkist Edward IV's renewed claim to the French throne, while King Louis supported the troubled Lancastrians. This proxy dispute certainly contributed to what Edward Meek describes as the "frosty" relations between the nations in the early 1460s.[26]

Just as Charles VII's crown had been defended by a Frenchwoman in his time of adversity, so was Henry VI's—by his French wife, Queen Margaret of Anjou, who, like Joan of Arc, hailed from Lorraine. Like Catherine of Valois's marriage to Henry V, Margaret's marriage was another attempt to reconcile the "contending kingdoms." After Henry's capture by Yorkist forces in 1460, she became the effective leader of the Lancastrians. Writing in 1611, John Speed called her the "true head and life of the contrary part."[27] However, amid the tumult of the events of 1460 and 1461 came allegations impugning Margaret's chastity and the legitimacy of her son Edward.[28] This particular strategy for damaging the reputation and credibility of a woman warrior foreshadows attacks on Joan of Arc's purity. Henry's brief return to power ended with his murder in 1471 and his posthumous sanctification.[29] The Yorkist supremacy itself did not last long and ended with the defeat of Richard III by Henry Tudor in 1485. Ironically, by marrying Elizabeth of York, Henry VII in his turn attempted to finesse any future strife—the same hope ultimately unrealized by the marriages of Henry V and Henry VI.[30]

In 1449, King Charles VII of France recaptured Rouen, where Joan of Arc's trial transcripts were housed, and the following year, for what appear to be purely political reasons, he initiated an inquiry into Joan's trial of condemnation. Association with the woman burned as a heretic had tainted the legitimacy of his reign. He also desired to repair his relationship with the papacy, damaged as a result of the Pragmatic Sanction of 1438, which appointed a French ecclesiastical council that in some ways superseded papal authority.[31] The nullification hearing was framed as an examination both of imperfect procedure and of personal malefaction on the part of Bishop Pierre Cauchon, as well as a response to a petition by Isabelle Romée for the restitution of her daughter's and her family's *fama* or good name—an important value in fifteenth-century France, especially, one assumes, for a family newly elevated to the nobility.[32] As well, incorporating frequent suggestions of English remorse into the transcripts was a useful tactic in removing additional stigma from Charles, who apparently never even secretly offered to negotiate a ransom, exchange, or escape for Joan.[33] Since Henry VI still upheld his claim to the French throne, it was in England's interest to keep alive such guilt by association. As news of the nullification was disseminated, there came increasingly categorical accusations that the English had stacked the deck against Joan. Craig Taylor reads the nullification testimony as specifically "blaming the English for exerting pressure to secure the death of Joan, and arguing that they had been frightened into cooperating with such a manifestly unjust action. In short, the primary goal of the Nullification trial may not have been to restore the reputation of the Pucelle but to expunge the legacy of collaboration with the English and to give added substance to her dream of a united France."[34] Around 1459, Pope Pius II opined, "It is possible that the English, who had been vanquished by her in so many battles, never regarded themselves as entirely safe with the virgin alive, even though she was a prisoner, and that they feared that she might escape or work some magic and therefore sought an excuse for her death."[35] The Burgundian chronicler Georges Chastellain, writing in the second half of the century, declared the trial to have been conducted "well and justly,"[36] but Martial d'Auvergne, who wrote a verse account of Charles' reign, declared the original judges "were biased." In his opinion, the original sentence was "iniquitous, abusive, defective, and she was condemned wrongly by very suspect judges."[37]

After Joan's trial had been declared iniquitous and her judges biased, and after the Yorkist Edward IV had established himself as king, an original defense of English magnanimity in the case appeared, supplementing the arguments for the justice of the trial in Henry VI's letter to Europe. The London chronicle was not the only source of fifteenth-century English history. The so-called *Brut*, a history of England from its legendary origins begun during the reign of Edward I (1272–1307) and written originally in Anglo-Norman, was, according to Lister Matheson, "the most popular secular work of the Middle Ages in England."[38] By the fourteenth century, it was translated into Middle English, and although many manuscript versions end with the reign of Edward III or Henry V, numerous continuations during the fifteenth century added material from the reign of Henry VI.[39] The story of Joan of Arc in one late continuation of the *Brut* prefigures the construction of Shakespeare's whorish witch, conjuring the legend of her purported pregnancy seemingly, yet purposefully, out of thin air. Once Joan was condemned, it tells us, "she said that she was with childe, wherby she was respited A while; but in conclusion it was found that she was not with child, and then she was brent in Roane."[40] Whether or not the printer William Caxton was responsible for inventing this calumny, as Matheson and others have suggested, his printed compilation, *The Cronycles of Englond* (1480) largely taken from the *Brut*, assured that it would be widely disseminated.[41]

As we have seen, after the nullification of Joan's conviction for heresy, there were ample political reasons for the English to rework the Maid's role in their history. Earlier in the century, it was enough to categorize her as a witch. However, after the verdict that had condemned her was nullified in 1456, the question of Joan's divine inspiration was no longer moot. From an English point of view, Joan's credibility had to be undermined. The most obvious way to demystify a heaven-sent virgin would be to show her to be promiscuous, the same tactic used to defame Margaret of Anjou. Even better to have her deny her virginity out of her own mouth. In its invention of a pseudo-pregnancy for the Maid, the *Brut* evokes English criminal law to show her sentence was neither precipitous nor arbitrary. At the same time, the *Brut* as well as some of the earlier narratives, consciously or not, also reflects a tradition of writing about women warriors.[42]

Although the earliest chronicles have been scrutinized for any hints of English opinion about Joan, her appearance as a military leader who is also a potentially fertile female, despite her vow of virginity, has been overlooked. Once Joan of Arc enters the English historical stream, she becomes part of a narrative including several other women warriors who led men in battle.[43] Unlike Joan, they are generally high-ranking women and mothers, notably Ælfleda of Mercia (d. 918), the daughter of King Alfred, and the Empress Maud (d. 1167), the daughter of Henry I.[44] It is instructive to compare how early chroniclers of English history present these leaders with how later ones situate Joan of Arc. The women's reproductive decisions and "masculine" behavior weigh heavily in the balance of chroniclers' evaluations of them, as did Joan's vow of virginity and her preference for men's clothing. Consistent in all eras is an unwillingness to uncouple a woman's leadership from her identity as a sexual being.

Medieval chroniclers' representation of women in military capacities varied considerably. In general, the seven extant manuscripts of *Anglo-Saxon Chronicle*, begun in the reign of King Alfred (reigned 871–99) report Ælfleda's activities following her husband Æthelred's death in 911 as part of a given year's important events: building fortresses, occupying Derby, and both sending out and leading military expeditions. In the year of her own death, 918, the *Chronicle* eulogized her as having ruled the Mercians "for eight years . . . with just authority," suggesting, as does her epithet, "Lady of the Mercians," that she wielded power independent of her brother, King Edward the Elder, or of her husband. Yet another manuscript merely notes without comment that she died in that year.[45]

Some time after the Norman Conquest, Anglo-Norman historian Henry of Huntingdon following the method of the *Anglo-Saxon Chronicle*, provides a year-by-year itemization of Ælfleda's political and military accomplishments. His language suggests he accepts her as a ruler in her own right: she ruled (*regebat*) for her infirm "father" (he confuses Alfred for Æthelred, her husband), and he consistently terms her *domina Merce*. In fact, Huntingdon writes, "Some call her not only lady, or queen, but even king." Ultimately, however, Huntingdon defines her valor as a masculine trait, eulogizing her in Latin verses as "O mighty Æthelflæd! O virgin, the dread of men [*terror virgo virorum*], conqueror of nature, worthy of a man's name! Nature made you a girl, so you would be more illustrious; your prowess made you acquire the name of man."[46] In the twelfth century, as well, chroniclers emphasized Ælfleda's marital chastity even before her widowhood. The monkish historian William of Malmesbury states, "She was a woman of great determination who, after having difficulties with the birth of her first, or rather her only, child, abhorred her husband's embraces ever after." Calling her a "virago," he adds, "It would be hard to say whether it was luck or character that made a woman such a tower of strength for the men of her own side and such a terror to the rest."[47]

As with Ælfleda, so with the Empress Maud, whose first husband was the Holy Roman Emperor, Henry V. Daughter of Henry I of England and at one point named as his heir, she went to war in 1139 to claim the English throne from Stephen of Blois, Henry's cousin, against the opposition of most of the English nobility. Chroniclers both praised and damned her behavior, based on their gender-driven expectations.[48] Equating her forthrightness with unfemininity, abbot William of Newburgh declared that both nobles and citizens were alienated by the empress's "intolerable female arrogance."[49] An account of King Stephen's reign, *The Acts of Stephen*, goes further: "She at once put on an extremely arrogant demeanour instead of the modest gait and bearing proper to the gentle sex, began to walk and speak and do all things more stiffly and more haughtily than she had been wont, to such a point that soon, in the capital of the land subject to her, she actually made herself queen of all England and gloried in being so called."[50] However, William of Malmesbury praises Maud as "unmindful of her sex and a worthy rival of the Amazons of old," who "led into battle, woman as she was, the columns of men clad in mail."[51] He admiringly calls her "virago."[52]

In her study of medieval women warriors, Megan McLaughlin observes that, in the Middle Ages, an increasing intolerance of unwomanly behavior and the professionalization of the military combined to increase the possibility of woman warriors being viewed as not only "anomalous," as she says, but threatening. She writes, "From the late eleventh century on, a variety of sanctions were directed at women who participated in warfare, sanctions ranging from restrictive legislation to ridicule to charges of sexual misconduct or even witchcraft." She provides the example of Richilde of Hainault, who acted as regent of Flanders in the early eleventh century. A contemporary account of the battle of Cassel (1070) merely reports Richilde of Hainaut's presence, while two hundred years later, her role was, in McLaughlin's words, "to throw 'magic powder' on the opposing army."[53] The association of a woman warrior with unnatural magic clearly did not originate in the career of Joan of Arc. Focusing on medieval queenship, Pauline Stafford also traces the effects of increasing misogyny and "gender definition that stressed the public, military man" on complicating the picture drawn by twelfth century and later chroniclers of those whom William of Malmesbury had praised as viragos.[54] Although warfare was always assumed to be the domain of men, these early chroniclers did not overlook women who fought, even as they unsexed them or presented them as agents of men. Joan of Arc, as we shall see, was also sometimes accused of being the tool of powerful men, while her virginity became the locus of her authenticity.

Historically, viragos were portrayed as women even if praised for acting like men. They were especially praiseworthy if they tempered their sexuality or fertility. Nancy Huston argues that "the idea that the loss of virginity makes women vulnerable, or that motherhood deprives them of their capacity to fight, is another proof of the specifically human nature of war."[55] An exception was the Amazon woman who might give birth but who also might remain a virgin, such as Homer's Penthesilea. Classical and medieval anxieties do seem to coalesce in the late fifteenth-century *Brut*. While, at least according to William of Malmesbury, chastity could be seen as favorable to a married woman's martial career and reputation, a "pucelle de dieu" could afford no hint of sexuality, except to eschew it.[56] Not only did the historical Joan of Arc testify that she had (secretly) avowed her virginity to God around the time of puberty,[57] Jean d'Alençon recalled her intolerance for the usual camp followers in her army.[58]

Thus, in the late fifteenth century, the *Brut*'s declaration that after being condemned, "she said that she was with child, whereupon she was spared a little while, but in conclusion it was found that she was not with child, and then she was burned," is carefully framed to lend verisimilitude to calumny. Having lost her virginity, Joan lost her protection, as the sixteenth-century Scots historian Hector Boece makes explicit: "Some say that as long as she kept her virginity inviolate, no adverse fortune befell her. But after her unchastity contaminated her, as I have said, evil betrayed her."[59] Joan herself was reported to have said that she was being harassed, possibly physically assaulted, if not actually raped, while in prison.[60] Nancy Bradley Warren reads Joan's and others' suggestive testimony about such threats as "ample grounds for Caxton's mention of a possible pregnancy (albeit not a pregnancy plea)" based on contemporary English prison conditions, including males guarding women and the mixing of the sexes.[61] Aside from reflecting current conditions, however, the invention of Joan's pregnancy plea defended the English decision to have her executed.

If a woman in an English prison had been sentenced to die yet claimed to be pregnant, then she had legal recourse. The allowed custom of "pleading the belly" (*de ventre inspiciendo*) is recorded in English writs from at least the thirteenth century.[62] In many instances, the plea hinged on questions of inheritance, not criminality, but a woman sentenced to death could make such a plea.[63] If such a writ were granted, the woman making this claim would be physically examined by a respectable group of women, commonly known as a "jury of matrons."[64] The purpose was to protect the unborn child, but the mere fact of pregnancy was not sufficient to delay punishment in the case of a capital indictment. Even for a delay in the execution of a woman's sentence (*in retardationem executionis*), the fetus must have begun to move. According to William Blackstone, if the matrons find the woman

> *quick with child* (for, barely, *with child*, unless it be alive in the womb, is not sufficient) execution shall be staid generally till the next session; and so from session to session, till either she is delivered, or proves by the course of nature not to have been with child at all. But if she once hath had the benefit of this reprieve, and been delivered, and afterwards becomes pregnant again, she shall not be entitled to the benefit of a farther respite for that cause. For she may now be executed before the child is quick in the womb; and shall not, by her own incontinence, evade the sentence of justice.[65]

Records for at least half a dozen cases from the thirteenth to the fifteenth centuries attest to the consistency of this procedure.[66] Fifteenth-century records of similar pleas are scant but show that the law had not changed. Katherine

Newport was found guilty of larceny in the north of England in 1468 and condemned to death. Her pregnancy being proved, she was sent to prison instead.[67] In 1488, one Elizabeth Thomson of London was "convicted of robbery, pleaded pregnancy and used the respite to purchase a pardon."[68] As Richard J. Sims reminds us, "in the medieval world, . . . expectancy would do nothing more than delay the inevitable and, as a result, few women would have feigned pregnancy,"[69] as Joan of Arc was alleged to have done. This is not to argue that in writing his account of the reign of Henry VI, Caxton was inspired by any particular case. However, he had found a way both to impugn the Maid's character and to promote the legality of her execution under *English* law. Indeed, albeit for a later period and in a slightly different context, Frances Dolan argues that "to the extent that printed texts refer to women's attempts to plead the belly, they usually do so in order to discredit the woman."[70] In short, the *Brut* represents Joan as a woman tried under English criminal law (not the Inquisition), resorting to a legal and time-tested strategy for extending her life, even if her pregnancy were disproved. The conclusion we are to draw is that the English treated her fairly and justly in granting her this respite.

The emphasis on the justice of English law becomes an emphasis on Joan's wickedness in the revised edition of Raphael Holinshed's *Chronicles* (1587), one of the texts that formed the basis of Shakespeare's *I Henry VI*—which portrayed Joan Puzel as a serial fornicator. Holinshed tells us Joan "stake [scrupled] not (though the shift were shamefull) to confesse hir self a strumpet, and (unmaried as she was) to be with child. For triall, the lord regents lenitie [leniency] gave hir nine moneths staie, at the end whereof she found herein as false as wicked in the rest."[71] The popularity of the *Brut* as promulgated in editions of Caxton and his successor printers doubtless contributed much not only to the perception that Joan of Arc's reputation in England throughout the sixteenth century was unremittingly hostile, but as Anke Bernau argues, that it was "expressed in a contestation of her virginity" even among those writers who do not repeat the tale of her pregnancy.[72]

The historian Hector Boece (or Boethius)'s *Scotorum Historiae*, or *History of Scotland* (1526) illustrates this contestation. As we have seen, Boece suggests a connection between Joan's execution and her unchastity, based on hearsay. Boece does not offer an explanation as to how Joan might have been defiled. Two versions of a translation by the poet John Bellenden, commissioned by James V of Scotland, differ substantially on these lines: a manuscript (Pierpont Morgan Library MS. M.527) and the first printed edition of 1536.[73] The manuscript follows Boece closely: "It is sayd, sa lang as scho kepitt hir virginite scho was victorious in every batall, but ony experience of fortoun adversair, and fra scho was corruppitt and tynt hir chaistite, scho fell in all thir inconvenientis afoir rehersitt."[74] The printed edition eliminates the qualification "some say" but, more importantly, states that Joan herself was aware of the protective power of her virginity: "Scho confessit, schortlie afore her deith, sa lang as scho keippit hir virginite, scho wes victorius in every battall, but ony experience of evill fortoun; and fra scho wes corruppit, scho wes maid sone pray to hir ennimes."[75] Ryoko Harikae points out that not only did Bellenden continuously revise his work before it was printed, but in doing so, he also consulted sources other than Boece. She notes that this occurs particularly in book 16 (which ends with Joan of Arc), where, under the influence of humanistic historiography, he strove more than in the earlier books to "provide useful moral or political lessons and models for readers."[76] Perhaps Boece's more direct accusation of Joan's "sorcery and incantations" and their consequences was intended as a moral lesson. (Such negative Scottish opinions of Joan of Arc are a little surprising. A hundred years earlier, the Scots had strongly supported their French allies, incurring devastating losses of life at the Battle of Verneuil [1424] and elsewhere.[77]) The link between Joan's virginity and her ill fortune was widely published: Boece's *Scotorum Historiae* was printed four times in the sixteenth century and Bellenden's translation thrice. The publication of so many editions suggests that "it was read all over north-west Europe" and "written as much for a European audience as for a purely Scottish one," according to Nicola Royan in her comparative study of the two texts.[78] Both Holinshed and Richard Baker cite Boece as a source for their later chronicles.

The tradition of chronicle writing in England essentially died out by the seventeenth century, with the notable exception of Sir Richard Baker's 1635 *Chronicle of the Kings of England*, which became a standard popular work of history—derided, but updated and reprinted well into the eighteenth century. Despite the comprehensiveness of Holinshed and John Speed, to whom I will return, Baker unselfconsciously sought to produce an encyclopedic compilation of available chronicles to date so that, in his own words, "if all other Chronicles should be lost, yet this onely would be sufficient to informe Posterity of all passages memorable or worthy to be knowne, which of any other generall Chronicle, cannot perhaps be said" (A2v).[79] Baker's work appealed to ordinary readers and was widely disseminated, so that, like the *Brut*, it serves as an important conduit for the English narrative of Joan of Arc. From 1643 to 1733, it was reprinted almost a dozen times, including as an abridgement and with continuations to the reign of Charles II, and was even translated into Dutch. Such contemporary historians as D. R. Woolf praise its "elegant summary of all earlier chronicles,"[80] while Martine Brownley notes that "Baker's longterm popularity with the general reader is particularly significant in view of the uniformly negative response to his work by educated men."[81] It was popular by virtue of his inclusion of vivid details, natural "wonders" such as dragons, and gossip. In his "Epistle to the Reader," Baker admits as much: "Where many have written the Reignes of some of our Kings, excellently as in the way of History, yet I may say they have not done it so well in the way of Chronicle; For whilst they insist wholly upon matters of State, they wholly omit meaner Accidents, which yet are Materials as proper for a Chronicle, as the other" (A2). Moreover, he acknowledges that at times he "may seeme rather to transcribe than to write," copying some passages verbatim. Yet Baker was not wholly indiscriminate in his use of sources. In writing of James I's reign, for example, he omits "some Passages of small moment" because "for want of knowing the particulars, I dare not venture upon making the Relation: which if some men would have done, the truth of our Chronicles should not have been mingled with so many falsities" (2:145). Overall, his comprehensiveness made the *Chronicle* precisely the kind of work that serious amateur historians loved to consult.[82] As such, it would be in Baker that many readers could find a lively and detailed narrative of Joan of Arc, printed in legible roman typeface and in an easy prose style.

Baker's account of Joan of Arc, however, is not entirely straightforward. Whether so intent on comprehensiveness that he hesitated to abridge or edit his sources lest he overlook some detail, or as a result of the challenge of conveying simultaneous events in sequence as had Fabyan and Rastell, as we shall see, or with some purpose to relegate Joan to the margins, Baker, like his fifteenth-century predecessors, rearranges the chronology of events that involved the Maid. He also eliminates any mention of Joan's cross-dressing. His praise for earlier viragos is tempered. While acknowledging that some of her brother's "glory . . . must be imparted to his sister *Elflede*," who "made choyce to follow the warres," he also writes that she was not acting on her own but "assisting her brother both against the *Welch*, and against the *Danes*" (1:12). Similarly, he devalues Empress Maud's valor, for her escape from the siege of Oxford "left such an impression of feare upon her, that she never after had any mind to appeare upon this stage of Warre, but left the prosecution of it to her Sonne Henry" (1:64).

Given his reluctance to allow that women could take autonomous action in war, perhaps it is not surprising that Baker, as had William Martyn, makes Jean, duc d'Alençon, not Joan of Arc, the hero of Orléans: "The Duke of Alanson . . . furnished the Towne with fresh Forces and Provision; which put such spirits into the Citizens, that they made a sally out, slew six hundred

English, and adventured upon the Bastile, where the Lord Talbot commanded, who repelled them with great slaughter of their men; but yet the next day the Earle of Suffolk gave over his siege, and dispersed his Army into their Garrisons" (2:66). Indeed, it was Jean (later styled "Dunois"), the so-called "Bastard of Orléans," who was in charge of the defense of the city, not Jean, duc d'Alençon, but whatever role Joan of Arc played, she was present and in the thick of battle during the raising of the siege, a fact that Baker, like some of his sources, chooses to understate.

With the "wheele of Fortune" turning in favor of the French, Baker narrates the victories led by Alençon in early summer 1429—Jargeau and Meun—and Charles's coronation. Only after Baker interrupts matters in France to mention the coronation of Henry in England does he add, "About this time, in France, a strange Impostor ariseth; a maid called la Pucelle, taking upon her to be sent from God, for the good of France, and to expell the English: and some good indeed she did, for by her subtle working, the King was received into Champaigne, and many Townes were rendered to him" (2:67).[83] This separation of events out of chronology follows a pattern established in the London chronicle with a similar effect, suggesting that Henry VI's arrival in Calais is a triumphal entry, associating the boy monarch with Joan's capture, but not her execution, which is not mentioned earlier. In Baker's *Chronicle*, Joan's real influence in leading Charles to Reims for the sacring that would transform him from dauphin to king is cleverly undercut by diverting attention to her "subtle working" on the road to, but not *into* Reims. According to Baker, although Charles's subsequent attempt to break the alliance between Bedford and Burgundy failed, the regent's absence from Paris persuaded him to besiege it. (In fact, Charles opposed Joan's determination to take Paris, absented himself from that action, and was in secret negotiations with Burgundy during the time.[84]) The remainder of her career is summarily dismissed. Captured after having earlier "caused an English Captaines head to be cut off, because he would not humble himselfe to her upon his knee," Joan was tried "as a Sorceresse, and deceiver of the King and his subjects [and] (after many delays of promise to discover secret practises, and lastly of her feigning to bee with childe) publickly burnt at Roan" (2:68).[85]

Baker followed in the tradition of the fifteenth-century English historians who dealt with Joan of Arc in various ways: from ignoring her, displacing her exploits, or making her an exemplar of rebellion, to impugning the virginity central to her authenticity. They also reflect continued English hopes for regaining a tangible foothold on the Continent and a reasserted claim to the French throne during periods of truce. It is, as Ellen Caldwell writes, "difficult to overestimate the importance of the Hundred Years' War in England's conception of itself as a nation"[86] and, thus, how its historians presented their country to Europe. During the early sixteenth century, the combination of regnal instability (Henry VII himself was threatened with uprisings more than once) with the loss of all its French possessions save Calais had so undermined English self-image that humanist historians, according to Nicola Royan, had to write "history that celebrates the realm to which [the historian is] attached"[87] so that it will be viewed as equal to its international counterparts.

From 1475, when Edward IV signed the Truce of Picquigny, until 1513, when Henry VIII sailed to invade France, English historians had the unusual opportunity to portray recent history against a backdrop of peace, not war, with France, even as Henry VII continued to uphold his claim to the French crown until his death in 1509.[88] Events during and after the reign of his son offered even more compelling reasons for redrafting the English past, which was marked by the king's three attempts to wrest back French territory in 1513–14, 1521–26, and 1544. With Henry VIII's death, the swift succession of Protestant Edward, Catholic Mary, and Elizabeth I provided a dizzying reversal of alliances and therefore new contexts for evaluating the French Catholic Maid. Untangled from the triangulation with France and Burgundy, England found two new legs to stand with, briefly placing its hopes in Spain and the papacy to offset France. The English Reformation added a new imperative to historical writing: to demonstrate England's distance from and independence of Catholicism and the papacy.[89] In his study of the printing history of Robert Fabyan's *New Chronicles* (1516), David Womersley argues that each subsequent reprinting reflects how the contemporary state of Reformation or reaction was "infus[ing] religious ideology into English historiography."[90] For this reason, Anke Bernau reminds us, John Foxe, in his *Boke of Martyrs* (1563), links "saintliness and Englishness," and Edward Hall, in his *Union of the Two Noble and Illustre Famelies of Lancastre & Yorke* (1548) contrasts the "effeminate" French and the manly English.[91] Not surprisingly, as we shall see, vituperation was Hall's solution to the enigma of a Catholic, French, and female warrior such as Joan of Arc, when viewed from the perspective of a reformed religion that on the one hand encouraged female piety, but on the other hand circumscribed her role to wife and mother. In England, after the dissolution of the monasteries under Henry VIII, a woman such as Joan of Arc no longer had recourse to cloistered communities where she could live with others who eschewed marriage. Throughout the early modern period, humanist methodology, post-Reformation politics, and the influence both of the "woman question" and fascination with witchcraft are reflected in English accounts of Joan of Arc.[92]

These changes in the audience and purpose of English history during the Tudor period coincided with the development of the so-called "new historiography," or, more broadly speaking, European Renaissance historiography in general.[93] As described by Matti Rissanen, such narratives considered the "concept of history as a coherent whole—not just as a series of isolated events; a more critical attitude toward sources; an analysis of cause and effect and an idea of the didactic value of history; a new interest in human character as an influence on the course of events; and, last but not least, the inclusion of argument in history—the use of history writing, for instance, to serve political purposes."[94] For example, Amos Lee Laine has written, once the Hundred Years' War had ended, "it [was] difficult to find an objective English viewpoint about contributions of the Normans [French] to the elements of English society thought to be unique."[95] With regard to the Tudor kingdom specifically, historians focused more on accuracy derived from multiple sources than on an encyclopedic inclusiveness that did not discriminate among them.[96]

What effect had shifts in diplomacy, internal politics, and historical methodology on narratives of Joan of Arc during the Tudor era and beyond? According to Nicola Royan, some pre-Reformation English and Scottish historians—Robert Fabyan, Polydore Vergil, and Hector Boece—were challenged by "fitting Jeanne into a recognisable narrative frame, for she breaks so many rules."[97] The three write from different perspectives: the Englishman Fabyan toward the end of Henry VII's reign; the Italian Vergil well into the reign of Henry VIII; and Boece as a Scotsman, but without the sympathy expected from a native of a country long allied with the French. But it is not just the narrative frame that stymied humanist historians; it was the problem of identifying a rhetorical stance that would, as Denis Hay writes in his study of Vergil, "justify the Tudors to the scholars of Europe,"[98] in part by downplaying the execution of Joan of Arc. It is in this context that later apologists have sought glimmerings of a shift in English opinion toward the Maid.

Early in the reign of Henry VIII, Robert Fabyan states his goal to make the history of England an international one in the "Prologus" to his *New Chronicles*:

> Nat for any pompe, or yet for great mede,
> This werke I have taken on hande to compyle;
> But of cause oonly for that I wolde sprede
> The famous honour of this Fertyle Ile,
> That hath contynued, by many a longe whyle,
> In excellent honour, with many a royall guyde,
> Of whom the dedes have sprong to the worlde wyde.[99]

Fabyan separates the histories of England and France, so that the overlapping reigns of their respective kings often appear many pages apart and must perforce be read as fragments of a whole.[100] His method results in a curious division in his accounts of Joan. He describes her childhood and mission at length under the rubric of Charles VII, while his account of her military career and eventual execution falls under the reign of Henry VI. For both, he refers copiously to the French historian Robert Gaguin's *Compendium de origine et gestis Francorum*, published in Paris in 1504, which drew on manuscripts of both of Joan's trials and thus provided English writers with new primary material.[101]

Because Fabyan's organization of material is chronological by reign, we read about Henry VI's accession before that of Charles VII. Fabyan dates the former from September 1, 1422 (Henry V died August 31), and the latter from "the moneth of October" that same year (Charles VI died October 21). Less than two months' difference results in a chronology that first mentions Joan near the height of her success (assuming the coronation of Charles as her apogee) in the account of the Battle of Patay, on June 18, which took place after the lifting of the siege of Orléans and proved an even more humiliating defeat for the English: "After some wryters it was for to strengthe and replenysshe certayne holdes, that wekyd [weakened] by reason of a conflut [conflict] that the Englysshmen had with the Frenshmen, at the which the lorde Talbot was taken prysoner, and the lorde Scalys, with many other, to the nombre of .iii.M. Englysshemen, were slayne and taken. But after the oppinyon of the Frenshe Cronycle, this victory shulde be o[b]tyened by Jane or Johane, callyd in Frenshe la Puzele de Dieu, in the .ix. yere of this kynge" (599).[102] Fabyan's skeptical acceptance of the role of Joan of Arc marks what must be a nationalistic, not gender, bias, for he had written admiringly and at length about Ælfleda, the Lady of the Mercians, clearly positioning her as a military leader of men (117). More than once, he criticizes "Robert Gagwyne, whiche levyth no thynge out of his boke that may sounde to the avauncement of the Frenshe nacyon" (415).

Although Fabyan dates English misfortunes from the death of Salisbury in Orléans in 1428, he does not further refer to the French raising of the siege. Like the London chronicle a century before him, Fabyan rearranges his narrative so that the coronation of Henry VI and his entry into Calais precede Joan's initial victories: "In this tyme and season that the kynge lay thus at Calays, many skyrmisshes were foughten atwene the Englisshmen & the Frenshmen in dyvers parties of Fraunce; and greatly the Frenshemen prevayled by the helpe of a woman, whiche they, as before is touched, named the Mayden of God" (601).

He provides a clear and indeed compendious narrative of Joan's early history, parentage, and "discovery" of the dauphin in hiding, not a close translation of Gaguin. He does not scoff at Joan's reported claims of "Goddys purveyaunce." He repeats, only to repudiate as "darke and fantastycall," the story of Joan finding her sword at Ste-Catherine-de-Fierbois by divine revelation, as Gaguin had written.[103] This may be the first information from the trial testimony to appear in English. While acknowledging that his author "affermyth" that "she by hyr provydence causyd the sayde Charlys, as kynge of Fraunce, to be crownyd at Raynys" in 1429, he adds that "nouther the Frensh Cronycle, nor other whiche I have [seen] testyfyeth that, but affermyn that he was not crowned durynge the lyfe of the duke of Bedforde" (642).[104] This unsubstantiated claim seems an attempt to bolster the regent's reputation as well as to distance Joan from the coronation. After all, at the time of Fabyan's writing, the Valois still ruled in France, in the person of Louis XII (reigned 1498–1515).

Fabyan's integration of a French source with the English chronicle tradition results in a disjointed account of the Maid's career. For neither king's reign does he describe her role in the siege of Orléans, ascribing the gradual loss of England's French possessions to the death of Salisbury during the siege. He further diminishes Joan's mythic reputation by choosing to term her "woman," "wenche," and "mayden," not "witch," "sorceress," or "prophetess."[105] He condemns Joan for contravening divine order in crowning Charles VII: "Almyghty God, which for a season sufferyth suche sorcery and develysshe wayes to prospere & reygne" (642), permitted Joan to be captured and executed. His phrase "suche sorcery and develysshe wayes" refers not to the identification of the hidden dauphin, or to the miraculous discovery of the sword of St. Catherine, or to the raising of the siege of Orléans, or the humiliation of Patay. It refers explicitly to the coronation. Therefore, despite providing some accurate information about Joan's early life and career, Fabyan continues a major theme from the London chronicle. While associating Joan with "sorcery," he never names her "witch." In the section on Henry VI, he repeats the tale of her pregnancy without comment and without suggesting that she was otherwise promiscuous. His *New Chronicles* thus offers a new way of integrating Joan into English history; along with Polydore Vergil's *Anglica Historia*, Fabyan's work influenced historical writers for the next century.

Yet, while Vergil's *Historia* was still in manuscript, John Rastell compiled and printed his *Pastyme of Pleasure* in 1529 based chiefly on Fabyan. Although Rastell was associated by marriage with the humanist Thomas More and his circle, his approach does not much reflect the influence of humanism on the writing of history. It is an old-fashioned work. The *Pastyme* is organized even more ambitiously than is Fabyan's history to present the separate histories of England, France, Northern Europe, the Holy Roman Empire, and the Papacy simultaneously, in parallel rows on each page.[106] Rastell seems fairly uninterested in Joan of Arc. Like Fabyan, he attributes all English misfortunes to the death of Salisbury, "for after his dethe, / the englysshemen lost ever in Fraunce theyr possessyons / moche more than they wanne" [E3r]. Immediately following, under the rubric "Charles," we read that "he had great warre with the englysshemen / to whose helpe there came a mayde of Fraunce / whome the frenchemen called la pusell de dieu / but she was take and brent by the englysshemen."[107] His grammar—specifically, "whome the frenchmen called le pusell de dieu / *but* she was taken and brent"—suggests either that she was not a "pusell de dieu" for, presumably, the English could not have captured and burnt her if she were really acting under God's protection and guidance, or that the English were in the wrong to doubt her heavenly inspiration.

By calling Joan "pusell de dieu" and "mayde of god" and by agreeing that she indeed played a military role in defeating the English, Rastell has been credited as the first English historian to present a neutral if not actually favorable view of the Maid.[108] But he took these epithets from Fabyan. He also omits most of Fabyan's section on her birth and background, and omits the finding of the sword at St. Catherine de Fierbois, which Fabyan found so "darke and fantastycall." He does not refer to her "sorcery and develysshe wayes," even though his modern editor notes his "belief in superstitions, omens, and devils."[109] He says nothing about male clothing, only that the French "gatte her armour." There is no hint of sexual misconduct, despite his dependence on Fabyan and possible knowledge of Vergil in manuscript.[110] He repeats without reservation Fabyan's own skepticism about the date of Charles's coronation, slightly changing the wording from Fabyan's "he was not crowned durynge the lyfe of the duke of Bedford" to "he was neuer crowned tyll after the dethe of the duke of Bedforde." This barebones approach is not unique to Rastell's account of Joan. He is equally economical and noncommittal when writing about earlier women leaders such as Ælfleda and Maud. In all these cases, Rastell's method seems to eschew sensationalism and to eliminate any individualizing details that might increase his audience's interest in anomalous situations. He neutralizes Fabyan's commentary on Joan by editing it, but is a lack of criticism to be read as approbation?

Unlike Fabyan and Rastell, the Italian humanist Polydore Vergil (ca. 1470–1555) spent the better part of three decades researching and writing his *Anglica Historia*. In 1502, under the sponsorship of his countryman Adriano Castelli, a favorite of Henry VII, Vergil traveled to England, where he resided until 1553.¹¹¹ Vergil had begun to study the history of his host country soon after his arrival, and around 1506, he related that "at the request of Henry VII . . . I wrote the deeds of his people and produced a historical work."¹¹² That diffidence belies his opinion that history "[redounds] as much to the glory of the author as to the usefulness of posterity."¹¹³ Even more than Fabyan or Rastell, he attempted to view his sources carefully. He methodically consulted his medieval predecessors yet scorned the Latin annals as "bald, uncouth, chaotic and deceptive, so that they are read with distaste by the learned and by the unlearned they are scarcely to be understood."¹¹⁴ Yet at the same time, as Denis Hay points out, he was willing to accept "the testimony of living tradition," including "the French belief in the divine mission of Joan of Arc."¹¹⁵

Vergil embeds his story of the Maid in the larger military and political context that interests him, as he does with another woman warrior, Ælfleda. The Lady of Mercia, he writes, "didde noe lesse upprightlie then wiselie administer the regiment a few yeares,"¹¹⁶ and his account of Empress Maud emphasizes her pragmatism. His chronological integration of Henry VI's and Charles VII's reigns imparts a welcome coherence to the story of Joan of Arc. His discussion of the decade of the 1420s is rich and not unduly critical of Charles VII's initial military leadership. He praises both the English preparations for the siege of Orléans and the inhabitants' valor. But just as Fabyan had done before him, he states unequivocally that after the death of Salisbury, "the English forrain affaires beganne to quaile; which infirmitie though the English nation, as a most sounde and strong body, did not feele at the first, yet afterward they suffered it as a pestilence and sicknes inwardly, by litle and litle decaying the strength: for immediatly after his death the fortune of warre altered."¹¹⁷ Unlike the Scots historian Boece, writing at about the same time, Vergil does not link Joan's downfall to her unchastity. He presents her plea of pregnancy as a claim on humanity, not law, writing that "the unhappie Maide, remembering, before execution done, what appertyened to humanitie, which naturally is bredd in every one, fained herselfe to be with childe, to thende she might eyther move her enemies to compassion, eyther els cause them to appoynt some more milde punishment." Indeed, he is highly critical of her execution:

> This saide sentence thus pronounced was thought the hardest that ever had beene remembred, which could neyther be mollified nor mittigated by tract of time. Surely it was of some thought that this woman thus excited to martiall manly prowesse, for defence of her country, was woorthy favour, especially seeing there were many

examples of mercie showed in such case, as that principally which Porsenna King of the Trurions hath left in memorie. For when as he, upon conclusion of peace with the Romanes, had receaved pledges, and amongst them Cloelia a virgin, who, conducting a company of others like, beguiled the watch, and amongst the middest of her enemies swam over Tiber and fledd to her owne people, notwithstanding that afterwarde she was by the league redelivered, yet he did not punish her, but with great commendation gave her part of the pledges, and sent her home againe. (38)

This passage is not in Vergil's manuscript.[118] Vergil's comment that the sentence could not be "mitigated" is of course literally true, although it does not seem that the many mitigating statements of English remorse, as stated in the nullification transcripts, were available to him.

The Italian's empathy for Joan of Arc was scorned by later English historians, notably in the 1587 edition of Holinshed's *Chronicles*: "In this tale of Tillets is she further likened to Debora, Jahell, and Judith, and unto Romane Clelia compared by Polydor, that shames not somewhat also to carpe at hir judgment, and much pitieth hir paine" (172). What Jean du Tillet had actually written in his monarchical history of France was in response to those French writers who thought Joan's achievements had been a ruse. He chides them, referring to Isaiah 59:1, for "having forgotten what is written about Deborah, Jael, and Judith, Behold, the Lord's hand is not shortened [unable to save]."[119] In the seventeenth century, the Italian historian Giovanni Francisco Biondi (Sir Francis Biondi) echoes Holinshed, in the words of his English translator Henry Carey: "I with *Polidorus* praise her as parallell to *Cloelia* since it so pleaseth him; but not as parallell to her in her actions. *Cloelia* fought not, fained not, did no harme to any: the Maid did hurt, and as much unto her selfe as others."[120] Vergil in fact addresses the mercy of Porsenna toward the escaped hostage Cloelia as a model for the English, not Cloelia as a model for Joan of Arc. To be sure, the second edition of Holinshed is neither linguistically incompetent nor politically disingenuous; the reviser deliberately inserted this cavil.

Although Baker does not seem to have used them, French accounts of the Hundred Years' War and Joan of Arc had become increasingly known in England throughout the sixteenth and seventeenth centuries, some eventually translated and published there. Notable among those, and equally important as Gaguin's *Compendium*, was Jean de Serres's *Inventaire général de l'histoire de France*, translated into English by Edward Grimeston (1607), which became an important source for the cartographer John Speed's lengthy narrative of

Joan's career in his *Historie of Great Britaine*. Unlike Vergil's carping about medieval chroniclers or Fabyan's dismissal of Gaguin, Grimeston admired de Serres because, as he writes in his address "To the Reader," he was

> as free from affection and passion, as any one that ever treated of this subject.... And if he hath not dilated at large the great attempts of Strangers in France, employed eyther for their Kings, or against them: he is not therefore to be blamed, nor to be held partiall.... You must consider, that he was a Frenchman: and although hee would not altogether smother and conceale those things, which might any way eclipse the glory of his Nation, least he should be taxed to have fayled in these two excellent vertues required in an Historiographer, Truth and Integritie, without passion, yet happily he hath reported them as sparingly as he could.[121]

But Grimeston's own larger purpose was both patriotic and didactic, so that he also includes "the sundry Battailes woon by our Kings of England against the French, and the worthie exploits of the English, during their warres with France, whereby you may bee incited to the like resolutions upon the like occasions."[122] This spirit of fair-mindedness was conveyed to, or shared by, John Speed, who drew extensively on Grimeston's translation of de Serres for his portrait of Joan of Arc.

Famous for his atlases, Speed has not received much praise for his history, yet it evinces methodologies born both of the humanists and of the antiquarians: selecting from among his sources; limiting marvels; and according to F. J. Levy, "judging kings on the basis of their ability to rule rather than on their morality, despite his belief in God's intervention in the world," for he "considered incompetent kingship a moral failing."[123] His proeme—"To the Learned and Lovers of Great Britain's Glory"—evokes a particular view of Britain, "this famous Empire." As far as Speed was concerned, Great Britain now enjoyed international cachet, for

> that this our Countrey and subject of History deserveth the love of her Inhabitants, is witnessed even by forraine writers themselves, who have termed it the Court of Queene Ceres, the Granary of the Westerne world, the fortunate Island, the Paradise of pleasure, and Garden of God.... Our Kings for valour and Sanctity, rancked with the worthiest in the world, and our Nations originals, conquests, and continuance, tried by the touch of the best humane testimonies, leave as fair a Lustre

upon the same stone, as doth any other, and with any Nation may easily contend (saith Lanquet) both for antiquity and continuall inhabitants, from the first time that any of them can claime their Originals. (A3)

It is tempting to find echoes of John of Gaunt's famous dying speech from Shakespeare's *Richard II* here.

Perhaps in part because he came to maturity during the reign of Elizabeth I (he was born in 1552), Speed's view of Joan of Arc is not based on conventional ideas about gender. Thus, he was not predisposed to subscribe to the view, then current among some French writers, that Joan of Arc was more mascot than martial maid. He understands that women may lead men into battle and risk their own lives, as well. He also shows that a woman can lead through tactical acumen, if not physical strength, for of Empress Maud he writes, "Shee, a woman (whose sexe hath often deceived wise men) resolved once againe to overreach her foe by wit, whom shee could not by force" (495). He is flummoxed by Margaret of Anjou, however. He praises her "manly courage," adding that in the military defense of her husband, she "addeth stratageme, and wit to her force" (863). Yet he also writes that upon her marriage to Henry, "the mournefull tragedies of our poore Country began" (845).

Speed's view of Joan is also informed by his reading of Henry VI's reign as a providential tragedy ultimately attributable to a woman:

Never any Princes raigne since the Conquest did better deserve to be described with a tragicall Stile, and words of horror and sorrow, although the beginning (like the faire morning of a most tempestuous day) promised nothing more then a continuance of passed felicities. For the State of the English affaires was great and flourishing, England without tumult, the naturall fierce humors of her people consuming or exercising themselves in France, and France her selfe ... was at their devotion. There wanted nothing which might advance the worke begun. Most noble and expert Leaders, as those which had beene fashioned in the Schoole of Warre, under the best Martiall-Master of that Age, the late Henry, armes full of veterant Souldiers, most of which were of skill sufficient to bee commanders themselves: their friends firme, no defect nor breach (by which dissipation might enter to the overthrow of the English greatness) as yet disclosing themselves. Wisdome, piety, riches, forwardnesse at home, courage and like forwardnesse abroad. It is a fruitfull speculation to consider how God carrieth his part in the workes of men, alwaies justly, sometimes terribly, but never otherwise then to bring all worldly greatnesse and glory into due contempt and loathing, that the Soule may be erected to her Creator, and aspire to a Crowne celestiall. (827)

This caution reminds his readers of the tragic future of the "fortunate island," a future in which Joan of Arc plays her own providential role, and whose short-term vanquishing of an internally contentious England was to be echoed—from Speed's point of view—in the utter destruction of the Lancastrian dynasty at the hands that "manly" woman from Lorraine—Margaret of Anjou.

Speed takes most of his description of Joan from Grimeston. He grants the "Martiall maide" a full measure of valor but adds parenthetically "some have written that it was a practise or imposure" (833). He places her by implication either in an advisory, leadership position or in the midst of battle, as he does with Margaret. He cautions his readers, however, "Doe not rashly beleeue Serres," a French source, after all, just as Fabyan had denigrated Gaguin. "Our Writers"—*English* writers—sometimes tell a different story (834).[124] Although, as Fabyan had done with Gaguin, Speed edits and critiques his principal French source, he mentions other works he consulted, not all English, including Vergil, Holinshed, Jean du Tillet, and Paulus Aemelius.[125] When faced with de Serres's emphasis on Bedford's personal animus toward Joan, as well as the claim that the English duke essentially bought off her examiners, Speed retreats to his English sources to depict the superiority of the English national character he had emphasized in his proem. Grimeston, too, had called attention to "the worthie exploits of the English, during their warres with France."[126] Of Bedford, de Serres had written, "The unbridled passion of his deadly hatred conceived against this maiden as having ruined his affaires in France carried away his reason. And not being able to put her to death, as a prisoner of war, he deliberates to make her a prisoner of justice." Grimeston's translation is accurate, but he leaves out de Serres's final sentence: "It was difficult to convert right into wrong, truth into falsehood" (731).[127]

Speed recognizes that Joan reinvigorated the French. While Joan's letter to the English before Orléans was "entertained by the English with laughter," Speed wryly acknowledges, "to some it may seeme more honourable to our Nation, that they were not to bee expelled by a humane power, but by a divine, extraordinarily revealing it selfe" (833). He continues, "Du Serres describes this Parragon in these words: Shee had a modest countenance, sweete, civill, and resolute, her discourse was temperate, reasonable, and retired, her actions cold, shewing great chastity without vanity, affectation, babling or courtly lightnesse. *Let us not dissemble what we find written* [emphasis added]: By her encouragements and conduct the English had Orleance pluckt out of their hopes" (834). After the coronation, he concedes, "shee might bee thought propheticall and fortunate." But at Compiègne, "here the glory of Joan unfortunately ended" (835) and, with it, her life.

Making Vergil's analogy (that so upset Holinshed) suit his own ends, Speed concludes, "Clalia was saved by Porsenna; and it is not to be doubted but that the magnanimity of the English would have spared her, had they not found it necessary to deface the opinion which the French, even with superstition, had conceived of her." As for Joan's end, notwithstanding the French historians, "our Writers"—his marginal note here refers to the hostile Holinshed—"shew how the course of her life being legally examined by the Bishop of Beauois (in whose Diocesse shee was taken) and she thereupon for sorcerie, blodshed, and unnaturall use of manlike apparell, and habiliments contrary to her Sexe, condemned to dye, was notwithstanding upon her solemne abjuring of such her lewde practises, pardoned her life, till againe convicted of perjurious relapsing, though acknowledging her self a strumpet, and fayning to be with child, she deservedly underwent that punishment which she sought to delay" (835). Speed pulls back only at the very end to justify his forebears' verdict as legal and Joan's own behavior as her downfall. But he definitively diminishes Joan of Arc's importance in English history, as a factor in turning the tide of war, to be sure, but one less important than were the deleterious effects of Margaret of Anjou on England's own soil.

During the reign of Charles I, historians were eager to provide a new political perspective on their nation's history. They do not follow Speed's lead in granting Joan some valor. John Trussell, the antiquarian mayor of Winchester, brought Samuel Daniel's popular *Collection of the History of England* (1612), which had ended with the reign of Edward III, forward to the reign of Henry VII, publishing his *Continuation* in 1636, with subsequent reprintings in 1641, 1650, and 1685. In his address "To the Courteous Reader," Trussell stresses his exhaustive research: "I left no Chronicle of this land, that purse, or prayer could purchase or procure, unperused" (A3) and "examined, though not all, (yet without touch of Arrogance, I may speake it) the most and best, that have written of those times" (A3v–A4).[128] Following more in the tradition of the chroniclers than of the humanist historians, but echoing the Tudor historian Edward Hall in his disapproval of Joan of Arc's transgendered behavior, Trussell gives an entirely negative view of Joan of Arc,

> that shee impostour Le pusill[,] who had bewitched the credulity of those times, and was for the more part esteemed as a prophetesse, and

shee againe to give some colour to settle this opinion, did dare, and doe many things beyond the reach, modesty, & strength of a Woman, riding manlike astride, and in armour, making show of manhood, and giving forth in speeches, not without some ostentation, that shee was a messenger sent from God, to reconquer out of the hands of the English, whatsoever they had now in possession there; By the subtile working of this Medean Virago, The French King was received into Champaigne. (130)

Trussell's disapproval of the "Medean Virago"—a wonderful coinage—is centered on Joan's unwomanly behavior, not on the effects of her valor on the war. Furthermore, his Royalist sympathies are on display when he states that she was burned after "judiciall proceeding against her as a Sorceresse, and deceiver of the King and his subjects, by her seeming show of sanctitie, and her inhumane cruelty, against the King of England and his subjects" (132). Joan of Arc offended against *both* kingdoms.

The epithets attached to Joan of Arc by English chroniclers and historians during the two centuries after her execution—from "witch" to "wench," "strumpet" to "mayden of God," "Martiall maide" to "Medean Virago"—clearly demarcate the diversity of judgments on a woman whose brief but stunning military successes and execution clashed with the nation's postmedieval reconstruction of its history. Yet English writers realized they could not "dissemble" what they found in the increasing number of French sources becoming available to them through print. Even as they record her condemnation as a "sorceress" or "witch," many make clear the political context that led to her execution. At the same time, as a woman *and* a virago, Joan became an exemplar for the literature of the *querelle des femmes* in England, as manifested in demonologies, defenses of women, and collections of curiosities, the subject of the next chapter.

CHAPTER 3

## "PENTHESILEA DID IT. WHY NOT SHE?"

### An English Virago

> Penthesilea did it. Why not she
> Without the stain of spels and sorcerie?
> Why should those acts in her be counted sin,
> Which in the other have commended bin?
> —Peter Heylyn, *Survey of the Estate of France*, 1656

Even as English historians writing about the reign of Henry VI were portraying Joan of Arc as a witch, or a "Martiall maide," or a "Medean Virago," those discrete identities led other writers to include her in works specifically focused on witchcraft or the status of women. The presentation of Joan of Arc as both a positive and negative exemplar demonstrates another approach for English writers to recreate her legend and displace her from their historical legacy. Thus, she is included in the first demonology printed in English. Her character is evoked to defend or disparage women in the *querelle des femmes*, or "woman question." She joins the tradition of the *femmes fortes*, or "female worthies," in which she is associated with Penthesilea, the Queen of the Amazons, and Biblical heroines Deborah, Esther, and Judith. She is grouped with English viragos such as Empress Maud in Thomas Heywood's 1624 history of women, *Gynaikeion*.[1] The cultural contexts in which women are called upon to represent ideologies underlie the analogies used to defend Joan; they also underlie how centrally or tangentially she is positioned within a catalog of argument. While the Maid's inclusion in such focused collections is sometimes predictable, as often as not it raises questions about both the status of her reputation in England and the author's criteria of selection. In parallel to the ongoing historical discourse, the career of Joan of Arc also becomes exemplary in compilations of witches, warriors, and women variously chosen and arranged to illustrate moral, philosophical, or political doctrines.

The earliest English reports of Joan in the London chronicle name her a witch. Although Joan's inquisitors reframed her prophetic utterances into demonic inspiration, the accusations of witchcraft or, more properly speaking, sorcery, against her preceded the height of witch scares, trials, and executions beginning in the late fifteenth century and finally dying out in the seventeenth. A number of the original seventy articles of indictment accuse Joan of forbidden practices. In the final twelve articles, however, these accusations are scattered. Their emphasis is everywhere on Joan's defiance of ecclesiastic authority and heresy. Yet heresy was closely linked to sorcery, and less than a decade after her execution, Joan became an exemplar of that association in the German theologian Johannes Nider's *Formicarius* (*The Ant Hill*; 1436–37). Michael Bailey characterizes this dialogue between master and pupil "as a kind of preacher's manual, a handy collection of ready-made edifying stories for use in sermons."[2] Joan of Arc is presented in book 5, "On Evildoers and their Deceptions." The master reports that recently an official in Cologne had told him about one of the false Joans who appeared after the Maid's death.[3] He then narrates the history of Joan of Arc, focusing on her masculine dress and her prophecies. However, Joan's downfall came when, having "sent threatening letters to the Bohemians, among whom there were then a multitude of heretics . . . layfolk and ecclesiastics, Regulars and Cloisterers began to doubt of the spirit whereby she was ruled, whether it were devilish or divine." Once she was captured "by God's will, as it is believed," she was tried, and "she at length confessed that she had a familiar angel of God, which, by many conjectures and proofs, and by the opinion of the most learned men, was judged to be an evil spirit, so that this spirit rendered her a sorceress."[4] Joan's own inquisitors had doggedly tried to elicit admissions of diabolism from her. Reportedly, the miter she wore to the stake included the words "heretic, relapse, apostate, idolater."[5] For Nider, the worst kind of heresy was, in Bailey's words, "the total apostasy of diabolical witches, who, in exchange for maleficent power, completely forsook Christ and worshiped Satan."[6] Nider clearly stated that the only possible fate for a convicted witch was to be hunted down and burned.[7] His *Formicarius*, including his endorsement of Joan's punishment, was widely disseminated, with twenty-five surviving manuscripts and seven printed editions from 1476 to 1692.[8] Thus, beyond her trial, Joan of Arc was associated with demonism almost from the time of her death.

On December 5, 1484, a generation later, Pope Innocent VIII issued the bull *Summis desiderantes affectibus*, expressly authorizing German inquisitors and approved notaries "to exercise their office of inquisition and to proceed to the correction, imprisonment, and punishment of [witches] for their said offences and crimes."[9] In 1486, two German Dominicans published a "handbook" to guide inquisitors in these particular procedures: *Malleus Maleficarum*, or *The Hammer of Witches*, codifying nearly two centuries of persecution of both men and women. Although its publication postdates by thirty years the nullification of Joan of Arc's original conviction for heresy in 1456, its modern translator Christopher Mackay's description of the mindset of the "witch craze" serves to encapsulate that of her Rouen trial:

> The world laid out in the *Malleus* is a place where demons inhabit the area above the earth, which is fixed at the center of the universe, and plot to ensnare humans (especially women) in their schemes and, after trapping the humans in their society, guide them in their evil-doing and have sex with them. It is a place where an implacable God reacts savagely to this betrayal of loyalty to him and in retribution gives the demons further permission to implement their nefarious plans. It is a place where the tenets of the Catholic Church are held to be absolutely true and it is the duty of the secular authorities to burn alive those convicted of deviating from the Church's truth. It is a place where clever inquisitors can make use of sagacious stratagems to track down the perpetrators of unspeakable crimes committed through magic and have them turned over to the authorities for burning as heretics.[10]

At Joan's trial, her inquisitors associated the folk customs of Domrémy, such as children dancing under an oak tree, with demons. She was asked sexually pointed questions about the physical manifestation of her voices, especially whether Saint Michael appeared to her clothed or naked. She was constantly admonished that she owed unquestioning obedience to the "Church Militant," and its earthly representatives of God. The Rouen inquisitors attempted many times, unsuccessfully, to trap Joan into self-indictment.

Yet, despite the dissemination of texts accusing or implicating Joan of Arc in such "unspeakable crimes," Reformation England was not the place conjured by the *Malleus*. Just as John Speed and others had evoked English law and magnanimity to justify Joan's execution, historian Diane Purkiss detects "a self-congratulatory note in discussions of English witchcraft; unlike the Europeans, we of course were too just and humane to use torture on the hapless accused."[11] Moreover, in England, witchcraft connoted inexplicable personal injury more than heresy.[12] In fact, executions for heresy and those for witchcraft seem *not* to have overlapped much in England, where the most common form of execution was beheading, not burning, but where the ultimate penalty was not very often imposed.[13] The prosecution for these forms of witchcraft came under Parliamentary scrutiny. The "Act against Conjurations, Witchcrafts, Sorcery, and Enchantments" (33 Hen. VIII c.8) addresses those who "unlawfully have devised and practised Invocacions and conjuracions of Sprites." Those convicted could face death, yet there is little evidence of persecutions under this act. The 1563 "Act against Conjurations, Enchantments, and Witchcrafts" (5 Eliz. I c.16) reduced the punishment to prison or pillory.[14]

The danger, however, was felt to be real. The first printed English treatise citing the notoriety and threat of individual practitioners of magic, sorcery, or witchcraft introduces Joan of Arc to the company of witches: Frances Coxe's *A Short Treatise declaringe the detestable wickednesse of magicall sciences* (1561). Coxe himself had been charged with sorcery and was made to confess publicly his "employment of certayne sinistral and divelysh artes."[15] His subsequent "grovelling and terror-stricken pamphlet," as characterized by Edward Heron-Allen, is an act of expiation by accusation.[16] He is eager to name the German theologian Cornelius Agrippa (who, as we shall see, had a sympathetic view of Joan) among those who trafficked with devils and came to a bad end. He cites Robert Fabyan, who "speaketh of a certayne mayde, experte in these sciences, called La pucelle de dieu, that is too saye: the mayde of God, who by her knowledge caused the Frenchmen marveylouslye too prevayle in their marciall affaires." He then reproduces Fabyan's moral almost verbatim: "But almightye God, whiche for a season suffereth suche sorcerye and dyvelishe wayes too prospere and raygne, too the correction of sinners: lastely too showe hys power, and that no good Christen menne shoulde falle intoo anye errroure: he sheweth the clearnes of such misticall thinges and so he did in this, for she by a knight Burgonion was taken, and after sent to Roane in Normandye, too the duke of Somerset, and there brente, for her demerites."[17] Coxe is just as vague as Fabyan about which particular "sorcerye and dyvelishe wayes" led Joan to her deserved punishment. Fabyan had stopped short of calling Joan a witch. Yet the passage suits its new context. Coxe's tone suggests that even accusing Joan of possible supernatural practices was sufficient to establish her guilt.

Rather few English tracts and treatises about witches and witchcraft after Coxe mention Joan of Arc; instead, as suggested above, they focus on the particular circumstances in England itself. Even though many of them couple "witchcraft" and "popery," their emphasis is on a Protestant interpretation of the Bible, or on recording the increasing local persecutions of women. And not everyone gave in to fear. In his 1584 *Discovery of Witchcraft*, Reginald Scot inveighs against a belief in witchcraft, strongly criticizing those who judged nefarious intent merely on appearance: "One sort of such as are said to be witches, are women which be commonly old, lame, blear-eyed, pale, fowle, and full of wrinckles; poor, sullen, supersticious, and papists."[18] Such unsightliness, he argues, should not be assumed to disguise inner evil. In his 1548 history of the fifteenth-century wars, Edward Hall ascribed Joan's virginity to her ugliness, "as some say, whether it wer because of her foule face, that no man would desire it, either she had made a vowe to live chaste, she kept her maydenhed, and preserved her virginite."[19] Or, perhaps by implication, because she *was* a witch.

Richard Bovet's *Pandaemonium, or, The devil's cloyster* (1684) also discusses the "hard case" of persons whose physical ugliness or deformity indicts them as witches—whether external appearance masks or proclaims internal virtue. "But," Bovet continues,

> tho I must confess that there is no reason that any person (by reason of those deformities which may be only the Effects of old Age, or the product of some disease) should be presently Indicted and trust up for a Witch; nor can I Imagine that ever such a thing hath been in a Civilized Nation, without the concomitant circumstances of some other proofs: That would be a hard case indeed! But I think it will not be difficult to prove that there have been some whose Insides have been blackned with as foul and damnable Confederacies as others; who have notwithstanding appeared with Faces very Charming and Angelical. For we have no account of any very Nauseous deformity that sate on the forehead of Jesabel, Joan of Arc, or Joan Queen of Naples. And perhaps the Attempts of these Hellish Agents may pass with less Suspicion, when under the plausible disguise of a handsom Face: For from Objects Nasty and deformed, men Naturally turn away, with a kind of Innate Aversion and Contempt; whilst under

the Charming Attraction of a fair Face, the Magical Enchantment Insensibly Steals upon men.[20]

Shakespeare's Joan Puzel exploits this "charming attraction" in order to gain the dauphin Charles's trust. In act 1 of *1 Henry VI*, she relates how her vision of the Virgin Mary transfigured her:

> In complete glory she revealed herself.
> And, whereas I was black and swart before,
> With those clear rays which she infused on me,
> That beauty am I blest with, which you may see.
> (1.2.83–86)[21]

As we shall see in chapter 4, this speech marks Joan Puzel as diabolical from the start. Bovet is also drawing on Thomas Fuller's association of Joan of Arc with Jezebel and Joanna, Queen of Naples, in his *Profane State* (1642), and we shall see how conflicted Fuller was about the Maid. Indeed William Marshall's engraving of Joan for that volume shows a face to be sure, not "charming" or "angelical," but equally not in any way physically deformed (see fig. 2).

Sixteenth- and early seventeenth-century demonologies reflected their writers' awareness of the active persecution of witches; by the eighteenth century, these collections took an antiquarian or skeptical view. At the dawn of the Age of Enlightenment, Daniel Defoe alluded satirically to Joan in his *Political History of the Devil* (1726). The Maid, along with Joan [Joanna], Queen of Naples, he notes, "were both sent home to their native Country [presumably Hell], as soon as it was discovered that they were real Devils, and that Satan acknowledg'd them in that Quality."[22] Richard Boulton's *Compleat History of Magick, Sorcery, and Witchcraft* (1715) conveys the lessening of both fear and belief in the supernatural. Offering examples of witchcraft and sorcery he writes, "it is reported of that infamous Woman amongst the French, Joan of Arc, who foretold a great many wonderful things to King Charles the Seventh, that upon her Encouragement and Assurance of Success, the French after encountered the victorious English, and contrary to all Reason and Expectation to their great Terror and Amazement suddenly counfounded them, though at last she was taken Prisoner by the English, and executed and burnt for her Witchcraft."[23] Like Coxe, Boulton hints that Joan's execution was due at least in part because her military prophecies were fulfilled, to the disadvantage of the English. Similarly, Francis Hutchinson's *Historical Essay Concerning Witchcraft* (1718) ascribes a political motive to Joan's fate.

FIGURE 2   Thomas Fuller, *The Profane State*, 1642. Library of Congress, Washington, D.C.

In his "Chronological Table" of trials and executions, Hutchinson writes that the "Earl of Bedford burnt her for a Witch," but he also acknowledges that conspiracy might have been as strong a motive as conjuring: "Dr. [Peter] Heylin doubts not to say, That she was neither Witch nor Prophetess, but was managed by the Earl of Dunois, to revive the drooping Spirits of the Beaten French."[24] Despite his acceptance of the allegations that Joan was a puppet, Heylyn vigorously defended her against imputations of witchcraft.

Peter Heylyn (1599–1662), a minister who wrote history in the form of travelogue, humorously but quite seriously champions Joan by asking "Penthesilea did it, why not she?," referring to the mythical Amazon, who fought with the Trojans but was slain by the Greek hero Achilles.[25] Heylyn mentions Joan several times in his geographical histories, beginning with the 1625 *Microcosmos*. In that early work, he merely links Joan with the town of Vaucouleurs in Lorraine, "the place of Joane the Virgin, to whose miracles and valour, the French attribute the delivery of their countrey from the Empire of the English; but being at last taken prisoner, she was by the Duke of Bedford then Regent of France, condemned, and burned for a Witch."[26] In his later works, however, he steadfastly refutes that accusation.

Nearly forty years later, in *Cosmographie*, a general history of the world, Heylyn expands on what he had written earlier. Speaking of Joan's execution for witchcraft, he opines, "Of which crime I for my part doe conceive her free. Nor can I otherwise conceive of her and her brave exploits, then of a lusty lasse of Lorrain, tutored and trained up by the practise of the Earl of Dunois commonly called the Bastard of Orleans; and so presented to Charles the seventh, French King, as if sent immediately from Heaven."[27] Heylyn disavows all forms of the supernatural in the case of Joan, whether witchcraft or divine inspiration. However, he includes some verses he says were written by a friend who had been inspired by seeing the Orléans monument, including the lines "She di'd a Virgin; 'Twas because the earth / Bred not a man whose valour and whose birth / Might merit such a blessing."

The verses praising Joan as another Penthesilea form the opening lines of that same poem, reproduced in Heylyn's *Survey of the Estate of France* (1656).[28] There, he elaborates on the Maid, defending her choice of men's clothing as a practical matter, and, as an ecclesiastic, denying that her achievements were in any way diabolical:

> As for that other imputation of being a Witch, saving the credit of those which condemn'd her, and theirs also who in their writings have so reported her: I dare be of the contrary opinion, for dividing her actions into two parts, those which preceded her coming unto Orleans, and those which followed it: I finde much in it of cunning, somewhat perhaps of valour: but nothing that is devillish. Her relieving of Orleans, and courage shewn at the battails of Patay and Gergeau, with her conducting of the King unto Rhemes: are not such prodigies, that they need to be ascribed unto witchcraft. (141)

After providing many examples of "heroical Ladies [of whom] I read no accusation of witchcraft," among them Amazons, Deborah, Judith, and Boudicca (the British queen who fought the Romans in the first century CE), Heylyn continues:

> As for her atchievements, they are not so much beyond a common being: but that they may be imputed to natural means: for had she been a Witch, it is likely she would have prevented the disgrace which her valour suffered, in the ditches of Paris, though she could not avoid those of Compeigne, who took her prisoner: the Devill at such an exigent only being accustomed to forsake those which he hath entangled. So that she enjoyed not such a perpetuity of felicity, as to entitle her to the Devils assistance, she being sometimes conqueror, sometimes overthrown, and at last imprisoned. (142)

He concludes, "Let those whom partiality hath wrested aside from the path of truth, proclaim her for a sorceresse, for my part I will not flatter my best fortunes of my Countrey to the prejudice of a truth: neither will I ever be enduced to think of this female warrior, otherwise then of a noble Captain" (143). There follows a longer version of the poem he had attributed to his friend in *Cosmographie*, although there is no evidence that he did not write it himself:

> Penthesilea did it. Why not she
> Without the stain of spels and sorcerie?
> Why should those acts in her be counted sin,
> Which in the other have commended bin?
> Nor is it fit that France should be deni'd
> This female souldier, since all Realms beside,
> Have had the honour of one: and relate
> How much that sexe hath re-enforc'd the state
> Of their decaying strengths.
> (143)

Perhaps Heylyn had read Sir David Lindsay's verses associating Joan of Arc with Penthesilia in his *Dialog Concerning the Monarchie* (ca. 1533):

> The proude Quene Pantasilia,
> The Princes of Amasona,

> With hir Ladyis tryumphandlye,
> Att Troye quhilk faucht so wailyeantlye,
> Nor yit the fair Madin of France,
> Danter of Inglis Ordinance,
> To Semeramis, in hir dayis,
> Wer no compare, as bukis sayis.
>
> (lines 2933–40)[29]

At some point, Peter Heylyn had read enough about Joan of Arc in English and French sources to develop a deep admiration for her. He defends her not merely against witchcraft and sorcery but against those who would downgrade her achievements merely on account of her sex.

Despite Heylyn's defenses, the association of Joan of Arc and witchcraft persisted, even among those who agreed with him. As late as 1779, the Scottish historian William Alexander's *History of Women* includes Joan in a chapter on witchcraft, an unusual categorization for her by that time. Making it clear that he did *not* believe Joan a witch, Alexander, like Francis Hutchinson, recognized the potential for judicial abuse in prosecuting witches. "Statesmen often availed themselves of witchcraft as a pretence to take off persons who were obnoxious to them, and against whom no other crime could be proved," he writes. He continues, "This was the pretence made use of for condemning the Maid of Orleans, well known in the history of England and of France; who, by her personal courage, and the power she assumed over the minds of a superstitious people, by persuading them that Heaven was on their side, delivered her country from the most formidable invasion which had ever threatened its subversion."[30] Less thoughtful writers continued to sensationalize Joan the witch. Near the end of the eighteenth century, in his *History of Witches* (1793) Malcolm Macleod baldly stated, "This damsel dealt in divination," although, after her successes, "a spirit of dejection prevailed amidst the English, who imbibed a notion that the maid was actually sent to war against them by the Almighty." Having narrated her victory at Orléans and nothing else of Joan's career, he concludes, "This young woman was afterwards burnt on a charge of witchcraft."[31]

The Joan of Arc in Sir Walter Scott's *Letters on Demonology*, one of his last published works (1830), is, like Alexander's, a heroine misplaced among the diabolical. Scott's historical novels are generally set earlier than the fifteenth century, with the exception of *Anne of Geierstein* (1829), but he alludes to the Maid in passing on several occasions.[32] He also cannily exploited the popular appeal of superstition. In *The Heart of Midlothian* (1818), set in the eighteenth century, Scott writes, "Witchcraft and dæmonology, as we have had already occasion to remark, were at this period believed in by almost all ranks, but more especially among the stricter classes of presbyterians, whose government, when at the head of the state, had been much sullied by their eagerness to enquire into, and persecute these imaginary crimes."[33] For the purposes of this fiction, it was "presbyterians" who manifested their fear of the supernatural in violence. For the purposes of Scott's *Letters*, however, the Catholic Church assumes the burden of guilt. In letter VII, he notes the frequency with which "an epidemic terror of witches" arose, and expresses his revulsion at the consequent "seas of innocent blood." The "truth of this statement" is to be seen, he continues, "in Catholic countries on the continent, [where] the various kingdoms adopted readily that part of the civil law, already mentioned, which denounces sorcerers and witches as rebels to God, and authors of sedition in the empire" (196). Like Hutchinson and Alexander, he understood both the power of superstition and how accusations of witchcraft were related to politics. He continues, writing that to "weed out of the land the witches and those who had intercourse with familiar spirits, or in any other respect fell under the ban of the church, as well as the heretics who promulgated or adhered to false doctrine," inquisitors were authorized "to use the utmost exertions on their part, that the subtlety of the examinations, and the severity of the tortures they inflicted, might wring the truth out of all suspected persons, until they rendered the province in which they exercised their jurisdiction a desert from which the inhabitants fled."[34] Both superstition and policy led to the downfall of Joan of Arc:

> The English vulgar regarded her as a sorceress—the French as an inspired heroine; while the wise on both sides considered her as neither the one nor the other, but a tool used by the celebrated Dunois, to play the part which he assigned her. The Duke of Bedford, when the ill-starred Jeanne fell into his hands, took away her life, in order to stigmatize her memory with sorcery, and to destroy the reputation she had acquired among the French. . . . The charmed sword and blessed banner, which she had represented as signs of her celestial mission, were in this hostile charge against her, described as enchanted implements, designed by the fiends and fairies whom she worshipped, to accomplish her temporary success. The death of the innocent, high-minded, and perhaps amiable enthusiast, was not, we are sorry to say, a sacrifice to a superstitious fear of witchcraft, but a cruel instance of wicked policy mingled with national jealousy and hatred. (198–99)

The last sentence encapsulates some two centuries of English opinion about the Maid, an opinion Scott was eager to pass on to a new generation. His view of Joan is more succinct and direct in his *Tales of a Grandfather*, a history of France for children (1831). He goes so far as to state that the English burned her "*to their eternal disgrace*" (original emphasis). "This execrable cruelty," he continues, "and the general haughtiness of the Duke of Bedford, so disgusted the duke of Burgundy (Philip the Good) that he abandoned the English."[35] Scott's adjective "execrable," applied to the English, not to Joan, echoes in reverse the 1587 edition of Holinshed's *Chronicles*, according to which Joan's "execrable abominations" justified her execution. If "witch" had been the one of the first epithets applied to Joan of Arc in all seriousness, it was also one of the most enduring, as authors exploited it to catch the reader's attention, perhaps, and then magnanimously exonerated Joan of any such transgression.

Some English demonologies indeed placed Joan of Arc in the company of sorcerers, magicians, and devils, yet others pronounced the accusation of witchcraft against her as spurious and the effect of uncontrolled popery or political machination. Her fate became an example of "wicked policy." Her actual conduct and undeniable accomplishments, while contrary to cultural and religious models for the behavior for women, were not always judged negatively in discussions of female vices and virtues. In the remainder of this chapter, I briefly examine the medieval deployment of exemplum in the specific case of women and then show how the trope served English writers working in different genres and to different purposes when considering Joan of Arc.

Exemplum—whether edifying or cautionary—is by its nature both selective and moral. As John D. Lyons explains, exemplum "is a way of taking our beliefs about reality and reframing them into something that suits the direction of the text" and is thus "the most ideological of figures."[36] When applied to women, Susan Wiseman suggests, repeated allusions to particular female exempla in the early modern period could signal an audience how to read the larger argument to which they are recruited. This function of example "shows gender at work in the interpretative acts of readers and writers," especially, as Wiseman suggests, when the same example is used to defend opposing points of view.[37] This is the case, as we shall see, when the playwright Thomas Heywood praises Joan in his 1624 *Gynaikeion* but calls her "Sorceress" in his 1641 *Life of Merlin*.

It was also the case in the early Middle Ages, when St. Jerome displayed his wide and consciously selective reading by culling exempla from both Christian and Classical sources to "show that virginity ever took the lead of chastity" in his famous treatise *Against Jovinianus*.[38] As do later writers, he chose what best suited his own purposes, ignoring inconsistencies of which he must have been aware.[39] The theological misogyny expressed by some of the church fathers had, by the close of the Middle Ages, been transmuted into a satirical stereotype, a literary trope that infused the debate about women. At least the gist, however distorted, of Jerome's letter must have been sufficiently embedded in English literary culture in the late fourteenth century to make recognizable Chaucer's Wife of Bath's allusion to "Seint Jerome, / That made a book agayn Jovinian."[40] In her Prologue, she laments her last husband Jankyn's collection of examples of "wikked wives" in a single book. But most collections focusing on women, as did some of those in Jankyn's manuscript, bind women of virtue as well as vice, as the Wife says, "in one volume." Also drawing on both the Classical and Christian traditions of exemplum, early defenders of Joan of Arc met the challenge of construing her spiritual authenticity by recourse to analogy with virtuous women. During Joan's own lifetime, theological defenders such as Jean Gerson, former Chancellor of the University of Paris, and literary ones such as the poet Christine de Pizan installed her among biblical heroes and Amazons. Later in the fifteenth century, Martin le Franc's defense of women *Le Champion des dames* sets Joan alongside her medieval counterparts Jeanne, Countess of Montfort and Jeanne de Bavière.[41] These fifteenth-century French writers who, like Jerome, selectively marshaled exempla to defend Joan of Arc, were deploying the strategy in the same way English writers were to do. Their common model was Italian humanist Giovanni Boccaccio's *De mulieribus claris* (*On Famous Women*, 1374).

Boccaccio's was the first Western collection of women's lives. The work praises women for their excellence despite their physical limitations: "If we grant that men deserve praise whenever they perform great deeds with the strength bestowed upon them, how much more should women be extolled—almost all of whom are endowed by nature with soft, frail bodies and sluggish minds—when they take on a manly spirit, show remarkable intelligence and bravery, and dare to execute deeds that would be extremely difficult even for men?"[42] Boccaccio chooses examples of Classical viragos who were to become standard in similar collections—Semiramis, Penthesilea, and Xenobia—but no biblical women. Following his lead, Christine de Pizan developed a more sophisticated dream-vision structure for her refutation of thoughtless misogyny in the *Le Livre de la cité des dames* (1405).[43] An English translation of the *City of Ladies* by Bryan Anslay was published in London in 1521. The chapter headings and text refer to the narrator as "Christine," but her authorship is not mentioned. Nevertheless, Stephanie Downes argues that "tropes and strategies developed in the *Cité des dames* are drawn upon by male authors contributing to the English debate about women," although such tropes and strategies were not unique to Christine.[44] When she came to praise Joan in her "Ditié de Jeanne d'Arc," Christine elevated the philosophical foundation of her earlier work to proclaim that God could work his will through a woman to save the kingdom of France.

Whether Christine de Pizan's work had any influence on English writers, the examples chosen by Gerson, Christine herself, and Martin le Franc foreshadow the ways in which Joan of Arc was integrated into the tradition of writing women's history. It is chiefly in the works of the followers of Boccaccio that Joan of Arc begins to take her place—often outside the military context that dominated the fifteenth-century chronicles. Especially in England, the three Old Testament viragos often associated with her—Judith, Deborah, and Esther—were also reappropriated, affecting the nature of the analogies. To some extent, they became part of a Protestant discourse on women and power, and provided, in Wiseman's words, "a repertoire which signalled to a reader that politics was being discussed."[45] Thus, when we see them associated with Joan of Arc in post-Reformation England, we must consider that larger religio-political dimension. Queen Elizabeth I, for example, was frequently depicted as an English Deborah. In his swift response to the theologian John Knox's attack on women rulers in *The First Blast of the Trumpet* (1558), Bishop John Aylmer evokes Deborah to defend ostensibly contradictory qualities. He writes that while "she sent [her husband Barake] to the warre, gave him his commission, and made him the generall, whereby apeareth that to be true, which we saide before: that a woman as a wife must be at commaundement, but a woman as a magistrate may lawfullye commaunde."[46] Yet Aylmer also evokes both the efforts of Empress Maud and Joan of Arc as examples of God's judgment on King Stephen and the English, respectively (F3v–F4), even though both women were rebelling against male authority.

Another example for early modern writers was Queen Esther. On the one hand, during the early seventeenth-century recurrence of the *querelle* in print, the pseudonymous "Ester Sowerman" evoked her namesake in the tract "Ester hath hang'd Haman" (1617), a response to Joseph Swetnam's 1615 *Arraignment of Lewd, idle, forward, and Unconstant Women*. On the other hand, during the seventeenth-century English Civil Wars, according to Wiseman, "petitions using the story of Esther as an example both hint at and retreat from claims to women having political rights."[47] Adapting examples of biblical women specifically to the woman question could also limit their universality, reducing them to the extremes of "the saint or the virago," as Alison Booth suggests is the case with Judith.[48]

Joan of Arc was similarly reappropriated in England, appearing often in collected exempla, some, but not all, marshaled to attack or defend her sex, and in contexts that sometimes emphasize gender norms against which to measure her. Such collections generally included but diluted serious philosophical and moral arguments, displacing them into the context of religious or cultural controversy. In the early sixteenth century, the German theologian Cornelius Agrippa defended the appropriateness of women having a voice in public life, and wrote an approving account of Joan of Arc that was "corrected" in one of its English translations. In Thomas Heywood's *Gynaikeion*, Joan is located not in the eighth book, with its catalog of "Witches," but in book 5, "of Amazons." At the outset of the English Civil war, in 1642, Thomas Fuller positioned the Maid among negative exemplars, including witches, in his *Profane State*. Yet—possibly inadvertently—he produced a sympathetic reading. These works demonstrate, as had the chronicles and John Speed, the malleability of Joan's story for English writers.

In 1509, shortly before Fabyan's *New Chronicles*—with its enduring influence on English historical accounts of Joan—was printed in England, Agrippa delivered a Latin declamation that reexamined centuries of critiques of women's virtue, reasoning, and physical attributes and concluded that women were not equal to men. They were superior beings. The extent of irony and hyperbole in his oration has been disputed, but its subsequent publication (Antwerp, 1529) did open new avenues in the debate.[49] The work was translated into English by David Clapham and printed in 1542 as *A Treatise of the Nobilitie and Excellence of Woman Kynde*.[50]

Agrippa addresses many admirable qualities in women, but toward the end of his *Declamation*, he turns to (in Clapham's translation) "many other moste noble women, whyche by theyr wonderfulle power and polycie, in moste extremytie, and whan there was no hope of helpe loked for, recovered theyre countrey, and restored it to wealthe ageyne" (F1). Of the Old Testament women to whom Joan of Arc is most often compared, Agrippa praises Deborah both for her wisdom and for her martial successes. In this context, Esther merits a single sentence: "So Hester, the wife of Kynge Assuer, not only delivered her people from the moste shamefull deth but also made theym ryght honorable" (F1v–F2). However, praising Judith adequately seems beyond Agrippa's own rhetorical powers; instead, he quotes St. Jerome: "Take Judith the wydowe, the example of chastite, declare her with triumphant prayse and perpetual commendation. For god gave her to be an example, not only for women, but also for men to folowe" (F–Fv).[51]

In the same provocative vein, Agrippa introduces Joan of Arc with a rhetorical challenge that Clapham alters in his translation. Agrippa's Latin asks, "Who in our day will be able to praise enough the noble young girl [Joan of Arc]?"[52] Clapham ascribes such praise to the French: "Nowe moche doo the Frenchemen prayse a yonge damsell, whiche beinge descended of a lowe linage, toke upon her after the maner of the Amazons, to leade the forward of the army: & she fought so valiantly, and hadde soo good chaunce, that the French men beleved verily, that by her prowesse, they recovered the relme of France out of the Englysshe mens handes" (F2–F2v). However, Agrippa does not enumerate any of Joan's singular achievements, other than her role in relieving the kingdom of France from English occupation. He disregards her execution entirely. Agrippa's praise for Joan is achieved both by its comparative length and by pride of place: it is last of all his examples of women, for "I am not soo presumptuous, to thynke my selfe able, to comprehend in few wordes, the infynite nobylities & vertues of women" (F3), an apologia that would be echoed a century later by Thomas Heywood, as will be discussed below.

A Restoration-era translation of Agrippa, *Female Pre-eminence* by Henry Care (1670), confirms Joan as a French national heroine, associating her not only with the Amazons but also with the English virago Ælfleda, the Lady of Mercia, who was instrumental in defeating the Danes in the early tenth century:

> The English Nation were most ungratefull, should they ever forget their Obligations to this Sex, to whose couragious resolution alone, they owe their deliverance from the insufferable tyranny of the Danes. . . . That strange ridling Prodigy of valour, Joan of Arc, (celebrated by some as a saint, and branded by others for a Witch,) when the English had almost spred their victorious Ensigns over the whole Kingdome of France, and wanted little to compleat its total conquest, taking Arms like an Amazon, arrested their fortune, put a stop to the torrent of their victories, and by degrees restor'd the withering de Luce [fleurs-de-lis] to their former lustre; in honour of which gallant Enterprise, a statue sacred to her memory stands erected on the Bridge at Orleans.[53]

Care was not merely translating. In his "Translator's Preface," he admits that he undertook the work "not without some Additions, and variation" (A2v).[54] He adds his own opinion of Joan from an English point of view and dramatizes

Agrippa's language, leaving no doubt of Care's admiration for the Maid who had defeated his ancestors so ignominiously. In 1657, Hugh Crompton similarly praised Joan, in this case by versifying Agrippa in English heroic couplets: "Who when the English had invaded France / Amazon-like her weapons did advance, / Driving the Armes of that cruell host / And did regain the Kingdome even lost" (lines 1105–8). Crompton also mentions the statue erected to Joan's memory in Orléans, but not her execution.[55]

David Clapham's earlier translation also effects significant changes to Agrippa, apart from somewhat abridging the Latin.[56] Clapham eliminates the opening rhetorical question, substituting for an authorial stance of implicit approval the establishment of distance between the European who can view Joan of Arc in the company of other illustrious women, and an Englishman who will impute any praise for her to "the Frenchmen." Next, following Fabyan, who wrote that it was only "after the *oppinyon* of the Frenshe Cronycle, this victory shulde be obteyned by Jane or Johane," Clapham also undercuts Joan's accomplishments: "The French men beleved verily, that by her prowesse, they recovered the relme of France out of the Englysshe mens handes" (F2v). But his syntax is unclear. Does he mean that only the French believe it was Joan's efforts that delivered France? Or was it the French belief that they now had a legitimate claim to their own kingdom? Agrippa states a fact, not a belief: Joan restored the kingdom that had been lost to its king. The German also ends with a reference to the Calvary monument in Orléans, which he calls a "sacra statua," a holy statue. Clapham alters the wording: "They made an ymage of a mayden to be sette up in Orliaunce on the bridge over the ryver of Liger or Loier" (F2v). Notably, he eliminates the Latin "sacra" and alters "statua" to "ymage," a fraught word. For in 1542, the year Clapham's translation was published, and amid growing Protestant iconoclasm, "image" suggests there is something idolatrous about such a memorial.[57] Indeed, the first edition of Edward Hall's *Union*, published just six years later, records that the Italian historian Paulus Aemilius Veronensis ("Paulus Emilius") reported "the citezens of Orleaunce, had buylded in the honor of her, an Image or an Idole."[58] Hall makes it very clear that "image" and "idol" are synonymous, not only with each other, but with idolatry itself. Not, I think, coincidentally, the late 1530s and 1540s also mark the issuance of a series of royal proclamations on religious observance, including ordering the removal of images from all churches in England.[59] The French who raised such a monument to their Pucelle are thereby idolaters just like Joan herself, as the miter she wore to her execution had proclaimed. Clapham therefore expresses a Reformation view of Joan even as he translates Agrippa's praise of her.

The word "idol" recurs in another Englishman's translated account of Joan, one that edits not by excision, as Grimeston had done in translating de Serres, but by amplification. In 1567, Geoffrey Fenton published *Certaine Tragicall Discourses written out of Frenche and Latin*, a translation of the *XVIII Histoires tragiques* by Pierre Boisteau and François de Belleforest.[60] The French was in turn based on the *Novelle* of the Italian writer Matteo Bandello.[61] In the original Italian story, Bandello's hero Filiberto meets Charles VII in Rouen, but the narrator does not mention the Maid's fate in that city. Belleforest, however, identifies Rouen as where, "some time ago, that is in 1430, the Duke of Somerset had the Maid Joan burned."[62] In his turn, for his English readers, Fenton expands on the significance of Rouen,

> wherein, not longe affore the Duke of Sommerset had burned the counterfait prophet of Fraunce, called La Pucelle Jeane; whome some pratinge Frenchmen do affirme to have wrought merveiles in armes during those warrs, but chiefly, that under the conduite of her, our countryemen lost Orleance, with diverse other holdes in those partes, and for a memory of that forged ydoll they kepe yet amongest other relikes in the abbay of S. Denys, which I sawe in May last, a greate roostie sworde, wherwith they are not ashamed to advowche that shee performed diverse expedicions and victories againste thinglishe nacion.[63]

Fenton completed the translation in Paris, although we cannot know whether he visited St. Denis specifically to view the purported relic, Joan's "great rusty sword." He might already have been reading about Joan, perhaps in Hall, given his choice of the word "idol." His amplification "corrects" the French account, bringing it in line with what his biographer Andrew Hadfield calls his own "staunchly protestant faith."[64]

The chains of additive translation—Agrippa to Clapham, Bandello to Fenton—illustrate one way in which English opinions of Joan were deliberately reconstructed. Edward Hall added polemic. In his *Union*, he appended to his lengthy account of Joan's career a declamation on the qualities of a good (i.e., English, Protestant) woman in order to demonstrate how far the Maid deviated from his model:

> For of this I am sure, that all aunoient writers, aswell devine, as prophane, alledge these three thynges, beside diverse other, to apparteine to a good woman. First, shamefastnesse, whiche the

Romain Ladies so kept, that seldome or never thei wer seen openly talkying with a man: which vertue, at this day emongest the Turkes, is highly esteemed. The seconde, is pitie: whiche in a womans harte, abhorreth the spillyng of the bloud of a poore beast, or a sely birde. The third, is womanly behavor, advoydyng the occasion of evill judgement, and causes of slaundre. If these qualities, be of necessitie, incident to a good woman, where was her shamefastnes, when she daily and nightly, was conversant with comen souldiors, and men of warre, emongest whom, is small honestie, lesse vertue, and shamefastnesse, least of all exercised or used? Where was her womanlie pitie, when she taking to her, the harte of a cruell beaste, slewe, man, woman, and childe, where she might have the upper hand? Where was her womanlie behavor, when she cladde her self in a mannes clothyng, and was conversant with every losell [profligate], gevyng occasion to all men to judge, and speake evill of her, and her doynges. Then these thynges, beyng thus plainly true, all men must nedes confesse, that the cause ceasyng, the effect also ceaseth: so that, if these morall vertues lackyng, she was no good woman, then it must nedes, consequently folowe, that she was no sainct. (159)

"Shamefastness" implies not only modesty of behavior, but of dress—of not wearing a man's clothing. Woman are exhorted to "shamfastnes" in 1 Timothy 2:9–15: "Lykewise also the wemen, that they araye them selves in comlye apparell wyth shamfastnes and discrete behaveour, not with broyded heare, ether golde or pearles, or costly araye: but as becommeth wemen that professe godlynesse thorowe good worckes."[65] By introducing arguments that would ably suit Knox's *First Blast of the Trumpet*, and in fact anticipating Knox by calling Joan a "monster," when he first mentions her,[66] Hall moves the historical discourse on Joan's disorderly conduct into the arena of the English *querelle*, an innovation that has not always been appreciated, given the attention paid to Shakespeare's adaptation of Hall's history, but not to this disquisition on womanhood.[67]

Joan of Arc was not generally evoked in the debate on women until it began to coalesce with the genre of collective female biography at the beginning of the seventeenth century. In addition to Agrippa, Aylmer had also singled her out in his response to Knox. Among numerous examples of women who bore sons who became kings, brought their husbands kingdoms as dowries, or fought for rulers, he praises Joan of Arc: "A maid defended Orliance, in armor, against the duke of Burgundie and the English army, and after with the same her army led the young king Charls the .7. to Rome, and ther crowned him. Before this maids time, the English ever prospered, and the french wer even at the last cast, geving up the goste, but she brought them into that condicion, that afterwarde, they grewe: and we appaired [weakened]."[68] A marginal note labels her "a woman noble and happye in warres," and another "the firste healpe of the french a woman."

Not all such defenses were as straightforward. The author's preface to Christopher Newstead's *Apology for Women* (1620), despite its fulsome dedication to "Lady Mary, Countess of Buckingham" (Mary Villiers), signals a satirical intent. The address begins, "Courteous Reader, if thy tongue hath not tyed thee to a curst wife, I doubt not, but the generall view of my Subject, wil winne at the least thy ordinarie acceptation."[69] Newstead's argument for women's valor is similar to Agrippa's: women "have the same vigour, and can, as well tolerate labours, as men, if they be accustomed to them" (18). He continues, "And was not France wholy overrunne by our English, untill (as the French brag) that valorous Joane gave life to the French, confronting our brave Bedford in the field?" (19). His marginal notation cites Grimeston's translation of de Serres, although neither of those texts speaks of a direct confrontation between Joan and the regent. As was no longer unusual, Newstead allows "Joane" to be valorous "as the French brag."

The early modern debate on women had praised, "translated," excoriated, and defended Joan of Arc well before the publication of Thomas Heywood's history of women *Gynaikeion* in 1624. While this is the first example of secular female biography in English, it must inevitably be read as part of the renewal of the *querelle*. Heywood had possibly already dipped his pen into that fray, for before 1620, his acting company mounted *Swetnam, the Woman-hater Arraigned by Women*.[70] Yet his address "To the Reader," Heywood slyly refuses to participate openly in the debate:

> Generous Reader, I have exposed to thy most judiciall view a Discourse of Women: wherein expect not, that I should either enviously carpe at the particular manners or actions of any living, nor injuriously detract from the Sepulchers of the dead; the first I could never affect, the last I did always detest. I only present thee with a Collection of Histories, which touch the generalitie of Women, such as have either beene illustrated for their Vertues, and Noble Actions, or contrarily branded for their Vices, and baser Conditions; in all of which, I have not exceeded the bounds and limits of good and sufficient Authoritie.[71]

Like Agrippa, who had also modestly protested his ability to convey "in few wordes, the infinite nobilities & vertues of women," Heywood anticipates one objection to his method of abridgement. "Now if any aske, Why I have shut up and contruded within a narrow roome, many large Histories, not delating them with everie Plenarie circumstance?," he answers in the age-old way: that he merely follows his models, who "epitomised great and memorable acts ... giving them notwithstanding their full weight, in few words" (A4–A4v).

Heywood organizes his nine books according to attributes of the nine Muses, beginning with Clio, the muse of History, and ending with Calliope, the muse of epic poetry. Joan of Arc appears in the central book 5, "inscribed Terpsichore. Intreating of Amazons: and other Women famous either for Valour, or for Beautie." Anticipating his readers' confusion about the association between the muse of dance and women of valor or beauty, Heywood asserts that this muse is most fitting, for like dance, "of what doth your martiall discipline consist; but upon time, number, measure, distance, and order?" (215).

Yet echoing the demonologies, Heywood begins book 5 with several cases "where a faire face meeteth with a corrupted mind" (216), as in the cases of Jezebel, Delilah, Helen, Lavinia, and others whose "beautie hath beene the cause of so much blood-shed" (218). His second group of exemplars consists of women whose "vertues of the mind solely acquire after fame and glory, conquer oblivion and survive envie" (218). After surveying Amazons and "other warlike Ladies," Heywood turns to a section "of English Viragoes. And of Joan de Pucil." Although I have suggested that chronicle accounts of early English viragos shed some light on how English historians wrote about Joan of Arc, Heywood is the first writer deliberately to include her in their company. In order, he writes about Guendoline "the wife of King Locrine";[72] Ælfleda, the Lady of Mercia; Empress Maud (mentioning in passing Stephen's queen, Matilda of Boulogne); Joan of Arc; the eleventh-century Queen Emma of Normandy, wife in succession to Æthelred and Cnut; and Margaret of Anjou. Having begun with English viragos, he continues, "And so much shall suffice to express the magnanimitie and warlike dispositions of two noble and heroicke English Ladies. A French Ladie comes now in my way, of whom I will give you a short character" (238). His principle of selection is, on the surface, merely associative: Maud and Matilda *remind* him of Joan of Arc.

Heywood does not seem to find the inclusion of the French virago, an enemy to the English, along with English viragos at all ironic. His "character" of Joan of Arc is the lengthiest in this section of book 5, yet he is also selective about which aspects of her career to include. He begins with historical context for the rise of the Maid: "When France ... was there governed by our English

Regents, the famous duke of Bedford, and others . . . whilest the English forraged through France at their will, and commanded in all places at their owne pleasure (the French in utter despaire of shaking off the English yoake) there arose in those desperate times, one *Joane Are*" (238). Heywood takes his details from Holinshed. For example, according to both, her visions were of "our blessed Ladie, S. Agnes, and S. Katherine" (238),[73] not Saints Michael, Margaret, and Katherine, as she later named them. Perhaps to enhance his praise of Joan as a military leader, he claims the "faire bright sword with five Flower-de-lyces upon either side engraven" she directed to be found at Fierbois was one "with which she after committed many slaughters upon the English" (238), an accusation Joan adamantly refuted in her trial testimony. She was very clear about what she actually *did* during battle: "She said that she herself carried the standard when she was attacking the enemy, in order to avoid killing anyone; and she said that she never killed anyone."[74]

Heywood relates in some detail the famous anecdote about Joan's meeting the dauphin at Chinon, but devotes exactly one sentence to the victory at Orléans: "Her first exploit was fortunately [i.e., successfully[75]] to raise the siege and releeve the town" (239).[76] He enumerates her subsequent victories, including "the great battaile of Pathay . . . in which were taken prisoners the lord *Talbot* (the skourge and terror of the French nation), the lord *Scales*, the lord *Hungerford*, with many others both of name and qualite." He grants her credit for the coronation of Charles, which he relates out of chronological order: "Shee passed to Reames, tooke the cittie and caused the Dolphin there to proclaime himself king, and take upon him the crowne of France." Heywood does not talk about the debacle of Paris. He does not speculate about Joan's career from the autumn of 1429 until her capture in May 1430, an interval that is still not entirely accounted for. He clearly states that Joan was betrayed and sold, and knew she would be: "The French Cronicles affirme that the morning before she was surprised, she tooke the sacrament, and comming from Church told to diverse that were about her, that she was betraide, her life sold, and should shortly after be delivered up unto a violent death, For sir John gave a great sum of money to betray her. The English comming to invest themselves before Mondidier, Joan was advised to issue out by Flavie and skirmish with them; who was no sooner out, but he shut the gates upon her" (239). She was sent to "Peter Bishop of Bevoise, who condemned her to the fire for a sorceresse." Heywood seems to justify Joan's credibility by referring to the nullification of her sentence. Only after "Charles the king *for a great summe of money* [emphasis added] procured an annichilation of the first sentence from the Pope" was she "proclaimed a Virago inspired with divine instinct." Whereas Holinshed dutifully records the reversal of Joan's sentence, but expresses contempt for writers who "make no consideration of her heinous enormities,"[77] Heywood comes to quite a different conclusion.

Other English writers had depicted Joan as a "Martiall maide," in John Speed's words, but Heywood's inclusion of her along with *English* viragos was unprecedented. We have seen that Coxe portrayed her as the witch who reveals herself in act 5 of *1 Henry VI*. Heywood made a deliberate choice as to where he included Joan in his history of women, for although he reports that she was "condemned to the fire for a sorceresse," he chose not to place her in book 8, which addresses witches. The subheadings in that book suggest that his interest in witchcraft was more carnivalesque than theological. These include, for example, "Of Witches transported from one place to another by the Devill" (406); "Of Witches that have eyther changed their owne shapes, or transformed others" (409); and "Of Witches that have confest themselves to have raised tempests in a most serene Skie, with other things of no lesse admiration" (413). Except for Joan Puzel's claim of a physical transformation, no version of the English construction of Joan of Arc would fit under such sensational rubrics. Moreover, in book 9, devoted to "Punishments appertaining to the Vitious, and Rewards due to the Vertuous," Heywood agrees in principle with Johannes Nider, who had written in his *Formicarius* that all witches should be sentenced to death: "All that have made any compact or covenant with the Devill [are] not worthy to live" (447). Heywood also ignored Joan's alleged pregnancy, yet shows he was aware of the practice of pleading the belly: "The Judges called *Areopagitæ*, when they deprehended a Witch, and were to deliver her to death, if shee were with child, stayed the execution till shee were delivered of her Infant, because they would not punish the innocent with the delinquent" (444). Heywood's Joan was simply the Virago.

Nearly two decades later, Heywood again had occasion to write of Joan of Arc. In 1641, he published his *Life of Merlin*, a compilation of English monarchical history through the reign of Charles I. This work presents "Joan de pusill, a Sorceresse," indicating that in terms of *English* history, Joan is no heroine, even though she might be seen as a virago in *women's* history. Thus, he relates, in the ninth year of Henry VI's reign, "the French for the most part prevailed, some said by the help of a woman called Joan de Pucil, whom they stiled, The Maiden of God, who was victorious in many conflicts." Not only is she a sorceress, but "she feigned her selfe with child, but the contrary being found, she was adjudged to death, and her body burnt to ashes."[78] In the decades before Heywood wrote, other Englishmen had been selective in what they wrote about Joan of Arc. Edward Hall emphasized what he viewed as her unnatural behavior. John Speed granted Joan her due, only to draw back at the end and blame the Maid herself for causing her own downfall. Heywood recognized that Joan was a malleable figure, and could not be shut into a single room.

Just as the Wars of the Roses followed hard upon England's losses in France in the fifteenth century, serious civil conflicts had again arisen in England between the time Heywood wrote his *Gynaikeion* and his history of the English monarchy. A year after *The Life of Merlin* was published, England was embroiled in a civil war precipitated by Parliamentary suspicions of Charles I, including that he was sympathetic to Catholics (he had married the French princess Henrietta Maria). Yet despite the widespread participation of women in this conflict, Joan of Arc does not seem to have served as a Royalist model, although her story was retold in new ways, notably by Thomas Fuller.

Fuller, a minister who preached against the war and, in 1660, became "chaplain-extraordinary" to the newly restored Charles II,[79] undertook to write biography in the ancient sense, as "a branch of rhetoric, specifically, a particular means or form of teaching a lesson" through examples.[80] In *The Holy State and the Profane State*, first published in 1642,[81] he presents types in a way that is similar to the character sketches of such writers as Sir Thomas Overbury and John Earle popular at the time, with illustrative lives drawn from the Bible, history, and contemporary biography. The figures described in the *Holy State* are examples to be emulated; those in the *Profane State* are so blatantly repugnant to civil and religious order as to require little overt moralizing. However, in the case of his "Life of Joan of Arc," Fuller seems reluctant to reduce her to such extremes, for despite his serious purpose, his humanity outweighed his didacticism.[82] He devotes four books to the holy, and only one to the profane. He disapproves of Joan of Arc on several grounds, but in the end, he humanely tries to imagine a punishment for her other than execution.

Fuller's exploration of vice, *The Profane State*, begins with the type "Harlot," followed by the example of Joan [Joanna], Queen of Naples. The type "Witch" is illustrated first by a biblical example, "The Witch of Endor" (1 Samuel 28:7–14) and then by the historical example "The Life of Joan of Arc." The remaining fourteen sketches focus on male types and exemplars. Fuller opens with a brief account of Joan's birth and the state of affairs in France "in her time." Like others before him, Fuller asserts that Joan was "set up" by French nobility "to make her pretend that she had a revelation from heaven, to be the leader of an army, to drive all the English out of France: and she being an handsome, witty and bold maid (about twentie years of age) was both apprehensive of the plot, and very active to prosecute it" (372–73). In a spirit of fairness Fuller continues, "But other Authours will not admit of any such complotting, but make her moved therunto either of her own, or by some Spirits instigation."[83]

After the victory at Orléans, Fuller writes, "this virago (call her now John or Joan) marched on into other countreys, which instantly revolted to the French crown" (374).[84] Fuller's wordplay, converting Fabyan's Latinized version of Joan's name to a masculine form, mocks the insignificance of gender markers to Joan and its mortal significance to her judges. She had insisted on the practicality of her male dress. Her judges saw it as a transgression of the laws of both God and man. Fuller especially disapproved of "two customes [Joan] had which can by no way be defended. One was her constant going in mans clothes, flatly against Scripture" and "as an occasion to lust" (376). In the chapter "Of Apparell" in *The Holy State*, Fuller defends "Sumptuary laws" on the basis of social class, in order to contain false pride, but he does not mention cross-dressing (165–66). Another "custome" was Joan's short hair; in his view, "she shaved her hair in the fashion of a Frier, against Gods expresse word, it being also a Solecisme in nature, all women being born votaries, and the veil of their long hair minds them of their obedience they naturally owe to man" (377).[85] Joan did wear her hair short, but only after she abjured her alleged crimes on May 24, 1431, did she agree to have it shaved off entirely, apparently to do away with a masculine style, just as she agreed to wear women's clothing.[86] (This might also have been a penitential gesture.) Even in his defense of women, Agrippa had written (in Clapham's translation), "Woman is endowed with a certaine dignitie and worthines of honestie, whiche is not gyven to man: for the heare of her head hangeth downe soo lowe, that yt wyll cover and hyde all the pryvy partes of her body."[87] At heart, though, Fuller is most outraged at Joan's Catholicism, which he terms her "smack of Monkery . . . as being sent to maintain as well the Friers as the French Crown" (377).

Fuller never grants the "She-General" a genuinely military identity: "What shall we say?" he asks, "when God intends a Nation shall be beaten, he ties their hands behind them" (374–75). Joan's was merely the power to rally men's spirits and appeal to their "Phancie" (imagination). Yet, regardless of whether he realized it, Fuller's sketch of "The Good Souldier" in *The Holy State* echoes the Maid's own leadership values. The Good Soldier, he writes, "chiefly avoids those sinnes, to which Souldiers are taxed as most subject. Namely common swearing, which impayreth ones credit by degrees, and maketh all his promises not to be trusted; for he who for no profit will sinne against God, for small profit will trespasse against his neighbour; drinking, whoring" (120). Joan, as discussed in chapter 2, famously abhorred swearing.

The most intriguing and initially puzzling aspect of Fuller's biography is his opinion of Joan's fate. He reports that after her capture, several arguments were advanced against putting her to death. First, "some held that no punishment was to be inflicted on her, because Nullum memorabile nomen / foeminea in poena. / Cruelty to a woman / Brings honour unto no man" (375). In Virgil's *Æneid*, Aeneas utters this conditionally as he contemplates taking his revenge on Helen.[88] A second argument against Joan's execution was that it would endanger English prisoners of war: "Putting her to death would render all English men guilty which should hereafter be taken prisoners by the French." Finally, "her former valour deserved praise, her present misery deserved pity. . . . Let them rather allow her an honourable pension, and so make her valiant deeds their own by rewarding them. However, she ought not to be put to death: for if the English would punish her, they could not more disgrace her then with life, to let her live though in a poore mean way, and then she would be the best confutation of her own glorious prophesies; let them make her the Laundresse to the English, who was the Leader to the French Army" (375–76). This curious "sentence" on Joan certainly reflects Fuller's humane view of earthly punishment. In the case of heretics, he preached, "where too much charity hath slaine her thousands, too little hath slaine her ten thousands. . . . So let our beliefes be composed of charity, mixt with our credulity."[89] Yet in his discussion of "the Heretick" in *The Profane State*, Fuller suggests that two crimes may indeed lead to the execution of heretics: sedition and blasphemy (395).

Because Joan of Arc's crimes were her "witchcraft and whoredomes" (376), however, Fuller suggests that she be punished by taking on one of the few roles a woman was permitted to play in the military, yet one that was sometimes equated with whore: laundress. This "sentence" for the Maid is on the surface difficult to elucidate. Laundress was a "poore mean" profession but one historically sanctioned by English military codes as the only authorized role—one specified in military rules—a woman could fulfill on military campaigns, except wife. Women were present in large numbers in the European armies of Fuller's time, when they served as sutlers (provisioners) as well as laundresses, but the assumption that many were indeed prostitutes prevailed.[90] The authorization of the laundress or washerwoman in combat is recorded at least from the First Crusade to distinguish them from those who might corrupt the morals of Crusaders.[91] Several statutes promulgated for crusaders in the twelfth century make this clear.[92] In writing about the fall of the Crusader citadel at Acre in 1291, the Norman poet Ambroise provides particulars of the washerwoman's function: "For all the women would remain in the city of Acre except for virtuous elderly women pilgrims, the laundresses who were on the pilgrimage, who washed the clothes and heads, and were as good as monkeys at getting rid of fleas."[93]

Importantly, the exception for laundresses persisted in English military regulations up to the time Fuller wrote.[94] For example, the laws and ordinances issued by Lord Northumberland in 1640, while not specifically enumerating approved occupations for women, could be interpreted to accommodate laundresses: "All idle persons, boyes, or women which have no particular imployment for the necessarie and honest use of the souldiers, and which be not allowed, shall be banished the camp."[95] By tradition, laundress was certainly for the necessary and ostensibly honest use of the soldiers. In practice, the laundress or washerwoman was distinct both from wives or other family members and prostitutes. She apparently held an almost gender-neutral position, her function overriding her sex, and her utility both acknowledged and protected. Fuller must have been familiar with the roles of women—licit and illicit—in the army of his time, for he served as chaplain to Robert, the First Baron Hopton, during the wars.[96] To be sure, washerwoman to the *English* would indeed be an insulting demotion for the Maid, especially, one supposes, if it including nit picking, as the poet Ambroise had described. But it was not inevitably equivalent either to servitude or prostitution,[97] despite Fuller's claim that Joan deserved death "for her witchcraft and whoredoms." So why consign Joan to the laundry? Fuller's source for his "Life of G[ustavus] Adolph[us] K[ing] of Sweden" in *The Holy State* provided him with the association of cleanliness and ungodliness. A marginal note at the beginning of the biography of the king refers to a translation of Gustavus Adolphus's military articles as *The Swedish Discipline* in 1632. There, Fuller could read in article 89 that "no Whore shall be suffered in the Leaguer: but if any will have his owne wife with him, he may. If any unmaried woman be found, he that keepes her may have leave lawfully to marry her; or els be forced to put her away."[98]

To illustrate the application of such rules in praise of Gustavus Adolphus's good generalship, Fuller relates the following anecdote, a version of which had been told previously in the military educator Johann von Wallhausen's *Defensio patriae* (1621).[99] Fuller attributed it to the Swedish king to illustrate his moral probity and humanity on the subject of women who followed the army:

> When first he entred Germany, he perceived how that many women followed his souldiers, some being their wives, and some wanting nothing to make them so but marriage, yet most passing for their landresses, though commonly defiling more then they wash. The King coming to a great river, after his men and the wagons were

passed over, caused the bridge to be broken down, hoping so to be rid of these feminine impediments; but they one a sudden lift up a panick schrick which pierced the skies, and the souldiers hearts on the other side of the river, who instantly vowed not to stirre a foot farther, except with baggage, and that the women might be fetch'd over, which was done accordingly. For the King finding this ill humour so generally dispers'd in his men, that it was dangerous to purge it all at once, smiled out his anger for the present, and permitted what he could not amend: yet this abuse was afterwards reformed by degrees. (332)

Fuller had hit upon an ingenious alternative punishment for Joan of Arc. Yet, answering his own "defense" of Joan, he concludes,

Against these arguments necessity of State was urged, a reason above all reason; it being in vain to dispute whether that may be done which must be done. For the French superstition of her could not be reformed except the idole was destroyed; and it would spoil the French puppet-playes in this nature for ever after, by making her an example. Besides she was no prisoner of warre, but a prisoner of Justice, deserving death for her witchcraft and whoredomes, whereupon she was burnt at Rohan the sixth of July 1461, not without the aspersion of cruelty on our Nation. Learned men are in great doubt what to think of her. Some make her a Saint, and inspired by Gods Spirit, whereby she discovered strange secrets and foretold things to come. (376)[100]

He thus ends with what became a frequently reprinted "Elegy":

Here lies *Joan of Arc*, the which
Some count saint, and some count witch;
Some count man, and something more;
Some count maid, and some a whore:
Her life's in question, wrong, or right;
Her death's in doubt, by laws, or might.
Oh innocence take heed of it,
How thou too near to guilt dost sit.
(Mean time France a wonder saw,
A woman rule 'gainst Salique Law.)
But, Reader, be content to stay

Thy censure, till the Judgement-day:
Then shalt thou know, and not before,
Whether Saint, Witch, Man, Maid, or Whore.
                    (377)

Fuller was not, of course, inventing these epithets. Shakespeare's "dolphin" Charles declares, "Joan de Puzel shall be France's saint" (1.5.68). The London chronicle described her as a "wycche." Edward Hall declared her a "manly woman." John Speed praised the "Martiall maide." English soldiers at Orléans called her "the Armagnacs' whore." Learned men such as Fuller were in doubt not only about Joan of Arc's true character but also about the cruelty of her punishment. Polydore Vergil called her sentence "the hardest that ever had beene remembred," while the 1587 edition of Holinshed's *Chronicles* justified her execution because of "her execrable abhominations."[101] Speed opined that English magnanimity sought to spare Joan. But Fuller offered the most original ruling of all and unintentionally established a paradigm for categorical considerations of the Maid in English to this day. He also, more importantly, reinforces the simultaneity of Joan's identities in England, confuting the tenability of any hypothesis that holds that her image was gradually amended from wholly negative to wholly adulatory.

After the 1660 Restoration of the English monarchy in the person of Charles II, William Winstanley, a minor poet and biographer, offered three accounts of Joan of Arc in miscellaneous collections that assembled anecdotes for humor and entertainment, inventing a new context for considering Joan of Arc. Winstanley has been identified as the pseudonymous author of the "Poor Robin" series of parodies and almanacs, which first appeared in 1662.[102] *Poor Robin's Character of France* (1666) includes "a brief Dialogue" between an Englishman and a Frenchman whose English is insultingly fractured. In his address "To the Judicious Readers," the author lampoons French mannerisms as well as "the fickleness of those people," reflecting the increasing tensions between England and France after the Continental realignments following the Thirty Years' War.[103] Having compared their respective patron saints, St. George and St. Denis, the Englishman spurns the French taste for the heroes of "Romances, wherein there is little danger in fighting," and turns to "real feats of Armes." He enumerates the great victories of the English during the Hundred Years' War: Poitiers, Crécy, and Agincourt. He boasts, "Have we not taken their Kingdom from them? the English King Crowned King of France in France? where was their Valour then? Why they were forced to have recourse to a Witch, one Joan of Arc, when France lay as it were expiring out her latest breath. How were they forced to pretend a Message to her from God, to breathe new courage into the hearts of their fanting Soldiers? and yet when they had wrought all these Forgeries, it was not so much their Courage as our own Divisions, that caused the English expulsion out of France" (26). The repetition of "forced" suggests that Joan of Arc was a last resort, and an unnecessary one for the French, as the English were the authors of their own destruction. Unwilling or unable to defend Joan, the Frenchman can only reply helplessly, "Me ha no skill in de History, me can no tell if de speak true" (26).

In a manual for the edification of the inarticulate, *The New Help to Discourse* (1680), Winstanley offers topics and anecdotes to spur polite conversation, some in question-and-answer form. He suggests one such leading question: "Who was accounted the most brave Virago woman that ever France bred?" The suggested answer is, of course, "Joan D'Arc . . . whom they call La Pusille; who when the English had almost over-run France, stoutly stood up for the defence of her Countrey."[104] But how odd a question, given that the answer is obvious. Why limit the conversation merely to viragos bred in France except to force attention on Joan of Arc alone? Winstanley writes an abridged version of Fuller's biography of Joan (correcting the year of Joan's death to 1431) and is willing—no doubt for the sake of sparking interesting conversation—to consider whether there might have been two sides to her character: "Some adjudge [her death] extream cruelty in the English, and that she was rather a Saint than Witch." But he is content merely to reprint Fuller's "epitaph" rather than express his own opinion.

Further insight into how Winstanley reappropriated Joan's reputation occurs in his 1684 *Historical Rarities*, wherein he places his story of Joan of Arc in tandem with that of Catalina de Erauso (whom he calls "Catarina d'Arcuso") as "two famous Viragos."[105] De Erauso (1592–1650), known as "La Monja Alférez" or "The Nun Second Lieutenant," was a seventeenth-century Basque woman who left a convent at age fifteen and dressed, traveled, and lived as a man. Erauso's life and afterlife differ markedly from Joan of Arc's. Her career was far longer and more sensational than was the Maid's, her transvestism eventually authorized by the pope.[106] Yet the Lieutenant Nun lived not merely dressed as a male, and she expressed her sexuality frankly, in ways Joan's judges attempted to elicit from her by questioning about her physical contact with her saints. The association of Joan with Catalina is, as far as I know, unique to Winstanley and would indeed prompt a lively and titillating conversation. Like Fuller, whose "epitaph" he reproduces, he refuses to pass final judgment on Joan: "Many sundry Opinions were conceived of this Woman, some judging her miraculously raised up by God for the good of France; others, that she was but a meer Impostor. We will suspend our Judgment herein."[107]

Over the next hundred years, Joan of Arc becomes a familiar presence in the burgeoning genre of female biography. And just as Fuller and Winstanley refused to admit their true opinions of her, many accounts express similar ambiguity. For example, John Shirley praises her in the introduction to his 1686 *Illustrious History of Women*, drawing his readers' attention to one of the "Noble Viragoes whose Courage and Conduct has been manifested to Admiration." He writes, "When France had stooped to English Valour, and all its courage drooped to a degree even of dispaire, this Warlike Maid by her courage and conduct put such Spirit and Life into the Feeble hearted French, that fatal to the English, soon after they stripped them out of almost all the Towns they held in that florishing Kingdom."[108] Yet in the chapter devoted to "Courage and Conduct in War," Joan is not further mentioned, although many of the viragos previously associated with her are—notably, as in Heywood, Ælfleda and Maud. She is initially dismissed in the anonymous *Biographium Fæmineum* (1766), an alphabetical dictionary of "The Female Worthies." The author admits that Joan of Arc, the "virago [who] rendered herself famous in history, by beginning the expulsion of the English out of France . . . seems entitled to some notice, tho' *otherwise, scarce worthy of a place in our memoirs* [emphasis added]."[109] Yet he writes her biography and admits she "fought with great conduct and bravery" at Compiegne. I will examine further the changing nature of Joan's biography in the eighteenth and early nineteenth centuries in chapter 5.

During her trial, Joan of Arc defied the judges who undertook to align her conduct with accepted categories of female behavior or who disputed her own conviction that her conduct was sanctioned by heaven, not inspired by hell. She occupied simultaneously domains that were deemed impossible to cohabit according to late medieval and early modern norms: *Pucelle* and *chef de guerre*. Visionary and idolater. A child of notable piety, yet an adult transvestite defiant of paternal and ecclesiastical authority. Nominating herself "Pucelle de Dieu," she situated herself as *sui generis*. Faced with the ineffable, in which language fails and faith or skepticism prevails, those attempting to define her by reference to multiple categories nevertheless determine to keep her, as Heywood writes, "shut up and contruded within a narrow roome." Indeed, perhaps only the Vatican succeeded—and that, belatedly—in furnishing an incontrovertible niche for Joan of Arc: in the company of saints.

CHAPTER 4

## "A PIEVISH PAINTED PUZEL"

### Joan of Arc and Mary Queen of Scots in 1 Henry VI

> It is an heretic that makes the fire, / Not she which burns in't.
> —William Shakespeare, *The Winter's Tale* (1611)

Whether or not Thomas Fuller was slyly winking when he refused to locate Joan of Arc definitively on a continuum of moral exemplarity—we cannot know "Whether Saint, Witch, Man, Maid, or Whore"—he was accurately conveying the contemporary range of English opinion about the Maid. Fuller might also have been throwing up his hands in the face of the same problem that literary critics have posed to themselves in trying to account for Joan's avatar "Joan Puzel" in 1 *Henry VI*.[1] Although the fifteenth-century London chronicle had called her "capytin," and "false prophetesse," it was the epithet "wycche," with its powerful evocation of fiendish inspiration, that resonated with the early modern era. Even so, Shakespeare's dramatization of Joan's fearsome but ultimately hollow demonic power could not entirely displace English depictions of her as a valiant warrior. If contemporary audiences had any notion of the historical Joan of Arc, then they might have expected her to appear at the outset of the play as Edward Hall's "peevish painted puzzle," or as Holinshed's "miraclemonger," "false miscreant," and "strumpet"[2]—and she does not disappoint. In the play, she first appears as a prophetess and, in

Richard Bovet's later words, "very *Charming* and *Angelical*" with no "very Nauseous deformity," a transformation from Edward Hall's "foule face" of which she herself brags.[3] In act 5, she amply demonstrates what Robert Fabyan had called her "sorcery and develysshe wayes" and not merely pleads her belly but convicts herself a whore.[4] In between, she generally evinces Polydore Vergil's "martiall manly prowesse, for defence of her country."[5] Just as she had for writers of history and participants in the *querelle des femmes*, the English depiction of Joan of Arc metamorphoses for the context and purpose in which she appears. In the late sixteenth century, Joan Puzel absorbs and reflects any number of political and religious threats to England.

Events of the late 1580s and early 1590s provided contemporary touchstones for many of the themes—some say anxieties—explored in *1 Henry VI*.[6] It was simultaneously an era deeply suspicious of powerful women and a time when women reigned in England (Mary Tudor, Elizabeth I) and Scotland (Mary Stuart) and acted as regent in France (Catherine de' Medici). Thus, the dramatized portrayal of such women, as Nina Levine argues, "whether in the [history] plays themselves, in their chronicle sources, or within Elizabethan society—are shaped not by cultural myths of gender alone but by the intersection of these myths with specific political situations."[7] Gender was integral to the political upheavals over Elizabeth I's succession. Although imprisoned in various locations after 1567, the Catholic Mary Stuart remained the focus of both international and domestic plots to place her on the English throne. Most notably in 1586, for example, a group of English Catholics led by Anthony Babington failed in their plans to assassinate Elizabeth, implicating Mary herself and leading to her execution. Even though Elizabeth had never indicated any willingness to name Mary as her heir, the question of who would succeed her—unmarried, childless, and approaching sixty years of age—had bedeviled Parliament for decades.[8]

Audiences for *1 Henry VI* might well have suspected references to such events in the play. Joan Puzel, especially, Leah Marcus observes in *Puzzling Shakespeare*, "could have given rise to many other associations with French and 'Popish' queens and claimants—with Elizabeth's half-sister Mary Tudor, for example, who had scourged English Protestants, or with Mary Queen of Scots, who had briefly been queen of France, who had plotted endlessly against Elizabeth and Protestantism until her execution in 1587, and who was much more openly (and justifiably) reviled as a whore than Elizabeth." But, she further argues, "the play's reverberations between Joan and Elizabeth are by far the most insistent and most troublesome."[9] Troublesome yes—but I will argue that reverberations between Joan Puzel and Mary Stuart are even more insistent. Like the Joan of Arc already represented in some English sources, Mary had long been associated with enchantments and witchcraft, sexual misconduct, and, most dangerously, "popery." As John Macleod puts it, for English Protestants, "Mary was perceived as a virtual Frenchwoman; a fanatical Romanist; a conniving, wanton woman capable of every viciousness and intrigue."[10] The 1569 pamphlet *A Discourse Touching the Pretended Match betwene the Duke of Norfolke and the Queene of Scottes* summarizes Mary's "crimes" in such a way as to parallel Joan of Arc's: "In religion she is either a Papist whilke is evill, or ells an Atheist whilke is werse. . . . Of inclination how she is geven, let her own horrible actes publikely knowen to the whole worlde witnesse, though now of late certaine seduced by practise, seeke to cloke and hide the same. Of aliances of the mother side how she is descended of a race that is both enemie to God and the common quiet to Europe, everye man knoweth, but alas to many have felt."[11] French, Catholic, and devious: shared attributes of two women who deserved to be executed, the power of whose memories, preserved in contemporary histories, continued to threaten or hearten vested interests from beyond the grave.[12]

One of those histories was a major source for *1 Henry VI*. Raphael Holinshed's *Chronicles* was first published in 1577, reissued with additional material in 1587, and promptly redacted.[13] On February 1, 1587, after Mary had been convicted of treason but a week before her execution, Elizabeth's Privy Council wrote to the archbishop of Canterbury expressing concerns about the addition of "sondry things which we wish had bene better considered" in the new edition, including matters of state and "such mention of matter touching the King of Scottes [the future James I] as may give him cause of offence."[14] Cyndia Clegg, who has closely analyzed the textual changes touching Mary's fate, concludes, "The text that had initially survived censorship reported the apprehension, trials, and executions of the Babington conspirators as well as the trial and condemnation of Mary, Queen of Scots. [Another] cancel retains substantially the same material, but in a version carefully edited to tame the violence and remove incendiary anti-Catholic language." She believes that final recension postdated Mary's execution.[15]

In contrast, the 1587 edition greatly expanded its narrative of Joan of Arc's judgment and execution in a passage attributed to the Protestant historian William Patten—a passage that could certainly be termed "incendiary." He added details drawn from the Burgundian chronicler Enguerrand Monstrelet and reworked Holinshed's original language to portray Joan as satanic.[16] In stark contrast to the *Chronicles*' silence about the Queen of Scot's execution (although not her guilt), Patten emphasizes that Joan of Arc deserved her fate:

"These matters may verie rightfullie denounce unto all the world hir execrable abhominations, and well justifie the judgement she had, and the execution she was put to for the same."[17] Patten displays as vehement a condemnation of her as had Edward Hall, without any attempt to show that English justice had prevailed by delaying her execution until her pregnancy was disproved, as had the *Brut*.

Despite the censors' tempering of Holinshed's anti-Catholicism, the *Chronicles* retained language summarizing Mary's crime of treason that was not much short of incendiary itself. During the debates over Mary's fate in the fall of 1586, it reports, the Speaker John Puckering told Parliament

> she hath alredie by hir allurements brought to destruction more noble men and their houses, togither with a greater multitude of the commons of this realme, during hir being here, than she should have beene able to doo, if she had béene in possession of hir owne crowne, and armed in the field against us. . . . She is the onelie hope of all discontented subjects, she is the foundation whereon all the evill disposed doo build, she is the root from whense all rebellions and trecheries doo spring: and therefore whilest this hope lasteth, this foundation standeth, and this root liveth, they will reteine heart, and set on foot whatsoever their devises against the realme, which otherwise will fall awaie, die, and come to nothing.[18]

Mary's "allurements," her military menace, and her ability to inspire rebellion are the same threats Joan Puzel represents in *1 Henry VI*: her sexual enticement of Charles, her military acumen, and her leadership of what the English characters saw as a French rebellion against their rightful king, Henry VI. Indeed, at the end of the play, the duke of York demands that Charles "swear allegiance to his majesty: / As thou art knight, never to disobey / Nor be rebellious to the crown of England" (5.3.169–71). The historical Henry VI's letter to Europe specifically accused Joan of sedition and inciting rebellion.[19]

From the time the Babington conspiracy was thwarted in September 1586, English writers transformed the Queen of Scots into an inflammatory figure. In the five years between her execution (February 8, 1587) and the first performance of the play Philip Henslowe, owner of the Rose Theatre, called "Harey the vj" (March 3, 1592),[20] Mary Stuart had been resurrected by John Lyly as the conspiring Tellus in his play *Endymion* (1588) and by Edmund Spenser variously as Duessa and Acrasia in *The Faerie Queen*.[21] In short, the life and fate of Mary Queen of Scots were of abiding fascination in the waning decade of

Elizabethan England, and it should not surprise us that contemporary drama reflects that interest. Some critics have hypothesized there was even a "Joan of Arc play" written before 1590 (and, therefore, closer in time to Mary's execution), later adapted into *1 Henry VI*.[22]

The reflection of contemporary affairs in the chronicle plays of the 1590s was not unique to *1 Henry VI*. George Peele had modeled the transformation of the narrative chronicle into drama in his *Troublesome Reign of John, King of England* (1589–90). Peele achieved, according to the play's editor, Charles Forker, "a more coherent and complex plotline, . . . better sustained and developing character relationships together with a richer integration of themes—themes that reflect the topical issues and concerns of Elizabethan England during the 1580s and early 1590s."[23] One of those themes is the problem that John Knox had identified in his polemic against women rulers: "To promote a woman to beare rule, superioritie, dominion or empire above any realme, nation, or citie, is repugnant to nature, contumelie to God, a thing most contrarious to his reveled will and approved ordinance, and finally it is the subversion of good order, of all equitie and justice."[24] Three chronicle plays written in the late 1580s and early 1590s, including *1 Henry VI*, dramatize that perceived problem.[25] Queen Elinor in Peele's *Famous Chronicle of Edward I* (1593), like Joan Puzel and Margaret of Anjou in *1* and *3 Henry VI*, is an example of those "unnaturally dominant females in positions of great power, [who raise] by implication disturbing questions about the subversion of male hegemony."[26] In Christopher Marlowe's *Troublesome Reign and Lamentable Death of Edward the Second* (ca. 1592), Edward's favorite Gaveston plays a similar thematic role: his danger to the stability of the realm lies not so much in his physical attraction for Edward, but in his disruption of the social order by his rapid rise in status.[27] Both *Edward II* and *1 Henry VI* dramatize the shortcomings of a monarch influenced by a social inferior, a theme not explored in the relationship between Joan Puzel and Charles.

Before exploring the affinities between Joan Puzel and Mary, Queen of Scots, however, I must emphasize that I do not claim Shakespeare was writing allegory, despite the symbolism of the white and red roses representing the feuding houses of York and Lancaster in act 2, scene 4 of *1 Henry VI* (the Temple Garden scene). Allusion and allegory might intersect, but we must not confuse suggestion with embodiment. In her study of allegory, Rosamund Tuve cautions that while Spenser's Duessa on one level "'is' the corrupt Roman church and the Queen of Scots, she must never be so equated with any of these" in such a way as to dominate the fictional narrative. The characters' "stories need not echo each other, but merely meet where meanings touch."[28]

As Nina Levine notes, what Shakespeare did was to "register [the] political concerns of the 1590s on the narratives on a fifteenth-century past."[29] This is what I argue for the play: Joan Puzel is not Mary, any more than she is Elizabeth, yet she touches meaningful elements of the Queen of Scots' story throughout.[30] Joan Puzel embodies the same anxieties as had Mary Stuart: of recusant Catholicism, of military threats from enemies old and new, of lingering fears of witchcraft and sorcery, and of the dangerous power of female sexuality that must be suppressed, even destroyed.

When York captures Joan Puzel in act 5, he likens her to the mythical sorceress Circe, a comparison made frequently to Mary in the aftermath of the Babington conspiracy:

> Damsel of France, I think I have you fast.
> Unchain your spirits now with spelling charms
> And try if they can gain your liberty.
> A goodly prize, fit for the devil's grace.
> See how the ugly witch doth bend her brows
> As if, with Circe, she would change my shape.
> (5.2.51–56)

In Greek mythology, Circe is a goddess who changes men into animals.[31] There is only one other allusion to Circe in Shakespeare's works,[32] and no such allusion in connection with Joan of Arc appears in Hall or Holinshed. Yet the allusion must have been recognizable to theater audiences, for in Marlowe's *Edward II*, Queen Isabel laments, "Would, when I left sweet France and was embarked, / That charming Circe, walking on the waves, / Had changed my shape" (1.4.171–73).[33]

Not long before, in the numerous paeans to the overthrow of the Babington plotters, several poems ascribed Mary's influence to Circean enchantments.[34] As we shall see, similar language finds its way into *1 Henry VI*, suggesting how quickly political allusions were integrated in the language of the dramatic poets. Some of these poems insinuate that Mary herself was the instigator of the plot, without actually naming her. In "The Triumph of Trophes In Saphic verse of Jubiles" (1586), Lodowick Lloyd blames "the onlie Circes, which hath this mischief wrought."[35] The Babington conspirators, he writes, were eager to accomplish their mission by using the black arts: "Of Simon Magus these men would faine be taught, / like Curres by Circes charm'd to be with Lions bold" (A3). Fear of Joan Puzel is also seen metaphorically as transfiguring "English dogs" to "whelps." Specifically, in the words of John Talbot,

> They called us, for our fierceness, English dogs;
> Now like to whelps we crying run away.
> Hark, countrymen—either renew the fight
> Or tear the lions out of England's coat.
> Renounce your soil, give sheep in lions' stead;
> Sheep run not half so treacherous from the wolf,
> Or horse or oxen from the leopard,
> As you fly from your oft-subdued slaves.
> 
> (1.5.25–32)

Charles uses similar imagery when the French are beaten back from Orleans: "What men have I? / Dogs, cowards, dastards!" (1.2.23–24). And Reignier replies that the English, "like lions wanting food, / Do rush upon us as their hungry prey" (1.2.27–28). Just as Circe magically transformed sailors into swine, in the play, soldiers are metaphorically changed into animals.

Another "Babington" poem, "A Joyfull New-yeares Guift" by the educator William Kempe (not to be confused with the actor), identifies Mary explicitly with Circe, addressing the conspirators as "faithless wights" who succumbed to the queen's eloquence:

> Now may you all with open crie, the hower and time both cursse
> That ever you lent your listening eares, to her, whose words have worse
> Bewitcht your wretched senceles mindes, that you could not forsee
> The guerdon alwaies incident, to workes of treacherie:
> Then ever Circes wicked charmes, did anye wight enchaunt:
> For God forbid, that traitor shoulde, of good successes vaunt.
> The Scottish Queene, with mischiefe fraught, for to perform the will
> Of him (whose Pupil she hath bene) hath used all her skill:
> By words most fair, and loving termes, & guifts of value great:
> For to perswade your hollowe harts, your dueties to forgette.[36]

Joan Puzel also uses "words most fair" to conjure spirits to aid her in act 5. She commands her demons: "You speedy helpers, that are substitutes / Under the lordly monarch of the north, / Appear, and aid me in this enterprise" (5.2.26–28). To be sure, the principal allusion here must be to Lucifer, or possibly a type of devil that Thomas Nashe referred to as "Northerne *Marcii*, called the spirits of revenge, & the authors of massacres, and seedsmen of mischiefe," such as "rapine, sacriledge, theft, murther, wrath, furie, and all manner of cruelties."[37] The English conspirators were surely the "seedsmen of mischief" and "helpers" of the former monarch of the north—Mary, Queen of Scotland.

English writers were not the first to associate Mary with dangerous mythical seductresses.[38] Shortly after her second husband, Henry Stuart, Lord Darnley, was murdered in March 1567, the "Mermaid and Hare" placard appeared in Edinburgh implicating the queen and James Hepburn, Earl of Bothwell, soon to be her third husband, as sexual partners and co-conspirators in regicide. In the late sixteenth century, a "mermaid" could denote not only "a woman who sings sweetly, or who charms, allures, or deceives," but also a prostitute.[39] Moreover, in a letter purportedly written by Mary to Bothwell, the writer shows clear knowledge of classical mythology by comparing her false lover to Jason and herself to Medea, who was the niece of Circe.[40] Mary herself must have been aware of these sorts of accusations against her both before and after she relinquished her throne. Shortly into her English captivity in July 1568, she wrote to Elizabeth (in French), "Alas! do not as the serpent that stops up its hearing, for I am not an enchanter, but your sister and natural cousin."[41]

In his study of the Renaissance figure of Circe, Gareth Roberts writes that the Catholic Church was also viewed as "seductive, glamorous, magical, bestially transforming, poisonous, enfeebling, effeminating."[42] Moreover, the Church itself was accused of complicity in the Babington plot. Maurice Kyffin, a Welsh poet, specifies Rome as the source of the conspirators' treason in "The Blessednes of Brytaine" (1587):

> What cursed Circes, could their minds so charme,
> As not to recke, to reave their Liege of breath?
> Fell Raging Rome, all this is long of thee,
> From whome, no Troubling Treasons, here are free.[43]

The dangers to England posed by the Circean Catholic Church are precisely those manifested by Joan Puzel from the start. In act 1, she makes immediately clear her underlying threat to the sixteenth-century English audience, even as she authenticates herself to her dramatized fifteenth-century French auditors as their savior chosen by "Heaven and Our Lady," whose "aid she promised and assured success" (1.2.74, 1.2.82).

During her trial, Joan of Arc named her voices as those of Saints Katherine and Margaret and the archangels Michael and Gabriel, but she never openly claimed she was inspired by the Virgin Mary. As a girl, she did frequent the shrine of Notre Dame de Bermont and possibly also visited the Marian chapel at Ruppes.⁴⁴ During the English Reformation, the theology of the Virgin Mary was complex. Most significant in terms of Joan Puzel's claim was the denial of Mary's role as the Queen of Heaven and intercessor, and the emphasis on her role as a humble vessel of God's grace that enabled the Incarnation. She was not to be worshiped as a saint and played no role in salvation.⁴⁵ In 1589, the theologian Thomas Rogers excoriated Catholics who "make [the Virgin Mary] another Christ" and take "the blessed Virgine, as they say, our Ladie ... for the Saviour of mankind, as wee do Christ."⁴⁶ Thus, an English audience would understand the danger in Joan Puzel's words:

> Heaven and Our Lady gracious hath it pleased
> To shine on my contemptible estate.
> Lo, whilst I waited on my tender lambs
> And to sun's parching heat displayed my cheeks,
> God's mother deigned to appear to me
> And, in a vision full of majesty,
> Willed me to leave my base vocation
> And free my country from calamity:
> Her aid she promised and assured success.
> In complete glory she revealed herself.
> And, whereas I was black and swart before,
> With those clear rays which she infused on me,
> That beauty I am blest with, which you may see.
> (1.2.74–86)

This speech identifies her with pre-Reformation theology. She calls the Virgin Mary "our lady." Among the Virgin's many attributes, she singles out "God's mother," emphasizing her role as intercessor with Christ, which some English reformers viewed as giving the mother authority over her son.⁴⁷ In David Womersley's words, Joan Puzel emphasizes "a prime point of difference between the reformed and unreformed churches."⁴⁸ And, as we have seen, she claims a miraculous transfiguration of her appearance, so that her inner corruption is masked by her outer beauty, as Richard Bovet would warn happens with some witches. Yet perhaps as a result of her unsuccessful conjurations in act 5, Joan Puzel's appearance may have reverted, for York addresses her as "ugly witch."

Charles's response to this revelation also evokes Reformation attitudes toward Mariolatry. He asks, "How many I reverently worship thee enough?" (1.2.145). After the French overtake Orléans, however, his worship becomes idolatry:

> In memory of her, when she is dead,
> Her ashes, in an urn more precious
> Than the rich-jewelled coffer of Darius,
> Transported shall be at high festivals
> Before the kings and queens of France.
> No longer on Saint Denis will we cry,
> But Joan de Puzel shall be France's saint.
> (1.5.62–68)

Later, Alençon promises to reward her similarly: "We'll set thy statue in some holy place / And have thee reverenced like a blessed saint" (3.3.14–15). In his account of the failed assault on Paris in 1429, Holinshed notes that the Parisians "repelled the Frenchmen, and threw down Jone their great goddesse."[49] Queen Elizabeth herself "threw down" such an idol during her 1578 summer progress. While she was staying at Euston Hall, hosted by the Catholic Edward Rokewood, an image of the Virgin Mary was discovered, about which Richard Topcliffe, later notorious for his pursuit and torture of Catholics,[50] wrote: "She rather seemed a beast, raysed uppon a sudden from hell by conjewringe, than the picture for whome it had bene so often and longe abused. Her Majesty commanded it to the fyer, which in her sight by the cuntrie folks was quickly done."[51] In that scene of burning, according to Helen Hackett, "the Virgin Mary is set up against the Virgin Queen Elizabeth; the 'false' virgin is destroyed, thereby reinforcing the authority of the 'true' virgin."[52] Like that false image, the false virgin Joan Puzel is also sentenced to burn, extinguishing one more Catholic threat to the kingdom.

That threat crystallized early in Elizabeth's reign. When Mary Stuart returned to Scotland from France as queen in the summer of 1561, John Knox expressed his distress at her swift reestablishment of the Catholic Mass. After the ensuing anti-Catholic protests abated, Knox recalled his friend Robert Campbell saying, "I have been here now five days, and at the first I heard every man say, 'Let us hang the priest'; but after that they had been twice or thrice in the Abbey, all that fervency was past. I think there be some enchantment whereby men are bewitched."[53] Knox also associated the queen's religion with "craft," opining, "If there be not in her (said he), a proud mind, a crafty wit, and an indurate heart against God and his truth, my judgment faileth me."[54]

Having established herself, like Mary Stuart, as the focus of Protestant anxiety about a religion that inappropriately venerated a woman, Joan Puzel temporarily discards her initial identification with the Virgin, only to reassume it when she prepares to suborn Burgundy, speaking as "thy humble handmaid," and later, even more outrageously, pleading "the fruit of my womb" to avoid execution.⁵⁵ Here, she echoes the Virgin's acceptance of her role as "hand maiden of the Lord." Joan Puzel's claim to pregnancy, however, argues against associating her with either Mary Queen of Scots or the Virgin Mary, for she claims serial fornication, and the fruit of Mary *Stuart's* womb was, by the early 1590s, commonly assumed to be Elizabeth's heir. At one time, it was held that by 1587, Mary's usefulness and effectiveness as the rightful Catholic successor of Elizabeth had so diminished by shifts in international affairs that her death was "the final assurance of the Union of England and Scotland" in the person of James VI and I.⁵⁶ But more recently, scholars have maintained that "uncertainties and worries about the succession did not disappear with Mary's removal, and the outcome was far from predictable."⁵⁷ Thus, continued anxiety about the succession question could plausibly be expressed in the chronicle plays well into the 1590s.

Indeed, when announcing the arrival of Joan Puzel in act 1, the Bastard of Orleans refers to one manifestation of succession anxiety: "The spirit of deep prophecy she hath, / Exceeding the nine sibyls of old Rome: / What's past and what's to come she can descry" (1.2.55–57). Prophecy had been outlawed in England in 1580, specifically with reference to foreknowledge of Elizabeth's death or the end of her reign. Death was the penalty "yf any person or persons of what Estate Condicion or Degree soever he or they bee . . . shall . . . by any Prophecieng Witchcrafte Conjuracions or other lyke unlawfull Meanes whatsoever seeke to knowe, and shall set forth by expresse Wordes Deedes or Writinges, howe longe her Majestie shall lyve or contynue, or who shall raigne as King or Queene of this Realme of England after her Highnesses Decease."⁵⁸ According to Glyn Parry, "the Protestant preacher William Harrison [who wrote "the Description of England" for the 1577 edition of Holinshed] firmly believed that Mary practised sorcery and that she hastily married Lord Darnley in 1565 partly because 'witches and sorcerers' had yet again promised that Elizabeth 'is but a dead woman and to end her life before the last of July.'"⁵⁹ Joan Puzel treacherously prophesies not only French victory but also "Henry's death" (1.2.136).

As we have seen, sorcery, sex, and politics were intertwined in the early modern mind. In act 3 of *1 Henry VI*, even as the English flee from Rouen, taunted by Joan Puzel and the French from the ramparts, John Talbot associates witchcraft with wantonness, jeering at the "Foul fiend of France and hag of all despite, / Encompassed with thy lustful paramours" (3.2.51–52).⁶⁰ She herself names them in act 5: Charles, Jean d'Alençon, and Reignier (René, duc d'Anjou, father of Margaret, Henry VI's future queen). Is the catalog of

Joan Puzel's lovers merely coincidental? Mary's first husband was the dauphin of France, later Francis II, and her third husband, James Hepburn, Earl of Bothwell, was, like Reignier, "a married man" at the time of his abduction of Mary.[61] The question of Mary's chastity had been debated in print from the English translation of the bishop of Ross, John Leslie's *Defence of the Honour of . . . Marie Quene of Scotlande* (1569) to Thomas Wilson's English version of George Buchanan's *Ane detectioun of the duinges of Marie Quene of Scottes* (1571), respectively arguing the extremes of her virtues and vices.[62]

Joan Puzel's inability to identify which of her lovers was the father of her child—as opposed to "merely" pleading her belly—does not appear in any previous English sources. The sixteenth-century French historian du Haillan, however, baldly claims, "Some say that she was the whore of John, the Bastard of Orleans, others of the Lord Baudricourt, and still others of Poton."[63] Jean Poton de Santrailles (or Xantrailles) was a mercenary and a companion of Joan who is mentioned in the play as the prisoner exchanged for John Talbot (1.4.27). Even though Henry Summerson's analysis of Holinshed's sources—named and unnamed—does not include du Haillan's history, I have not identified any other source for this particular calumny.[64] Throughout the play, Joan Puzel's true nature is consistently enunciated by the clear-eyed Talbot—"Puzel or pussel," "witch," "strumpet"—safeguarding the English audience from succumbing to her eloquence and valor. Joan Puzel's incantations in act 5 may make good theater, but they are *not* unexpected.[65] Talbot had clearly prophesied her true nature.

Nor are the praises showered on Joan Puzel in act 1 by the besotted Charles—"Thou art an Amazon / And fightest with the sword of Deborah," (1.2.104–5)—unambiguously laudatory. Both epithets, "Amazon" and "Deborah," would seem to package Joan Puzel neatly within the debates over women; we have seen how they were applied to her in both medieval and early modern texts.[66] Yet these misdirected allusions demonstrate how thoroughly her compatriots are taken in. David Clapham's translation of Agrippa reported that it was the *French* who regarded Joan of Arc as an Amazon: "Nowe moche doo the Frenchemen prayse a yonge damsell, whiche beinge descended of a lowe linage, toke upon her after the maner of the Amazons, to leade the forward of the army."[67] In his *First Blast of the Trumpet* (1558), John Knox coupled an allusion to Circe's enchantments with a marginal note on Amazons, "monstruouse women, that coulde not abide the regiment of men, and therfore killed their husbandes," inveighing against the mere thought of a woman bearing scepter and crown: "Suche a sight shulde so astonishe them, that they shuld judge the hole worlde to be transformed in to Amazones, and that suche a metamorphosis and change was made of all the men of that countrie, as poetes do feyn was made of the companyons of Ulisses, or at least, that albeit the owtwarde form of men remained, yet shuld they judge that their hartes were changed frome the wisdom, understanding, and courage of men, to the foolishe fondnes and cowardise of women."[68] The ever-taunting York calls Queen Margaret an "Amazonian trull" (3 *Henry VI*, 1.4.114), recalling Burgundy's characterization of Joan Puzel as the Dolphin's "trull." In that play, the widowed queen sends a message to King Edward IV warning him that "my mourning weeds are done, / And I am ready to put armour on" (4.1.104–5), to which the king responds, "Belike she minds to play the Amazon" (4.1.106).[69] In Shakespeare's *King John*, the Bastard, recognized by John as his nephew, rebukes the rebels as

> you degenerate, you ingrate revolts,
> You bloody Neroes, ripping up the womb
> Of your dear mother England, blush for shame:
> For your own ladies and pale-visag'd maids
> Like Amazons come tripping after drums,
> Their thimbles into armed gauntlets change,
> Their needl's to lances, and their gentle hearts
> To fierce and bloody inclination.
>                           (5.2.151–58)[70]

Notably, Shakespeare disarms, domesticates, and sexualizes the one actual Amazon in his plays, Hippolyta in *A Midsummer Night's Dream*, who chastely longs for the consummation of her marriage with Theseus. Even so, Titania accuses Oberon of making "the bouncing Amazon, / Your buskin'd mistress and your warrior love" (2.1.70–71).[71] As Leah Marcus points out, "popular materials from the immediate post-Armada years [after 1588] display an upsurge of similar fascination with, and horror of, the Amazonian confusion of gender," even as such writers as James Aske compared Queen Elizabeth to "the Amazonian Queene."[72] Still, in the early 1590s, the word seems in some of these cases to retain a pejorative connotation.

If "Amazon" was generally a term of dispraise, allusions to Deborah were generally admiring, perhaps because she was not a virago. Agrippa had grouped Joan of Arc with Deborah, Hester, and Judith in the final section of his *Declamation*. Knox acknowledged Deborah as a prophetess and instrument of God's will, but he explains at length that she never put herself above any man: "But all this, I say, she did by the spirituall sworde, that is, by the worde of God, and not by any temporall regiment or authoritie, whiche she did usurpe over Israel."[73] She did not lead her armies with an actual sword, as Charles mistakenly asserts in praising Joan Puzel, but with her words. In certain contexts, Deborah was praised for her eloquence, yet women's speech was viewed as potentially subversive in the Reformation era, signaling disobedience as well as unchastity.[74]

The association of speech and unchastity brings us back to the sexual allurements of Circe's song and to the association of both Joan Puzel and Mary Queen of Scots with speech that leads men astray. William Kempe claims that Mary's words had "bewitched" the Babington conspirators. In response to Joan Puzel's persuasion, Alençon acknowledges that corrupting power: "Women are shrewd tempters with their tongues" (1.2.123), and this is proven by Burgundy's admission that "I am vanquished" by "these haughty words of hers" (3.3.78). Throughout the play, the purpose of her speech becomes progressively corrupted. Ultimately, it fails, as she exits with a curse: "May never glorious sun reflex his beams / Upon the country where you make abode" (5.3.87–88). Michele Osherow argues this curse "inverts" the blessing at the end of Deborah's song of praise in Judges 5, further complicating the association of the prophetess and the pucelle.[75] And this prophecy *does* come true, at least onstage. The phrase "glorious sun" anticipates the opening soliloquy of *The Tragedy of Richard III* spoken by another object of Tudor political demonization: "Now is the winter of our discontent / Made glorious summer by this sun of York" (1.1.1–2).[76] The "sun" in splendor was a common Plantagenet device also used by Henry V and Edward IV. Lisa Dickson reminds us that "with [Joan Puzel's] assertion, 'Expect Saint Martin's summer, halcyon days / Since I have entered in these wars' (1.2.131–32), Joan appropriates the most powerful image of Henry [V]'s spectacular kingship, the sun."[77] In many ways, *1 Henry VI*—indeed, the entire tetralogy, encompassing the three Henry VI plays as well as *Richard III*—is all about "disruptions in succession,"[78] in Brian Walsh's words, beginning with Bedford's futile invocation of the "ghost" of Henry V, continuing with Joan Puzel's curse, and ending only when Henry Tudor assumes the throne.

At the end of act 1, after the French enter Orléans, Charles apostrophizes Joan Puzel as "Divinest creature, Astraea's daughter." Frances Yates demonstrates the applicability of the goddess of Justice not only to Elizabeth, but also as "a symbol of the imperial justice of the French crown," even "the sign of the horoscope of France."[79] Astraea was also associated with Mary. Just before the queen returned to Scotland after the death of her first husband, Francis II, the French monarchy also drew on such classical associations in a "propaganda campaign," in which "Venus and Astraea became key metaphors:

political union would be achieved only through love; Astraea was the restorer of harmony to a world in chaos," according to Michael Lynch.[80] To call Joan Puzel a "daughter" of the virgin goddess suggests an uneasy analogy with her claim that "God's mother" had singled her out as the English scourge. When she was imprisoned in England, Mary Stuart had also placed herself under the Virgin Queen's maternal protection. In the early years of her English captivity, Mary addresses Elizabeth in her letters not only as "sister" and "cousin," but also frames their relationship as mother and daughter. In October 1570, placing her son James in Elizabeth's care, Mary offers her "humble submission and obedience . . . *as if I had the honor of being your daughter* [emphasis added]."[81] Using the same metaphor, John Leslie, the bishop of Ross, had defended Mary's right to reign in Scotland and to succeed to the English throne: "Yea she ys, as yt were her dawghter, bothe by dawgheterlye reverence she bearethe her majestie, and by reason she ys of God called to the daughters place in the succession of the crowne, yf her majestie faile of issewe."[82] That was an extraordinarily provocative statement. Equally provocative was the claim that virgin mothers nursed their metaphorical children.

In her "Ditié de Jeanne d'Arc," Christine de Pizan alludes to Isaiah 49:23—"And kings shall be thy nursing fathers, and their queens thy nursing mothers"—describing Joan as nourishing France with a mother's milk: "a young maiden [who] . . . feeds France with the sweet, nourishing milk of peace."[83] The same trope was applied to Elizabeth, a trope that "so perfectly fit the needs of those celebrating a female head of the English church that it became a commonplace," observes Peter McCullough. He quotes a 1594 sermon by Richard Eedes, one of Elizabeth's chaplains, that concisely makes the point: "God hath honored her . . . so far beyond other princes, as to make a virgin Queen the best nurce of the religion of him, who had a virgin to his Mother."[84] Joan Puzel's speech attempting to suborn Burgundy exploits that powerful metaphor of mothers and daughters, rulers and subjects:

> Look on thy country, look on fertile France,
> And see the cities and the towns defaced
> By wasting ruin of the cruel foe,
> As looks the mother on her lowly babe
> When death doth close his tender-dying eyes.
> See, see the pining malady of France,
> Behold the wounds, the most unnatural wounds,
> Which thou thyself hast given her woeful breast.
> 
> (3.3.44–51)[85]

Having lost Rouen through a failure of her martial leadership, Joan Puzel returns to the talent that had inaugurated her career: her eloquence. Her stirring, if stereotypical, appeal to Burgundy's loyalty echoes the Bastard's speech in *King John* as well as the rhetoric in such tracts as William Lightfoot's *Complaint of England* (1587). There, a personified "England" bewails the treason of the Babington conspirators: "How can I but blushe to call them sonnes, who violating the sacred laws of nature, have sought to prefer an unjust stepdame before their most loving mother?" (B1v). England further laments "there yet liveth many a one, whose father, mother, brother, sister, kinsman or friend, this savage Antichrist [the pope] hath wrongfully murthered, & by untimely death abridged the date of theyr days; confiscating their goods, and leaving their posterity not onely fatherless children, but also comfortles orphans" (C3v). The Calvinist poet and translator Abraham Fleming's censored exhortation on the Babington conspirators in Holinshed's *Chronicles* sounds the same note: "O caitives most execrable, begotten and borne to miserie! How much better had it beene for you, never to have bene conceived to have prooved an untimelie frute, to have beene overthrowen in your cradles, to have perished in your swathling clowts; than in so unhappie an houre, under so infortunat constellations, to so unluckie a life, and so reprochfull a death to be reserved; whome none can pitie without suspicion of impietie, none lament but with lacke of loialtie, none favorablie speake of without great note of ingratitude and privie trecherie?"[86] Elizabethan politicians had taken great care to frame a just and legal case for Mary's treason. In the play, such care was unnecessary. Even as Joan Puzel begs "I prithee, give me leave to curse awhile," York flings epithets of guilt at her: "ugly witch," "fell banning hag, enchantress," and "miscreant" (5.2.55–65). Interestingly, according to an account by Mary's physician, when Queen Elizabeth's commissioners interrogated the Scots queen at Fotheringay in October 1586, the judges "flew into a rage" at her answer, reciting all her misdeeds "without letting her respond clearly to what they said."[87] The play's promised administration of justice on Joan Puzel is to be brutal, if unseen, as grisly as Mary's own botched execution.[88] Whatever supposed trial Joan Puzel undergoes is conducted offstage. For in act 5, scene 3, she is already "that sorceress condemned to burn," suggesting that she is on her road to the stake.

Although Joan Puzel is established as a religious and, therefore, political threat in the earliest scenes of the play, it is her physical courage and skill that test John Talbot, the exemplar of English virtue and valor. He does not react at all to the Messenger's appellation of "Joan de Pucelle" in act 2 as a "holy prophetess," already knowing her to be diabolical. Within a dozen lines, he calls her true: "Deveil or devil's dam," "strumpet," and "a woman clad in armour" and thus, by contemporary lights, subversive of the natural order. When she establishes her prowess against this greatest of English soldiers (her "buckle" with Charles presented no challenge), Talbot is amazed by the "witch by fear, not force," reflecting the 1429 English decrees against desertion supposedly inspired by the Maid (discussed in chapter 1). In the play, Bedford also expresses disbelief: "A maid? And be so martiall?" (2.1.21). Polydore Vergil had called Joan "martial," but even though Hall consulted the earlier work, he omits the admiring "martial" from his history, and it is not reintroduced in Holinshed.

Respecting the Maid's courage was not unprecedented in sixteenth-century England. Vergil, Agrippa, and Aylmer had praised Joan's valor. Closer to Shakespeare's time, in the marginalia to his *Commonplace Book* (1584), poet Gabriel Harvey noted her courage and leadership, and was, I believe, the first in English to call her "virago." Harvey mentions Joan of Arc three times within six pages, citing the Italian philologist Giovanni Egnazio's 1554 *De exemplis illustrium virorum*, although a copy of the work was not, apparently, in his library.[89] First, he associates her with Alexander and David, probably because of their youth: "Alexander, an Unexpert youth, a most incomparable Warrior. ye French Virago, A young wenche, A very excellent warrior with woonderfull victoryes: David, A forward stripling, vanquisshed A huge Giant" (90). Two pages later, "after quoting the story of Joan" from Egnatius, beside the marginal note "Daring Women: Joan of Arc," Harvey writes "A gallant Virago: . . . A most worthy valiant young wenche, General of ye fielde, worthy to be Queene of France at least, for her Labor. . . . What may not an Industrious, & politique man do, with lyke, or more coorage; when A lusty adventurous wenche might thus much praevayle? Nothing in her, but A lively praesumptuous Audacity, and brave vigour. . . . She cowld have no other great value at those yeares" (92). In a further marginal note, he reminds himself to "Meditate on the deeds of Joan of Arc, The French Viragos Imperatory, and Militair Industry; acheving wunderfull Exploytes and assuring curragious Industry of ani victory, even against all hope of possibility" (96).

This last passage aptly describes the Joan Puzel in act 2 of *1 Henry VI*, who briskly dismisses Charles's ingratitude and halts the dispute among the French captains as to the blame for the breach of the walls at Orléans. Her leadership is sound:

Question, my lords, no further of the case
'How, or which way?'; 'tis sure they found some place

> But weakly guarded, where the breach was made.
> And now there rests no other shift but this—
> To gather our soldiers, scattered and dispersed,
> And lay new platforms to endamage them.
> (2.1.72–77)

One of those new platforms is the stratagem Joan devises in act 3, when she and others make their way into Rouen masquerading as peasants. Such a trick was time-honored and even successful, although in some cases no doubt embellished in both French and English chronicles.[90] Perhaps because it is based on deception, not valor, the subsequent—brief and fictitious—French capture of Rouen is the height of France's military success.

During Mary's reign, loyal Scots had their own military successes, some led by their queen. The physical valor of Mary Stuart was never in dispute, although her few military excursions did not result in her actually fighting in the field. As reported in Holinshed, Puckering's speech to Parliament had emphasized the threat of Mary's "allurements" over any military action she might undertake. The only reference to Mary as a "virago" that I have seen appears in George Buchanan's *De Maria Scotorum* (1571) in an anonymous poem that was not included in the English translation.[91] Still, during the queen's Highland tour in 1562, when she was threatened by John Gordon, Lord Huntly, Thomas Randolph (the English ambassador to Scotland) wrote William Cecil: "In all these garbullies [tumults], I assure your honour I never sawe her merrier, never disamayde, nor never thought that stomache to be in her that I fynde! She repented nothynge but when the lardes and other at Ennernes [Inverness] came in the mornynges from the wache, that she was not a man to knowe what lyf yt was to lye all nyghte in the feeldes, or to walke upon the cawsaye [causeway] with a jacke and knapschall, a Glascowe buckeler [shield] and a broode swerde."[92] A "knapscall" (later translated as "steel cap"), according to the *OED*, is "some kind of helmet or headpiece; generally worn by persons of inferior rank; perhaps originally by the servants of the men-at-arms."[93] Randolph chose a term that insults Mary's status, but not her pluck.

Three years later, at the outset of the brief uprising known as the Chaseabout Raid, led by Mary's half brother James Moray, Randolph again writes to Cecil: "I take it for a tale, though constantly reported, that herself sometimes bears a 'pystolet,' and had one in her hand when near Hamilton she looked to have fought."[94] Once the rebels had been defeated, he writes that "what safety and assurance she thinks herself in, (if it be true that I heard) that she has a 'secret or previe' defence on her body, a 'knapescalle' for her head, and a 'dagge' at her saddle."[95] He suggests that Mary herself wore some kind of protective vest, perhaps a "jacke." Even John Knox, no promoter of female assertiveness, allowed Mary courage at the outset of the Raid. He writes that as the king (Henry Stuart, Lord Darnley) and queen marched from Glasgow to Edinburgh, there was a great storm, so that "with great difficulty went they forward. And albeit the most part waxed weary, yet the Queen's courage increased man-like, so much that she was ever with the foremost."[96] Holinshed, while not portraying Mary as armed, clearly describes her as a military leader: "The queene assembled an armie, and went to Glascow to pursue [the rebels]"; she "assembled foorth of all the parts of the whole realme an armie"; "about this time, the queene tooke the castell of Tantallon from the earle of Morton"; after this, "the queene returning to Edenburgh in September, prepared all things necessarie for the armie."[97] Such adventures were anathema to John Calvin, who in the 1550s presciently preached on Deuteronomy 25:11–12 that women "must always consider what their sexe will allowe them to doe, and that they become not like launceknightes, as we see some are, which will handle an Harquebuse as boldely as anie man, and march with ensigne displayed as couragiously. It is so monstrous a sight to beholde such wicked women, that a man ought, not onelie to spitte at them, but also to take up durt and cast at such impudent creatures."[98]

Mary's youthful delight in "playing the Amazon" aligns with Joan Puzel's eagerness to fight, and both women are represented as unmoved by violent death. Joan Puzel's impassiveness at the sight of Talbot's body is not only coarse but recalls what George Buchanan had written about Mary's viewing her murdered husband Henry Stuart's body. Observing Talbot, who "stinking and fly-blown lies here at our feet," Joan Puzel permits Sir William Lucy to take him and his son off for burial, for "to keep them here, / They would but stink, and putrefy the air" (4.4.188 and 4.4.201–2). This speech is another example of how language marks the debasement of Joan Puzel's character, and compared to the heartfelt English eulogies over Talbot, it also demonstrates her increasing indifference to any human life but her own. Mary was reported to have been wordless when viewing Darnley's body, but her former tutor in the classics George Buchanan, in Thomas Wilson's Scottish translation, interpreted her silence as "a strange example of crueltie, and sic as never was heard of befoir, that as she had satisfied her heart with hys slaughter, sa she would nedes fede hir eyes with the sight of hys bodie slayne. For she lang beheld, nat only without grefe, but alswa with gredy eyes, hys dead corps, the gudlyest corps of any gentleman that ever lived in this age."[99]

The account in Buchanan's *Historia Scotorum* is more temperate yet still hints at Mary's heartlessness: "The King's Body, having been left a while as a Spectacle to be gaz'd upon, and a great Concourse of People continually [flockt] thither, the Queen order'd, That it should be laid on a Form or Bier turn'd upside down, and brought by Porters into the Palace. There she her Self viewed the Body, the fairest of that Age, and yet her Countenance discover'd not the secrets of her Mind, neither one way or other."[100] For all his own dislike of Mary, Knox's recollection of the scene is nonjudgmental: "[The queen] beheld the corpse without any outward show or sign of joy or sorrow."[101] She was doubtless fearful and in shock; her own letters, as well as Bothwell's account, show her to be distraught.[102] The 1577 Holinshed does not record the queen's reaction, but immediately turns to Bothwell's abduction of her; the 1587 version, however, is much expanded in such ways as to complicate the reader's response.[103]

Joan Puzel, too, might be a coldhearted virago, but of all the epithets applied to her, diabolical labels predominate. Hall provides a veritable thesaurus of calumny: "witch or manly woman," an "enchanteresse, an orgayne of the devill, sent from Sathan, to blind the people and bryng them in unbelife." He reproduces Henry's letter to Burgundy, including the accusation that "she made diverse to beleve, and trust in her faithe, promisyng to them great and notable victories, by the which meane, she did turne the hartes of many men and women, from the truthe and veritie, and converted them to lies and errors,"[104] language that echoes both the official and popular accusations against Mary.

Just as Joan Puzel and the Queen of Scots were similarly cast as satanic sorcerers for political reasons, so their last-minute defenses exhibit uncanny resemblances as well. Once she is captured and her pregnancy defense mocked, Joan Puzel warns the English that they are about to execute a royal personage "descended of a gentler blood" and "issued from the progeny of kings" (5.3.8, 38).[105] Just prior to her own execution, Mary was reported by the eyewitness Robert Wingfield to have warned, "I am Cozen to your queene and descended from the bloud Royall of H[enry] the 7th;"[106] Henry VII was her great-grandfather. Joan Puzel continues with a shrewd indictment of English preconceptions: "Because you want the grace that others have, / You judge it straight a thing impossible / To compass wonders but by help of devils" (5.3.46–48). During her trial, Joan of Arc had admonished Bishop Pierre Cauchon in similar terms: "You say you are my judge; I do not know if you are, but I warn you not to judge me amiss, lest you place yourself in great peril."[107] Mary Stuart, as well, questioned the legality of the proceedings against her, stating on the first day of her trial that "she was borne a Queene, and that she would not prejudice hir rancke and state" by undergoing their examination as if she were merely another subject.[108] The next day, she reiterated that "as a queen and sovereign princess she could not submit herself to the jurisdiction of the Queen of England."[109] Mary Stuart in her own lifetime baffled her contemporaries as Joan of Arc had done in hers, and the threat each one represented to an England in political turmoil could be removed only by execution.

"Harey the vj" proved a financial success for Lord Strange's Men, performed sixteen times between March 3, 1591, and January 31, 1593, although no further record of its production exists before the publication of the First Folio, the only surviving text. Some have speculated that this version represents a revision.[110] Before the play was performed again, nearly 150 years later, Restoration politics echoed many of its topical concerns. Going even further than it had in 1587, Parliament authorized the execution of King Charles I on January 30, 1649, precipitating the English Civil Wars. "Anti-popery" flourished during and well beyond the Interregnum, especially with the uncovering in 1678 of the concocted "Popish Plot," that Jesuits were planning to assassinate King Charles II.[111] Just as Elizabethan statesmen feared Catholic Europe's ambition to place Mary Stuart on the English throne, their Restoration counterparts feared the potential influence of Catholic Louis XIV of France on the kingdom, especially after the conversion of the duke of York, the future King James II, to Catholicism in 1669 became public.[112] Despite *his* mother's Catholicism, Mary's son, James I, had been safely raised a Protestant, but his lineal right to succeed the childless Elizabeth had been contested. In the face of Charles II's failure to produce a legitimate heir, the public revelation of James II as a Catholic presented the choice of a hereditary or a Protestant succession. In that atmosphere, a revival of *1 Henry VI*—so thematically appropriate to those similarly parlous post-Restoration succession issues, and featuring an actress playing the virago after the theaters reopened in 1660—would seem to have offered a profitable opportunity to an entrepreneurial theater manager.

Despite its title, however, John Crowne's *Henry VI, The First Part* (1681) is based on *The First Part of the Contention of the Two Famous Houses of York and Lancaster*, that is, *2 Henry VI*. Crowne's *Miseries of Civil War*, also known as *Henry the Sixth, The Second Part* adapts the last two acts of that play and much of *3 Henry VI*.[113] Neither play makes use of *1 Henry VI*. Civil, not foreign, wars were Crowne's concern. The influence of queens and mistresses suited his political agenda far more than that of a French sorceress. According to Matthew Wikander, "Crowne devotes most of his energy to heightening parallels between the murder of Duke Humphrey and the contemporary sensation, the murder of Sir Edmund Berry Godfrey," a direct or indirect victim of the Popish Plot.[114] Joan of Arc or Joan Puzel had no relevance to such matters.

In the eighteenth century, the Folio *1 Henry VI* was apparently revived only once, on March 13, 1738, sponsored by the "Shakespeare Ladies Club," which not only supported the installation of the Shakespeare monument in Westminster Abbey but also "began a movement which restored many of Shakespeare's neglected plays to the boards."[115] The members described themselves as "Ladies of Quality,"—very high quality, in fact, as their leader was Susannah Ashley-Cooper, Countess of Shaftesbury.[116] They were motivated in part by a nationalistic backlash against, among other foreign entertainments, "French Vagrants" performing pantomime on the English Stage.[117] However, other women who promoted the history plays on the same nationalistic basis, including the social and literary critic Elizabeth Montagu (1718–1800), were silent on *1 Henry VI*.[118] Coincidentally, because they were revivals, Shakespeare's works did not fall under the Theatrical Licensing Act of 1737, so they provided "alternatives to new plays that would have been subject to censorship."[119]

John Genest's history of the post-Restoration English stage provides a list of *dramatis personae* that confirms this production as the play included in the First Folio. "Mrs. [William] Hallam," Anne Hallam, played the part of Joan Puzel.[120] Although the advertisement for the performance claimed that it had not been performed for "50 years" (i.e., since 1688), probably referring erroneously to Crowne's play, Genest's own comment makes more sense: "This play seems not to have been repeated—in all probability this was the only night on which it was ever acted since the Restoration—perhaps since the time of Shakespeare. This play, Henry 4th part 2d, and Henry 5th are said not to have been acted for 40 or 50 years—if this really meant any thing, it implied that these 3 plays had been performed 40 or 50 years ago—but there seems no ground for such a supposition."[121]

Anne Hallam, it therefore seems, was the only contemporary actress who had the opportunity to speak the speeches Shakespeare wrote for Joan Puzel. Two eighteenth-century playwrights recalled the historical Joan in backhanded praise for the power of women's eloquence. The Epilogue to "the new *Tragedie of Edward the Black Prince*" by William Shirley (1750) laments the decline of "English warriors" in Edward's day to the present-day "arrant Beaux," asserting "The mightiest Talkers, are the poorest Doers, / Such to subdue, requires no martial Fire, / One Joan of Arc wou'd make 'em all r[e]tire."[122] In George Keate's Epilogue to *The Play of King John* (1769), Constance (mother of Prince Arthur) proclaims the power of a woman's tongue in the persons of Xantippe, Roxana, and Cleopatra, and exhorts the audience to "Think of the Maid of Orleans, Joan of Arc, / There was an enterprizing, female spark! / Whole Armies she harrangu'd, whole hosts withstood; / Her tongue was surely more than flesh and blood!"[123] These allusions indicate an expectation of the audience's familiarity, and even sympathy, with Joan of Arc, as well as a transformation from fear to admiration of her speech. Yet for nearly three centuries, Joan Puzel was realized in only two dimensions, as text and image, at a time when illustrated editions, acting editions, and nascent scholarly editions of Shakespeare proliferated, and portraits of actresses were popular forms of advertising and promotion. The existence of only the Folio text left editors with little to say either about the play or about Joan Puzel, except to make historical observations or to object to some of the language.

Importantly, the antiquarian Joseph Ritson in 1783 expressed a wholehearted admiration for the historical, if not the theatrical, figure. He first corrects the editor George Steevens's comment that the word "trull," which Burgundy uses to refer to Joan Puzel, "did not anciently bear so harsh an interpretation as it does at present."[124] Ritson's comment goes beyond the etymological, however: "It is to be regretted that Shakspeare should have so far followed the absurd and lying stories of his time, about this celebrated heroine, whom the French called the maid of God, as to represent her not onely a strumpet, but a witch. If we may believe the most authentic historians she was no less distinguished for virtue than courage. She was burnt, indeed, by the barbarous English, whom she had so frequently driven before her, and who, to excuse their want of courage or policy, and to justify their inhumanity, pretended that she had dealt with the devil!"[125] Beginning with the first illustrated edition of Shakespeare in 1709, many artists and engravers also met the challenge of depicting Joan Puzel and, in doing so, projected visual images of Joan of Arc, congruent or incongruous with her textual presence in literature and history.[126]

Nicholas Rowe's illustrated Shakespeare of 1709 and 1714, *Bell's Edition of Shakespeare's Plays* (1774), and the Boydell Shakespeare Gallery exhibits of paintings based on the plays (1789) offer a surprising number of portraits of Joan Puzel, given her absence from the stage. Hanns Hammelmann believed that it was a "general convention of theatrical illustration" in the eighteenth century to "[take] salient incidents from each drama, mostly in fairly close relation to current stage practice," as the basis of illustrations.[127] Editors and illustrators had to choose how to represent a scene or character in a single static image. As Jonathan Bate observes, "An illustration of a dramatic text is a peculiar thing. It makes meaning by freezing a single moment, whereas the unstoppable motion of time, the piling of action upon action upon reaction, is the very essence of drama."[128] If the play were based on history, moreover, illustrators might feel constrained by audience expectations.[129] The French artist François Boitard, who executed most of the pictures for Rowe in 1709,

FIGURE 3  Frontispiece to *1 Henry VI*, ed. Nicholas Rowe, 1709. Folger Shakespeare Library, Washington, D.C.

"appears to have looked, where possible, at contemporary staging of the plays for ideas."[130] In the case of *1 Henry VI*, of course, the illustrations could not have been directly inspired.

Rowe's edition was set from the Fourth Folio (1685) and was the first to add *dramatis personae*.[131] "Joan la Pucelle" is designated as "a Maid pretending to be inspir'd from Heaven, and setting up for the Championess of France."[132] Despite the playwright Thomas Nashe's opinion that Talbot was the most memorable character in the play,[133] the frontispiece to *1 Henry VI* features an engraving of Joan Puzel leading her soldiers on foot into the gates of Orléans (see fig. 3). Boitard's engraving is wholly in accord with the stage direction in act 1, scene 5, from the first four Folios, reproduced in Rowe: "A short Alarum: Then Enter the Town with Soldiers."[134] The direction interrupts Joan Puzel's exit speech to Talbot so that it seems logical that she flings these lines over her shoulder at him as the French rejoin her on the stage and march into the town.[135]

FIGURE 4  Frontispiece to *1 Henry VI*, ed. Nicholas Rowe, 1714. Folger Shakespeare Library, Washington, D.C.

Boitard's illustration suggests both the confines of a proscenium stage and a medieval walled city.¹³⁶ A cathedral spire against a clearing sky overlooks the scene below. The figure of Joan Puzel, her gaze directed into the town, strides confidently toward the open city gate, above which is carved "Orleans." She rather jauntily bears a sword or pike over her left shoulder, and wears a plumed helmet, likely a morion, under which her long hair waves. Her helmet does not have a gorget, unlike those of the two principal male soldiers who flank her. Below her skirted armor, her slim and shapely calves and dainty feet, shod in tapered sabatons, signal her femininity. Furthermore, two rondels, rather than protecting the area under her arms, are set just below her shoulders, seeming to suggest breasts. In Rowe's second edition of 1714, the image engraved by Louis du Guernier is based on Boitard's, but reversed. Contrary to Stuart Sillars' conclusion that for the most part "The woodenness of the earlier designs has been replaced by a greater anatomical accuracy,"[137] du Guernier has made Joan la Pucelle much less feminine. Gone are her shapeliness and dainty feet. Gone are the rondels suggesting breasts. Still skirted, she is rather *more* wooden and less dynamic (see fig. 4).

Boitard's feminized portrayal of Joan Puzel as imagined onstage accords with later eighteenth- and early nineteenth-century illustrations of the character. Although "breeches roles" were popular and actresses were willing to display, as Jean Marsden puts it, a "well-turned feminine ankle,"[138] Joan Puzel, as depicted in such illustrations, tends to wear skirts, not breeches. John Bell's "acting" editions of Shakespeare in the 1770s featured engravings of popular (or notorious) actresses because Bell "believed that attractive portraits of actors would boost sales." As with Boitard's engraving, readers were to take these as the performer "purportedly in action," an imagined performance in the case of *1 Henry VI*.[139] Two actresses embody Joan the virago brandishing a weapon—each a feminine virago dressed in yards of fabric and each with an elaborate feathered headdress. Elements of the pose—the upraised sword and the feathers—somewhat resemble the famous "Alderman" portrait of Jeanne d'Arc installed in the town hall of Orléans in 1581 and widely copied in both France and England through the eighteenth century. William Nelson Gardiner, for example, was to engrave a quite altered version for Sylvester Harding's *Shakespeare Illustrated* (1790), reproduced in his illustrated edition of Shakespeare published in 1793 (see fig. 5).[140]

The actress Sophia Baddeley, drawn by portrait artist James Roberts, appears against a plain background. There is nothing in the drawing but the quotation from 1.2—"I am prepar'd, here is my keen edged Sword"—to indicate context (see fig. 6).[141] The embroidered bodice in Baddleley's costume does resemble armor, although the multilayered skirts would surely impede any combative movements. The weight of her headdress seems to tip her backward. The entire image is static, despite the raised sword in her right hand. Joan Puzel as impersonated by Ann Stuart (painted by the German-born J. H. Ramberg), however, is a dynamic figure, enclosed within in oval, clearly depicting the quotation below: "Advance our waving colours on the walls; Rescued is Orleans" (1.5.40–41) (see fig. 7).[142] Her flowing overskirt and the "waving colors" she faces are caught by a breeze as she is captured in midstride. Moreover, while her upper arms seem to be encased in armor, her

FIGURE 5   W. N. Gardiner, *La Pucelle d'Orleans*, Harding's Shakespeare, 1793. Folger Shakespeare Library, Washington, D.C.

ample bosom is shown to flattering advantage. She holds a spear vertically, not offering any hint of battle. Her left arm is raised, and she extends her forefinger as if to admonish any opposition.

Perhaps reflecting the growing interest in the "gothic" in the last quarter of the eighteenth century, Joan of Arc continued to be associated with witches, although the fear expressed in the sixteenth century was much diluted. As we have seen, William Alexander's *History of Women* includes Joan in a chapter on witchcraft as an example of judicial abuse. Several artistic depictions of *1 Henry VI* focus on Joan's evocation of "choice spirits" in act 5, scene 2. William Hamilton's "Joan of Arc and the Furies," now in the Vassar College collection, was painted for the Boydell Shakespeare Gallery in 1795 and engraved by Anker Smith for the 1802 printed edition of the plays (see fig. 8). In the painting, Joan Puzel's blood-red cape swirls behind her against a dark sky. The background of infernal storm clouds reflects the stage direction "Thunder." Three mostly naked figures sullenly refuse to meet her eyes, while other, indistinct forms fade into the background. The stage direction requires that "they shake their heads" as they move away with Joan Puzel's realization: "See, they forsake me." Yet Joan's own facial expression is almost indiscernible, in deep shadow: neck and head form a thick cylinder that defies human anatomy.

FIGURE 6 "Mrs. Baddeley in the Character of Joan la Pucelle," 1776. Folger Shakespeare Library, Washington, D.C.

FIGURE 7 "Miss Stuart as Joan la Pucelle," 1776. Folger Shakespeare Library, Washington, D.C.

Although her left (sinister) arm is raised, her sword lies as if the rejection of the fiends has forced her to relinquish the symbol of her martial power.

Charles Turner Warren also captured that moment in an engraving of a drawing by John Thurston for an 1806 edition of Shakespeare's plays.[143] Here is a woman not defiant, but suppliant (see fig. 9). Bending her left knee to the ground, she extends her sword with her left hand and reaches out to the larger figure of a cloaked "fiend" with her disproportionately large right hand, palm up. Her long hair is pinned up, visible because her plumed helmet has fallen aside; her armor is swathed in a surcoat embroidered with fleurs-de-lis. A cloak curves over her back, emphasizing her submissive posture. In his own account of Joan of Arc in his *History of England* (1762), David Hume observed that during her imprisonment, Joan "betrayed neither any weakness

FIGURE 8  William Hamilton, "Joan of Arc and the Furies," 1795. Folger Shakespeare Library, Washington, D.C.

FIGURE 9  Charles Turner Warren, "King Henry VI, Part I," 1806. Folger Shakespeare Library, Washington, D.C.

nor womanish submission."[144] But as we shall see, in the Romantic era, Joan of Arc was increasingly criticized for overstopping the bounds of contemporary redefinitions of femininity.

The engraver Allen R. Branston published a number of wood engravings to illustrate the plays, also based on drawings by John Thurston.[145] He imagines a longhaired Joan clad in a Roman tunic or chiton; she seems to plant a banner in a cloud (see fig. 10). She kneels on a sort of promontory, a crenelated fortification in the distance, her abandoned sword before her, as two cloaked fiends, somewhat reminiscent of Hamilton's, seem to float off into the vapors. The Swiss-born painter Henry Fuseli created a stunningly modern realization of this scene for the Shakespeare edition annotated by Alexander Chalmers in 1805 (see fig. 11).[146] This Joan is entirely dressed in armor, her face in shadow, the only hints as to her sex an outline of a small breast below her

FIGURE 10   Alan R. Branston, "Then take my soul," 1810. Folger Shakespeare Library, Washington, D.C.

FIGURE 11   Henry Fuseli, "Enter Fiends," 1805. Folger Shakespeare Library, Washington, D.C.

raised arms and, as art historian Irene Dash notes, "the brilliantly integrated design of her long braided hair hanging down her back."[147] Four skulking demons showing the whites of their eyes seem almost to flee before her, as if it were she dismissing them, not they forsaking her. The prolific Thurston drew *Illustrations of Shakspeare* "adapted to all editions" in 1826.[148] Each play is illustrated by six vignettes on a single page. The first for *1 Henry VI* literally illustrates York's curse in act 5: "Break thou in pieces and constume to ashes, / Thou foul accursed minister of hell." A torso with its head blown off smolders in flames (see fig. 12).

Only Hamilton's painting of Joan formed part of the Boydell Gallery project, whose object, according to John Boydell, was to "establish an English School of Historical Painting."[149] Boydell himself admits, "It must not then be expected, that the art of the Painter can ever equal the sublimity of our Poet,"

FIGURE 12  John Thurston, "Break thou in pieces!," 1826. Folger Shakespeare Library, Washington, D.C.

*York.* Break thou in pieces and consume to ashes,
Thou foul accursed minister of hell!

and the essayist Charles Lamb writes of the "injury" he felt viewing the paintings, lest a single image "confine the illimitable."[150] The illustrators' ideal was, it seems, to allow readers to picture Joan Puzel (or Joan of Arc) according to their personal taste and bias, but the textual editors were in no way reluctant to comment on her character or the language of the play. Thus, as Shakespeare's plays gained in popularity into the nineteenth century, editors resorted not to creative etymology, such as the editor George Steevens's attempt to temper the meaning of "trull," but to outright censorship.

Even though *1 Henry VI* was likely not performed again by a major company after 1738 until 1906,[151] the play came under the scrutiny of the actor and playwright Francis Gentleman, who edited Bell's acting edition of Shakespeare, omitting "scenes and passages highly derogatory to [the Bard's] incomparable general merit."[152] Gentleman objects to Joan Puzel for her Catholicism. He calls her claim of a vision of Mary "heathen" and will not excuse it on the basis of Classical precedent: "Poets of antiquity always brought deities into war; but to bring in the *Virgin Mary* similarly, is not justifiable."[153] He diminishes her identity as a virago, finding the dauphin's challenge "ridiculous" (99) and the single combat with Talbot "laughable" (108). She is, he writes "of so outré and masculine a nature, that she is, through the whole offensive to true criticism," adding, in response to her comments over the corpse of Talbot, "This lady is as indelicate in her sentiments, and expression, as in her actions: this Act is too cold for representation, and little better for perusal." Her "interviews with fiends, and her witchcraft are totally disallowable; delusive to youth, and ridiculous to age" (155–56). Finally, he scorns her plea of pregnancy, for she "cannot fix on a father" (168).

More egregious censorship than comments about language and indelicacy marked the Bowdlers' *Family Shakespeare*, although the name is eponymous with expurgation intended to protect the sensibilities of women and children. The original 1807 edition published anonymously by Henrietta (also known as Harriet) Bowdler did not even include *1 Henry VI*.[154] The second edition, credited to her brother Thomas, includes all three of the Henry VI plays in volume 6. The full title explains the siblings' purpose and audience: *The Family Shakespeare in Ten Volumes; in which nothing is added to the original text; but those words and expressions are omitted which cannot with propriety be read aloud in a family*. In his preface to the 1818 edition, Thomas Bowdler explains the reasoning behind his editorial principles: to excise indecency, which he defines as "profaneness or obscenity," specifically language that "can give pain to the most chaste, or offence to the most religious of his readers" (1:viii).[155] He speaks only of expletives, but in the case of *1 Henry VI*, at least, his delicacy leads to serious abridgement of act 5.

In her unpublished master's thesis, Emily Burden closely compares the texts of the second edition of the Oxford Shakespeare (2005), Isaac Reed's 1813 edition based on Johnson and Steevens, and the *Family Shakespeare*.[156] She shows that the "editing" falls into three categories. The first echoes the 1606 "Act to Restrain Abuses of Players," which forbade "any Person or Persons" in any public entertainment "jestingly or profanely [to] speak or use the holy Name of God, or of Christ Jesus, or of the Holy Ghost, or of the Trinity, which are not to be spoken but with Fear and Reverence."[157] While phrases such as "king of kings" or "Lord of hosts" in some of the plays are left intact, even the seemingly respectful "God's mother" spoken by Joan Puzel in act 1 changes to "our lady." Talbot's reference to "Devil or devil's dam" (1.5.5) was cut, as well as his despairing "Heavens, can you suffer hell so to prevail?" (1.5.9). "That damned sorceress" (3.2.37) becomes "that cursed sorceress."[158] Steevens's attempt to redefine "trull" foreshadowed the final category of the Bowdlers' censorship: striking not only specific words such as "whore" and "pucelle or puzzle" but also all direct or indirect references to sex or sexual conduct. In his 1723 edition of Shakespeare, Alexander Pope relegates Talbot's speech in 1.5 to a footnote, expurgating these words from the main text. Similarly, Pope moves four of Talbot's lines before he bids "farewell" to Joan Puzel to a footnote, doubtless because they include "strumpet." Lewis Theobald, who corrected many of Pope's emendations and oversights, restores the passage for his own edition in 1733.[159] In his edition, Samuel Johnson refuses to understand the connotation of "pussel," suggesting emendation to "Pucelle or puzzle," although he was no prude.[160] He amended his original gloss on "Winchester goose" from "a clap, or rather a strumpet"[161] to the more precise "strumpet, or the consequences of her love," alluding more directly to the bishop of Winchester's illegitimacy.[162]

Not content with linguistic cleansing, however, the Bowdlers excised nearly all of Joan Puzel's role in act 5. After the first seven lines of her "conjuration" in the modern edition, her speech resumes at line 25, after the spirits depart. Apart from her promise to "lop a member off" as a token of "further benefit," perhaps the double entendre in "My body shall / Pay recompense if you will grant my suit" is the key to this deletion. But Joan Puzel never reappears, leaving the audience no clue as to her fate. Although Thomas Bowdler claimed that the few additions he made to the texts were "inserted to connect the sense of what follows the passage that is expunged, with that which precedes it" (1:x), he did not succeed in this case.

The reputation of Joan of Arc was constructed by language, but her words were mediated from the start. In 1431, her trial testimony had been transcribed in French and Latin, in indirect discourse, in the third person. Her actual words, her tone of voice, are muted. Around 1591, the speeches Shakespeare invented for her, particularly the defiant ones, ring true as the voice of an idiosyncratic personality, although a full English translation of her testimony was not published until the twentieth century.[163] By the end of the sixteenth century, excerpts from the trial were already being reproduced in French histories, but the English sources of the history plays seemed unaware of them.[164] So Joan Puzel's speech shared some of the forthright defiance conveyed in the chronicle histories, yet also echoed metaphors associated not with fifteenth- but sixteenth-century anxieties about how the leadership of a woman threatened patriarchal norms. Even after the London stage found its voice again in the mid-seventeenth century, including the voices of women on stage, Joan of Arc for the most part remained a mute witness to her own burgeoning presence in English letters.

CHAPTER 5

## "TOM PAINE IN PETTICOATS"

*Domesticating Joan of Arc*

> She unbound
> The helm of many battles from her head,
> And, with her bright locks bow'd to sweep the ground,
> Lifting her voice up, wept for joy, and said,—
> "Bless me, my father, bless me! and with thee,
> To the still cabin and the beechen-tree,
> Let me return!"
> —Felicia Hemans, "Joan of Arc in Rheims" (1826)

The "cursed breeches" that, according to *The Gentleman's Magazine*, led to Joan of Arc's execution had been a focus of her reputation from the time she first donned armor in the spring of 1429. In the course of the eighteenth and early nineteenth centuries, as we have seen in chapter 4, most illustrations of the Maid, usually meant to represent Shakespeare's Joan Puzel, portray her with long hair and flowing garments, even if they also indicate some form of trousers. Only Henry Fuseli depicts her entirely in male dress—long braids her sole unambiguous gender marker in his image—with one exception. The Folger Shakespeare Library possesses a unique image of unknown origin from the late eighteenth or early nineteenth century that epitomizes fascination about her female body, especially when she is dressed in male clothing (see fig. 13).[1] Standing just to the right of center and framed by a portcullis archway, a

FIGURE 13  Joan of Arc donning armor. Folger Shakespeare Library, Washington, D.C.

woman in full armor raises her helmet, her long, blonde hair cascading down her back, framing her upper torso. Although her breasts are not exposed, the impossibly skintight armor displays a female body with admirable musculature, even the suggestion of a navel. Rather than a more conventional surcoat, she wears a short skirt, emphasizing her female form. She stands *contrapposto*, with her weight on her left foot, and tilts her head coquettishly. Despite her armor, she is entirely feminine.

In the Middle Ages, as we have seen, chroniclers sidestepped the perceived conflict between masculine and feminine gender roles by focusing on women's obstetrical histories, as in the case of Ælfleda, the Lady of Mercia. In the late eighteenth century, depicting a woman warrior as erotically alluring expresses both male expectation and male anxiety—often obscene—about female cross-dressing and, by extension, female sexuality itself. Revealing his own expectations for how the Maid should appear on stage, the author Horace Walpole writes to Lady Ossory that he had mistaken "a dame with a helmet on, a spear and shield, and one leg bare" for Joan of Arc in scene one of the comic opera *The Reduction of Paris* in 1775.[2]

Some years later, when the playwright Lady Eglantine Wallace (whose *The Ton* was about to open) wore breeches in the Gallery of the House of Commons, the *Times* of March 12, 1788, noted that "Lady Wallace, it is asserted, means to *dramatize* the late debate on the Declaratory Bill, and introduce some of the rising Members in her piece." The quip recalls the sexual insults flung at Joan of Arc from the English ramparts in Orléans. On March 14, the newspaper added that "though Lady Wallace, like Joan d'Arc, chuses to appear in male attire, yet, on certain occasions, her Ladyship, like Joan, is no friend to coats of mail." Like earlier associations between Joan's male attire and her supposed promiscuity, the *Times* hints at a sexual identity based on her male attire alone. Along with these excerpts, Daniel J. O'Quinn offers this analysis: "The implication is that by appearing in breeches and by promoting her comedy Lady Wallace was showing and hence advertising her body and her 'piece' respectively for future consumption. This parallel between body and 'piece' gives some indication of how some parts of her audience understood the consumption of her comedy as somehow not altogether distant from the consumption of her. Underlying this entire assemblage is a widespread assumption of the proximate nature of female publicity and prostitution."[3] For the *Times* in 1788, as for Edward Hall in 1548, transgressive dress signaled sexual transgression, no matter the purpose of the "breeches." For Lady Wallace, doubtless her attire was a successful publicity stunt. For Joan of Arc, as she disingenuously testified during her trial, it was the least important thing, a practical decision.[4]

The allusions in Walpole's letter and the *Times* confirm that the Maid's history, including aspersions on her chastity, was thoroughly integrated into British popular culture. A major source of that integration was the burgeoning of historical literature. During the eighteenth century, the craft of historiography was responding to contemporary impulses of nationalism, revolution, and feminism, consequently altering the English reimagining of Joan of Arc.[5] In addition to monarchical histories, chronological narratives, and biographical compilations, historiography began to accommodate such genres as memoirs and letter writing to appeal to a broader reading audience.[6] Oliver Goldsmith, for example, framed his *History of England*, published anonymously in 1764, as a series of letters from a father to his son. William Guthrie's narrative of Joan in his *General History of England* in 1744 sometimes reads like historical fiction.[7] As the century progressed, the extended family of historiographical genres somewhat slipped the bonds of a linear, primarily male, discourse to reshape itself under the hands of historians such as Hester Thrale Piozzi (*Retrospection*, 1801), Helen Maria Williams (*Letters from France*, 1790–96), and Mary Hays (*Female Biography*, 1803).[8] The genres that women chose in some cases upended the conventions of mainstream historical narrative in which women's achievements came to be measured against a domestic rather than a public ideal.

Not all those who brought new historiographical impulses to the fore were women, and not all who wrote traditional history were men. Catharine Macaulay's *History of England* (1763–83), for example, was an important political analysis. Even so, in analyzing women's historiography in this period, Greg Kucich attributes to women "a more comprehensive kind of alternative historical vision, which foregrounds sympathy as the central component of historical understanding."[9] Yet such an approach was not confined to women. In 1790, a book review in the London *Monthly Review* noted approvingly a trend in historiography from "the recital of warlike transactions" to a concern for "the private situation of individuals."[10] Nor, like their male counterparts, did female historians share a single view of society, revolution, women's education, or, for that matter, historical method. One "alternative historical vision" that many did seek was the inclusion of women in mainstream historical discourse. As early as 1705, Mary Astell, who wrote extensively in favor of women's education and intellectual development, argued, "The Men being the Historians, they seldom condescend to record the great and good Actions of Women; and when they take notice of them, 'tis with this wise Remark, That such Women *acted above their Sex*. By which one must suppose they wou'd have their Readers understand, That they were not Women who did those Great Actions, but that they were Men in Petticoats!"[11] Astell was prescient, for this insight became manifest in later representations of Joan of Arc.

How, then, did the English image of the Maid of Orleans fare as she became a new kind of exemplar in an era when the *querelle des femmes* was reframed both in response to and reaction against revolution? If there is any common element, it is the trend toward domesticating, feminizing, and to a lesser extent, sexualizing, the Maid. Unwittingly, Samuel Taylor Coleridge's critique of Robert Southey's depiction of Joan of Arc as "a Tom Paine in petticoats" encapsulates the revolutionary era's approach to her story.[12] Astell had understood the word as derogatory. By the end of the century, "petticoats" applied particularly to women who transcended society's expectations by "meddling" in male domains, particularly in response to excesses of the French Revolution.[13] Walpole rebuked Mary Wollstonecraft as "a hyena in petticoats" for "discharge[ing] her ink and gall on Marie Antoinette."[14] In a review of her *Letters*, Helen Maria Williams was likewise critiqued as a "politician in petticoats" for directing her commentary on the French Revolution to a female audience.[15] The Maid's male attire also inspired versifiers from the mid-eighteenth through early nineteenth centuries to use both "breeches" and "petticoats" as metonymy when making light of her fate.

In just one example, anonymous verses on "Mother Ross"—Mrs. Christian (or Catherine) Davies, who, disguised as a man, served in the British army in the early eighteenth century—include a comparison to Joan of Arc:

> England can boast a greater Joan than France,
> To use the Pistol, as she did the Lance:
> Grant us, kind Heav'n! thy Fate be not the same
> With Joan of Arc, that famous Gallic Dame!
> The Frenchman call'd her Saint; the English, Witch,
> And basely clapp'd a Flambeau to her Breech.[16]

If the *Times*' report on Eglantine Wallace had demonstrated a woman's "breeches" marked her as an object of sexual attention—verbal or otherwise—a woman's "petticoats" marked her either as a meddler in men's affairs, or vulnerable to love and sexual jealousy. Joan might have been overtly sexualized in the anonymous engraving with her flowing hair and in her body-revealing armor, but she was also rendered susceptible to "being made subservient to love or lust," as Wollstonecraft had cautioned.[17] One extreme example of such subservience was enacted in the graphic dénouement of some editions of Voltaire's *La Pucelle d'Orléans:* Joan's loss of virginity.[18]

In his own epic poem *Joan of Arc* (1796), Robert Southey's chaste Maid inspires the devotion of Conrade, a French soldier. But although his "converse most the Virgin loved,"[19] they are not lovers. A more egregious example of Joan's subservience to love was enacted in *Joan of Arc; or, The Maid of Orleans*, a pantomime presented at Covent Garden in February 1798, with lyrics by J. C. Cross and music by William Reeve. In a letter to his brother Thomas, Southey provides a lively description of the plot, the gist of which is that Joan and her sister Blanche keep an "ale-house." When English soldiers "behave somewhat uncivilly" to the women, John Talbot saves them and both women fall in love with him. When he chooses to reciprocate Blanche's affections, Joan, along with Alençon, tries to poison him. When the plot fails, Southey writes, she

> goes to a rocky desert place, and there calls up the devil (don't swear, Tom!). Up comes old Lucifer—red-hot, hissing from hell; he gives her a compact to sign—she hesitates. The rock opens, and discovers Talbot and Blanche in a bower, with Cupids hovering over them. She resolves, and signs her name in letters which appear traced in fire as

she writes them. Lucifer gives her a banner—she proclaims her mission—takes the armour from the tomb, which falls to pieces—defeats the English—captures Talbot and her sister, and throws them into a dungeon—they escape—another battle ensues—her sword and shield break—she is taken prisoner, but pardoned at the intercession of her sister—out she rushes to the place of her incantation, and up comes Lucifer—the rock opens and discovers the mouth of hell, like a large cod-fish—the mouth opens—a legion of Beelzebubs come out, and bear in Joan amid fire and flames.[20]

This dénouement precipitated such demonstrations that, as Southey wrote in the preface to the 1806 edition of *Joan of Arc*, "after a few nights, an Angel was introduced to rescue her."[21] The poet had anticipated such a reaction to Joan's damnation in his original preface: "If among my readers there be one who can wish success to injustice, because his countrymen supported it, I desire not that man's approbation."[22] The audience may also have been reacting to the depiction of Joan as a sexually jealous female who fights the English out of revenge. Despite Walpole and the *Times*, her predominant reputation in English letters was one both of valor and female virtue. Indeed, the lyrics to "Victorious La Pucelle" sung during the show unreservedly praise her "Warlike deeds," while claiming "the Laurel wreath fresh blowing thy future Deeds foretell."[23] This glorification of Joan the warrior was undercut, however, by the historical pageant that followed the pantomime. There a woman's role in warfare was swiftly relocated to her proper, subordinate one.[24] A parade of British heroes, presided over by the national symbol Britannia, ended with "Henry V—The Triumphs of Agincourt, and his Marriage with Catherine,"[25] overlooking Joan of Arc's historical role in nullifying the promise of that union.

By the turn of the nineteenth century, then, a reasonably accurate version of Joan's history was sufficiently familiar to the public that radical deviations from its outline, as in the original ending of the 1798 pantomime, occasioned outrage. Southey's own choice of Joan of Arc as the heroine of an *English* national epic was hotly debated in the reviews of the first two editions, reflecting the influence of the French Revolution and its aftermath on English opinions about the Maid. The first edition of *Joan of Arc* (1796) was sometimes harshly criticized for the faulty aesthetic of its hasty composition, and critics were also divided on the subject matter. The conservative *Critical Review*, for example, called Joan a "singular woman," "whose enthusiasm and valour were the means of raising the siege of Orleans and of restoring the true heir to the crown of France."[26] It raises the question of whether Southey "has chosen a subject scarcely suited to the dignity of epic poetry," especially in light of "recent occurrences" in France. But the anonymous author of the review concludes that Joan possesses many qualities desirable in the hero of an epic.[27]

The physician-turned-writer John Aikin also raises the problem of Southey's subject matter in the *Monthly Review:* "How far the story of the Maid of Orleans is happily chosen for an epic poem is a question which will, doubtless, be differently decided by different persons." He suggests that Voltaire's "supremely witty, splendid, and licentious poem, has almost . . . unfitted la Pucelle for becoming a heroine."[28] A similar thought was advanced in the ultraconservative *Anti-Jacobin Review*'s article on the second edition of 1798: "There are some (ourselves in the number) who, having read [Voltaire], cannot dismiss from their minds that ludicrous association of ideas which must, for ever, operate against the dignity of the heroine."[29] In his preface, Southey claims not to have read Voltaire.

Neither the politically neutral *Monthly Mirror* nor the radical *Analytical Review* found the choice of Joan objectionable. The critic for the former writes, "Joan of Arc has often struck us as an admirable subject for an epic poem;—we thought, like Mr. Southey, that its want of nationality was an objection too trivial to be considered; it can, and ought only, to weigh with such as entertain a blind and fastidious veneration for the ancients, or are too much the slaves of custom and prejudice, to admire even the traditional valour of an enemy to their country; as if virtues were the growth of a particular soil, and courage alone estimable in the breast of an Englishman."[30] The anonymous writer for the *Analytical Review* calls Joan's story "one of the most interesting in the history of France," and shows a good understanding of the culture in which she lived, remarking, "Though, in this incredulous age, it will not be commonly believed that she was really inspired, it must at least be admitted, that she thought herself so, and that this was the common opinion among the vulgar at the time when she performed her great exploits."[31]

Reviewers of the revised edition of *Joan of Arc* (1798) uniformly praised the changes Southey had made, particularly his elimination of Joan's heavenly inspiration. As he writes in the preface to this edition, "The palpable agency of superior powers would destroy the obscurity of her character, and sink her to the mere heroine of a Fairy Tale."[32] The *Monthly Review* especially approves of the revision of Joan's early life, writing, "The Maid is more naturally introduced, and more conformably to real history," adding that she "must not be a mere fanatical maid of an inn."[33] The *Critical Review* also finds "her birth and infancy are more properly represented with regard to place and circumstance."³⁴ The strongest criticism is expressed by the *Anti-Jacobin*: "The established rule for the epic, that the subject be national, is, surely, founded on true patriotism. To this rule Mr. S. has acted in direct opposition and chosen . . . the ignominious defeat of the English. . . . Is there not a squint of malignity—a treacherous allusion in such a picture? And was it not rather a seditious rather than a poetic spirit that first contemplated the Maid of Orleans, as the heroine of an English epic?"³⁵ The suggestion of sedition recalls *1 Henry VI*, which considered Joan's leadership as rebellion against France's rightful king, Henry VI. And although she shared Southey's antiwar sentiments, the poet Anna Seward also objected to his perceived lack of patriotism. By criticizing the English glories of Agincourt, she writes, he "[branded] / The hallow'd lustre of thy ENGLAND'S name / With slavish Meanness."³⁶ Yet she defends English magnanimity, a trait not exercised in Joan's behalf, despite John Speed's declaration in 1611 that "it is not to be doubted but that the magnanimity of the English would have spared her." Seward, too, defines her country by its beneficence, lauding

> ENGLAND, whose martial fire
> Applauding ages have pronounc'd, adorn'd
> With fair Munificence, and temper'd still
> By dove-ey'd Mercy's sway.
> (lines 30–34)

Like some early modern historians, these critics used the story of Joan of Arc to discuss the nature of historiography itself.

During the heyday of English revolutionary fervor in the 1790s, Southey was not alone in expressing his politics through the life and death of the French heroine. Helen Maria Williams provides a female revolutionary perspective on Joan in her *Letters From France* (1790–96). Williams was briefly imprisoned under the Reign of Terror in Paris, and lost many of her friends to the guillotine.³⁷ Before those events, the first volume of her *Letters* (1790) reflects her staunch support for the French Revolution. Her *Letters* provide a sympathetic, sometimes uncritical view of the historical individuals associated with the places she visits. Writing about Rouen, she admits

> I always feel a little ashamed of my country, when I pass the spot where the Maid of Orleans was executed, and on which her statue stands, a monument of our disgrace. The ashes of her persecutor, John Duke of Bedford, repose at no great distance, within a tomb of

black marble, in the cathedral, which was built by the English. One cannot feel much respect for the judgment of our ancestors, in chusing, of all places under the sun, the cathedral of Rouen for the tomb of him whose name is transmitted to us with the epithet of the *good* Duke of Bedford: for you have scarcely left the cathedral, before the statue of Jeane d'Arc stares you in the face, and seems to cast a most formidable shade over the *good* Duke's virtues."[38]

She acknowledges that "in France it is not what is *antient*, but what is *modern*, that most powerfully engages attention," and sees no irony in the contrast of her admiration of Joan (who fought to establish a monarch) with the French Revolution's destruction of monarchy.

In a later edition of the *Letters*, originally written in the summer of 1790, Williams devotes an entire missive to the memory of Joan of Arc in Orléans, beginning with the Calvary Monument, which would be destroyed in 1792: "The statue of the celebrated Jeanne d'Arc, the maid of Orleans, is erected in the principal street of the town. Wherever I travel in France it seems as if I were haunted by this Jeanne d'Arc. I left her lately at Rouen, and here I find her at Orleans; and in both places I fancy she looks at me with an air of reproach."[39] She describes the "solemn procession" on May 8 and listens to a sermon in which "the preacher never fails to paint in the darkest colours the crimes of the English, and their detestable cruelty towards this heroine, to whom, as Mr. Hume the historian justly remarks, the more generous superstition of the ancients would have erected altars. When the guilt of our nation has been made sufficiently manifest, the sermon concludes" (42–43). In another letter, she describes a visit to the Maison de Ville (town hall), where "we saw a picture of Jeanne d'Arc, painted two hundred years ago. The countenance is uncommonly beautiful. It seems that nature, while she bestowed on the Maid of Orléans the heroic qualities of the other sex, did not deny her the soft attractions of her own" (66). This is the famous Alderman portrait of Jeanne d'Arc. Williams states what many other writers had begun to suggest: Joan of Arc must be seen as a woman first, and, preferably, an attractive one.

By mentioning Hume, Williams reminds us that while histories no longer excluded or displaced Joan from her genuine triumphs, many struggled with the very idea of the porous borders between the material and the spiritual in the Middle Ages, and thus struggled with how to account for her inspiration. While David Hume, for one, approached the struggle philosophically, yet another approach was mockery, as in the article on Joan of Arc in the May 1737 issue of *The Gentleman's Magazine*.[40] The article is headed "Fog's Journal.

May 7. No. 442." Unfortunately, only a few issues of *Fog's Journal* survive, not including this one, so the existence of this view of Joan must be credited to the editor Edward Cave. Cave's *Gentleman's Magazine* was to function much as the *Reader's Digest* did in twentieth-century America: "to give Monthly a View of all the Pieces of Wit, Humour, or Intelligence, daily offer'd to the Publick in the News-papers," which, amounting to "no less than 200 Half-sheets per Month," would be impossible for any reader to obtain or peruse.[41] The original author of the article on Joan of Arc was likely the playwright and translator John Kelly, who became editor of *Fog's* in 1737, but was writing for it earlier.[42] I postulate Kelly's authorship not only because he was briefly in charge of the magazine but also because he published a partial translation of Rapin de Thoyras's *Histoire d'Angleterre* in the early 1730s, and thus was familiar with at least one popular source of Joan's story.[43]

The article on Joan of Arc, dated May 7, one day before the annual observances in Orléans, assumes a skeptical and ironic tone. As we have seen in the introduction, Kelly begins by establishing the French view of Joan as a victim of the English for "having very successfully served her King and Country." Despite English remorse, he claims, the English insist she "was no other than a daring, resolute, enterprising Woman, of whom Charles VII's Courtiers made most advantageous Use to re-establish the tottering Affairs of the Kingdom." Kelly adopts the view of the early French historians who maintained she was the tool (even the whore) of Robert Baudricourt. He maintains his belief in her virginity but is skeptical about its power: "I am not of Opinion, that the Quality of a Virgin carries with it that of a Prophetess, and a Deliverer of Nations. I concur with the French Historiographers, that Joan of Arc never had a Bastard." Nevertheless, he maintains she was an imposter, referring his readers to "Stephen Pasquier," although his language suggests he is closely adapting Rapin (his translation differs only slightly from Nicholas Tindal's, first published in 1726).

Kelly further displays his skepticism about Joan's chastity by alluding to a tale by Jean de la Fontaine (1621-1695) and to the more recent sensational story of Marie-Catherine Cadiere. First, he writes, "had I not admitted our Maiden's Virginity, I might parallel the Story she tells with that of Friar *Luce*, put into Verse by the most ingenious *M. de la Fontaine*." He refers to the *conte* "L'Ermite," in which a lascivious Friar seduces a young girl by claiming their union would result in the birth of the next pope.[44] His "parallel" refers both to certain dishonest writers who claimed that Joan was the whore of Baudricourt, and, of course, to the English invention of her pregnancy.[45] Less fanciful, perhaps, is his recollection of the case of Marie Cadiere, a young Frenchwoman who had been accused of witchcraft in 1731, after likely having been seduced by a priest. She was condemned to death, but then reprieved. Her trial was a sensation, and she was saved from burning only at the last minute, unlike Joan.[46] Kelly details their similarities: "Both were alike desirous of deluding the Publick, and of acquiring a Reputation of Sanctity. Both wanted to be ranged among the Number of the Beatified. And Joan even gave herself out for the Almighty's Confident." He finds his proof of "the Absurdity of this Pious Romance" in Joan's imprisonment.

For despite being promised that she could hear Mass and receive the Sacrament if she changed to woman's attire, Joan "would needs retain her Breeches, which she preferred to all the Riches upon Earth, and chose rather to continue a considerable While under the Bar of Excommunication, than put on a Petticoat." This was blasphemy, which he insists she *chose* "rather not to receive the Communion, than to quit her Male Apparel." Despite the opinions of various ecclesiastics and theologians, however,

> the English would have spared Joan's Life, but they insisted on her laying aside those cursed Breeches, of which she was so obstinately fond. The Holy Heroine, at length finding that she absolutely must resolve to die, or return to wearing Petticoats, determined on the latter. But the Mischief of all was, that she put on the Petticoat, without advising with S. Catherine, who, on returning to make her a Visit in Prison, was very angry at finding her dressed like a Woman. She read her a severe Lecture thereupon, saying; "what is it you mean by wearing this F**t in the Air [Pet en l'air], when I told you it was convenient for you to wear Breeches? Down with these Petticoats: Let me see you do it, even should all the Bishops, Doctors, and Batchelors burst with Rage at it." Joan obeyed; and she had abundantly better have done otherwise.[47]

John Kelly's mockery departed radically from the history of Joan of Arc transmitted by the French historians Pasquier and Rapin de Thoyras. The Scottish historians William Guthrie and David Hume culled some of the same materials as the journalist. Yet they crafted the story differently, and while both were skeptical of her divine inspiration, they did not mock it.

Now mostly forgotten, William Guthrie (1708–1770) wrote four versions of Joan's story in different contexts over the span of a quarter century. The most extensive was in his *General History of England* (1744).[48] Interestingly, Guthrie began his own career as a contributor to *The Gentleman's Magazine*, as what we would now call a parliamentary journalist, and this experience allowed him "to bring considerable journalistic flair to the contemporary popularization of historiography," as his biographer notes.[49] In the preface to his *History of England*, Guthrie clearly expresses his purpose and style: "to give a general view of our fundamental liberties and constitutions, and to describe the great scenes of action, with the characters of its chief performers, in as warm and animating a manner as possible, without deviating from truth" (1:iii). He criticizes earlier authors for "their dependence upon, or deference to, papal or ecclesiastical power," continuing "the priests of the reformation could not bear with any alteration of those characters, which had been rendered venerable by the priests of Rome" (1:ii). His skepticism is indeed reflected in his retelling of the story of Joan of Arc, which he nevertheless presents both with sympathy and an eye to the political realities of the Hundred Years' War, albeit with a touch of Kelly's eye for scandal.

Guthrie's expansive account (eighteen double-columned folio pages) seriously discusses fifteenth-century policies and politics. He is evenhanded about Bedford's leadership in France. He admires Joan as a woman of sterling character and astonishing gifts. He fulfills his promise to write "in as warm and animating a manner as possible" by occasionally employing the fiction writer's techniques of an omniscient point of view and foreshadowing. For example, he imagines Joan daydreaming of glory: "But we are now to behold her eyes, hitherto intent upon rural or menial duties, flash terror through the deepest array of the bravest veterans; we are to see the hand, which a distaff filled before, tear the wreathe from the temples of the laurelled warrior; and the arm, which before managed a sheep-hook, brandish the sword which is to cut an empire from its roots" (531). He imagines that "no doubt, she had often already, within her cottage, triumphed over the English battalions, and put her foot on the neck of the regent duke" (532). In time, "her impatience for action first put her blood in a violent ferment, her brain catched the infection, till the whole constitution both of her mind and body was all over one glow of enthusiasm." For Guthrie, enthusiasm is merely "a sincere, warm, disinterested operation of mind" (533), which as we shall see, differs sharply from Hume's meaning.

Anticipating some of his readers' familiarity with the legend of Joan's pregnancy, Guthrie adapts a passage from Gabriel Daniel's *Histoire de France* (1713) to illustrate the power of her chastity. He writes that Baudricourt at first determined Joan's brain was "distempered," yet "willing to be satisfied of what temperament the female adventurer was composed, he turned her over to some young gentlemen, who put her to a very dangerous proof of her virtue. But Joan, in this, was an overmatch for them all" (532). Daniel had written that "at first, Baudricourt regarded her as a madwoman, and putting her in the hands of his men, put her to a most dangerous proof. Not only did she evince a modesty that perfectly conformed to the piety she professed from her tenderest youth; but those among them who had designs to corrupt her vowed that they had felt themselves to have been seized in accosting her with a particular feeling of terror and respect which prevented them from saying even the least unseemly word to her."[50] The anonymous English translator of Daniel excised this passage nearly completely, retaining only the first sentence: "Baudricourt looked upon her at first as a mad woman."[51] Guthrie also claims that while Joan was in prison, "in vain did the duchess of Bedford, with curiosity more than female, make searches and experiments, in hopes to blast her pretence to the glorious character she assumed of a virgin" (548); Daniel had said nothing of the kind. On the contrary, we know Anne Bedford attempted to protect Joan. The salacious tone recalls Guillaume Boisguillaume's equally distasteful claim that the duke of Bedford spied on the gynecological examination in Rouen.[52]

More than once, Guthrie's authorial voice dismisses any thought that Joan was divinely inspired as "ridiculous," an adjective he also uses to describe the charges against her. Of course, she recognized the disguised dauphin, "as if we can suppose that Joan, who was now about seven or eight and twenty years of age, might not have seen Charles before, or received previous information how she might distinguish him" (533). But neither will he accept that "the whole [was] a contrived juggle." Not until after Bedford had left Paris and Charles approached the city, according to Guthrie, does Joan reconsider her mission, "to express a wish, that she was to return to domestic tranquillity, and pass the remainder of her days with her aged parents." However, called to a sense of duty, "she seemed perfectly resigned, and went forward with the greatest chearfulness" (543). Despite that encouragement, Guthrie suggests that Joan was betrayed at Compiègne by her own side: "She fell perhaps a sacrifice to the mean, but reigning, jealousy which the other general officers had of her glory" (547), a claim Daniel considered likely.[53] After her capture, "the maid, instead of being considered as the fairest, the brightest example of true courage and piety, was treated, by the gazing vulgar, great as well as small, as the agent of hell, and a minister of Satan. We know not of a soul in all the English party which was so unfettered by prejudices as not to behold her in this light" (547). Yet despite all his previous reservations, Guthrie asserts that "the purity of the virgin, her blameless conversation, her intrepid virtue, and superior sense, disappointed the eye of malice, and blunted the sting of calumny" (548).

Even so, at her trial, "the root of enthusiasm was still in her breast; nor had her brain yet wholly cooled from her visionary dreams" (549). Resuming her male clothing proved that Joan's "madness, though stifled, had not been yet fully extinguished." If at first it was Baudricourt who thought her mad, at the last it is Guthrie the author who pronounces her "enthusiasm" to be "madness." This does not, however, alter his sympathy for Joan's fate and his opprobrium for those who executed her: "If all-wise providence ever deigns to avenge the perfidy, the cruelty, the injustice of particulars upon a whole nation, well may the English read, in the miseries that soon after befel them, their punishment for the death of this matchless virgin, who, being no native under their government, and taken in fair war, could neither legally be tried by their courts, nor put to death by their award" (549).

However, Guthrie's later versions, written for different audiences and different purposes, tell a different story. In 1766, in collaboration with John Gray "and others," Guthrie published a *General History of the World*, with only five pages devoted to Joan of Arc.[54] He repeats the sixteenth-century French claim that "the whole of her appearance and conduct was the contrivance of Charles and his courtiers, assisted by her amazing courage, sagacity, and strength of body," hypothesizing that "Baudricourt was himself her instructor; but he pretended ignorance and surprize" (193). Notwithstanding, he still finds much to praise in her military tactics and "the grandeur and intrepidity of her deportment" (194). He repeats, "Her captivity is said to have owing to the meanness of the French officers, who were jealous of the glory and reputation she had acquired" (197). In his *General History of Scotland* (1767), Guthrie assumes the reader knows enough of Joan's military career to understand a brief allusion to her: "The capture and death of the maid of Orleans served only to render Charles the more sollicitous to oblige and caress his Scotch allies."[55]

According to Guthrie's final effort, the *New Geographical, Historical, and Commercial Grammar* published in 1770, the year he died, Joan is both an imposter *and* a martyr: "All the efforts of Charles against the English must have been ineffectual, had he not found a young woman who had formerly served as ostler to several inns, and persuaded her to feign an divine commission for driving the English out of France" (321). She "acted her part with such judgment and courage," but "they most barbarously put her to death, after a sham trial for witchcraft and heresy." After Guthrie's death, later editions substitute a different paragraph: "The siege was raised by the valour and good conduct of the Maid of Orleans, a phenomenon hardly to be paralleled in history, being born of the lowest extraction, and bred a cow-keeper, and sometimes a helper in stables at public inns. She must, notwithstanding, have possessed an amazing fund of sagacity as well as valour. After an unparalleled train of glorious actions, and placing the crown on her sovereign's head, she was accidentally taken prisoner by the English, who burnt her alive for being a witch and a heretic (391).[56] Joan of Arc continued to be a fortuitously malleable figure in English history, one whose story could be retold to suit its context.

Guthrie's fellow Scot David Hume might have known his countryman's work, but since they consulted some of the same sources, it is difficult to be certain.[57] Unlike Guthrie's, Hume's *History of England*, originally published in six volumes from 1754 to 1761, became a standard reference in the latter part of the eighteenth century, revised and expanded after his death by Tobias Smollett and others. In fact, Hume wrote the volumes on the Middle Ages last, in part because he had great difficulty in understanding the power of a belief in Christianity to influence political events.[58] His well-known view of the Middle Ages as "barbarous" pertains generally to the era before the reign of Henry VII.[59] He was not alone in viewing the medieval period, with its credence of the supernatural, with what Susan Mosher Stuard calls "rationalist fastidiousness."[60] But he did not denigrate his ancestors as, for example, did John Lockman, who in his *New History of England* attributes the English loss at Orléans to "the unaccountable frenzy and surprize with which they were seized, from the chimerical supposition that they were to encounter a witch; so silly were mankind in those dark ages."[61] It is not Hume's generalized prejudice against an age that underlies his narrative of Joan of Arc. It is his specific inability to enter into the thought processes of religious mysticism. He accepted Joan of Arc's military leadership but was skeptical about her divine inspiration, for reasons he explored in his 1741 essay "Of Superstition and Enthusiasm," which establishes a linguistic paradigm for his evaluation of the Maid.[62]

In that essay, Hume couples superstition and enthusiasm as "two species of false religion." But, he argues, they are different. "The mind of man is subject to certain unaccountable terrors" that result from any variety of causes. Where the mind permits itself to dread "infinite unknown evils . . . from unknown agents; and where real objects of terror are wanting, the soul, active to its own prejudice, and fostering its predominant inclination, finds imaginary ones, to whose power and malevolence it sets no limits."[63] Superstition, with its attendant rituals, some associated with organized religions—although he does not say so outright—attempts to "appease" such imagined terrors. However, "enthusiasm" arises because "the mind of man is also subject to an unaccountable elevation and presumption" (74). The "summit of enthusiasm" is reached when "the inspired person comes to regard himself as a distinguished favourite of the Divinity" (74). Nevertheless, other influences could come into play in accounting for an "extraordinary" human agent, such as Joan of Arc.

Hume viewed Joan's role, as well as the belief of her adherents, as, in Donald Siebert's words, "a manifestation of wish-fulfillment."[64] As we have seen, the anonymous reviewer of Southey's *Joan of Arc* in the *Analytical Review* would say the same: "She thought herself [inspired], and that this was the common opinion among the vulgar at the time when she performed her great exploit."[65]

The beginning of Hume's narrative is peppered with conditionals and passive constructions, reflecting the genuine difficulty he had in understanding how religious belief could outweigh human reason. The first two pages alone employ such phrases as "it is easy to imagine," "could not fail," "it is uncertain," and "it is pretended." By this "constant reassertion, of a common ground," Fiona McIntosh-Varjabédian writes, Hume invites his readers into his own skepticism.[66] In narrating Joan's fate after her capture, Hume sympathetically argues that her recantation was a result of "enthusiasm," which he had asserted in his essay "Of Superstition and Enthusiasm" is made up of "hope, pride, presumption, a warm imagination, together with ignorance," degenerating into "superstition," the result of "weakness, fear, melancholy, together with ignorance" (74).

Hume rephrases those qualities of enthusiasm in his *History* when he states that Joan of Arc had a "visionary and enthusiastic spirit" (341) but an "unexperienced mind" that "mistook the impulses of her passion for heavenly inspirations" (336). Yet he is not immune to the "extraordinary" in her story. Famously, he writes that "it is the business of history to distinguish between the *miraculous* and the *marvelous*; to reject the first in all narrations merely profane and human; to scruple the second; and when obliged by undoubted testimony, as in the present case, to admit of something extraordinary, to receive as little of it as is consistent with the known facts and circumstances" (336–37). Joan's discovery of the dauphin, her revelation of his "secret," the discovery of the famous sword of St. Catherine of Fierbois—all such "miraculous stories were spread abroad, in order to catch the vulgar" (337). Moreover, according to Hume, Joan's very identity was reinvented, from a servant in her late twenties to a "shepherdess" in her teens. As a result, "all the sentiments of love and chivalry, were thus united to those of enthusiasm, in order to inflame the fond fancy of the people with prepossessions in her favour" (337). Hume's evocation of "chivalry" in this context implies that a grown woman who was used to physical labor would be less appealing to the protective instincts of the nobility than a teenaged peasant girl would. In an appendix to the first volume of his *History*, he writes that the elevation of knighthood "begat that martial pride and sense of honour, which, being cultivated and embellished by the poets and romance writers of the age, ended in chivalry. The virtuous knight fought not only in his own quarrel; but in that of the innocent, of the helpless, and above all, of the fair, whom he supposed to be for ever under the guardianship of his valiant arm" (423). Chivalry, then, begotten of the fancy of poets, is akin to "enthusiasm," the result of another form of imagination.[67]

Once Joan sets off on her mission to Orléans, Hume writes, the French begin to see her as a "prophet." In his 1748 essay "On Miracles," he equates prophecy with miracle, and dismisses both: "Mere Reason is insufficient to convince us of its Veracity: And whoever is moved by Faith to assent to it, is conscious of a continued Miracle in his own Person, which subverts all the Principles of his Understanding, and gives him a Determination to believe what is most contrary to Custom and Experience."[68] Despite his own disdain for this way of thinking, Hume allows Joan such determination: "She insisted, in right of her prophetic mission, that the convoy should enter Orleans, by the direct road" (338). Her success, which the people of her own time viewed as "miracles ... convinced the most obdurate incredulity of her divine mission." Nor could the English disabuse their troops of "the prevailing opinion of supernatural influence" (340). After her success, Charles "resolved to follow the exhortations of his warlike prophetess" and so led his army to Reims. Once he was crowned, "no one doubted of the inspirations and prophetic spirit of the Maid" (342). Finally, once Joan was dissuaded from her desire "to return to her former condition, and to the occupations and course of life, which became her sex," Hume writes, without irony, that she persevered "till, by the final expulsion of the English, she had brought all her prophecies to their full completion" (344).

Like Guthrie, Hume accepts the tradition that Joan was betrayed at Compiègne: "The common opinion was, that the French officers, finding the merit of every victory ascribed to her, had, in envy to her renown, by which they themselves were so much eclipsed, willingly exposed her to [capture]" (344). His indignation that she was not treated properly as a prisoner of war could have been written by her most "enthusiastic votaries":

> She had never, in her military capacity, forfeited, by any act of treachery or cruelty, her claim to that treatment: She was unstained by any civil crime: Even the virtues and the very decorums of her sex had ever been rigidly observed by her: And tho' her appearing in war, and leading armies to battle, may seem an exception, she had thereby performed such signal service to her prince, that she had abundantly compensated for this irregularity; and was even, on that very account, the more an object of praise and admiration. It was

> necessary, therefore, for the duke of Bedford *to interest religion in some way in the prosecution* [emphasis added]; and to cover under that cloak his violation of justice and humanity. (345)

While it is not surprising that Hume should evoke "religion" as the machine of Joan's destruction, Thomas Carte had earlier written much the same in his *General History of England* (1747–55): "[The English] view was to cure their countrymen of the terror which her pretences of being sent from Heaven to drive them out of *France*, had inspired into their minds: and this could not be done so effectually in any manner, *as by interesting religion in the case* [emphasis added], by proceeding in the forms of the church against heretics, and by getting her condemned as an heretic, a sorceress, and an imposter."[69] It is not surprising in this light that it was Joan of Arc's cultural context rather than her personal courage to which Hume objected.

As he narrates Joan's trial, Hume is clearly impressed by Joan's "firmness and intrepidity: Tho' harassed with interrogatories . . . she never betrayed any weakness or womanish submission" (345–46). But in the end, Joan, "browbeaten and overawed by men of superior rank, and men invested with the ensigns of a sacred character, which she had been accustomed to revere; felt her spirit at last subdued" (346). At this point, consciously, or unconsciously, Hume has recourse to the formula of his earlier essay on superstition. He continues, "Those visionary dreams of inspiration, in which she had been buoyed up by the triumphs of success and the applauses of her own party, gave way to the terrors of that punishment to which she was sentenced." Joan of Arc's "hope, pride, and presumption" gave way to "weakness, fear, [and] melancholy." In short, "enthusiasm" gave way to "superstition."

Hume made one major revision to his account of Joan in the final, corrected edition of the *History* (1778). He eliminated a note that defended her role in the death of Franquet d'Arras and expounded on her chastity, which Graeme Slater attributes to a "narrative repatterning."[70] After the sentence "Even the virtues and the very decorums of her sex had ever been rigidly observed by her," Hume originally noted:

> We learn from her trial in Pasquier, that when accused of having put to death Franquet d'Arras her prisoner, she justified herself by saying, that he was a known robber, and lay under sentence of death by a civil magistrate. She was so careful of observing decorums, that, when she was in any town or garrison, she always went to bed with some women of character in the place: When in the camp, she lay

in armour, and always had one of her brothers on each side of her. The English never reproached her with any thing in regard to her morals. (345n)

In this, Hume is again following Carte, who had written that Joan's "reputation in point of chastity was never attacked, even by her enemies."[71] The elimination of the reference to Franquet might have been the result of what Slater terms "new information." The elimination of the "proof" of Joan's virtue is consistent with the rest of his narrative. Apart from the brief references to her female decorum, Hume never uses the words "virgin," "virginity," or "chastity" to refer to Joan. He never refers to any test of the Maid's virtue.

Hume's *History* remained popular throughout the eighteenth and nineteenth centuries—cited, plagiarized, expanded and reprinted, abridged, and adapted for different audiences. After Hume's death in 1776, and after the brief copyright of the time expired, the *History*, like Shakespeare's plays, was often reissued with illustrations. None of these, however, is as carefully tied to the text as those in the contemporaneous Shakespeare editions. Even when Hume's text is straightforward, the illustrators take a fair bit of license in interpreting it.[72]

Robert Bowyer's folio edition of the *History* issued from 1793 to 1806 featured commissioned paintings in the manner of Boydell's gallery of Shakespeare. Several of the artists contributed to both, including Hamilton and Fuseli, but none who had depicted Shakespeare's Puzel reimagined the historical Joan. For Bowyer, John Opie (1761–1807), who specialized in historical paintings, depicts "Joan of Arc Declaring Her Mission," although nothing in the engraving distinguishes Joan from any other person (see fig. 14).[73] Hume described Joan's initial interrogation at Poitiers: "An assembly of grave doctors and theologians cautiously examined Joan's mission, and pronounced it undoubted and supernatural. She was sent to the parliament, then residing at Poictiers; and was interrogated before that assembly: The presidents, the counselors, who came persuaded of her imposture, went away convinced of her inspiration" (2:337). In the illustration, Joan, with her hair caught up as if blown by a wind, raises her right arm before a group of four distinctly dubious men and gazes upward. Seated in the foreground, one man consults a heavy tome. Standing, an elderly man in a cap combs his beard as he faces Joan. To his right, another man looks past Joan. A fourth, seated facing the viewer, gestures as he holds another heavy volume. One could read hostility, fear, or credulity into their faces.

A different editorial view of Joan appears in an 1803 edition of Hume's *History* published in London by J. Wallis. The work appears to be that of the

FIGURE 14  John Opie, "Joan of Arc Declaring Her Mission," 1806. Folger Shakespeare Library, Washington, D.C.

FIGURE 15  John Thurston, "Joan of Arc in Prison," from Hume, *History of England*, 1803.

engraver Charlton Nesbit and based on designs by John Thurston.[74] Reprinted below the illustration is a passage that focuses on her clothing, which Hume had reenvisioned as a direct source of "temptation" while Joan was in prison: "Suspecting, that the female dress, which she had now consented to wear, was disagreeable to her, they purposely placed in her apartment a suit of men's apparel; and watched for the effects of that temptation upon her"[75] (see fig. 15). An androgynous prisoner sits on a low bench, left hand over the heart, and right hand grasping the hilt of a sword. The hair is long and waving, indicating a female, but the thick neck and overall musculature indicate a male. The figure is clad in a sort of toga, with one leg bare and one swathed in fabric. A jailer is walking through an archway to the rear, eyes toward the central figure. A bundle of what *might* be clothing lies on the stone floor. As Rosemary Mitchell points out, this ambiguous engraving seems an example of the commonplace use of stock engravings for different historical scenes.[76]

Unlike Carte, Lockman, Guthrie, and Hume, who composed chronological histories of England, Hester Thrale Piozzi (1741–1821) in *Retrospection* (1801) conceived of a kind of universal history in the tradition of Guthrie's *General History of the World*. During the gestation of her ideas for the book, Piozzi wrote to her daughter that she was collecting "Anecdotes of the last Century—not a History."[77] In the 1770s, the literary critic Elizabeth Montagu had argued for the value of anecdotes "to explain the great text of History. They shew the manners and sentiments of the times, and sometimes the causes, sometimes the consequences and effects of great Events."[78] No doubt, Piozzi hoped to repeat the success of her method in *Anecdotes of Dr. Johnson* (1786), which quickly sold out but was criticized for not conforming to the "impersonal register of the classic biography,"[79] even though, as an intimate of Johnson for many years, she was writing the memoir of a friendship. The subtitle of *Retrospection* promises *A Review of the Most Striking and Important Events, Characters, Situations, and their Consequences*. By labeling her collection a "review," she does not promise new material or a new approach to historiography. As she states in the preface, she intended her work both for younger readers and as an *aide-mémoire* for "those who long ago have read, and long ago desisted from reading histories" (vii). Her words echo the preface to Goldsmith's *History of England*: "The present publication is designed for the benefit of those who intend to lay a foundation for future study, or desire to refresh their memories upon the old, or who think a moderate share of history sufficient for the purposes of life."[80] Over a century earlier, William Howell had also offered his monarchical history (1679) as a stimulus to memory, "to serve as a Remembrancer to those who have already studied the History of England; that in a short View they may refresh and rub up their Memories."[81] However, by Piozzi's time, such an approach to history, especially written by a woman, was expected to appeal more narrowly to "other women or children, to turn history into appropriate moral lessons, and to defer to historical authorities," as Devony Looser observes.[82] Nor did Piozzi dress up her work to resemble mainstream histories. Unlike historians from the sixteenth century onward, she did not provide marginal source citations. The book did not have a table of contents or an index, although such apparatus was not yet standard, as Marnie Hughes-Warrington's analysis of over two dozen histories has shown.[83] The first two published volumes of Hume's *History* did not cite his authorities.[84] Moreover, Piozzi did plan to include one of the touchstones of "real" history—an annotated index. Writing to her daughter in 1798, she explains that her book would include "a Table of immense Length in the last of four 8vo. Volumes with the Names of all Cities mentioned in the Course of the Work, as called by Ancients and moderns; French, Italian, English, and Latin."[85]

When Piozzi begins to narrate the reign of Charles VII near the end of volume 1 of *Retrospection*, she follows Hume in crediting the dauphin's success to women: "It seems as if the highest and lowest of our sex had been, without their expectation, oddly enlisted to serve as instruments towards this man's re-instatement on the throne of his ancestors: for in this place a strange phenomenon presses upon our powers of *Restrospect*, and claims a transient glance for Joan of Arc."[86] Piozzi's "transient glance" is both summary and selective. In a mere two pages, she focuses on how Charles came to trust Joan, choosing two anecdotes to prove her case. She introduces the Maid as "artless and illiterate, ... born in a cottage, bred a cow-keeper [who] at the age of twenty-seven years advanced to menial service in a course country inn." There, "after some nights passed in strange perturbation [she] was suddenly and, as she said, involuntarily impelled to seek the tent of an old French officer, then upon guard, and to demand of him safe convoy and entrance into a far distant church, St. Catharine, Fier à Bois, where, she informed him, was deposited a sword and standard sevenscore years before, with which she was commissioned to defeat the English army ... raise [the siege of Orleans], and see the rightful monarch crowned at Rheims" (444–45).

Piozzi embellishes the anecdote of the sword, adding a banner to the cache. Joan had her famous banner made for her during the muster to Orléans.[87] Piozzi also invents a connection between Joan's mission and the crusades. "Seven score," or 140 years, prior to 1431, the year of Joan's death, would have been 1291, when the forces of Sultan al-Ashraf Khalil defeated the Templar defenders of Acre. Without stating how or even why Joan had arrived at Charles VII's court, Piozzi focuses on two public proofs of Joan's authenticity: Joan's "discerning [the dauphin] from all his courtiers, dressed in the same uniform," and her "steady and minute description of this all-conquering sword and banner brought from the Holy Land so long ago, upon a great occasion she ne'er heard of, and laid up in a place she could never have visited" (445). Joan's reputation did indeed strike fear in some of the English soldiers in France. Piozzi attributes that fear to the discovery of this sword: "The fame of

Joan's strange enterprize and errand to the church at Fier à Bois, flew to the English camp, and facilitated her future victory by previous amazement."

When Piozzi relates Joan's desire to retire "to her cot again" after Charles's coronation, she makes Charles's refusal the occasion to allude to a prophecy overlooked in most histories of that time—that Joan predicted she would last only one year: "She assured the king that victory would not in any preternatural mode further attend her steps. This sad assertion, never believed or listened to in the French camp, was notwithstanding, verified too early; and our shocked sight sees with affliction their long-dreaded antagonist made prisoner by some French troops in English pay, who, under pretence of heresy and witchcraft, *burned her alive*" (445). Piozzi otherwise downplays Joan's prophetic utterances.[88] What is both intriguing and idiosyncratic about this "transient glance" is Piozzi's indifference to Joan's gender or cross-dressing. Piozzi does not anywhere say that Joan wore man's clothing or armor. Aside from feminine pronouns and the epithet "maid," one could substitute the name "John" for "Joan" throughout. Piozzi suggestively transposes guilt for the Maid's execution from the English to the French allies of her foes. In *Retrospection* Piozzi makes Joan's death sound like a French lynching, obviating any question of English culpability or retroactive apology. She mentions neither trial. Piozzi's account of Joan of Arc does draw a firm conclusion about the effects of the Maid on the English. Having burned her, she writes, "ill success followed their savage decision; our invading armies were driven home baffled, or cut to pieces on the continent" (445–46).

Piozzi was writing universal history, not women's history. In the last quarter of the eighteenth century, however, a number of female biographies appeared. Contending with the identity of a woman warrior in revolutionary and post-revolutionary times, some realigned Joan's achievement with more gender-appropriate (i.e., domestic) aspirations, in keeping with a growing debate on what actually constituted femininity and the influence of what Jeanne Wood terms "the general conservative backlash of the late 1790s against radical politics."[89] In the sixteenth century, many treatises defended the virtue and military valor of women, including Joan of Arc. However, in the eighteenth century, "conduct books, sermons, homilies, novels and magazine articles insisting that good order and political stability necessitated the maintenance of separate sexual spheres" proliferated, according to Linda Colley.[90] Increasingly, during the last quarter of the eighteenth century, as Miriam Burstein argues, "the 'events' of women's history take place in the domestic and spiritual domains: women 'conquer' on the battlefield of the soul rather than on the bloody fields that interest historians who chronicle men's deeds."[91]

Echoes of John Knox also resound in such texts as John Brown's 1765 sermon "On the Female Character and Education." If women manifest "masculine Boldness and indelicate Effrontery" and "affect a self-sufficiency and haughty Independency; assert an unbounded Freedom of Thought and Action; and even pretend to guide the Principles of Taste, and the Reins of Empire," then "it is inevitably the consequence that 'the Reality of national Virtue vanisheth, and its Shadows occupy is Place; Sincerity is no more.'"[92] Even a figure so historically remote as Joan of Arc presented a challenge for historians, biographers, and polemicists in the context of this backlash against women worthies. In the early seventeenth century, Thomas Heywood had seen no conflict in placing Joan among English viragos in his *Gynaikeion*, but he relegated her to the ranks of "sorceress" in his monarchical history, *Life of Merlin*. In the late eighteenth century, however, the challenge was how to grant that a woman's courage might be praiseworthy in certain circumstances but was not to be emulated.

As Bonnie Smith observes in her study of the origins of female historiography, "Because moral qualities remained important in a heroine's past ... her life could not be narrated by the simple toting up of achievements. Rather it had to be interpreted in terms of the changing moral standards for the behavior of womankind."[93] William Alexander makes this clear in his 1779 history of women:

> We could give innumerable instances of women, who ... have distinguished themselves by their courage ... such was the Maid of Orleans. But we do not chuse to multiply instances of this nature, as we have already said enough to shew, that the sex are not destitute of courage when that virtue becomes necessary; and were they possessed of it, when unnecessary, it would divest them of one of the principal qualities for which we love, and for which we value them. *No woman was ever held up as a pattern to her sex, because she was intrepid and brave* [emphasis added].[94]

Fortuitously for writers aware of the "changing moral standards," two widely repeated historical anecdotes sanctioned the view that Joan of Arc accepted the social limitations of her gender: her reported longing for home after Charles VII's coronation and her ability to transform from warrior to woman by the simple act of dismounting.

During the nullification hearing, Jean Dunois recalled the archbishop of Reims, Regnault of Chartres, asking, "Joan, where do you hope to die?" We must perforce read this as a leading question, for the archbishop was no friend of Joan's and, after her capture, was reported to have criticized her willfulness and pride.[95] Joan replied, "Where it shall please God. Would it please God, my creator, that I now retreat, laying down my arms, and go to the service of my father and mother in tending their sheep, with my sister and brothers, who will rejoice greatly to see me."[96] Even though we cannot guarantee the accuracy of Dunois's memory, Joan's longing to return home to her domestic occupations gave English historians an opening to realign her aspirations with those increasingly prescribed for women. Likely disseminated through David Hume's popular *History*, this anecdote became an essential part of the English reimagination of Joan's identity. Felicia Hemans made it the core of her 1828 poem "Joan of Arc in Rheims," as we shall see.

Closely associated with the trope of longing for home was the Maid's transformation from warrior to woman when she dismounted, suggesting that Joan, like Shakespeare's Rosalind, although "caparison'd like a man," did not have "a doublet and hose in [her] disposition."[97] Both Southey and Hays reprinted Thomas Fuller's association of Joan's horsemanship with her "masculine" vigor and her dismounting to her femininity: "Ever after she went in mans clothes, being armed cap-a-pe, and mounted on a brave Steed: and which was a wonder, when she was on horseback, none was more bold and daring; when alighted, none more tame and meek; so that one could scarce see her for her self, she was so changd and alterd, as if her spirits dismounted with her body" (373–74).[98] In her 1804 *Biographical Dictionary of the Celebrated Women of Every Age and Country*, Matilda Betham neatly summarizes, "Her manner is recorded to have been mild and gentle, when unarmed, though courageous in the field!"[99]

Indeed, toward the end of the eighteenth century, women warriors and Amazons fell astonishingly quickly out of favor.[100] The updated collections of "female worthies" emphasized British, not international, and literary, not political, accomplishments, as in George Ballard's *Memoirs of Several Ladies of Great Britain* (1752). The traditional canon of female worthies, chiefly "foreign" viragos from Penthesilia to Joan of Arc was partially displaced by what Harriet Guest terms "the emergence of a national canon of celebrated women."[101] The downgrading of viragos is manifest in the anonymous *Biographium Fæmineum* of 1766. The preface offers an apologia for the inclusion of certain women whose careers might not seem obvious inspirations to domestic virtue: "It will probably be objected, that the characters of some of these ladies very indifferently comport with the title of our book, The Female Worthies, which seemingly implies, that none but such are honoured with a place in it" (viii). Nevertheless, the author implies that negative exemplars may offer useful moral lessons, as in the case of Joan of Arc: "As this virago has rendered herself famous in history, by beginning the expulsion of the English out of France, after the death of our brave king Henry V, she seems entitled to some notice, tho,' otherwise, scarce worthy of a place in our memoirs."[102] Joan is nevertheless allowed "a valour and resolution uncommon in her sex," and to have "fought with great conduct and bravery" before her capture.

Around 1800, several biographical compilations of famous women written *by* women appeared: Mary Hays's *Female Biography* (1803), and Matilda Betham's *Dictionary* and Mary Pilkington's *Memoirs of Celebrated Female Characters*, both in 1804. Perhaps the same unease expressed in the *Biographium Fæmineum* about the appropriateness of a French virago as an exemplar for young Englishwomen led to her exclusion from avowedly didactic works. Neither Pilkington's moral guide *A Mirror for the Female Sex* (1799) nor Lucy Aikin's *Epistles on Women Exemplifying Their Character and Condition* (1810) includes the Maid.

Hays's and Betham's works, especially, have been singled out as representative of how women themselves commented on contemporary issues of gender through their portrayals of history. Stereotypically, Hays is the radical feminist, Betham the conservative upholder of historical precedent. Yet Hays omitted Mary Wollstonecraft from her *Female Biography*, having already written a posthumous appreciation of her,[103] and a youthful Betham acknowledged her support for women's equality and wrote in defense of George IV's wife, Caroline of Brunswick, when he attempted to divorce her in 1820.[104] Both women defended Joan's inspiration in Hume's skeptical terms. But they did not castigate her for staying in Charles's service after his coronation, despite her expressed wishes to return home.

Mary Hays had earlier considered Joan of Arc in her 1798 *Appeal to the Men of Great Britain in Behalf of Women*, in which she seems to follow Alexander's lead in observing, "Nature dictates with a force not to be misunderstood, that women are not formed for warlike enterprises. . . . Necessity has indeed upon pressing occasions, lent strength to women, and boldness, for any given purpose. . . . But every one is aware of the absurdity of adducing particular cases, to establish general rules."[105] That is, Joan's career could be excused because of the dire situation France was in, as Alexander had suggested. However, for Hays, ultimately a woman's choice was always clear: "If the pursuit of knowledge, or accomplishments of whatever kind, interferes with her duty in any of the leading characters of the sex, as daughter, sister, wife, or mother; a woman of sense and virtue will not for a moment balance between these" (202–3). A woman must choose her domestic duty over any other aspirations, notwithstanding her natural talents.

Hays's stated purpose in writing female biographies was more general: to present "to the rising generation" a "memorial of those women, whose endowments, or whose conduct, have reflected lustre upon the sex" (v–vi).[106] Inevitably, in Gina Luria Walker's view, the very scope of her work sets forth "a rich, variegated history of women in which they struggled against male intolerance in a variety of forms."[107] The story of Joan's life and death that Hays told in *Female Biography* needed little fine-tuning to suit this theme. While emphasizing—as Hume had—Joan's adherence to female decorum, Hays continually points out how men both disregarded and used her "as a political engine in a credulous and fanatic age" (148). In a backhanded compliment to Joan's leadership at the battle of Patay, for example, she writes that "the conduct of the troops, the military operations, and even the decisions of the council, were politically attributed to Joan, to whose sagacity and promptitude in availing herself of the suggestions of more experienced commanders no mean praise is due" (156). Hays also continually attributes the psychological effects of Joan's valor—reanimating French morale and undermining English—to the "fanaticism" of "an unenlightened age" (155). She moves Joan's plea "to be allowed to retire" (160) *after* the retreat from Paris, with the effect of suggesting Joan fleeing after loss, rather than withdrawing at the high point of achievement just after Charles's coronation.

Hays emphasizes that it was men—"French officers, jealous of the glory of the maid" (162)—who betrayed Joan at Compiègne. Men—Bedford and the bishop of Beauvais—conspired against her in the name of religion. Men, too, forced her to recant, "brow-beaten by men of superior rank [and] basely deserted by the monarch she had served" (167). Worst of all, "no steps were taken by Charles to rescue from destruction the deliverer of himself and the saviour of his dominions; nor, while he held in his hands, as prisoners of war, English of the first distinction, were any proposals offered to exchange them for the heroic Joan:—a memorable example of the gratitude of princes" (167–68).

In her *Biographical Dictionary*, Matilda Betham reverses Hays's emphasis on Joan's victimization by men. She begins with fulsome praise for Bedford and dubiety about Joan. The duke, she writes, was "one of the most accomplished princes of the age, whose experience, prudence, valour, and generosity, enabled him to maintain union among his friends, and to gain the confidence of his enemies" (57). She follows Hume in depicting Joan as an impressionable patriot whose belief in her mission overcame "that bashfulness so natural to her sex, her years, and low condition" (58). Similarly to Speed, she suggests a direct connection between Joan's giving in to the importunities of Dunois to remain with the court and her capture, trial, and condemnation: "Dunois, sensible of the great advantages which might still be reaped from her presence in the army, exhorted her to persevere, till the final expulsion of the English. In pursuance of this advice, she threw herself into the town of Compiegne." At last, the "admirable heroine was cruelly delivered over alive to the flames" (60).

Hester Piozzi's decision not to relate Joan of Arc's story at length tells us that English readers were familiar with it, even as Hays and others recast it to make a medieval virago comprehensible to a post-revolutionary mindset. In fact, increasing familiarity with French sources, as well as English histories, inspired commentary on nationalism or patriotism, just as Southey's poem had done. Thomas Carte's midcentury *General History* did not escape the critical eye of Nicolas Lenglet-Dufresnoy in his *Histoire de Jeanne d'Arc dite la Pucelle d'Orléans* (1753–54), translated into English and published in an abridged version by Geo. Ann Grave in 1812. Just as Lenglet-Dufresnoy had appended to his excerpts from Carte's work a lengthy diatribe against the English historian's diminution of Joan's role, Grave offered his own views in "Supplementary Remarks":

> The perusal of English historians, as far as relates to the subject of the foregoing memoirs, has always left on my mind some impression of inconsistent, not to say unfair animadversion; professing to seperate the credible from the marvellous, they generally end in heightening the wonders of an event, in itself sufficiently extraordinary. Those universally established facts which ought to speak for themselves, have been so clouded, by confounding her agency with that of others, as to veil more than half their lustre. Joan's youth is either denied, or only used to discredit her operative sufficiency; Joan's ignorance is dwelt upon, not the ignorance of that age; her enthusiasm, not her genius. They grant her unblemished integrity, yet represent it as conniving at the most unnecessary deceptions.[108]

He then answers each perception that reduces Joan's "operative sufficiency" or agency, such as her age, her occupation as a servant, her facility in riding, her lack of education, and her standing as "a kind of military automaton," concluding, "The merits and glories of Joan, though extraordinary, are neither marvellous nor unnatural, and after all, may perhaps be best summed up in this one simple fact, she promised nothing that was not eventually performed!" (158). Grave's work was received with both condescension and criticism, but in a larger sense, the reviews demonstrate how the historiography of Joan of Arc had become part of a wider conversation, just as the reviews of Southey's *Joan of Arc* had done. *The Literary Panorama*, with its patriotic emphasis and protective attitude toward women, fusses, "More appropriate examples of patriotism for British ladies, might have been selected, from the annals of our own country."[109] Dismissing charges of demonology and heavenly inspiration alike, the reviewer acknowledges, "Nevertheless Jeanne d'Arc was a remarkable person. To France a fortunate tool for policy to work with. To England a scourge for foolish superstition, or wicked dissension: an occasion of panic without cause, in the judgment of reason and common sense; but of angry debate and contradictory opinion where statesman-like jealousy was not checked by more truly statesman-like forbearance and magnanimity" (69).

The critic for the *Monthly Review* went much further, demonstrating that he had read widely. He unfairly calls Grave to task for not consulting manuscripts published by Clement de l'Averdy in 1790, which Southey had praised: "To undertake a new life of Joan of Arc, without carefully examining this recent treasury of information concerning her, is not respectful to the public."[110] But Grave was translating exceprts from a work published decades before the appearance of those documents. The critic's own "corrections" to Grave display both cynicism and bias. Joan was a tool of the church, as well as "the Armagnac party" (132). His view that Joan's execution, "this deed of inhumanity, not the sword of Joan of Arc, expelled the English from France," (130) echoes Piozzi's conclusion in *Retrospection*. The reviewer also evinces an enduring strain of English derision for the Maid and her times.

Shortly thereafter, the literary reimagining of Joan of Arc according to the standards of her time was complete, in the work of Felicia Hemans. By the time Hemans published her poetic *Records of Women*, in 1828, she was established and respected, a woman who "marketed herself as a poet who celebrated the 'domestic affections,' as a defender of hearth and home."[111] But what she *actually* records is the ironic dissonance between women's fortitude and willingness to transcend the "decorums" of their sex, and the anguished recognition that their power is limited to upholding, not determining, the workings of the wider, masculine, world.[112] Yet while the lives of many of her characters end in death, despair, or estrangement, the *Records* often doubly memorialize their heroines: through the poems that tell their stories, and the physical monuments or living memories of those left behind. A major theme of the work is, in Gary Kelly's view, the "contradictory effects of memory on the individual, the family, the community, and the nation."¹¹³ "Joan of Arc in Rheims" is a study in such effects—not just on the reader, but also on "Joanne" herself. In his *Joan of Arc*, Southey allows, but did not require, the reader to "remember" Joan's tragic end at her moment of triumph, for the poem ends at Reims. In Heman's poem, Joan's future martyrdom similarly lies outside the narrative frame yet simultaneously resides in the reader's memory.

"Joan of Arc in Rheims" opens with a series of appeals to the senses that convey Joan's awe at the coronation of Charles VII. The first seven lines contrast sound and silence, the peals of "mighty music" with the hush of the crowd straining to hear "what was done within" the cathedral. Shifting perspective to the inside, images of light and dark set off the central figures. The king stands within the ring of his vassals, "shadow'd by ancestral tombs," in the "rich gloom" (line 8) of the stained glass windows. Another figure, however, stands "alone / And unapproach'd, beside the altar-stone, / With the white banner, forth like sunshine streaming, / And the gold helm thro' clouds of fragrance gleaming, / Silent and radiant" (lines 17–21). This is not Joan of Arc, but the devout Jeannette, "glorified, with inspiration's trace," gazing upward to an image of the Virgin, with a "soft light in that adoring eye" (line 31). Her helmet "was raised," not yet doffed; it is the helmet, not her hair, framing "Woman's cheek / And brow" (lines 24–25). She is simultaneously warrior and woman. Karen Laird suggests that by showing Joan as a votary of the Virgin Mary, "embraced by this powerful icon of motherhood, . . . Hemans implies that Joan chose wrongly in prioritizing political action over family security."¹¹⁴ Yet Mary, too, heeded an angel's message and accepted *her* mission, although Joseph "was minded to put her away privily" (Matthew 1.19), ashamed of her pregnancy. Only now, a third of the way through the poem, does the narrator name "the shepherd's child, / Joanne, the lowly dreamer of the wild!" (lines 33–34). The apposition initially defines Joanne as ordinary, but it is followed by the narrator's triumphant distinguishing of her as unique:

> Never before, and never since that hour,
> Hath woman, mantled with victorious power,
> Stood forth as *thou* beside the shrine didst stand,
> Holy amidst the knighthood of the land;
> And beautiful with joy and with renown,
> Lift thy white banner o'er the olden crown,
> Ransom'd for France by thee!
>
> (lines 35–41)

Hemans's readers might expect the poet to dramatize the moment when the peasant child, victorious warrior, and devout "votaress" expressed her longing to return home, only to be persuaded to continue her military career by the king or Dunois. But the poet's own ambivalence about "renown" leads her first to describe its temptations, for as Joanne emerges from the cathedral,

> Then rose a nation's sound—
> Oh! what a power to bid the quick heart bound,
> The wind bears onward with the stormy cheer
> Man gives to glory on her high career!
> (lines 50–53)

Momentarily, the cacophony of "shouts that fill'd / The hollow heaven tempestuously, were still'd" (lines 56–57), and into that brief silence breaks the voice of her father calling "Joanne," only the second occurrence of her name at about the two-thirds point of the poem.

Neither the triumphant music nor the shouts of the crowd prompt a reaction from Joanne. But her father's voice and the sight of him and her two brothers loosen her tongue—her cry "Father! and ye, my brothers!"—transforms the "woman, mantled with victorious power" into the girl from Domrémy.[115] Not just her thoughts but "her spirit turn'd" to the memory of a Wordsworthian paradise, where a chapel displaces the cathedral, and the sound of birds drowns out the "warlike melodies" in "a music heard and felt / Winning her back to nature" (lines 81–82).[116] Southey had also established his Joan as a child of nature. In his poem, she tells the priests examining her in Poitiers that she "fled the house of prayer" and found the voice of God in nature:

> 'Tis true my youth,
> Conceal'd in forest gloom, knew not the sound
> Of mass high-chaunted, nor with trembling lips
> I touch'd the mystic wafer: yet the Bird
> That to the matin ray prelusive pour'd
> His joyous song, methought did warble forth
> Sweeter thanksgiving to Religion's ear
> In his wild melody of happiness,
> Than ever rung along the high-arch'd roofs
> Of man.
> (Book the Third, 420–29)

Both poets contrast the formal music of indoor worship with Nature's music both heard and felt.[117]

By saying Joanne's aural memories succeeded in "*winning* her back to nature" (emphasis added), Hemans suggests that Joanne was not immune to the pull of fame, an enticement the poet herself understood. In 1826, Hemans wrote the short lyric "Woman and Fame," whose first verse was printed as the epigraph to "Joan of Arc in Rheims":

> Thou hast a charmed cup, O Fame!
>     A draught that mantles high,
> And seems to lift this earth-born frame
>     Above mortality.
> Away! to me—a woman—bring
> Sweet waters from affection's spring.
>                   (lines 1–6)[118]

This poem contrasts the "charmed cup" of Fame, envisioned here, as in the longer poem, as necessarily public, with "home-born love." Yet the voice that banishes Fame acknowledges its allure, with the repetition in its last line: "Where must the lone one turn or flee?— / Not unto thee—oh! not to thee!" (lines 29–30). Anna Brownell Jameson expresses a more cynical view in her 1826 novel, *Diary of an Ennuyée*. Her thinly disguised narrator declares, "I do not pity Joan of Arc: that heroic woman only paid the price which all must pay for celebrity in some shape or other: the sword or the faggot, the scaffold or the field, public hatred or private heart-break; what matter?"[119]

Joanne has sacrificed her "domestic tranquility," in William Guthrie's phrase, for France's cause. But she is not lost to the lure of Fame. Fleeing that temptation cannot be accomplished merely by pulling off her helmet and releasing her long hair. Susan Wolfson argues that elsewhere in Heman's *Records of Women*, this gesture "signals [women's] emergence from customary restraints," but it is not true for Joanne.[120] She releases her hair not only to express nostalgia for her youth but also to beg remission from sin. Her prayer in "Joan of Arc in Rheims"—"Bless me, my father, bless me" (line 86)—"echoes the traditional beginning of the confessional: 'Bless me, Father, for I have sinned,'" as James McGavran reminds us.[121] Hemans restages Joanne's temptation from that of resuming male clothing in her prison to relinquishing her military mission for her domestic life. The poet also transforms the source of her anguish from abjuring her testimony to abjuring "the still cabin / And the beechen-tree." Wolfson terms the appearance of Joanne's family a "domestic plot," but it functions more significantly as a competing temptation: Can one sent by God abjure her mission?

The answer comes not from her father, but from the narrator, who directs the reader's memory to Joanne's impending fate:

> Oh! never did thine eye
> Thro' the green haunts of happy infancy
> Wander again, Joanne!—too much of fame
> Had shed its radiance on thy peasant-name;
> And bought alone by gifts beyond all price,
> The trusting heart's repose, the paradise
> Of home with all its loves, doth fate allow
> The crown of glory unto woman's brow.
> (lines 89–96)

Had Joan of Arc's story not been a familiar one in English culture by 1828, one might have read her plea "as the moment when Joan finally becomes a legible, historical figure because she evinces her true, female nature," as Chad Edgar argues.[122] But what is "legible" in the ending of the poem is the book of memory that troubles history itself.

The English story of Joan of Arc was to be troubled again shortly after Hemans completed her poem and after Sir Walter Scott had declared Joan of Arc's execution an "execrable cruelty."[123] In 1841, the French historian Jules Michelet canonized Joan of Arc in essence eighty years before the Vatican was to do so in fact.[124] Nadia Margolis describes the effect of his post-Romantic portrait of Joan: "As her historian, Michelet implies his role as prophet and 'voice of the people,' allowing Joan's virtues to become collective traits of the French people, so that anyone admiring Joan automatically possessed or acquired these virtues, and also proved him/herself a true French citizen as well as a child of God—the French as divinely favoured (over the English). . . . Ultimately, his words also issued a mandate to historians of Joan, and their readers, as arbiters of the truth of her legend, or perhaps more appropriately, the legend of her truth."[125] Margolis calls his work "Joan's *real* rehabilitation trial," which not only indicts Charles VII as her enemy but, in the process, "rekindles his French readers' lasting odium for the English as eternal foe." The English poet Thomas de Quincey engaged that argument in an essay published in *Tait's Edinburgh Magazine* in 1847.[126] His sentimental retelling of Joan's story accords with Michelet's emphasis on her greatest accomplishment, her martyrdom, and her essential character as a humble servant of

God. Nevertheless, Michelet's Christlike Joan forever changed how any writer could approach her story.

In the eighteenth and early nineteenth centuries, England's Joan of Arc is simultaneously Guthrie's "matchless virgin" and Hume's "admirable heroine," yet a deluded victim of religious enthusiasm. She is Southey's "mission'd Virgin" and Hays's "prophetess." She is Piozzi's "artless and illiterate maid" and Hemans's "shepherd's child," longing to return to her "cot." I have paired these epithets deliberately, for they encapsulate a movement toward the ultimate domestication of Joan of Arc in English letters. Not the publication of Hume's *History* and its indirect dissemination in dozens of subsequent texts, nor the increasing availability of the trial transcripts in both French and English, nor Mary Hays's diligent synthesis of historical research and sympathy were powerful enough to counter English writers' persistent uneasiness about Joan of Arc. The unease in the Romantic period is partly the repercussion of political and social anxiety about revolution and feminism. Yet underlying it is the English inability to exonerate Joan herself from complicity in English injustice by clinging to her "cursed breeches" and giving in to the importunities of her king to remain at his side rather than retiring to her "cot," in "the green haunts of happy infancy" to pursue "the occupations and course of life which became her sex." At the end of four hundred years, while Joan of Arc was fully integrated into British history, her name a catchword for both female valor and feminine waywardness, the English reimagined Joan of Arc as the simple shepherd girl.

AFTERWORD

*"Is That Meant to Be Me?"*

> We used to buy candles to burn before Joan of Arc. "But what do *you* want with candles?" the sacristan would say. (The God who made all the Creeds knew, but we did not.) And, two years after our last visit together in peace time, there remained only the gutted shell of the Cathedral, but, in a corner of the void, lay a metal candleholder—I tried to believe that very one on which we had spiked our useless offerings.
> —Rudyard Kipling, *Souvenirs of France*, 1933

From the sixteenth century onward, English travelers to France visited and remarked on monuments to the Maid, notably the one in Orléans first erected in 1458 and at least twice destroyed and rebuilt. Some tourists reacted with sophisticated indifference, such as Robert Montagu, Lord Mandeville. Some, such as Peter Heylyn, used their visit as an occasion to defend her. Still others, such as Helen Maria Williams, found "reproach" in her gaze. Later travelers also responded to her image and memory. Rudyard Kipling was one of those. He had visited Reims cathedral before World War I—Joan had been beatified in 1909—lighting his candles, but the structure was heavily damaged by German shelling in 1914.[1] During the war, both French and English propagandists evoked Joan's image of heroism, and in the succeeding decade she became a symbol of French and English unity. After the war, after she was canonized, the English themselves began to construct monuments to her, as virago and saint. I began with the image of Joan's statue in the retrochoir of Winchester Cathedral. I end

FIGURE 16  Leicester Cathedral East Window.

with another English tribute, the stained glass memorial window in Leicester Cathedral. Comparing these two English images of the Maid, designed and installed in the aftermath of "the war to end all wars" crystallizes centuries of English ambivalence and makes clear how they reconciled it.

At St. Martin of Tours church (now Leicester Cathedral) in April 1920, as part of a daylong celebration of its patron saint and commemoration of the fallen soldiers from the city, the bishop of the diocese dedicated the new memorial East Window, designed by Christopher Whall (see fig. 16).[2] Surmounted by a rayed sun, the upper window features Christ in Majesty. The Cathedral website describes the lower window as "sorrowful with the dead body of Jesus lain beneath the bold, dark wood of the cross. Mary, his mother standing, receives her dead son. St. John and the other Mary in the gospel story flank the other side of his body, as together they form a new human family borne out of suffering."[3] On the far left facing the Virgin stands Joan of Arc, whose halo reflects her imminent canonization (on May 16). But this Joan is not the kneeling virago of Orléans or the stoic warrior of Winchester Cathedral.

FIGURE 17 Leicester Cathedral, detail: Joan of Arc.

AFTERWORD | 163

The background of this window depicts "the Cloth Hall in Ypres burning standing for France *and all that women did* in the Great War." Rather than the military garb depicted in those monuments, here Joan's head is encircled by the halo of her sainthood, not the helm of her mission. Her hair is bobbed, her visage soft and sad. Only glimpses of armor show under her encompassing blue cape, festooned with gold fleurs-de-lis. A small peasant girl huddles by her left side, evoking the similar fiery depredations fourteenth- and fifteenth-century French peasants suffered at the hands of brigands. Like the "Joanne" of Felicia Hemans's poem, Joan represents womanhood. Her deeds are acknowledged, but displaced. Although not herself a mother, she is the protector of children traumatized by war. Although she wears armor, she wields her banner, not a sword, while the three male militant saints who also figure in the window stand with swords drawn. To the far right of the lower window is St. Martin, patron saint of soldiers. On guard in the upper window are St. George on the left, his sword pointed toward the dragon he has slain, and on the right, St. Michael, patron saint not only of warriors, but of the sick and suffering.

On the surface, in both English memorials, Joan stands for "the friendship of two peoples, confirmed in the heroisms of the 20th century," as the Dean of Winchester declared at the statue's dedication.[4] But they also stand for enduring English ambivalence about her identity and her legacy. In Winchester, overlooking the tomb of her prosecutor, she is the virago, the valorous warrior, wielding a sword, not a banner. There, another blue cape with its golden fleurs-de-lis drapes behind her, framing and setting off the golden armor. Nevertheless, in remarks during the dedication of the statute, even as he praised Joan's valor, the Lord Lieutenant declared, "no wonder that Christian men—*and above all, Christian women* [emphasis added]—throughout the world now unite to do her honour."[5]

George Bernard Shaw remarks ironically on the Winchester statue in the epilogue to *Saint Joan*, from the same year, 1923. De Stogumber, one of the ghosts who visits Charles VII in the night, comments, "Sir: I was chaplain to the Cardinal of Winchester once. They would always call him the Cardinal of England. It would be a great comfort to me and to my master to see a fair statue to The Maid in Winchester Cathedral. Will they put one there, do you think?" A "Gentleman" answers, "As the building is temporarily in the hands of the Anglican heresy, I cannot answer for that." A stage direction follows: "*A vision of the statue in Winchester Cathedral is seen through a window.*" Joan is surprised: "Is that meant to be me? I was stiffer on my feet."[6] Joan of Arc might well ask the same question of every English attempt to capture her essence, in words or pictures, then and now.

# NOTES

In citing works in the notes, I have generally used shortened titles. Complete citation information is in the bibliography. Works frequently cited are identified by the following abbreviations.

Duparc   Pierre Duparc, ed. *Procès en Nullité de la Condamnation de Jeanne d'Arc.* 5 vols. Paris: C. Klincksieck, 1977–88.

ODNB   Oxford Dictionary of National Biography

OED   *Oxford English Dictionary*

Tisset   Pierre Tisset and Yvonne Lanhers, eds., *Procès de Condamnation de Jeanne d'Arc*, 3 vols. Paris: C. Klincksieck, 1960–71.

A NOTE ON THE TEXT

1. Tisset, 1:40. On "Darc," see Pernoud and Clin, *Joan of Arc: Her Story*, 220–21.
2. C. Taylor, *Joan of Arc*, 48.

INTRODUCTION

1. The statue was designed by the ecclesiastical architect John Ninian Comper, who patterned it after the one inside Reims Cathedral. "Joan of Arc Memorial in Winchester Cathedral," appeal leaflet, Hampshire Archives and Local Studies, DC/E4/5/2/1. For Beaufort's tears, see Doncoeur and Lanhers, *Réhabilitation de Jeanne la Pucelle*, 38. For testimony on Joan's ashes, see Duparc, 1:456, 459, 470.
2. "Joan of Arc Memorial in Winchester Cathedral," appeal leaflet; Geddes, "Icon Betrayed." I appreciate Mr. Geddes's referring me to the Hampshire archives.
3. M. Darmesteter, "Joan of Arc in England," 3; M.-R. McLaren, *London Chronicles*, 86; Fuller, *Holy State and Profane State*, 377.
4. J. Kelly, "Joan of Arc," 287b–89. I discuss this article and its authorship in chapter 5.
5. Tisset, 1:396.
6. Duparc, 1:434.
7. Duparc, 1:427.
8. Coleridge, *Marginalia*, 119.
9. Thickett postulates that the number of editions and their wide distribution "[indicate] that they were printed in a large number of copies": *Bibliographie des oeuvres d'Estienne Pasquier*, 9–10, 31.
10. Pasquier, *Oeuvres*, 537. "Bonne guerre" is not the same as war undertaken in the name of God; see Novack, *Double-Edged Sword*.

11. Curry translates the treaty in "Two Kingdoms, One King."
12. H. Nicolas, *Proceedings and Ordinances*, 4:222–23.
13. Hall, *Union*, 159.
14. G. Paris, "James Darmesteter," 504.
15. M. Darmesteter, "Joan of Arc in England," 33 (895). The parenthetical page numbers refer to the original French. This claim was revived as recently as 1949 by Henri Carré, who based his argument on Charles the Dauphin's adulatory speech to Puzel in act 1, scene 5. Carré, "C'est Shakespeare."
16. M. Darmesteter, "Joan of Arc in England," 3 (883).
17. Southey, *Robert Southey: Poetical Works*, 1:xxxv–xxxvii.
18. M. Darmesteter, "Joan of Arc in England," 57 (907).
19. W. S. Scott, *Jeanne d'Arc*, 168.
20. K. Sullivan, "Justice magnanime des Anglais," 116.
21. Vale, *Ancient Enemy*, 91, 97. In an earlier work, Vale chides both Andrew Lang and Régine Pernoud for being "over-indulgent" toward Joan, revealing his disagreement over the importance of the Maid's role in establishing Charles as consecrated monarch and therefore highlighting the (admittedly) political motivations for the nullification of her original indictment: Vale, *Charles VII*, 53 n. 2. Ironically, the cover of Juliet Barker's 2012 *Conquest* features Jean-Jacques Scherrer's 1887 oil painting *L'Entrée de Jeanne d'Arc à Orléans*.
22. Butterfield, *Familiar Enemy*, 360.
23. Lanéry d'Arc, *Livre d'or*, 241.
24. Lanéry d'Arc, *Livre d'or*, 244.
25. Guthrie, *General History of England*, 2:533.
26. Guthrie, Gray et al., *General History of the World*, 193. Guillaume du Bellay explains, "they say that it was the King who devised this stratagem, to give hope to the French": *Instructions sur le faict de la guerre*, 56.
27. Thurston, "Blessed Joan of Arc in English Opinion," 450–51.
28. Thurston, "Blessed Joan of Arc in English Opinion," 453.
29. Thurston, "Blessed Joan of Arc in English Opinion," 458–59.
30. Lingard, *History of England*, 420. Later editions greatly amplify Joan's story.
31. Lightbody, *Judgements of Joan*, 155.
32. Full reference to these and other works mentioned below may be found in the bibliography. The French view that the English unremittingly demonized Joan, to the extent of using her name as a bogey to frighten children, is enthusiastically expressed by Lorenzi de Bradi, "Jeanne d'Arc dans la littérature anglaise. I," 194.
33. Dunand, "Légende anglaise de Jeanne d'Arc," 15.
34. These include Sevin, *Jeanne d'Arc dans la littérature anglaise contemporaine*; Rapp, *Jeanne d'Arc in der englischen und amerikanischen Literatur*; Newman, "Joan of Arc in English Literature"; Keyser, *Joan of Arc in Nineteenth-Century English Literature*; C. B. Saunders, *Women Writers and the Nineteenth Century*, 79–102. I show that the domestication of Joan of Arc began earlier than Saunders considers—with Hume.
35. Flower, *Joan of Arc*, 2.
36. Margolis, "Rewriting the Right."
37. De Quincey, "Joan of Arc," 185.
38. Fuller, *Holy State and Profane State*, 376.
39. Bandel, "English Chroniclers' Attitude Toward Women," 113–18.
40. Baker's *Chronicle* was reprinted almost a dozen times until 1733, including a translation into Dutch, an "Abridgement," and a continuation through the reign of Charles II.
41. Sir Walter Scott, *Letters on Demonology and Witchcraft*, 199.

CHAPTER 1

Preliminary material from this chapter was presented at the Forty-Eighth International Congress on Medieval

Studies, Western Michigan University in May 2013.

1. For Henry's presence in the city, see Basin, *Histoire de Charles VII*, 160, and Wolffe, *Henry VI*, 59. According to Grummitt, "Henry kept a splendid court while at Rouen": *Henry VI*, 78.
2. Du Fresne de Beaucourt, *Histoire de Charles VII*, 281.
3. M.-R. McLaren, *London Chronicles*, 86; Kingsford, *English Historical Literature*, 84. The earliest manuscript of the Chronicle cannot be dated definitively, but its account of the events of 1431 was nearly contemporaneous.
4. According to the testimony of Thomas Marie in Duparc, 1:238–39. Tellingly, although several of the original seventy articles of indictment emphasize Joan's trafficking with demons and her witchcraft (*sortilegiis*), none of the final twelve articles does so. See Tisset, 1:193 and 290–97. A recent study of Jan Hus's 1415 heresy trial summarizes the canon law also underlying Joan's case: Fudge, *Trial of Jan Hus*. C. Taylor translates a 1430 letter to Hus's followers purporting to be from Joan but signed by her confessor, Jean Pasquerel, that places her in the role of scourge of heretics: *Joan of Arc*, 132–33.
5. Duparc, 1:352.
6. Doncoeur and Lanhers, *Réhabilitation de Jeanne la Pucelle*, 55; cf. Duparc, 1:435.
7. Duparc, 1:454.
8. Otway-Ruthven, *King's Secretaries*, 89–90; Le Cacheux, *Actes de la Chancellerie d'Henri VI*, 370–71.
9. Duparc, 1:224–25.
10. Duparc, 1:348–49.
11. Lefèvre-Pontalis, *Panique anglaise en mai 1429*, but see Waugh, "Joan of Arc in English Sources," 387–88.
12. Duparc, 1:320.
13. Monstrelet, *Chronique*, 4:326. Cf. Wavrin, *Recueil des croniques*, 294–95.
14. Duparc, 1:412.
15. Duparc, 1:447–48. Vale attributes such claims to politically based self-exculpation in the "carefully staged rehabilitation trial": *Ancient Enemy*, 96.
16. C. Taylor, *Joan of Arc*, 73 (his translation). These conclusions are from a summary; the actual record of the hearing does not survive.
17. Christine de Pizan, "*Ditié de Jehanne d'Arc*," lines 241–44.
18. Challet and Forrest, "Masses," 292; Barnay discusses spiritual dimensions in "Jeanne d'Arc et le prophétisme féminin," 237–44.
19. *De mirabili victoria*, in C. Taylor, *Joan of Arc*, 81.
20. *De bono et malo spiritu*, in C. Taylor, *Joan of Arc*, 126–30.
21. Barker, *Conquest*, 103, for example.
22. Tisset, 1:169.
23. Tisset, 1:242.
24. Tisset, 1:153.
25. Contamine, Bouzy, and Hélary, *Jeanne d'Arc: Histoire et dictionnaire*, 509.
26. On the origins and development of the conflict, see Curry, *Hundred Years War*, and Allmand, *Hundred Years War*.
27. As Curry notes, the treaty did not stipulate a *male* heir, and it "had the effect of ending Salic law in France": "Two Kingdoms, One King," 32.
28. Vaughan, *John the Fearless*, 266–68.
29. Stratford, "John, duke of Bedford (1389–1435)," *ODNB* online edition.
30. Vale, *Charles VII*, 25–26.
31. At the beginning of her trial, Joan was asked her name. The French *Minute* records, "She answered that, in the place where she was born, she was called Jeannette, and in France, Jeanne": Tisset, 1:40–41. I have chosen, where possible, to translate Joan's testimony from the *Minute française* as it was reprinted in Tisset, hoping it captures a trace of Joan's actual words and tone; see Hanawalt and Noakes, "Trial Transcript, Romance, Propaganda," 607, and Tisset, 1:xxi–xxx. The notes of each day's interrogation were transcribed

contemporaneously by some of the notaries present and later used as the basis for the Latin redaction. Karen Sullivan argues that the transcripts represent an ultimately irreconcilable clash between the worldviews of the ecclesiasts and ordinary people: *Interrogation of Joan of Arc*. Translations from the Latin are to be found in C. Taylor, *Joan of Arc*, and in Hobbins, *Trial of Joan of Arc*. Any similarities in phrasing or word choice are coincidental, not intentional.

32. Charles's chamberlain Perceval de Boulainvilliers wrote to the duke of Milan in June 1429 that Joan was born "in nocte Epiphaniarum Domini" (on the evening of the Lord's Epiphany): Quicherat, *Procès*, 5:116. Given the fantastic content of other parts of the letter, the date seems spurious, if appropriate for constructing a legend. Nevertheless, Vita Sackville-West incorporated it as part of the title of her biography, *Saint Joan of Arc: Born, January 6th, 1412*. Krumeich reviews the inauthenticity yet widespread acceptance of that date in "La date de la naissance," 21–31.

33. Tisset, 1:41. Around May 1429, Jean Dupuy, bishop of Cahors, included in his *Collectarium historiarum* the statement that Joan was "seventeen years of age": C. Taylor, *Joan of Arc*, 90. An anonymous letter dated June 1429 states that she was eighteen years old "or thereabouts" (91). See also Pernoud, *Joan of Arc: By Herself*, 28, and Pernoud, *Jeanne d'Arc par elle-même*.

34. Tisset, 1:47.

35. Tisset, 1:48.

36. In addition to C. Taylor's *Joan of Arc* and Hobbins's *Trial of Joan of Arc*, several books provide a thorough background to the career of Joan of Arc: Pernoud, *Joan of Arc: By Herself*, which intersperses primary documents with commentary; Pernoud, *Retrial of Joan of Arc*; Pernoud and Clin, *Joan of Arc: Her Story*; Fraioli, *Early Debate*; L. J. Taylor, *Virgin Warrior*; and Castor, *Joan of Arc*.

37. Tisset, 1:426–30.

38. Doncoeur and Lanhers, *Réhabilitation de Jeanne la Pucelle*, 33.

39. Tisset, 1:221–22.

40. Duparc, 1:393.

41. Tisset, 1:128. The Latin is consistent: "in Angliam."

42. Tisset, 1:84. On the political implications of Cauchon's question about the language St. Margaret spoke, see Butterfield, *Familiar Enemy*, 364–66.

43. C. Taylor, *Joan of Arc*, 109 (his translation). Even though Chartier uses the word "nation," Vale cautions that "we may . . . have to be rather careful about how we define 'nacion' or *natio* at this time. 'Nation' in the modern sense will probably not do, as the medieval *natio* could mean a 'people' rather than the inhabitants of a sovereign nation-state": *Ancient Enemy*, 77. This caution seems pertinent to how a medieval woman such as Joan of Arc might have perceived the matter. See also Ruggier, "Nation," 23–26.

44. C. Taylor, *Joan of Arc*, 4 and map, xiii.

45. Tisset, 1:46.

46. Tisset, 1:63.

47. Duparc, 1:279. It is possible that they had a closer relationship. The translator of Pernoud, *Joan of Arc: By Herself*, glosses the word as "godfather" (32n). L. Taylor suggests that Joan was godmother to d'Epinal's son: *Virgin Warrior*, 220 n. 60. D'Epinal was among several villagers who went to Châlons in July to see Joan accompany Charles on the road to Reims.

48. Tisset, 1:63–64. Presumably, what the Burgundians "must" do is to ally with the king of France.

49. Tisset, 1:295. "Revelation" is a complex theological term. According to the *Catholic Encyclopedia*, it connotes

"The communication of some truth by God to a rational creature through means which are beyond the ordinary course of nature": Joyce, "Revelation." The original article 38, addressing the question of whether Joan's voices told her to hate the Burgundians, does not employ this term; rather, she was asked whether the voice told her. Tisset, 1:239.
50. Tisset, 1:38.
51. Perroy, *Hundred Years War*, 282. Luce writes, "This border of Lorraine, on the frontiers of Germany, was not the route of the English. The Treaty of Troyes had established them in Champagne, but they occupied only a small number of positions": *Jeanne d'Arc à Domrémy*, xix.
52. For the era of Joan of Arc, see Armstrong, *England, France, and Burgundy*, 343–74. For the reign of Charles VII, see J. Ferguson, *English Diplomacy*, 1–34.
53. During her trial, she was asked if she had cited a man from Toul, and she answered, "I did not have him cited, but it was he who had me cited . . . and finally [said] that she had not made him any promise": Tisset, 1:123. See Beaulande-Barraud, "'Fiançailles' rompues de Jeanne."
54. Longnon, "Limites de la France," 527–28; Duparc, 5:139–42.
55. Girardot, "Entre France, Empire et Bourgogne," 201. See also Hamy, *Livre de Gilles de Bouvier*, 45; Contamine, "Le Barrois et la Lorraine"; and Dauphant, "'Fille de la frontière.'"
56. The map on p. 38 of Curry, *Hundred Years War*, shows Edward III's army in 1359–60 as far east as Châlons. The map on p. 62 depicting the major campaigns of 1415–28 shows no fighting near the Meuse. The map on p. 87, however, suggests that English control did extend to the Meuse. Aimond claimed that "[the English] had likewise already crossed the Meuse, and beyond the regions of Verdun and Bar, the English influence had reached with its weapons, even so far as the region of Toul": *Relations de la France et du Verdunois*, 244.
57. Grateful thanks to Aleksandr Lobanov, then a doctoral student working with Anne Curry, for this information, from an email dated October 20, 2013. Nogent-le-Roi and Montigny-le-Roi are now part of Val-de-Meuse. The names of two of the soldiers mentioned in documents relating to these garrisons printed in Luce, *Jeanne d'Arc à Domrémy*, 191–92, appear in Curry's database, "The Soldier in Later Medieval England."
58. Luce, *Jeanne d'Arc à Domrémy*, cli–clii and note; for the regent's reply, see 317–18.
59. Curry, "English Armies," 52. According to Newhall, "the Earl of Warwick had jurisdiction over the frontiers of France, Vermandois, Champagne, Brie and the Gâtinais": *Muster and Review*, 46.
60. L. Taylor, *Virgin Warrior*, 5.
61. Girardot, "Entre France, Empire et Bourgogne," 202. Bouzy reproduces a document dated 1425 showing Jacques was living in Vouthon at that time: "Famille de Jeanne d'Arc," 36.
62. Servais, *Annales historiques du Barrois*, 96–99.
63. *Chronicle of Jean de Venette*, 131.
64. Quicherat, "Récit des tribulations," 359. The English translation is by Birdsall: *Chronicle of Jean de Venette*, 253.
65. C. J. Rogers, "By Fire and Sword," 35. See also Boutruche, "Devastation of Rural Areas," 23–59, and C. Taylor, *Chivalry and the Ideals of Knighthood*, 217–27.
66. Buirette, *Histoire de la ville de Sainte-Ménehould*, 168.
67. Luce, *Jeanne d'Arc à Domrémy*, xlvii and note. See also Ayroles, *Vraie Jeanne d'Arc*, 2:263–64.

68. Luce, *Jeanne d'Arc à Domrémy*, lxii–lxiv; Gillet, *Sermaize et Jeanne d'Arc*, 63–65; L. Champion, *Jeanne d'Arc, écuyère*, 29–30.
69. Curry, "English Armies," 40.
70. Calmet, *Histoire de Lorraine*, 7:clxxxix; Debout, *Bienheureuse Jeanne d'Arc*, 1:82–83.
71. Aimond, *Relations de la France et du Verdunois*, 244.
72. Girardot, "Entre France, Empire et Bourgogne," 202.
73. J. H. Rowe, "John Duke of Bedford and the Norman 'Brigands,'" 583–600. A fair amount is known about English brigands marauding throughout Normandy, including the famous Richard Venables; less is known about what was happening in the east.
74. N. Wright, *Knights and Peasants*, 89–95; see also J. H. Rowe, "John Duke of Bedford and the Norman 'Brigands,'" 585–86.
75. Gillet describes two possible routes: *Sermaize et Jeanne d'Arc*, 63–65. L. Champion proposed another: *Jeanne d'Arc, écuyère*, 28–29.
76. Fraioli touches on what Joan might have known about the circumstances of the war itself: *Joan of Arc and the Hundred Years War*, 58–61.
77. Luce, *Jeanne d'Arc à Domrémy*, lv.
78. Martin, *Métier de predicateur*, 12.
79. Briand, "Foi, politique et information," 90.
80. L. Taylor, *Soldiers of Christ*, 146–47.
81. Marot, *Neufchâteau en Lorraine au Moyen Age*, 113.
82. Allmand, *Hundred Years War*, 33.
83. Duparc, 1:305.
84. Duparc, 1:290.
85. L. Paris, "Écosse," 27, items 4838 (James I's letter, dated July 19, 1428) and 4839 (Charles VII's letter dated October 30, 1428).
86. Raknem, *Joan of Arc in History*, 10. Several itineraries for Joan from 1428 until the spring of 1429 have been essayed by Pernoud and Clin, *Joan of Arc: Her Story*, 266–67, and Bouzy, "Essai d'itinéraire de Jeanne d'Arc," 13–20.
87. Duparc, 1:258.
88. Tisset, 1:64.
89. Duparc, 1:305. Jean Morel of Greux also testified to having heard this; see Duparc, 1:253–54.
90. De Bouteiller and de Braux, *Famille de Jeanne d'Arc*, 27.
91. Chevreux and Louis, *Département des Vosges*, 7:242.
92. According to Jean Morel. Duparc, 1:253.
93. Duparc, 1:467. Jean Moreau, also from Viville, testified to his knowledge about Joan and her family: Duparc, 1:462.
94. Liébaut, *Mothe*, 13–14.
95. Duparc, 5:172–81, discusses her travels during this period taking into account the distances.
96. Duparc, 1:294; C. Taylor, *Joan of Arc*, 142 n. 12.
97. Duparc, 1:295–96.
98. Duparc, 1:305. Easter fell on April 4 that year, so Ascension Day was May 13. Cheny, *Handbook of Dates*, 110.
99. Tisset, 1:126–27.
100. At her trial, Joan testified that "for fear of the Burgundians, she left her father's house and went to Neufchâteau, in Lorraine, to the home of a woman named La Rousse, where she stayed for about fifteen days": Tisset, 1:46.
101. Pernoud and Clin, *Joan of Arc: Her Story*, 19.
102. Neufchâteau lay along the old Roman road from Langres to Trèves. "From this route a road branched off at Neufchâteau that ran along the valley of the Meuse, and passing by Domrémy, Vaucouleurs and Verdun led towards Belgium": Marot, *Neufchâteau en Lorraine au Moyen Age*, 22. As well, "by its geographical situation, Toul was an important commercial crossroads, at the heart of a vast diocese. It was a fortified and prosperous location": Heilig, "Collections."
103. Duparc, 1:290.

104. Duparc, 1:306.
105. Mark Twain puts Bedford's later words into the soldier's mouth: *Personal Recollections of Joan of Arc*, 89.
106. Du Fresne de Beaucourt, *Histoire de Charles VII*, 197 n. 1.
107. Pernoud, *Joan of Arc: By Herself*, 43–44; Henzler, *Die Frauen Karls VII. und Ludwigs XI.*, 126–27; and Beaune, *Jeanne d'Arc*, 97–99; this hypothesis is disputed by L. Taylor, *Virgin Warrior*, 35.
108. J. Ferguson, *English Diplomacy*, 178–85. The list of envoys from England to France demonstrates that most of the traffic took place after the Treaty of Arras in 1434.
109. For the letter, see C. Taylor, *Joan of Arc*, 74–76.
110. Quicherat transcribes a manuscript discovered in the mid-nineteenth century outlining justifications for the celebration of May 8 in Orléans that preserves the account of an older citizen recalling what he knew or witnessed of Joan's presence in the city: *Procès*, 5:290.
111. Duparc, 1:363.
112. K. DeVries, *Joan of Arc*, 61. A "boulevard," according to DeVries, "was a low earthwork defense that was generally placed before a vulnerable gate or wall. In essence, it was a gunpowder artillery fortification, its defense derived from a large number of guns and, in English boulevards at least, longbowmen."
113. Duparc, 1:363–64. Pernoud and Clin identify Granville as "a 'renegade' Norman": *Joan of Arc: Her Story*, 42.
114. *Journal du siège d'Orléans*, 79.
115. Godefroy, *Dictionnaire de l'ancienne langue française*, 7:183; "Ribaud," *Dictionnaire du Moyen Français*.
116. K. DeVries, *Joan of Arc*, 60.
117. *Journal du siège d'Orléans*, 79.
118. Quicherat, *Procès*, 5:290–91, adding, "And so he did, just as will be made known hereafter." On Glasdale's earlier career, see Lefèvre-Pontalis, "Épisodes de l'invasion anglaise," 501.
119. Duparc, 1:321.
120. *Journal du siège d'Orléans*, 80.
121. Duparc, 1:393.
122. Duparc, 1:394. "Armagnacs" refers to those Frenchmen who sided with Charles.
123. Duparc, 1:395.
124. Quicherat, *Procès*, 4:463.
125. Quicherat, *Procès*, 5:291.
126. Duparc, 1:392.
127. Duparc, 1:366.
128. Monstrelet, *Chronique*, 4:388.
129. Jouffroy, *Ad Pium Papam II*, 138.
130. Quicherat, "Supplément," 65–66.
131. Gilles de Roye, *Chronique*, 1:208. Ayroles establishes the date as June 6: *Vraie Jeanne d'Arc*, 3:459n.
132. Nicolas and Tyrrell, *Chronicle of London*, 170.
133. Duparc, 1:264, 291.
134. Duparc, 1:473, 367.
135. Duparc, 1:340. Several other deponents said essentially the same, such as Guillaume de Ricarville, who said, "She stopped the armed troops when they blasphemed the name of God or swore in vain; and when they committed any evil, or did any violence, she reproved them": Duparc, 1:330.
136. Duparc, 1:407–8. See also the *Chronique de la Pucelle*, which, relying largely on this deposition, differs in small details, but repeats the phrase "[nous] remenerons un godon" (292). Perhaps this was on May 3, when one Raoulet de Recourt was reimbursed 20 *sous parisis* from the town accounts for a shad presented to Joan: Pernoud, *Joan of Arc: By Herself*, 85.
137. Duparc, 1:327.
138. Duparc, 1:431–32.
139. Duparc, 1:349.
140. Quicherat, *Procès*, 5:142. C. Taylor translates the French word "bran" as "shit": C. Taylor, *Joan of Arc*, 235. The word "bran" could mean excrement, although Godefroy does not gloss the word as obscene. But the *Dictionnaire du Moyen Français* suggests that in the

fifteenth century, it was equivalent to today's *merde*.
141. Duparc, 1:406.
142. Hillman analyzes the broader connotations of the word in the fifteenth century in "La Pucelle and the Godons," 167–88. See *Mystère du siège d'Orléans*, lines 4741–42 and 10913–14. Olivier Maillard inveighs against corrupt priests as "gross *goddons*, damned, infamous, and written in the book of the devil": *Sermones de adventus*, fol. 31v.
143. Gérold, *Manuscrit de Bayeux*, 103, chanson 87.
144. Rickard, *Britain in Medieval French Literature*, 176–77. An eighteenth-century note states, "*La Godale* derives from the sweet beer that fattens the English." Agrippa d'Aubigné, *Avantures du Baron de Fœneste*, 382. See also Thurston, "Fleur de Lys and Two Godons," 416–20.
145. Ditcham, "'Mutton Guzzlers and Wine Bags,'" 1–13. Le Roux de Lincy includes a song that calls for an uprising against "ces godons, panches à poys" (these paunchy godons): *Recueil de chants historiques français*, 300. Citing a lyric that refers to "ces paillars godons d'Angleterre" (these bawdy godons of England), Montaiglon adds, "The word was applied especially to the English, and Joan of Arc nearly always called them that": *Recueil des poésies françoise*, 79. "Nearly always" is an exaggeration.
146. Cotgrave, *Dictionarie of the French and English Tongues*, fol. Tti r.
147. Sainte-Palaye, *Dictionnaire historique de l'ancien langage françois*, 6:402. Rickard concludes that *godon* derives "from the addiction of English soldiers to blasphemous utterance," and notes "a verb 'godoner' ([meaning] 'to swear' and by extension 'to grumble') survives in the Cotentin region of Normandy": *Britain in Medieval French Literature*, 176 n. 4.
148. Quicherat, *Procès*, 3:122.
149. Godefroy, *Dictionnaire de l'ancienne langue française*, 4:301. Luce glosses it as "a popular nickname given to the English": *Jeanne d'Arc à Domrémy*, v. Duparc glosses "un godon" as "blasphemateur anglais" (English blasphemer): 4:89. I had accepted this etymology before undertaking research for this chapter, and perpetuated the error in my annotations to Mary Hays's biography of Joan: Orgelfinger, "Joan d'Arc"; Hays, *Female Biography*.
150. *OED* online edition, s.v. "God-damn(-me)."
151. Articles 47 (Tisset, 1:246) and 66 (Tisset, 1:283).
152. Monstrelet reproduced the French version addressed to Philip of Burgundy: *Chronique*, 4:442–47. Wijsman details the dissemination of Monstrelet's work in the sixteenth century: "History in Transition," 204–23.
153. M.-R. McLaren, *London Chronicles*, 86–87.
154. Tisset, 1:427.
155. Not only based on his testimony to the Privy Council. An ugly story surfaced during the nullification hearings, related by the notary Boisguillaume (Guillaume Colles). He had heard it said—but he could not remember by whom—that while certain matrons, including Anne, Duchess of Bedford, examined Joan to ascertain her virginity, "the Duke of Bedford stood in a secret place from which he could see Joan visited": Duparc, 1:438. Bedford was indeed resident in Rouen at the time.
156. Tisset, 1:221.
157. Monstrelet, *Chronique*, 4:341. Is there a sardonic echo in this admittedly formulaic "greeting" of Joan of Arc's letter of challenge to the English assembled before Orléans in March? Jeffrey Jerome Cohen suggested to me that this verbal echo might have been deliberate. For chroniclers of the various factions in the fifteenth century, see Le Brusque,

"Chronicling the Hundred Years War," 77–92.
158. According to Wolffe, the source of rumors that Bedford had mishandled the war is not known: *Henry VI*, 71–72. C. Taylor attributes the accusations "almost certainly" to Gloucester: *Joan of Arc*, 238.
159. H. Nicolas, *Proceedings and Ordinances*, 222–23. The Earl of Salisbury had died of wounds suffered at Orléans in the fall of 1428.
160. Harriss discusses Bedford's regency and how his and Salisbury's "alternative and conflicting strategies" crystallized around the siege of Orléans: *Shaping the Nation*, 551–53. See also C. Taylor, *Joan of Arc*, 238–39.
161. Barker, *Conquest*, 95–97.

CHAPTER 2

1. J. Howell, *Epistolae Ho-Elianae*, 139–40.
2. Evelyn, *Diary*, 137. Descriptions of the statue vary widely because it was at least twice destroyed and rebuilt. See Brun, "Premier Monument à Jeanne d'Arc," 70–76, and Heimann, *Joan of Arc in French Art and Culture*, 7, 45, and plate 4.
3. Brennan, *Origins of the Grand Tour*, 83.
4. G. C. Moore Smith, *Gabriel Harvey's Marginalia*, 90, 92, 96. The term "virago" is not so simple. Its English definition as "warrior" coexisted with a negative gender connotation from the third quarter of the fourteenth century: *OED* online edition, s.v. "virago."
5. On English hostility to Joan, see Goy-Blanquet, "Shakespeare and Voltaire."
6. Martyn, *Historie and Lives of Twentie Kings of England*, 221–23.
7. Vale, *Ancient Enemy*, 96.
8. Duparc, 1:454.
9. M-R. McLaren, *London Chronicles*, 85.
10. Waugh, "Joan of Arc in English Sources," 392. Clermont-Ferrand summarizes the chroniclers' attitude toward Joan as "silence, absence, and demonization": "Joan of Arc and the English Chroniclers," 154.
11. Perroy, *Hundred Years War*, 281.
12. Rollison, *Commonwealth of the People*, 267–72 (Sharpe) and 275–78 (Cade).
13. Tisset, 1:283, trans. Hobbins, *Trial of Joan of Arc*, 153.
14. M.-R. McLaren, *London Chronicles*, 81.
15. Given-Wilson, *Chronicles*, 185–86.
16. Scholars do not agree about the dating of these manuscripts, but for my purposes, exact dates are not crucial. See Kingsford, *Chronicles of London*, viii–ix; M.-R. McLaren, *London Chronicles*, 100 n. 6.
17. Representing this version, M.-R. McLaren quotes St. John's College MS 57, which she identifies as a copy of an earlier source: *London Chronicles*, 86.
18. British Library MS Cotton Julius B II, quoted in Kingsford, *Chronicles of London*, 96.
19. British Library MS Cotton Cleopatra C IV, quoted in Kingsford, *Chronicles of London*, 133.
20. M.-R. McLaren, *London Chronicles*, 85.
21. M.-R. McLaren, *London Chronicles*, 89.
22. M.-R. McLaren argues that mentioning Joan dressed in armor is sufficient "to indicate her perversion": *London Chronicles*, 86 n. 89.
23. Kingsford, *English Historical Literature*, 93; *Brut*, 2:478–82. Keen notes the political dimension of both Dame Eleanor's and Joan of Arc's trials: *England in the Later Middle Ages*, 308, 337.
24. M.-R. McLaren, *London Chronicles*, 89.
25. Wolffe, *Henry VI*, 270, and Harriss, *Shaping the Nation*, 627–31. Henry's maternal grandfather, Charles VI of France, also suffered increasingly debilitating mental illness. See Green, *Hundred Years War*, 105–6.
26. E. Meek, "Practice of English Diplomacy," 64.
27. Speed, *Historie*, 857. All citations to Speed are to the second, revised edition of 1623. Maurer, *Margaret of Anjou*, 187.
28. Maurer, *Margaret of Anjou*, 175–78.

29. Wolffe, *Henry VI*, 4–7 and 351–58.
30. Henry VII was the grandson of Catherine of Valois by her second husband, Owen Tudor, although his claim to the throne derived from his mother, Margaret Beaufort, a great-great-granddaughter of Edward III of England.
31. Vale, *Charles VII*, 61–64.
32. Akehurst, "Good Name, Reputation, and Notoriety." Unsurprisingly, King Henry's letter scorns this elevation: "And she dressed herself also in arms bestowed on knights and squires, raised a standard, and with the greatest contempt, pride, and presumption, demanded to have and to bear the most noble and excellent arms of France": Tisset, 1:426.
33. Vale examines Joan and Charles's association in *Charles VII*, 45–69. Mention of "deux entreprises secretes" involving Jean Dunois in the spring of 1431 are suggestive, but in no way confirm a plan to rescue Joan; Du Fresne de Beaucourt, *Histoire de Charles VII*, 255 and note. The ambiguities of status and the intricacies of ransom are discussed by Green, *Hundred Years War*, 221–29. As he notes, there was "friction between obligations of honour and the pragmatism of national self-interest" (222).
34. C. Taylor, *Joan of Arc*, 42.
35. C. Taylor, *Joan of Arc*, 352.
36. Chastellain, *Chronique*, 2:203.
37. Martial de Paris, *Poésies*, 120, 122.
38. Matheson, "Historical Prose," 210.
39. Matheson, *Prose Brut*, 3.
40. *Brut*, 2:501.
41. Matheson concludes that Caxton "was the compiler of the continuation from 1419 to 1461," the version of the *Brut* that includes the story of Joan's pregnancy: *Prose Brut*, 164. See also Matheson, "Printer and Scribe."
42. Hanawalt, "Golden Ages."
43. Even though women in the context of war are important ethical touchstones in medieval English literature, "especially rare is the image of the woman who takes up arms," according to Corrine Saunders, "Women and Warfare in Medieval English Writing," 209. However, in France, at least, they were not seen to be anomalous: Contamine, *War in the Middle Ages*, 241–42.
44. Bandel, "English Chroniclers' Attitude Toward Women." Maud is the English version of Matilda, which I use to avoid confusion with other contemporary royal Matildas, particularly the wives of Henry I and Stephen of Blois.
45. Plummer and Earle, *Two of the Saxon Chronicles Parallel*, 1:105, 103; Wainwright, "Æthelfled, Lady of the Mercians."
46. Henry, Archdeacon of Huntingdon, *Historia Anglorum*, 309.
47. William of Malmesbury, *Gesta regum Anglorum*, 1:199. It is not at all clear where Malmesbury got this anecdote, or if there was any truth in it. Dockray-Miller suggests that a difficult first birth along with her husband's debilitating illness might have led to Ælfleda's chastity "by default rather than design": *Motherhood and Mothering in Anglo-Saxon England*, 63.
48. Beem reads accounts of Maud's career as gendered in "Virtuous Virago," 85–98.
49. William of Newburgh, *History of English Affairs*, 63.
50. *Gesta Stephani*, 119.
51. William of Malmesbury, *Gesta regum Anglorum*, 2:381.
52. For Malmesbury's diction, see K. Fenton, *Gender, Nation, and Conquest*, 50–52. See also LoPrete, "Gendering Viragos," 17–38.
53. McLaughlin, "Woman Warrior," 200.
54. Stafford, "Portrayal of Royal Women in England," 157.
55. Huston, "Matrix of War," 163.
56. In the sixteenth century, French detractors would impugn Joan's chastity. Notable among them was du

Haillan, who alleged, "Some say this Joan was the whore [garce] of Jean, the Bastard of Orleans, others say of the Lord Baudricourt, Marshal of France": *De l'Estat et succez des affaires de France*, 69.
57. Tisset, 1:123.
58. Duparc, 1:387.
59. Boethius, *Scotorum Historia*, fol. CCCLVIII (my translation).
60. According to Isambart de la Pierre, Joan said that "she had been subject to many wrongs and injuries in prison": Doncoeur and Lanhers, *Réhabilitation de Jeanne la Pucelle*, 37. Guillaume Manchon testified that certain guards had tried to violate her: Duparc, 1:181. Later, he elaborated that she resumed her male clothing to protect her virginity against such threats: Duparc, 1:427. Martin Ladvenu said that "a certain great English lord had entered her cell and attempted to seize her by force": Duparc, 1:442. See also C. Taylor, *Joan of Arc*, 26.
61. Warren, "Joan of Arc, Margaret of Anjou, and Malory's Guenevere," 142–43. Caxton, who resided in Bruges for many years, would presumably have known about European prison conditions. (It is intriguing to speculate whether Caxton, who was close to the Burgundian court, had heard something about the nullification trial.) See also C. Taylor, *Joan of Arc*, 26. Nevertheless, from the end of the fourteenth century in England, there is evidence of segregation of the sexes in prisons: Pugh, *Imprisonment in Medieval England*, 357–58.
62. Oldham, "On Pleading the Belly," 2; De Haas and Hall, *Early Registers of Writs*, lxxvii–lxxviii.
63. Forbes, "Jury of Matrons," 24–25.
64. For different reasons, a similar practice was evidently customary in France, as Joan's virginity was examined by women at least twice. C. Taylor, *Joan of Arc*, 48.
65. Blackstone, *Commentaries*, 388. See Hale, *Historia placitorum coronæ*, 368, and Hanawalt, "Women Before the Law," 189.
66. Forbes cites three cases from the thirteenth century: "Jury of Matrons," 26. For additional examples, see *Close Rolls of the Reign of Henry III*, 501; Sayles, *Select Cases*, 56; Oldham, "On Pleading the Belly," 3; and De Haas and Hall, *Early Registers*, 75.
67. Neville, "Gaol Delivery in the Border Counties," 57–58; Oldham, "On Pleading the Belly," appendix 2, 37.
68. Blatcher, *Court of King's Bench*, 52.
69. Sims, "Secondary Offenders," 71.
70. Dolan, "Tracking the Petty Traitor," 156. Levin examines the *Brut's* claim in the political and cultural contexts of Shakespeare's *1 Henry VI*, concluding that "presenting Joan as lying about a pregnancy and fearful of death would be another way for the English to destroy her reputation and credibility": "'Murder not then the fruit within my womb,'" 79–80.
71. Holinshed, *Chronicles*, 3:171. As we shall see in chapter 4, the 1587 edition added much material, all of it denouncing Joan.
72. Bernau, "'Saint, Witch, Man, Maid or Whore,'" 214.
73. According to Royan, "neither version is an entirely reliable witness to Boece's text": Royan, "Bellenden, John (c.1495–1545x8)," *ODNB*, online edition. See also Royan, "Relationship."
74. Bellenden, *Chronicles of Scotland compiled by Hector Boece*, 2:379.
75. Boece, *History of Scotland* (trans. Bellenden), 2:495.
76. Harikae, "John Bellenden's *Chronicles of Scotland*," 138.
77. Brown, "French Alliance or English Peace."
78. Royan, "Relationship," 138.
79. The book was published in one volume, but beginning with the reign of Richard II, the foliation/pagination

recommences. For clarity, I cite as if there were two volumes.
80. Woolf, "Genre into Artifact," 345.
81. Brownley, "Sir Richard Baker's Chronicle," 481.
82. Brownley, "Sir Richard Baker's Chronicle," 482.
83. Baker was not the first to refer to Joan as "subtle," with an undertone of its secondary meanings of "crafty," "devious," or "treacherous." At the opening of Charles VII's inquiry into the validity of the proceedings that had condemned Joan, Jean Beaupère, canon of Rouen and one of the chief questioners, recalled that "she was very subtle with the subtlety of a woman, as it seemed to him": Doncoeur and Lanhers, *Réhabilitation de Jeanne la Pucelle*, 57.
84. Vale, *Charles VII*, 58.
85. This probably refers to Monstrelet's claim that Joan ordered the Burgundian mercenary Franquet d'Arras to be beheaded shortly before she was captured: *Chronique*, 4:384–85. Joan had once jokingly threatened to cut off Dunois's head if he were tardy in informing her of fighting at Orléans, according to Jean d'Aulon, her steward. Duparc, 1:478.
86. Caldwell, "Hundred Years' War and National Identity," 245.
87. Royan, "National Martyrdom," 463.
88. Giry-Deloison, "France and England at Peace."
89. Maccoll, "Construction of England"; Schwyzer, "Archipelagic History," 599–601.
90. Womersley, *Divinity and State*, 32.
91. Bernau, "'Saint, Witch, Man, Maid or Whore,'" 218, 222.
92. I will discuss the two most famous sixteenth-century historians, Edward Hall and Raphael Holinshed, in the context of the "woman question" in chapter 3 and Shakespeare's *1 Henry VI* in chapter 4. For approaches to writing history in this period, see Kelley and Sacks, *Historical Imagination in Early Modern Britain*; Woolf, *Reading History in Early Modern England*; Shrank, *Writing the Nation in Reformation England*; Mottram, *Empire and Nation*; and A. B. Ferguson, *Clio Unbound*.
93. Trimble, "Early Tudor Historiography"; Hardin, "Chronicles and Mythmaking."
94. Rissanen, *Studies in Style and Narrative Technique*, 13.
95. Laine, "John Rastell and the Norman Conquest," 301.
96. Levy, *Tudor Historical Thought*, 200–201. This is somewhat the case for Robert Fabyan, for example; see Trimble, "Early Tudor Historiography," 33–34, and Bean, "Role of Robert Fabyan."
97. Royan compares the treatment of Joan of Arc and William Wallace as "icons of national identity": "National Martyrdom," 466–68.
98. Hay, *Polydore Vergil*, 9.
99. Fabyan, *New Chronicles*, 3. Goy-Blanquet concludes, "It is Fabyan, not Vergil, who inspires Hall's irate tones and sectarian views": "Shakespeare and Voltaire," 9.
100. In Ellis's edition of Fabyan, these accounts of Joan of Arc fall some forty pages apart.
101. On Gaguin's knowledge of the trial transcripts, see Contamine, "Jeanne d'Arc après Jeanne d'Arc (IV)," 408–9.
102. "Johane" is Latin, following Gaguin, not masculine, but later writers would make it so.
103. "Deus est qui revelavit": Gaguin, *Compendium*, fol. CXVII.
104. This is a mysterious comment, for neither Gaguin nor Monstrelet nor any of Fabyan's other named sources makes any such claim.
105. At this time, "wench" generally referred to a young female or one from the lower classes. But it did also refer to wantons. In the context in which Fabyan uses the word, it does not seem to be purposefully derogatory. See *OED* online edition, s.v. "wench."

106. Harashima, "Narrative Functions," 43–86.
107. Rastell, *"Pastyme of People,"* E3v.
108. Thurston, "Blessed Joan of Arc in English Opinion," 450–51. Thurston's perception of Rastell's lack of hostility toward Joan might be because he "liked to compare differing accounts, but he often refrained from choosing sides": Geritz and Laine, *John Rastell*, 68. Herman reads these abridgments of Fabyan's commentary as sympathetic: "Rastell's *Pastyme of People*," 283–84.
109. Rastell, *"Pastyme of People,"* 20.
110. Geritz suggests that it is possible Rastell had access to portions of Vergil's history in manuscript because of their mutual connections with the More circle: Rastell, *"Pastyme of People,"* 56 n. 102.
111. For Vergil's biography, see Vergil, *Anglica Historia*, ix–xi.
112. Vergil, *Anglica Historia*, xx n1.
113. Vergil, *Anglica Historia*, xxvii (ed. and trans. Hay): "It is in the dedication to Henry VIII of the *Anglica Historia* that we find the fullest of Vergil's statements of purpose.... The specific function of history [is] 'the only unique, certain, and faithful witness of times and things." It also reflects his obvious desire "to put a favourable interpretation on the rise of the house of Tudor" (xix).
114. Vergil, *Anglica Historia*, xxviii.
115. Hay, *Polydore Vergil*, 92.
116. Vergil, *Three Books of English History*, 227 (from an anonymous sixteenth-century translation).
117. Vergil, *Three Books of English History*, 22.
118. Hay, *Polydore Vergil*, 194.
119. Du Tillet, *Recueil des roys de France*, 163. He merely suggests that God may have acted through Joan as he had through the Old Testament heroines. The reference to disbelievers may be to Guillaume du Bellay de Langey who had asserted that "it was the King who had coached her in this deception"— that is, to claim she had been sent by God: *Instructions sur le faict de la guerre*, 56.
120. Biondi, *History of the Civill Warres*, 1:69.
121. Grimeston, *Generall Historie of France*, "To the Reader." G. N. Clark observed that de Serres's *Inventaire* "was well suited in style and contents to make French history known to foreign protestants": "Edward Grimeston, the Translator," 591. According to Boas, Grimeston both added to and abridged de Serres: "Edward Grimeston," 400.
122. Grimeston, *Generall Historie of France*, "To the Reader."
123. Levy, *Tudor Historical Thought*, 198–99.
124. In his *History of the Civill Warres*, Biondi observed of de Serres, "he is noted of falshood by his owne country men" (1:58).
125. Paulus Emilius Veronensis, *De rebus gestis Francorum*, 459–61. Paulus had died in 1529 before completing his work, which appeared first in 1543. Since Speed also cites Holinshed, who himself mentioned Du Tillet, it is not clear whether Speed ever read the French source directly.
126. Grimeston, *Generall Historie of France*, "To the Reader."
127. De Serres, *Inventaire général*, 732–33.
128. Trussell, *Continuation of the Collection*.

CHAPTER 3

Preliminary material from this chapter was presented at the 31st International Congress on Patristic, Medieval, and Renaissance Studies, Villanova University, October 2006, and the 50th International Congress on Medieval Studies, Western Michigan University, May 2015.

1. I will consider eighteenth-century collections such as Mary Hays's 1803 *Female Biography* in chapter 5 because they were influenced by Enlightenment

views of history and add a different social dimension to exemplarity. On the myriad connections between gender and history, see Spongberg, *Writing Women's History*. On the many genres that in some way encompass the "woman question," see Utley, *Crooked Rib*, and Woodbridge, *Women and the English Renaissance*.

2. M. Bailey, *Battling Demons*, 99.
3. See Elliott's reading of this passage in *Proving Woman*, 294–96. For the imposters, see Pernoud and Clin, *Joan of Arc: Her Story*, 233–35.
4. Nider, *Formicarium*, 387–88. Nider writes that he heard of the trial from one "Nicolao Amici," probably Nicholas Midi, of the University of Paris, tr. Coulton, 212n.
5. *Journal de Clément de Fauquebergue*, 3:13.
6. M. Bailey, *Battling Demons*, 28.
7. Nider, *Formicarium*, 351.
8. M. Bailey, *Battling Demons*, 3.
9. Kors and Peters, *Witchcraft in Europe*, 179.
10. *Malleus Maleficarum*, 1:1.
11. Purkiss, *Witch in History*, 239. For the religious, social, and political dimensions of witchcraft in the sixteenth century, see Sharpe, *Monuments of Darkness*.
12. Wrightson, *English Society*, 202.
13. Perhaps the most famous examples of heretics burned in England were Dr. Robert Barnes (in 1540, under Henry VIII) and Anne Askew (under Edward VI in 1546).
14. Gibson, *Witchcraft and Society*, 1–3.
15. Arber, *Transcript of the Registers*, 36. Coxe's statement was issued as a broadside by John Allde in 1561.
16. Heron-Allen, "Coxe, Francis (fl. 1560–1575)," rev. Kassell, *ODNB*, online edition.
17. Coxe, *Short Treatise*, fol. Biiii–Biiiiv. The second sentence is taken almost verbatim from Fabyan.
18. Scot, *Discovery of Witchcraft*, fol. C3.
19. Hall, *Union*, 148.
20. Bovet, *Pandaemonium*, 82–83.
21. Shakespeare, *King Henry VI Part I*.
22. Defoe, *Political History of the Devil*, 296.
23. Boulton, *Compleat History of Magick*, 172.
24. Hutchinson, *Historical Essay concerning Witchcraft*, 20.
25. Milton, "Heylyn, Peter (1599–1662)," *ODNB*, online edition; Rose, "Penthesilea," *Oxford Classical Dictionary*, 662.
26. Heylyn, *Microcosmos*, 127.
27. Heylyn, *Cosmographie*, 2:63.
28. Heylyn, *Survey of the Estate of France*, 143.
29. Lyndsay, *Works*, 97.
30. Alexander, *History of Women*, 2:62–63. Burstein situates Alexander's work in the philosophical debates about history and gender in the late eighteenth century: *Narrating Women's History*, 43–49.
31. M. Macleod, *Macleod's History of Witches*, 19–20.
32. As in *Quentin Durwood* (1823), *Minstrelcy of the Scottish Border* (1802–3), and *A Legend of Montrose* (1819).
33. Sir Walter Scott, *Heart of Midlothian*, 135. Boatright, "Demonology," 78–79.
34. Sir Walter Scott, *Letters on Demonology*, 196–7. See the discussion of the letter in Stabler, *Burke to Byron*, 245–51.
35. Sir Walter Scott, *Tales of a Grandfather*, 292.
36. Lyons, *Exemplum*, ix.
37. Wiseman, *Conspiracy and Virtue*, 34.
38. Jerome, *Against Jovinianus*, book 1, par. 41 (ed. Schaff and Wace, 6:379).
39. McLeod, *Virtue and Venom*, 43–47.
40. Benson, *Riverside Chaucer*, 114, lines 674–81.
41. Martin le Franc, *Champion des dames*, 4:104–5.
42. Boccaccio, *Famous Women*, 9. On Boccaccio and his immediate followers, see the summary in Spongberg, *Writing Women's History*, 38–39.

43. Curnow, "*Livre de la cité des Dames*"; Christine de Pizan, *Book of the City of Ladies*.
44. Downes, "Fashioning Christine de Pizan," 73.
45. Wiseman, *Conspiracy and Virtue*, 57.
46. Aylmer, *Harborowe*, D3. See also Osherow, *Biblical Women's Voices*, 83–84. For the complexity of the analogy, see A. N. McLaren, *Political Culture*, 23–31.
47. Wiseman, *Conspiracy and Virtue*, 48.
48. Booth, *How to Make It as a Woman*, 110.
49. Agrippa, *Declamation*, 27–29. Both Rabil's introduction to the text and the editors' introduction to the series (The Other Voice in Early Modern Europe, edited by Margaret King and Rabil) provide succinct and clear background to this genre.
50. The English quotations and all page citations are to Clapham, who generally abridges the Latin.
51. *PL* 29:37–39.
52. "Iam quis satis laudare poterit puellam illam nobilissimam." Agrippa, *De nobilitate*, C5; trans. Rabil, 88.
53. Care, *Female Pre-eminence*, 66–67. Through his mother, Henrietta Maria, daughter of Henri IV of France, Charles II of England (presumably "the most Christian King") was a direct descendent of Charles VII of France.
54. According to Schwoerer, Care was setting himself up as a defender of women as if the *querelle* had reignited, in order to sell more books: *Ingenious Mr. Henry Care*, 30.
55. Crompton, "The Glory of Women," 37–38.
56. The translation is not, as James Turner states, "straightforward": *One Flesh*, 110.
57. On iconoclasm, see Duffy, *Stripping of the Altars*.
58. Hall, *Union*, 159.
59. See "Injunctions for Religious Reform" in Hughes and Larkin, *Tudor Royal Proclamations*, 1:394.
60. Originally, Boisteau translated only six tales. An expanded collection with additional translations by Belleforest appeared in Paris, 1559; another edition was printed in Lyon in 1564.
61. Bandello, *Novelle*, part 3, novella 17, 1595–1607.
62. Belleforest, *18 Histoires tragiques*, 390.
63. G. Fenton, *Certaine Tragicall Discourses*, 244. *OED* online edition, s.v. "forged." In the mid-sixteenth century, "forged" could connote "counterfeit, false, spurious." Joan did indeed testify that she offered up a sword and armor at St. Denis: Tisset, 1:170.
64. Hadfield, "Fenton, Sir Geoffrey (*c.*1539–1608)," *ODNB* online edition.
65. *Byble in English*, 511.
66. When first introducing Joan, Hall writes that "she as a monster was sent to the Dolphin, by Sir Robert Bandrencort": *Union*, 148.
67. Stow also called Joan "a monstrous woman, named Ioan la pucelle de dieu" in his *Annales* (606). Rabbe maintains that this is Stow's mistranslation of Gaguin's "prodigue," or prodigal/prodigious: *Jeanne d'Arc en Angleterre*, 65. Grene, for one, overlooks the end of Hall's account, stating that "Hall had so very little time for Joan that he gave hardly any details of her story": *Shakespeare's Serial History Plays*, 71.
68. Aylmer, *Harborowe*, fol. F4.
69. Newstead, *Apology for women*, A3.
70. L. B. Wright, *Middle-Class Culture in Elizabethan England*, 490 n. 45.
71. Heywood, *Gynaikeion*, fol. A4. The title page gives the first word in Greek, which refers to an interior domestic space reserved for women. Parenthetical page numbers refer to this edition.
72. According to Geoffrey of Monmouth, Gwendolyn married one of the sons of the legendary founder of Britain, Brutus. When her husband died, she murdered his mistress and ruled the

kingdom in her own right until her son came of age: *History of the Kings of Britain*, 60–61.

73. As early as 1547, the *Mirouer des femmes vertueuses* had identified Joan's voices as "la Vierge Marie, et . . . madame saincte Katherine et madame saincte Agnès" (fol. A.ii).

74. Joan had just been questioned about the various swords in her possession at different times. She said she carried a sword she had captured from a Burgundian "right up to Compiègne, because this was a good sword for war, and good for giving hard clouts and strong blows": Tisset, 1:76–78, and C. Taylor, *Joan of Arc*, 155–57, whose English translation I quote here.

75. *OED* online edition, s.v. "fortunately."

76. This and all subsequent quotes from Heywood's account of Joan appear on p. 239.

77. Holinshed, *Chronicles*, 3:172.

78. Heywood, *Life of Merlin*, 250. All page numbers refer to this edition.

79. Patterson, "Fuller, Thomas (1607/8–1661)," *ODNB*, online edition.

80. Houghton, *Formation of Thomas Fuller's Holy and Profane States*, 170.

81. *The Profane State* has its own title page, following p. 354. All citations are to this edition. There is a facsimile edition: *Thomas Fuller's The Holy State and the Profane State* in two volumes, ed. Maximilian Graff Walten (1938; New York: AMS Press, 1966).

82. Houghton, *Formation of Thomas Fuller's Holy and Profane States*, 189.

83. The idea that Joan was a not acting on her own had arisen in two pro-Burgundian texts from the mid-fifteenth century. Chronicler Jean de Wavrin wrote that Joan "was sent before the king of France by a knight named Sir Robert de Baudricourt [who] introduced her and taught her what to do and say": *Recueil des croniques*, 262. In an oration on Duke Philip of Burgundy, Bishop Jean Jouffroy had claimed that French nobles made use of Joan to raise the morale of the dispirited army: *Ad Pium Papam II*, 137.

84. Fuller is perhaps deliberately misreading Fabyan, who had written, "this victory shulde be obtyened by Jane or Johane": *New Chronicles*, 599. "Johane" was his rendering of the Latin form of Joan's name.

85. In the margin, Fuller cites "Gerson," meaning the theologian Jean Gerson, long believed to be the author of *De quadam puella*, which states, "it is further reported that she had had her hair cut in the style of a man and that, when she wants to go to war, she puts on male clothing and arms, and climbs on to a horse": C. Taylor, *Joan of Arc*, 112–13. Closer to Fuller's time, a 1620 pamphlet *Hic-Mulier* (The Man-Woman) had condemned a fad of "masculine women" who adopted men's clothing and cut their hair.

86. Tisset, 1:394.

87. Clapham, *Treatise*, B8.

88. Virgil, *Eclogues, Georgics, Aeneid*, 32, lines 583–84.

89. Fuller, *Joseph's Partie-Colored Coat*, 9.

90. Hacker, "Women and Military Institutions," 648–51.

91. Siberry, *Criticism of Crusading*, 45. See also Kostick, "Women and the First Crusade," 57–68.

92. William of Newburgh, *Historia rerum Anglicarum*, 274; Roger of Hovedon, *Chronica*, 337; and *Itinerarum peregrinorum et gesta Regis Ricardi*, 248.

93. Ambroise, *Estoire de la Guerre Sainte*, 1:92 (text); 2:110 (translation). See also Donagan, *War in England*, 141–56; and Griffin, *Regulating Religion and Morality*, 1–21.

94. "Laws and Ordinances set down by Robert Earl of Leicester," in Strype, *Annals of the Reformation* (part 2), 356.

95. Clode, *Military Forces of the Crown*, 436.

96. Patterson, "Thomas Fuller," *ODNB*, online edition.
97. Importantly, the *OED* does not record "laundress" or "washerwoman" as a synonym for "prostitute."
98. Watts [attrib.], *Second Part of the Swedish Discipline*, 55.
99. Quoted in Haberling, "Army Prostitution and Its Control," 42–43. I have not identified Fuller's actual source for this anecdote.
100. The Catholic historian John Lingard, however, *did* regard Joan as a prisoner of war: "By the humanity of later ages, the life of the prisoner of war is considered as sacred: a few centuries ago he remained at the mercy of the captor, who might retain him in custody, liberate him for money, or put him to death": *History of England*, 418–19.
101. Holinshed, *Chronicles*, 3:171.
102. W. E. Burns, "Winstanley, William (d. 1698)," *ODNB* online edition.
103. Winstanley [attrib.], *Poor Robin's Character of France*, 26.
104. Winstanley, *New Help to Discourse*, 48–49.
105. Winstanley, *Histories and Observations*, 177–81.
106. Velasco, *Lieutenant Nun*, 2.
107. Winstanley, *Histories and Observations*, 181.
108. J. Shirley, *Illustrious History of Women*, A10.
109. *Biographium Fæmineum*, 8–10.

CHAPTER 4

1. For simplicity, I refer to the play's author as "Shakespeare," although there were multiple authors. In the First Folio of Shakespeare's works (1623), Joan of Arc in *1 Henry VI* is referred to variously as "Joane," "Joane de Puzel," "Pucell," and "Puzel." I follow Edward Burns, editor of the Arden Shakespeare edition of *1 Henry VI*, in referring to her as "Joan Puzel." All citations are from this edition. Michael Taylor analyzes the "disjunctiveness" of Joan Puzel's characterization in his introduction to the Oxford edition: *Henry VI, Part I*, 44–50. That disjunctiveness may well result from the play's having several authors, and the possibility of its revision between the time it was played in the 1590s and the publication of the Folio. For a summary of these issues, see Burns's introduction to Shakespeare, *King Henry VI Part I*, 73–84; Vickers, "Incomplete Shakespeare"; Chernaik, "Shakespeare as Co-Author"; and Taylor and Loughnane, "Canon and Chronology," 513–17.
2. Hall, *Union*, 159; Holinshed, *Chronicles*, 3:170–71.
3. Bovet, *Pandaemonium*, 82–93; Hall, *Union*, 148.
4. Fabyan, *New Chronicles*, 642.
5. Vergil, *Anglica Historia*, 38.
6. For this and related issues, see Marcus, *Puzzling Shakespeare*; Howard and Rackin, *Engendering a Nation*; Kirk, *Mirror of Confusion*, 131–54; and Levine, *Women's Matters*.
7. Levine, *Women's Matters*, 14.
8. Somerset, *Elizabeth I*, 103–6.
9. Marcus, *Puzzling Shakespeare*, 74.
10. J. Macleod, *Dynasty*, 83.
11. *Discourse*, A2v.
12. Ton Hoenselaars presents several documents that associate the French (and thus Joan) with inconstancy, lasciviousness, and sorcery, although many of his examples postdate Shakespeare's play: "Jeanne d'Arc de Shakespeare," 19–28. See also Ascoli, *Grande-Bretagne devant l'opinion française*.
13. The textual history of these editions is extremely complex. See Heal and Summerson, "Genesis of the Two Editions," 3–19. For simplicity, I refer to the work in general as "Holinshed."
14. Dasent, *Acts of the Privy Council*, 311–12.
15. Clegg, "Censorship," 57–58.
16. Djordjevic, "'W. P.,'" 40–43. Djordjevic compares how Joan of Arc is presented

in both editions in *Holinshed's Nation*, 160–65.
17. Holinshed, *Chronicles*, 3:171.
18. Holinshed, *Chronicles*, 4:932.
19. Tisset, 1:427.
20. Greg, *Henslowe's Diary*, 13.
21. Bevington, "Lyly's *Endymion* and *Midas*"; Neill, "Spenser's Acrasia," 682–88; O'Connell, "Mary Queen of Scots," 462; and McCabe, "Masks of Duessa."
22. Bullough, *Narrative*, 34.
23. Peele, *Troublesome Reign*, 1; Vickers, "*Troublesome Raigne*," 78–116.
24. Knox, *First Blast of the Trumpet*, 9.
25. See Eggert, *Showing*; and Campbell, *Shakespeare's Histories*, 127–44.
26. Peele, *Troublesome Reign*, 2.
27. Marlowe, *Edward the Second*, 26–32; all quotations are from this edition. See also Hopkins, "Christopher Marlowe"; and Kewes, "History Plays," 498–504.
28. Tuve, *Allegorical Imagery*, 404.
29. Levine, *Women's Matters*, 18.
30. Although several critics have associated Mary Stuart with Joan Puzel (for example, Hardin, "Chronicles and Mythmaking," 34), I have found only one outright claim that the execution of Mary in 1587 was "dramatized as the execution of Joan of Arc." E. Clark, *Hidden Allusions in Shakespeare's Plays*, 569–70. For the Queen and her reign, I relied on Fraser, *Mary Queen of Scots*. A contemporary French ode excoriating Elizabeth for Mary's execution alludes directly to Joan: "Vous estes les fils / De ceux qui furent deconfits / Par les armes d'une pucelle" (You are the sons of those who were vanquished / By the might of a maid). Ascoli, *Grande-Bretagne devant l'opinion française*, 315, lines 112–14.
31. Rose, "Circe," *Oxford Classical Dictionary*, 193.
32. In Shakespeare, *Comedy of Errors*, 5.1.271, 100n. See Bevington, "Domineering Female," 54.

33. The verbal echoes might be coincidental. Gary Taylor summarizes the case that Marlowe had a significant hand in a play that was later "adapted by Shakespeare": Taylor and Loughnane, "Canon and Chronology," 513–15.
34. Neill, "Spenser's Acrasia," 686–87.
35. Lloyd, *Certaine English verses*, A2v. The alternate title heads the text of the poem.
36. Kempe, *A Dutiful Invective*, fol. 3v.
37. Nashe, *Pierce Pennilesse*, 230.
38. Neill, "Spenser's Acrasia," 684–85.
39. *OED* online edition, s.v. "mermaid." See Barrett-Graves, "Mermaids, Sirens, and Mary," 69–70, and Fraser, *Mary Queen of Scots*, 383–84.
40. This was the fourth of the so-called Casket Letters, produced to implicate Mary in the death of her husband Henry Stuart, Lord Darnley: Fraser, *Mary Queen of Scots*, 478–507. For the text, see *Calendar of the Manuscripts*, 377. The Queen herself had stated, "Thay ar false and feinzeit, forgit and inventit": Labanoff, *Lettres, instructions et mémoires*, 2:203. My argument does not hinge on the authenticity or authorship of these letters, but any allusion to Jason and Medea in a love letter strikes an odd note. On Circe and Medea, see Clauss and Johnston, *Medea*, 31.
41. Labanoff, *Lettres, instructions et mémoires*, 2:134 (my translation).
42. Roberts, "Descendants of Circe," 202.
43. Kyffin, *Blessednes of Brytaine*, fol. B2.
44. Ann Astell argues that Joan's devotion to the Virgin Mary significantly informed her conception of the workings of heavenly inspiration as an organic whole: "Virgin Mary," 37–60.
45. Peters, *Patterns of Piety*, 207–45; Woods, *Shakespeare's Unreformed Fictions*, 30–45. Woods reads the play in terms of its pre- and post-Reformation tensions.
46. T. Rogers, *Historical Dialogue*, 24.
47. Espinosa provides several examples in *Masculinity and Marian Efficacy*, 42. He

suggests that "the play appears to speak to the post-Reformation fear of the Virgin Mary's . . . unrestrained power" (47). See also T. Rogers, *Historical dialogue*, 29.
48. Womersley, *Divinity and State*, 245.
49. Holinshed, *Chronicles*, 3:168.
50. Richardson, "Topcliffe, Richard (1531–1604)," *ODNB* online edition.
51. Letter from Topcliffe to the Earl of Shrewsbury, August 20, 1578, in Goldring, Eales, Clarke, and Archer, *John Nichols's "Progresses and Public Processions,"* 2:773.
52. Hackett, *Virgin Mother, Maiden Queen*, 2–3.
53. Knox, *History of the Reformation in Scotland*, 12.
54. Knox, *History of the Reformation in Scotland*, 20 and note 2.
55. The English version of the "Hail Mary" that invokes "the freute of thy wombe Jesus" appears to have originated in the 1506 translation of *Compost et Kalendrier des Bergiers* (the *Kalendar of Shepardys* printed by Richard Pynson). Thurston, "Our Popular Devotions. V.," 499; Sommer, *Kalendar of Shepherdes*, 3:76 (Giiiiv).
56. Holmes, "Mary Stewart in England," 215.
57. Doran and Kewes, *Doubtful and Dangerous*, 4. See also McCabe, "Poetics of Succession," 197–99.
58. *Statutes of the Realm* 4, part 1, 659–60.
59. Parry, *Arch-Conjurer of England*, 70. See also Mason, "Scotland," 656.
60. The Sixth Earl of Shrewsbury (a descendant of John Talbot) had been Mary's jailer and was relieved of his duty in 1584. Scoufos argues, "the Talbot scenes [in *1 Henry VI*] . . . were written to exonerate" him: *Shakespeare's Typological Satire*, 136.
61. Mary's abduction occurred on April 26, 1567, and at least one witness believed that Bothwell forced her sexually. Bothwell's marriage to Lady Jean Gordon was dissolved by Protestant authority on May 3 and, at Mary's request, annulled by Catholic authority on May 7. They wed on May 15. See Fraser, *Mary Queen of Scots*, 393–99.
62. Hutson calls Wilson's work an "effective forgery": "Fictive Acts," 726. She explains how Wilson created a dossier from which later attacks on Mary could draw by adding his own material, including letters purporting to have been written by Mary.
63. Du Haillan, *Histoire générale des rois de France*, DDdi r, 1145. This work was printed five times between 1576 and 1585.
64. Summerson, "Holinshed's Sources" and Summerson, "Sources: 1587."
65. Purkiss writes, "the sensational uncovering of her identity as witch in the final act . . . constitutes the principal revelation or discovery of the truth of witchcraft to the audience": *Witch in History*, 190. Similarly, while arguing that "the English demonise Joan" and that throughout the play, "there are a series of clues to her real spiritual identity," Lake maintains that "at the outset, and for a good deal of the play, Joan's precise status is left deliberately ambiguous": *How Shakespeare Put Politics on the Stage*, 133.
66. Schwarz notes that at least in part, "Joan is described in the language of exemplary catalogues," and (like Mary Stuart, as I argue below) that Margaret is not an Amazon but "amazonian," a player of Amazons: *Tough Love*, 82, 101.
67. Clapham, *Treatise*, Fii–Fiiv.
68. Knox, *First Blast of the Trumpet*, 11.
69. Shakespeare, *King Henry VI Part Three*.
70. Shakespeare, *King John*. Woodbridge labels Shakespeare's allusions to Amazons "disturbing": *Women and the English Renaissance*, 160.
71. Shakespeare, *A Midsummer Night's Dream*.
72. Marcus, *Puzzling Shakespeare*, 66; Aske, *Elizabetha triumphans*, 23.
73. Knox, *First Blast of the Trumpet*, 45.

74. Osherow, *Biblical Women's Voices*, 89.
75. Osherow, *Biblical Women's Voices*, 90.
76. Shakespeare, *Richard III*.
77. Dickson, "No Rainbow Without the Sun," 143.
78. Walsh, *Queen's Men*, 109.
79. Yates, *Astraea*, 82.
80. Lynch, "Reassertion of Princely Power in Scotland," 213.
81. Dated October 16, 1570, Labanoff, *Lettres, instructions et mémoires*, 3:107–8.
82. Leslie, *Defence*, "Author to the Gentle Reader."
83. Christine de Pizan, "Ditié," lines 188–91.
84. P. McCullough, "Out of Egypt," 139. See Strauss, "Virgin Queen as Nurse of the Church," 185–202. In contrast, Topcliffe reports that everyone was glad to see the Norfolk statue of the Virgin burned except "some one or two who had sucked out the idoll's poisoned mylke": Goldring, Eales, Clarke, and Archer, *John Nichols's "Progresses and Public Progressions,"* 2:773.
85. Bellis reminds us of the similarity of this language to Burgundy's speech at the end of *Henry V*. See Bellis, *Hundred Years War in Literature*, 224–25.
86. Holinshed, *Chronicles*, 4:899. Archer identifies Fleming as the author of this section of the *Chronicle*: "Social Order and Disorder," 409.
87. Chantelauze, *Marie Stuart, son procès*, 526.
88. As Cecil's agent, Robert Wingfield, described it in a letter the day of Mary's execution. "The Examynacon and Death of Mary the Queen of Skottes," in Dack, *Trial, Execution and Death*, 1–17.
89. G. C. Moore Smith, *Gabriel Harvey's Marginalia*, 90, 92, 96; Stern, "Bibliotheca of Gabriel Harvey." Under the general rubric of "De fortitudine," Egnazio lauds "Joan the French virgin," especially for her courage in exhorting the French to victory at Orléans despite an arrow wound: Egnatius, *De exemplis illustrium virorum*, 3, part 2:85–86.
90. Burns points to a similar ruse employed by the English in 1441 reported by Hall: Shakespeare, *King Henry VI Part 1*, 205n. The famous French hero Bertrand du Guesclin had also supposedly used such a strategy: Vernier, *Flower of Chivalry*, 42–43. Gutierrez reads this ruse as being in line with the feminization of the French men in the play: "Gender and Value in *1 Henry VI*," 191–92.
91. "In Mariam Stuartam Reginam Scoticam, satyra," signed "P. R. Scotus": Buchanan, *De Maria Scotorum Regina*, Q3v, p. 124. It begins, "Quae fuit egregio Derlino juncta Stuarta: / sustulit illa suum saeva virago virum" (The Stuart, a fierce warrior, who was joined to the excellent Darnley, upheld her husband). I thank Robert Wright for help with the translation. Jackson sees the term "virago" as "almost entirely positive" in English: "Topical Ideology," 49 n. 29. But the remainder of the Latin poem makes clear that here it is pejorative.
92. *Calendar of State Papers Relating to Scotland and Mary, Queen of Scots, 1547–1603*, 1:651 (henceforth *CSPS*).
93. *OED* online edition, s.v. "knapscall." I am grateful to Jane Dawson, University of Edinburgh, and John Guy, Cambridge University, for discussing Mary's "steel cap" with me in email correspondence, February and March 2015.
94. *CSPS*, 2:202.
95. *CSPS*, 2:222.
96. Knox, *History of the Reformation in Scotland*, 162 and note 3.
97. Holinshed, *Chronicles*, 5:615–16.
98. Calvin, *Sermons*, 884. The Deuteronomy sermons were preached in 1555–56: D. DeVries, "Calvin's Preaching," 114.
99. Buchanan, *Ane Detectioun*, Eii–Eiiv.
100. Buchanan, *Historia Scotorum*, 191.
101. Knox, *History of the Reformation in Scotland*, 202.

102. Fraser, *Mary Queen of Scots*, 381.
103. McElroy, "Genres," 267–83, esp. 278.
104. Hall, *Union*, 157.
105. The "Bastard theory," that Joan was the illegitimate daughter of Queen Isabeau of Bavaria, was not promulgated in print until the nineteenth century. See Pernoud and Clin, *Joan of Arc: Her Story*, 222.
106. Dack, *Trial, Execution and Death*, 5.
107. Tisset, 1:59.
108. Labanoff, *Lettres, instructions et mémoires*, 7:37–38.
109. Labanoff, *Lettres, instructions et mémoires*, 6:441.
110. Burns, *King Henry VI Part 1*, 69–73.
111. Kenyon, *Popish Plot*, 52–53.
112. Maguire, "Factionary Politics," 72.
113. White, *John Crowne*, 107–8. White provides a scene-by-scene comparison of Crowne's plays to Shakespeare's.
114. Wikander, *Play of Truth and State*, 114.
115. Avery, "Shakespeare Ladies Club," 153.
116. Dobson, *Making of the National Poet*, 148–49.
117. Ritchie, *Women and Shakespeare*, 149–50, and Ritchie, "Influence of the Female Audience," 57–69.
118. G. Taylor, *Reinventing Shakespeare*, 205–6; see Montagu, *Essay on the Writings*.
119. Nussbaum, *Rival Queens*, 142–43.
120. Highfill, Burnim, and Langhans, *Biographical Dictionary*, 50.
121. Genest, *Some Account of the English Stage*, 555–56.
122. W. Shirley, *Edward the Black Prince*, 71.
123. Keate, *Poetical Works*, 149.
124. Steevens, *Plays of William Shakespeare in 10 volumes*, 210. Steevens rejects that meaning because he finds the word uttered "in a song sung by a young man in the presence of the young lady to whom he was instantly to be married."
125. Ritson, *Remarks on Shakespeare*, 113–14.
126. Boase, "Illustrations of Shakespeare's Plays," 83–108; Merchant, *Shakespeare and the Artist*; Sillars, *Illustrated Shakespeare*. In chapter 5, I analyze Enlightenment and Romantic texts and images.
127. Hammelmann, "Shakespeare's First Illustrations," 1. He also establishes the attribution to Boitard. See also Sillars, *Illustrated Shakespeare*, 31–42.
128. Bate, "Pictorial Shakespeare," 33.
129. Bann considers theatrical representations of history in *Clothing of Clio*, 58–59.
130. Allen, "Early Illustrators of Shakespeare," 49. The composition of the scene closely resembles Boitard's drawing "Joseph est jeté dans un puits par ses frères": Sillars, *Illustrated Shakespeare*, 40, fig. 12.
131. Dobson and Wells, *Oxford Companion to Shakespeare*, 402.
132. N. Rowe, *Works of Mr. William Shakespear: in six volumes* (1709), 3:1378.
133. Nashe, *Pierce Penilesse*, 212.
134. N. Rowe, *Works of Mr. William Shakespear: in six volumes* (1709), 3:1393.
135. There seems no need, as some modern editors have done, to emend the direction to specify that it is "the French" or "Charles" who "pass over the stage" and enter Orléans (by, respectively, M. Taylor and Burns in their editions). Ryan retains the Folio stage direction in the Signet Classics edition. Shakespeare, *King Henry VI, Parts I, II, and III*, 68. For the staging, see Bevington, *Wide and Universal Theater*, 75.
136. Dash, "*Henry VI* and the Art of Illustration," 256.
137. N. Rowe, *Works of Mr. William Shakespear: In Nine Volumes* (1714), 171; Sillars, *Illustrated Shakespeare*, 64.
138. Marsden, "Rewritten Women," 44. See also P. Rogers, "Breeches Part," 255–56. For a discussion of theatrical transvestism and transgendered casting, see

Dugaw, *Warrior Women and Popular Balladry*, 175–82.
139. Burnim and Highfill, *John Bell*, 20–21, item 8.
140. Harding and Harding, *Shakespeare Illustrated*, n.p.
141. Burnim and Highfill, *John Bell*, 41.
142. Burnim and Highfill, *John Bell*, 77.
143. M. Wood, *Plays of William Shakspeare*, vol. 8, following p. 104.
144. Hume, *History of England* (1762), 2:346.
145. Branston, *Illustration of Shakespeare*, n.p.
146. Shakespeare, *Plays of William Shakspeare*, vol. 8, following p. 220.
147. Dash, "*Henry VI* and the Art of Illustration," 258.
148. *Illustrations of Shakespeare*, 21.
149. Boydell, *Catalogue*, i.
150. Boydell, *Catalogue*, x; Lamb and Lamb, *Letters*, 985.
151. Shakespeare, *King Henry VI Part I*, 304.
152. Burnim and Highfill, *John Bell*, 11.
153. Bell, *Shakespeare's Plays*, 99n. Parenthetical page numbers refer to this edition.
154. H. Bowdler, *Family Shakespeare*.
155. T. Bowdler, *Family Shakespeare in Ten Volumes*, 1:vii.
156. Burden, "Pre-Victorian Prudery." See also Perrin, *Dr. Bowdler's Legacy*, 60–86.
157. *Statutes at Large, of England and of Great-Britain*, 678–79.
158. Burden, "Pre-Victorian Prudery," 211–13.
159. Pope, *Works of Mr. William Shakespear*, 23, 24; Theobald, *Works of Shakespeare*, 128.
160. S. Johnson, *Plays of William Shakespeare*, 4:511n: "I know not what *pussel* is: perhaps it should be *Pucelle* or *puzzle*. Something with a meaning it should be, but a very poor meaning will serve." On the critical rivalries among early editors, see Seary, "Early Editors of Shakespeare," 175–86.
161. Johnson, *Plays of William Shakespeare*, 4:506n.
162. Steevens, *Plays of William Shakespeare in ten volumes*, 194n. See Sherbo, *Samuel Johnson, Editor of Shakespeare*, 112.
163. Barrett, *Trial of Jeanne d'Arc*.
164. According to Margolis, François de Belleforest in *Les Grandes Annales*, first published in Paris in 1579, was the "first historian to quote from [the trial transcripts] at length": *Joan of Arc in History, Literature, and Film*, 90–91.

CHAPTER 5

1. I have located no other copies of this image; the Folger catalogs it as "Joan of Arc." I am grateful to Nora Heimann for discussing it with me. Joan had long been eroticized, most notably in illustrations to Voltaire's *La Pucelle d'Orléans*: Peccatte, "Figurations sensuelles et érotiques."
2. Walpole, *Correspondence with the Countess of Upper Ossory*, 32:268–69.
3. O'Quinn, "Introduction to Wallace's *The Ton*," par. 6. According to Cobbett, women had been banned from the House gallery in 1778: *Parliamentary History*, 672–47.
4. Tisset, 1:75. Crane, *Performance of Self*, chapter 3, discusses Joan's cross-dressing.
5. See O'Brien, "English Enlightenment Histories"; Woolf, "Feminine Past."
6. Phillips, *Society and Sentiment*, 343.
7. The first English novel devoted to Joan of Arc was not published until 1841. Thomas James Serle's *Joan of Arc: The Maid of Orleans*, a first-person recollection by "Jacques Alain," anticipates Twain's *Personal Recollections of Joan of Arc*. In "Tales of Other Times," Anne Stevens suggests that historical fiction should also be considered part of an expanded definition of historiography.
8. G. Kelly, *Women Writing, and Revolution*, 4–9.
9. Kucich, "Women's Historiography," 4.
10. *Monthly Review*, unsigned review of *History*, 1. O'Brien sees Enlightenment

historians, including Hume, "extending... the emotional range of historical narrative": *Narratives of Enlightenment*, 65.
11. M. Astell, *Christian Religion*, 293.
12. Coleridge, *Marginalia*, 119.
13. *OED* online edition, s.v. "petticoat."
14. Walpole, *Correspondence with Hannah More*, 31:397. Wollstonecraft had written that Marie Antoinette was "a woman... whose conduct in life has deserved praise, though not, perhaps, the servile elogiums which have been lavished on the queen": *Vindication of the Rights of Man*, 53.
15. Kennedy, "Benevolent Historian," 329.
16. *British Heroine*, appendix, 18. According to the *OED*, at that time "breech" could also refer to buttocks.
17. Wollstonecraft, *Vindication of the Rights of Woman*, 27.
18. For a discussion of the variations in that text concerning Joan's virginity, see Heimann, *Joan of Arc in French Art and Culture*, 26–31.
19. Southey, *Joan of Arc* (1796), book 10, line 142. Unless otherwise indicated, all quotations refer to the edition by Lynda Pratt and to the 1796 edition of the poem.
20. Warter, *Selections from the Letters of Robert Southey*, 51.
21. Southey, *Joan of Arc* (1806), 1:18. Hogan reconstructs the performance of February 16: *London Stage*, 2043–44.
22. Southey, *Joan of Arc*, 5. Goy-Blanquet has described *Joan of Arc* as republican panegyric written "to atone for his country's crime in burning Joan": "Shakespeare and Voltaire," 29.
23. Cross, "Victorious La Pucelle." I thank the librarians at the University of Colorado Boulder for providing me with copies of the sheet music from the Early American musical theater collection, Sister Mary Collection, American Music Research Center.
24. Wahrman, *Making of the Modern Self*, 331, n46. Wahrman discounts the lyric that celebrates Joan as a warrior.
25. Hogan, *London Stage*, 2044.
26. *Critical Review*, unsigned review of *Joan of Arc* (February 1796), 191–92.
27. *Critical Review*, unsigned review of *Joan of Arc* (May 1796), 183.
28. J. Aikin, "*Joan of Arc*," 361.
29. *Anti-Jacobin Review*, unsigned review of *Joan of Arc* (April–August 1799), 120. For the political bias of this and the other periodicals mentioned, see A. Sullivan, *British Literary Magazines*.
30. *Monthly Mirror*, unsigned review of *Joan of Arc* (1795–96), 355.
31. *Analytical Review* 23 (1796), 171.
32. Southey, *Joan of Arc* (1798), 202.
33. *Monthly Review*, unsigned review of *Joan of Arc*, 59, 61.
34. *Critical Review*, unsigned review of *Joan of Arc* (1798), 197.
35. *Anti-Jacobin Review*, unsigned review of *Joan of Arc* (April–August 1799), 120–21.
36. Seward, "Lines Written by Anna Seward," 29–30. Seward later regretted her harshness. See Kairoff, *Anna Seward*, 106–9.
37. Kennedy, *Helen Maria Williams*, 107.
38. Williams, *Letters Written in France*, 103–4. It was Humphrey, Duke of Gloucester, Bedford's brother, who was posthumously dubbed "the good duke." Wagner, *Encyclopedia of the Hundred Years War*, 156. Bedford had died in Rouen in 1435, but by Williams's time, only a plaque marking his original tomb remained in the Cathedral: Stratford, "John, Duke of Bedford," *ODNB*, online edition.
39. Williams, *Letters from France*, 41.
40. J. Kelly, "Joan of Arc," 287–88. Subsequent quotations from this article are found on these two pages.
41. Cave, "Introduction"; Carlson, *First Magazine*, 51–52.
42. Lockwood, "John Kelly's 'Lost' Play," 31.
43. Keymer, "Kelly, John (c.1684–1751)," *ODNB*, online edition; Keymer and Sabor, *Pamela in the Marketplace*, 70–72. Only the first volume of the

1732 translation bears Kelly's name on the title page. I am grateful to Catherine Maguire and the staff at the Maryland Law Library in Annapolis for providing access to this work. Volume 5 of Rapin de Thoyras's hugely popular *History of England* included a lengthy "Dissertation on the Pucelle d'Orléans." See also Rapin de Thoyras, *Histoire d'Angleterre*.

44. La Fontaine, *Contes et nouvelles en vers*, 54–61. Thanks to Lisa Gasbarrone, professor of French at Franklin and Marshall College, for identifying the *conte*.
45. Pasquier, *Oeuvres*, 1:541.
46. Choudhury, *Wanton Jesuit and Wayward Saint*.
47. *OED* online edition, s.v. "petenlair." A *pet en l'air* or "petenlair" was a type of women's short jacket popular in the eighteenth century, but in French slang "pet" could also mean "fart," so Kelly manages to pun in English on a truncation of "petticoat" as well as on "*pet*."
48. Guthrie, *General History of England*, 3:531–49. Subsequent page numbers refer to this edition.
49. Allan, "Guthrie, William (1708?–1770)" *ODNB*, online edition. Okie praises both his eschewal of partisan politics and his research: *Augustan Historical Writing*, 171–88. See also Dew, "Economic Turn," 79–83.
50. Daniel, *Histoire de France*, 1056 (my translation). This paragraph, unlike much of Daniel's text, does not indicate a source. There are many similarities between Guthrie and Daniel, but not enough to task the Scot with mere translated paraphrase.
51. Daniel, *History of France*, 425.
52. Duparc, 1:438.
53. Daniel, *Histoire de France*, 1082. Such claims or rumors were current even in the fifteenth century, P. Champion, *Guillaume de Flavy*, 282–85.
54. Guthrie, Gray et al., *General History of the World*, 193–98.
55. Guthrie, *General History of Scotland*, 3:324–25.
56. Guthrie, *New Geographical, Historical and Commercial Grammar* (1770), 321. The revised paragraph appears in the 1776 edition (391).
57. Okie offers useful comparisons between the two: *Augustan Historical Writing*, 198–99.
58. Black, *Art of History*, 103–5.
59. Hicks, *Neoclassical History and English Culture*, 190–92.
60. Stuard, "Fashion's Captives," 60.
61. Lockman, *New History of England*, 8th ed. (1752), 123–24. Having examined several earlier editions, I believe this is the first to add the final phrase.
62. Cléro, "Jeanne d'Arc," 39–41.
63. Hume, *Essays, Literary, Moral, and Political*, 73–74. All citations are to this edition.
64. Siebert, *Moral Animus of David Hume*, 127.
65. *Analytical Review*, unsigned review of *Joan of Arc* (1796), 171.
66. McIntosh-Varjabédian, "Probability and Persuasion," 112. Hume, *History of England*, 1:335–47. Parenthetical page numbers refer to this edition.
67. On imagination in Hume, see Costelloe, "Fact and Fiction," 181–99.
68. Hume, *Philosophical Essays*, 203. See also Schmidt, "Hume as a Philosopher of History," 170–71.
69. Carte, *General History of England*, 709.
70. Slater, "Hume's Revisions of the *History of England*," 136.
71. Carte, *General History of England*, 708.
72. Mitchell, *Picturing the Past*, 34–43.
73. Boase, "Macklin and Bowyer," 175–77; Mitchell, *Picturing the Past*, 39–41. Boase mentions a photographic reproduction of the painting in the Witt collection of the Courtauld Institute entitled *Sapphira before the Apostles*: "Macklin and Bowyer," 177.
74. For the identification of Thurston, see Chatto, *Treatise on Wood Engraving*, 613.

75. Hume, *History of England. [. . .] Embellished with engravings*, 401.
76. Mitchell, *Picturing the Past*, 23.
77. Bloom and Bloom, *Piozzi Letters*, 2:233. I am grateful to Orianne Smith who first drew my attention to Piozzi.
78. Quoted from Guest, *Small Change*, 54.
79. D'Ezio, *Taste for Eccentricity*, 58.
80. Goldsmith, *History of England*, 338.
81. W. Howell, *Medulla historiæ*, b2–b2v.
82. Looser, *British Women Writers*, 156.
83. Looser points out that Piozzi justified this omission in her second volume: *British Women Writers*, 166. See also Hughes-Warrington, "Writing on the Margins," 892–93.
84. Mossner, "Apology for David Hume, Historian," 685–86.
85. Bloom and Bloom, *Piozzi Letters*, 3:11.
86. Piozzi, *Retrospection*, 444. The history of Joan of Arc occupies pages 444–45.
87. Tisset, 1:78.
88. Jean d'Alençon recalled, "Sometimes he heard Joan say to the King that she would last for one year and no more": Duparc, 1:387. On Piozzi's own prophetic self-identification, see O. Smith, *Romantic Women Writers*, 96–98.
89. J. Wood, "'Alphabetically Arranged,'" 130.
90. Colley, *Britons*, 259.
91. Burstein, *Narrating Women's History*, 11.
92. Quoted in Guest, *Small Change*, 38.
93. B. Smith, "Contribution of Women," 718.
94. Alexander, *History of Women*, 2:78–79.
95. Quicherat, *Procès*, 5:168–69.
96. Duparc, 1:325. Although Joan was often referred to as a "shepherdess," the term might have been used to emphasize her lower social status: Pernoud and Clin, *Joan of Arc: Her Story*, 22.
97. Shakespeare, *As You Like It*, 3.2.189–91.
98. Fuller cites Gerson in the margin, although his authorship is disputed. See C. Taylor, *La Pucelle*, 112–13.
99. Betham, *Biographical Dictionary*, 60–61.
100. Wahrman, "Percy's Prologue," 133–36; Hicks, "Women Worthies," 180–81.
101. Guest, *Small Change*, 49–50.
102. *Biographium Fœmineum*, 8.
103. Hays, "Memoirs of Mary Wollstonecraft," 411–16.
104. E. Bailey, "Lexicography of the Feminine," 397.
105. Hays, *Appeal to the Men of Great Britain*, 193–94.
106. Hays, *Female Biography*, 1:146–72. Parenthetical page numbers refer to this edition.
107. Walker, *Mary Hays*, 222. See also K. M. Rogers, *Feminism in Eighteenth-Century England*, 206.
108. Grave, *Memoirs of Joan d'Arc*, 137. On Lenglet, see Gury, "L'Historien," 269–71.
109. *Literary Panorama*, unsigned review of *Memoirs* (1813), 68–69.
110. *Monthly Review*, unsigned review of *Memoirs*, 126.
111. Hemans, *Records of Women*, xx. All quotations are from this edition.
112. Kucich, "Romanticism and Re-Engendering," 25.
113. G. Kelly, "Gender and Memory," 131.
114. Laird, "Adapting the Saints," 502.
115. Edgar, "Felicia Hemans," 127.
116. C. D. Clark, "Call from the Wild," 26–35.
117. Hemans referred to Southey's *Chronicle of the Cid* in her "Songs of the Cid," so it seems plausible she was familiar with his *Joan of Arc*: Hemans, *Felicia Hemans*, 203 n. 2. It was this passage that prompted Coleridge to note "how grossly unnatural an anachronism thus to *transmogrify* the fanatic votary of the Virgin into a Tom Paine in Petticoats, a novel-palming Proselyte of the Age of Reason." Coleridge, *Marginalia*, 119.
118. Hemans, *Felicia Hemans*, 351–52.
119. Jameson, *Diary of an Ennuyée*, 5.
120. Wolfson, "'Domestic Affections,'" 156. Many, if not most, "portraits" of Joan from the fifteenth century onward show her with long hair, as did both

the original Orléans monument and its replacement.
121. McGavran, "Felicia Hemans's Feminist Poetry," 544.
122. Edgar, "Felicia Hemans," 128.
123. Sir Walter Scott, *Tales of a Grandfather*, 292.
124. Beginning in that same year, 1841, Jules-Jacques Quicherat began publishing his five volumes of documents, including the transcripts of both trials as well as dozens of contemporary chronicles, letters, treatises, and poems.
125. Margolis, "Rewriting the Right," 61.
126. De Quincey, "Joan of Arc," 535–42.

AFTERWORD
1. Kipling, *Souvenirs*, 23–24.
2. Cormack, "Whall, Christopher Whitworth (1849–1924)," *ODNB*, online edition.
3. Leicester Cathedral, "Remembering." Peter Cormack notes that by this date, Whall's daughter Veronica was "a very accomplished artist and craftswoman. Her contribution to the studio's work is increasingly evident in post-war commissions, such as the east windows of the Royal Military Academy Chapel, Woolwich (1919), and Leicester Cathedral (1920)." Cormack, *Arts and Crafts Stained Glass*, 273. How intriguing to consider a woman's hand in this portrait of Joan.
4. "Joan of Arc," *Western News and Mercury*, May 31, 1923, 4.
5. Hampshire Record Office: DC/E4/5/2/1. By kind permission.
6. George Bernard Shaw, *St. Joan*, 156.

# BIBLIOGRAPHY

Agrippa d'Aubigné, Théodore. *Les Avantures du Baron de Foeneste par Théodore Agrippa d'Aubigné.* Vol. 2. Cologne: Chez les hériteurs de Pierrre Mareau, 1729.

Agrippa, Henricus Cornelius. *Declamation on the Nobility and Preeminence of the Female Sex.* Edited and translated with an introduction by Albert Rabil, Jr. Chicago: University of Chicago Press, 1996.

———. *De nobilitate et praecellentia foeminei sexus.* Antwerp: Michael Hellenius, 1529.

Aikin, John. "*Joan of Arc*, an Epic Poem. By Robert Southey." *Monthly Review* 19 (April 1796): 361–68.

Aikin, Lucy. *Epistles on Women Exemplifying Their Character and Condition in Various Ages and Nations.* London: J. Johnson & Co., 1810.

Aimond, Charles. *Les Relations de la France et du Verdunois de 1270 à 1552.* Paris: Champion, 1910.

Akehurst, F. R. P. "Good Name, Reputation, and Notoriety in French Customary Law." In *Fama: The Politics of Talk and Reputation in Medieval Europe*, edited by Thelma Fenster and Daniel Smail, 75–94. Ithaca: Cornell University Press, 2003.

Alexander, William. *The History of Women from the earliest antiquity to the present time, giving some account of almost every interesting particular concerning that Sex, among all Nations, ancient and modern.* 2 vols. London: W. Strahan and T. Cadell, 1779.

Allen, Brian. "The Early Illustrators of Shakespeare." In *Shakespeare in Art*, edited by Jane Martineau, 49–51. London: Merrel, 2003.

Allmand, Christopher. *The Hundred Years War: England and France at War, c.1300–c.1450.* Rev. ed. Cambridge: Cambridge University Press, 2001.

Ambroise. *The History of the Holy War: Ambroise's Estoire de la Guerre Sainte.* Edited by Marianne Ailes and Malcolm Barber. Woodbridge, U.K.: Boydell, 2003.

*Analytical Review.* Unsigned review of *Joan of Arc, an Epic Poem*, by Robert Southey. 23 (January–June 1796): 170–77.

Anslay, Bryan. *Here begynneth the boke of the cyte of ladyes.* London: Henry Pepwell, 1521.

*Anti-Jacobin Review.* Unsigned review of *Joan of Arc*, by Robert Southey. 3 (April–August 1799): 120–27.

Arber, Edward. *A Transcript of the Registers of the Company of Stationers in London, 1554–1640 A.D.* Vol. 5. London: Privately printed, 1875. Reprint, New York: Peter Smith, 1950.

Archer, Ian. "Social Order and Disorder." In Kewes, Archer, and Heal, *Oxford*

*Handbook of Holinshed's Chronicles*, 389–410.

Armstrong, C. A. J. *England, France, and Burgundy in the Fifteenth Century*. London: The Hambledon Press, 1983.

Ascoli, Georges. *La Grande-Bretagne devant l'opinion française depuis la guerre de cent ans jusqu'à la fin du XVIe siècle*. Travaux et Mémoires de l'Université de Lille. Droit-Lettres. Nouvelle Série 11. Paris: Librairie Universitaire J. Gamber, 1927.

Aske, James. *Elizabetha triumphans*. . . . London: Printed by Thomas Orwin, for Thomas Gubbin, and Thomas Newman, 1588.

Astell, Ann W. *Joan of Arc and Sacrificial Authorship*. Notre Dame: Notre Dame University Press, 2003.

———. "The Virgin Mary and the Voices of Joan of Arc." In *Joan of Arc and Spirituality*, edited by Ann Astell and Bonnie Wheeler, 37–60. New York: Palgrave Macmillan, 2003.

Astell, Mary. *The Christian Religion, As Profess'd by a Daughter of the Church of England*. London: R. Wilkin, 1705.

Avery, Emmett L. "The Shakespeare Ladies Club." *Shakespeare Quarterly* 7, no. 2 (Spring 1956): 153–58.

Aylmer, John. *An Harborowe for faithfull and Trewe Subjects agaynst the late blowne blaste concerning the government of women*. London: John Day, 1559.

Ayroles, Jean-Baptiste-Joseph. *La Vraie Jeanne d'Arc*. 5 vols. Paris: Gome et Cie, 1890–1902.

Bailey, Elaine. "Lexicography of the Feminine: Matilda Betham's *Dictionary of Celebrated Women*." *Philological Quarterly* 83, no. 4 (2004): 389–413.

Bailey, Michael. *Battling Demons: Witchcraft, Heresy, and Reform in the Late Middle Ages*. University Park: Pennsylvania State University Press, 2003.

Baker, Sir Richard. *A Chronicle of the Kings of England from the time of the Romans government unto the reaigne of our soveraigne lord, King Charles*. . . . London: Printed by R. C. and R. H. for Daniel Frere, 1643.

Ballard, George. *Memoirs of Several Ladies of Great Britain, who have been celebrated for their writings or skill in the learned languages arts and sciences*. Oxford: W. Jackson, 1752.

Bandel, Betty. "The English Chroniclers' Attitude Toward Women." *Journal of the History of Ideas* 16, no. 1 (January 1955): 113–18.

Bandello, Matteo. *Novelle*. In *Tutte le opera de Matteo Bandello*, edited by Franceso Flora. Milan: Mondadori, 1942. http://www.letteraturaitaliana.net/pdf/Volume_4/t77.pdf.

Bann, Stephen. *The Clothing of Clio: A Study of the Representation of History in Nineteenth-Century Britain and France*. Cambridge: Cambridge University Press, 1984.

Barker, Juliet. *Conquest: The English Kingdom of France, 1417–1450*. Cambridge: Harvard University Press, 2012.

Barnay, Sylvie. "Jeanne d'Arc et le prophétisme féminin: une parole habitée." In Guyon and Delavenne, *De Domremy . . . à Tokyo*, 237–44.

Barrett, W. P. *The Trial of Jeanne d'Arc*. New York: Gotham House, 1932.

Barrett-Graves, Debra. "Mermaids, Sirens, and Mary, Queen of Scots: Icons of Wantonness and Pride." In *The Emblematic Queen: Extra-Literary Representations of Early Modern Queenship*, edited by Debra Barrett-Graves, 69–100. New York: Palgrave Macmillan, 2013.

Basin, Thomas. *Histoire de Charles VII*. Edited and translated by Charles Samaran. Vol. 1. Paris: Société d'Édition "Les Belles Lettres," 1964.

Bate, Jonathan. "Pictorial Shakespeare: Text, Stage, Illustration." In *Book Illustrated: Text, Image, and Culture, 1770–1930*, edited by Catherine J. Golden, 31–59. New Castle, Del.: Oak Knoll Press, 2000.

Bean, J. M. W. "The Role of Robert Fabyan in Tudor Historiography of the 'Wars of the Roses.'" In *Florilegium Columbianum: Essays in Honor of Paul Oskar Kristeller*, edited by Karl-Ludwig Selig and Robert Somerville, 167–85. New York: Italica Press, 1987.

Beaucourt, Gaston du Fresne, marquis de. *Histoire de Charles VII*. Vol. 2. Paris: A. Picard, 1881.

Beaulande-Barraud, Véronique. "Les 'Fiançailles' rompues de Jeanne: un non-événement?" In Guyon and Delavenne, *De Domremy . . . à Tokyo*, 227–36.

Beaune, Colette. *Jeanne d'Arc, vérités et légendes*. Paris: Perrin, 2008.

Beem, Charles. "The Virtuous Virago: The Empress Matilda and the Politics of Womanhood in Twelfth-Century England." In Levin and Stewart-Nuñez, *Scholars and Poets Talk About Queens*, 85–98.

Bell, John. *Bell's Edition of Shakespeare's Plays 1774*. Facsimile edition. Vol. 7. London: Cornmarket Press, 1969.

Belleforest, François de. *18 Histoires tragiques, extraictes des oeuvres Italiennes de Bandel, et mises en langue françoise*. Lyon: Benoist Regaud, 1596.

Bellenden, John. *The Chronicles of Scotland compiled by Hector Boece*. Edited by Edith C. Batho and H. Winifred Husbands. Translated into Scots by John Bellenden, 1531. 2 vols. Edinburgh: William Blackwood & Sons for the Scottish Text Society, 1941.

Bellis, Joanna. *The Hundred Years War in Literature, 1337–1600*. Cambridge: D. S. Brewer, 2016.

Benson, Larry D., ed. *The Riverside Chaucer*. Boston: Houghton-Mifflin, 1986.

Bernau, Anke. "'Saint, Witch, Man, Maid or Whore?' Joan of Arc and Writing History." In *Medieval Virginities*, edited by Anke Bernau, Sarah Salih, and Ruth Evans, 214–33. Toronto: University of Toronto Press, 2003.

Betham, Matilda. *A Biographical Dictionary of the Celebrated Women of Every Age and Country*. London: Printed for B. Crosby and Co., etc., 1804.

Bevington, David M. "The Domineering Female in *1 Henry VI*." *Shakespeare Studies* 2 (1966): 51–58.

———. "Lyly's *Endymion* and *Midas*: The Catholic Question in England." *Comparative Drama* 32, no. 1 (Spring 1998): 26–46.

———. *The Wide and Universal Theater: Shakespeare in Performance Then and Now*. Chicago: University of Chicago Press, 2007.

*Biographium Fœmineum. The Female Worthies: or, Memoirs of the Most Illustrious Ladies, of all Ages and Nations*. London: S. Crowder and J. Payne, 1766.

Biondi, Sir Francis. *An History of the Civill Warres of England Between the two Houses of Lancaster and Yorke*. Englished by the Right Honourable Henry Earle of Monmouth, in two volumes. London: T. H. and I. D. for John Benson, 1641.

Black, J. B. *The Art of History: A Study of Four Great Historians of the Eighteenth Century*. New York: F. S. Crofts, 1926.

Blackstone, William. *Commentaries on the Law of England. Book IV: Public Wrongs*. With an introduction, notes, and textual apparatus by Ruth Paley. Oxford: Oxford University Press, 2016.

Blatcher, Marjorie. *The Court of King's Bench, 1450–1550: A Study in Self-Help*. London: The Athlone Press, 1978.

Bloom, Edward A., and Lillian D. Bloom, eds. *The Piozzi Letters: Correspondence of Hester Lynch Piozzi, 1784–1821 (formerly Mrs. Thrale)*. Vols. 2–3. Newark: University of Delaware Press, 1989, 2002.

Boas, F. S. "Edward Grimeston, Translator and Sergeant-at-Arms." *Modern Philology* 3, no. 4 (April 1906): 399–400.

Boase, T. S. R. "Illustrations of Shakespeare's Plays in the Seventeenth and Eighteenth Centuries." *Journal of the Warburg and Courtauld Institutes* 10 (1947): 83–108.

———. "Macklin and Bowyer." *Journal of the Warburg and Courtauld Institutes* 26, nos. 1–2 (1963): 148–77.

Boatright, Mody C. "Demonology in the Novels of Sir Walter Scott: A Study in Regionalism." *Studies in English* 14 (1934): 75–88.

Boccaccio, Giovanni. *Famous Women*. Edited and translated by Virginia Brown. Cambridge: Harvard University Press, 2001.

Boece, Hector. *The History of Scotland*. Translated by John Bellenden. Edinburgh: W. and C. Tait, 1821.

Boethius, Hector. *Scotorum Historiae a prima gentis origine*. Paris: Iodoci Badii, 1526.

Booth, Alison. *How to Make It as a Woman: Collective Biographical History from Victoria to the Present*. Chicago: University of Chicago Press, 2004.

Boulton, Richard. *Compleat History of Magick, Sorcery, and Witchcraft*. Vol. 1. London: E. Curll, 1715.

Bouteiller, Ernest de, and G. de Braux. *La Famille de Jeanne d'Arc. Documents inédits. Généalogie. Lettres de Jean Hordal et de Ch. du Lys. Publiées pour la première fois*. Paris: A. Claudin, 1878.

Boutruche, Robert. "The Devastation of Rural Areas During the Hundred Years War and the Agricultural Recovery of France." Translated by G. F. Martin. In *The Recovery of France in the Fifteenth Century*, edited by Peter S. Lewis, 23–59. New York: Harper and Row, 1972.

Bouzy, Olivier. "Essai d'itinéraire de Jeanne d'Arc." In *Jeanne d'Arc: Histoire et Dictionnaire*, edited by Philippe Contamine, Olivier Bouzy, and Xavier Hélary, 13–20. Paris: Éditions Robert Laffont, 2012.

———. "La Famille de Jeanne d'Arc, ascension sociale d'un lignage roturier du XIV$^e$ au XVI$^e$ siècle." In Guyon and Delavenne, *De Domremy . . . à Tokyo*, 33–42.

Bovet, Richard. *Pandaemonium, or, The devil's cloyster*. London: J. Walthot, 1641.

Bowdler, Henrietta. *The Family Shakespeare*. 4 vols. Bath: Richard Cruttwell, 1807.

Bowdler, Thomas. *The Family Shakespeare in Ten Volumes; in which nothing is added to the original text; but those words and expressions are omitted which cannot with propriety be read aloud in a family*. Vol. 1. London: Longman, Hurst, Rees, Orme, and Brown, 1818.

Boydell, John. *A Catalogue of the Pictures in the Shakspeare Gallery Pall-Mall*. London: Sold at the Place of Exhibition, 1789.

Branston, Allen R. *An Illustration of Shakespeare: 38 Engravings on Wood*. London: Vernor, Hood and Sharpe, 1809.

Brennan, Michael G., ed. *The Origins of the Grand Tour: The Travels of Robert Montagu, Lord Mandeville (1649–1654), William Hammond (1655–1658), Banaster Maynard (1660–1663)*. London: The Hakluyt Society, 2004.

Briand, Julien. "Foi, politique et information en Champagne au XV$^e$ siècle." *Revue Historique* 312, no. 653 (January 2010): 59–97.

*The British Heroine: or, an Abridgment of the Life and Adventures of Mrs. Christian Davies, commonly call'd Mother Ross*. London: n.p., 1742.

Brown, Michael. "French Alliance or English Peace? Scotland and the Last Phase of the Hundred Years War, 1415–53." In *The Fifteenth Century VII: Conflicts, Consequences and the Crown in the Late Middle Ages*, edited by Linda

Clark, 81–99. Woodbridge, U.K.: The Boydell Press, 2007.

Brownley, Martine Watson. "Sir Richard Baker's *Chronicle* and Later Seventeenth Century English Historiography." *Huntington Library Quarterly* 52, no. 45 (1989): 481–500.

Brun, Pierre-Marie. "Le Premier Monument à Jeanne d'Arc." *Dossiers d'archéologie* 34 (1979): 70–76.

*Brut, or The Chronicles of England*. Part 2. Edited by Friedrich W. D. Brie. London: Early English Text Society, 1908.

Buchanan, George. *Ane detectioun of the duinges of Marie Quene of Scottes thouchand the murder of hir husband, and hir conspiracie, adulterie, and pretensed marriage with the Erle Bothwell. . . . Translatit out of the Latine quhilke was written by G. B.* London: John Day, 1571.

———. *De Maria Scotorum Regina totáque eius contra Regem coniuratione. . . .* London: John Day, 1571.

———. *Historia Scotorum. The History of Scotland written in Latin by George Buchanan; faithfully rendered into English*. London: Printed by Edw. Jones, for Awnsham Churchil, 1690.

Buirette, Claude. *Histoire de la ville de Sainte-Ménehould et de ses environs*. Sainte-Ménehould: Chez Poigné-Darnauld, 1837.

Bullough, Geoffrey. *Narrative and Dramatic Sources of Shakespeare*. Vol. 3. London: Routledge and Kegan Paul; New York: Columbia University Press, 1966.

Burden, Emily Caroline Louise. "Pre-Victorian Prudery: *The Family Shakespeare* and the Birth of Bowdlerism." Master's thesis, University of Birmingham, 2006.

Burnim, Kalman A., and Philip H. Highfill, Jr. *John Bell, Patron of British Theatrical Portraiture: A Catalog of Theatrical Portraits in His Editions of Bell's Shakespeare and Bell's British Theatre*. Carbondale: Southern Illinois University Press, 1998.

Burstein, Miriam Elizabeth. *Narrating Women's History in Britain, 1770–1902*. Aldershot, U.K.: Ashgate, 2004.

Butterfield, Ardis. *The Familiar Enemy: Chaucer, Language, and Nation in the Hundred Years War*. Oxford: Oxford University Press, 2009.

*Byble in English*. London: Edward Whytchurch, 1540.

Caldwell, Ellen C. "The Hundred Years' War and National Identity." In *Inscribing the Hundred Years' War in French and English Cultures*, edited by Denise Baker, 237–65. Albany: SUNY Press, 2000.

*Calendar of State Papers, Foreign Series, of the Reign of Elizabeth 1572–1574*. Edited by Allan James Crosby. London: Longman and Co., 1876.

*Calendar of State Papers Relating to Scotland and Mary, Queen of Scots, 1547–1603*. Vols. 1–2, edited by Joseph Bain. Edinburgh: H.M. General Register House, 1898–1900.

*Calendar of the Manuscripts of the Marquess of Salisbury at Hatfield House Hertfordshire*. Part 1. London: Eyre & Spottiswoode, 1883.

Calmet, Augustin. *Histoire de Lorraine . . . depuis l'entrée de Jules César dans les Gaules, jusqu'à la cession de la Lorraine, arrivée en 1737 inclusivement*. Nancy: Veuve Leseure, 1757.

Calvin, John. *The Sermons of M. John Calvin upon the fifth booke of Moses called Deuteronomie faithfully gathered word for word as he preached them in open pulpet*. Translated out of French by Arthur Golding. London: Printed by Henry Middleton for George Bishop, 1583.

Campbell, Lily B. *Shakespeare's Histories: Mirrors of Elizabethan Policy*. San Marino, Calif.: The Huntington Library, 1947.

Campbell, Matthew, Jacqueline M. Labbe, and Sally Shuttleworth, eds. *Memory and Memorials, 1789–1914: Literary and Cultural Perspectives. London: Routledge, 2000.

Care, Henry. Female Pre-eminence, or, The dignity and excellency of that sex above the male an ingenious discourse / written originally in Latine by Henry Cornelius Agrippa . . . ; done into English with additional advantages by H. C. London: T. R. and M. D., 1670.

Carlson, C. Lennart. The First Magazine: A History of The Gentleman's Magazine. Brown University Studies 4 (1938). Reprint, Westport, Conn.: Greenwood, 1974.

Carré, Henri. "C'est Shakespeare qui a, le premier, rehabilité Jeanne d'Arc dans l'opinion anglaise." Figaro Littéraire, May 7, 1949, 3.

Carte, Thomas. A General History of England. Vol. 2. London: Printed for the Author, 1747–55.

Castor, Helen. Joan of Arc: A History. New York: HarperCollins, 2015.

Cave, Edward. "Introduction." Gentleman's Magazine 1 (1731): n.p.

Challet, Vincent, and Ian Forrest. "The Masses." In Government and Political Life and England and France, c.1300–c.1500, edited by Christopher Fletcher, Jean-Philippe Genet, and John Watts, 279–316. Cambridge: Cambridge University Press, 2015.

Champion, Louis. Jeanne d'Arc, écuyère. Paris: Berger-Levrault & Cie, 1901.

Champion, Pierre. Guillaume de Flavy, capitaine de Compiègne; contribution à l'histoire de Jeanne d'Arc et à l'étude de la vie militaire et privée au XV$^e$ siècle. Paris: H. Champion, 1906.

Chantelauze, F. R. Marie Stuart, son procès et son exécution, d'après le journal inédit de Bourgoing, son médecin. Paris: Plon, 1876.

Chastellain, Georges. Chronique. In Oeuvres de Georges Chastellain publiés par M. le Baron Kervyn de Lettenhove. Vol. 2, Chronique 1430–31, 1452–53. Brussels: F. Heussner, 1863.

Chatto, William Andrew. A Treatise on Wood Engraving, Historical and Practical. London: Charles Knight, 1839.

Cheny, C. R., ed. Handbook of Dates for Students of English History. London: Offices of the Royal Historical Society, 1970.

Chernaik, Warren. "Shakespeare as Co-Author: The Case of 1 Henry VI." Medieval and Renaissance Drama in England 27 (January 2014): 192–220.

Chevreux, Paul, and Léon Louis. Dictionnaire historique et statistique. Vol. 7 of Le Département des Vosges: description, histoire, statistique, edited by Léon Louis. Épinal: Imprimerie E. Busy, 1889.

Choudhury, Mita. The Wanton Jesuit and the Wayward Saint: A Tale of Sex, Religion and Politics in 18th-Century France. University Park: Pennsylvania State University Press, 2015.

Christine de Pizan. The Book of the City of Ladies. Translated by Earl Jeffrey Richards. New York: Persea Books, 1982.

———. "La Ditié de Jeanne D'Arc." Edited and translated by Angus J. Kennedy and Kenneth Varty. Part 1, Nottingham Medieval Studies 18 (1974): 29–55. Part 2, Nottingham Medieval Studies 19 (1975): 53–76.

Chronicle of Jean de Venette. Translated by Jean Birdsall. Edited, with an introduction and notes, by Richard A. Newhall. New York: Columbia University Press, 1953.

Chronique de la Pucelle, ou Chronique de Cousinot. Edited by Auguste Vallet de Viriville. Paris: Adolphe Delahays, 1859.

Clapham, David. A Treatise of the Nobilitie and Excellencie of Woman Kynde. London: Thomas Bertheletus, 1541.

Clark, Cheryl D. "A Call from the Wild: Woman's Inner Self in Records of Woman." Publications of the Mississippi Philological Association (January 2005): 26–35.

Clark, Eva Turner. *Hidden Allusions in Shakespeare's Plays: A Study of the Oxford Theory.* New York: William Farquhar Payson, 1931.

Clark, G. N. "Edward Grimeston, the Translator." *English Historical Review* 43, no. 172 (October 1928): 585–98.

Clauss, James J., and Sarah Iles Johnston, eds. *Medea: Essays on Medea in Myth, Literature, Philosophy and Art.* Princeton: Princeton University Press, 1997.

Clegg, Cyndia Susan. "Censorship." In Kewes, Archer, and Heal, *Oxford Handbook of Holinshed's Chronicles*, 43–60.

Clermont-Ferrand, Meredith. "Joan of Arc and the English Chroniclers: Monstrous Presence and Problematic Absence in *The Chronicle of London, The Chronicle of William of Worcester*, and *An English Chronicle, 1377–1461*." *Medieval Chronicle* 7 (2001): 151–65.

Cléro, Jean-Pierre. "Jeanne d'Arc dans *l'Histoire d'Angleterre* de Hume." In *Images de Jeanne d'Arc*, edited by Jean Maurice and Daniel Couty, 35–43. Paris: PUF, 2000.

Clode, Charles Mathew. *The Military Forces of the Crown: Their Administration and Government.* Vol. 1. London: John Murray, 1869.

*Close Rolls of the Reign of Henry III, Preserved in the Public Record Office.* Vol. 7: *A.D. 1251–1253.*. London: H.M. Stationery Office, 1927.

Cobbett, William. *The Parliamentary History of England.* Vol. 19. London: T. C. Hansard, 1814.

Coleridge, Samuel Taylor. *Marginalia.* Part 5, edited by H. J. Jackson and George Whalley. Vol. 12 of *Collected Works of Samuel Taylor Coleridge*, edited by H. J. Jackson. Princeton: Princeton University Press, 2000.

Colley, Linda. *Britons: Forging the Nation, 1707–1837.* New Haven, Conn.: Yale University Press, 1992.

Contamine, Philippe. "Le Barrois et la Lorraine dans la Guerre de Cent Ans." In Guyon and Delavenne, *De Domremy . . . à Tokyo*, 103–16.

———. "Jeanne d'Arc après Jeanne d'Arc (IV): Sous l'Ancien Régime (1456–1789): persistence d'une mémoire et d'un enjeu, naissance d'une historiographie savante." In *Jeanne d'Arc: Histoire et dictionnaire*, edited by Philippe Contamine, Olivier Bouzy, and Xavier Hélary, 396–441. Paris: Robert Laffont, 2012.

———. "Naissance d'une historiographie. Le Souvenir de Jeanne d'Arc, en France et hors de France, depuis le 'proces de son innocence' (1455–1456) jusqu'au debut du XVI$^e$ siècle." *Francia* 15 (1987): 233–56.

———. *War in the Middle Ages.* Translated by Michael Jones. Oxford: Basil Blackwell, 1984.

Contamine, Philippe, Olivier Bouzy, and Xavier Hélary, eds. *Jeanne d'Arc: Histoire et dictionnaire.* Paris: Robert Laffont, 2012.

Cormack, Peter. *Arts and Crafts Stained Glass.* New Haven, Conn.: Yale University Press, 2015.

Costelloe, Timothy M. "Fact and Fiction: Memory and Imagination in Hume's Approach to History and Literature." In *David Hume: Historical Thinker, Historical Writer*, edited by Mark G. Spencer, 181–99. University Park: Pennsylvania State Press, 2013.

Cotgrave, Randle. *A Dictionarie of the French and English Tongues.* London: Adam Islip, 1611.

Coulton, C. G., ed. *Life in the Middle Ages.* New York: Macmillan, [1910?]. https://sourcebooks.fordham.edu/source/nider-stjoan1.asp.

Coxe, Francis. *A Short Treatise declaringe the detestable wickednesse of magicall sciences, as Necromancie, Conjurations of Spirites, curiouse astrologie and such lyke.* London: John Alde, [1561].

Crane, Susan. *The Performance of Self: Ritual, Clothing, and Identity During the Hundred Years War*. Philadelphia: University of Pennsylvania Press, 2002.

*Critical Review; or Annals of Literature.* Unsigned review of *Joan of Arc, an Epic Poem*, by Robert Southey. 2nd ser., no. 16 (February 1796): 191–95.

*Critical Review; or Annals of Literature.* Unsigned review of *Joan of Arc, an Epic Poem*, by Robert Southey. 2nd ser., no. 17 (May 1796): 182–92.

*Critical Review; or, Annals of Literature.* Unsigned review of *Joan of Arc*, 2nd ed., by Robert Southey. N.s., 23 (1798): 196–200.

Crompton, Hugh. *The Glory of Women, or a Looking Glasse for Ladies*. London: Printed by T. H. for Francis Coles, 1652.

Cross, John C. "Victorious La Pucelle." A Favorite Song. Sung by Mrs. Clendening at the Theatre Royal, Covent Garden, in *Joan of Arc*. Written by J. C. Cross. Composed by William Reeve. London: Longman and Broderip, 1798.

Curnow, Maureen Cheney. "The *Livre de la cité des dames* of Christine de Pisan: A Critical Edition." Ph.D. diss., Vanderbilt University, 1975.

Curry, Anne. "English Armies in the Fifteenth Century." In *Arms, Armies and Fortifications in the Hundred Years War*, edited by Anne Curry and Michael Hughes, 39–68. Woodbridge, U.K.: Boydell Press, 1994.

———. *The Hundred Years War, AD 1337–1453*. London: Routledge, 2003.

———. *The Soldier in Later Medieval England*. Accessed May 17, 2018. http://www.medievalsoldier.org.

———. "Two Kingdoms, One King: The Treaty of Troyes (1420) and the Creation of a Double Monarchy of England and France." In *The Contending Kingdoms*, edited by Glenn Richardson, 23–41. Aldershot, U.K.: Ashgate, 2008.

Dack, Charles. *The Trial, Execution and Death of Mary Queen of Scots*. Northampton, U.K.: The Dryden Press, 1889.

Daniel, Gabriel. *Histoire de France, depuis l'établissement de la monarchie française dans les Gaules*. Vol. 2. Paris: J.-B. Delespine, 1713.

———. *The History of France: from the time the French Monarchy was Establish'd in Gaul, to the Death of Lewis the Fourteenth. Written originally in French by Father Daniel, of the Society of Jesus. And now Translated into English. In Five Volumes.* London: Printed for G. Strahan, 1726.

Darmesteter, James. "Jeanne d'Arc jugée par les Anglais." *Nouvelle Revue* 22, nos. 5–6 (1883): 883–916.

Darmesteter, Mary. "Joan of Arc in England." In *English Studies by James Darmesteter*, 1896. Reprint, Freeport, N.Y.: Books for Libraries Press, 1972.

Dasent, John Roche, ed. *Acts of the Privy Council of England*. Vol. 14, *1586–1587*. London: H.M. Stationery Office, 1897.

Dash, Irene. "*Henry VI* and the Art of Illustration." In *Henry VI: Critical Essays*, edited by Thomas A. Pendleton, 253–71. New York: Routledge, 2001.

Dauphant, Léonard. "'Fille de la frontière' ou 'vierge des marches de Lorraine.' Espace vécu et identité régionale de Jeanne d'Arc." In Guyon and Delavenne, *De Domremy . . . à Tokyo*, 117–26.

Debout, Henri. *La Bienheureuse Jeanne d'Arc, 1412–1431*. Paris: Maison de la Bonne Presse, 1905.

Defoe, Daniel. *Political History of the Devil, as well Ancient as Modern*. London: T. Warner, 1726.

De Haas, Elsa, and G. D. G. Hall, eds., *Early Registers of Writs*. Selden Society Publications 87. London: Bernard Quaritch, 1970.

De Quincey, Thomas. "Joan of Arc: In Reference to M. Michelet's *History of France*." *Tait's Edinburgh Magazine* 14 (1847): 184–90, 535–42.

DeVries, Dawn. "Calvin's Preaching." In *The Cambridge Companion to John Calvin*, edited by Donald K. McKim, 106–24. Cambridge: Cambridge University Press, 2004.

DeVries, Kelly. *Joan of Arc: A Military Leader*. Gloucestershire: Sutton Publishing, 1999.

Dew, Benjamin. "An Economic Turn? Commerce and Finance in the Historical Writing of Paul de Rapin Thoyras, William Guthrie and David Hume." In *Historical Writing in Britain, 1688–1830: Visions of History*, edited by Benjamin Dew and Fiona Price, 73–91. Basingstoke, U.K.: Palgrave Macmillan, 2014.

D'Ezio, Marianna. *Hester Thrale Lynch Piozzi: A Taste for Eccentricity*. Newcastle upon Tyne, U.K.: Cambridge Scholars Publishing, 2010.

Dickson, Lisa. "No Rainbow Without the Sun: Visibility and Embodiment in 1 Henry VI." *Modern Language Studies* 30 (2000): 137–56.

*Dictionnaire du Moyen Français (1300–1500)*, version 2015. ATILF-CNRS et Université de Lorraine. http://www.atilf.fr/dmf.

*A Discourse Touching the Pretended Match betwene the Duke of Norfolke and the Queene of Scottes*. London: Printed by John Day?, 1569?

Ditcham, Brian G. H. "'Mutton Guzzlers and Wine Bags': Foreign Soldiers and Native Reactions in Fifteenth-Century France." In *Power, Culture, and Religion in France, c.1350–1550*, edited by Christopher Allmand, 1–13. Woodbridge, U.K.: Boydell Press, 1989.

Djordjevic, Igor. *Holinshed's Nation: Ideals, Memory, and Practical Policy in the Chronicles*. Farnham, U.K.: Ashgate, 2010.

———. "W. P.: The Case for William Patten's Contribution to Holinshed's *Chronicles* (1587)." *Notes and Queries* 53, no. 1 (March 2006): 40–43.

Dobson, Michael. *The Making of the National Poet: Shakespeare, Adaptation and Authorship, 1660–1769*. Oxford: Clarendon Press, 1992.

Dobson, Michael, and Stanley Wells, eds. *The Oxford Companion to Shakespeare*. Oxford: Oxford University Press, 2001.

Dockray-Miller, Mary. *Motherhood and Mothering in Anglo-Saxon England*. New York: St. Martin's Press, 2000.

Dolan, Frances E. "Tracking the Petty Traitor Across Genres." In *Ballads and Broadsides in Britain, 1500–1800*, edited by Patricia Fumerton, Anita Guerrini, and Kris McAbee, 149–72. Farnham, U.K.: Ashgate, 2010.

Donagan, Barbara. *War in England, 1642–1649*. Oxford: Oxford University Press, 2008.

Doncoeur, Paul, and Yvonne Lanhers, eds. *La réhabilitation de Jeanne la Pucelle: L'enquête ordonnée par Charles VII en 1450 et le codicille de Guillaume Bouillé*. Paris: Librairie d'Argences, 1956.

Doran, Susan, and Paulina Kewes, eds. *Doubtful and Dangerous: The Question of Succession in Late Elizabethan England*. Manchester: Manchester University Press, 2014.

Downes, Stephanie. "Fashioning Christine de Pizan in Tudor Defences of Women." *Parergon* 23, no.1 (2006): 71–92.

Dronsart, Marie. "Jeanne d'Arc en Angleterre." *Correspondent* 128 (1891): 596–627.

Du Bellay de Langey, Guillaume. *Instructions sur le faict de la guerre*. Paris: Michel Vascosan, 1548.

Duffy, Eamon. *The Stripping of the Altars: Traditional Religion in England, 1400–1580*, 2nd ed. New Haven, Conn.: Yale University Press, 2005.

Dugaw, Dianne. *Warrior Women and Popular Balladry, 1650–1850*. Cambridge: Cambridge University Press, 1996.

Du Haillan, Bernard de Girard. *De l'Estat et succez des affaires de France*. Paris: Olivier de l'Huillier, 1571.

———. *L'Histoire générale des rois de France jusqu'à Charles VII inclusivement*. Paris: P. L'Huillier, 1576.

Dunand, Philippe-Hector. "La Légende anglaise de Jeanne d'Arc, de 1431 à 1903." In *Études critiques d'après les textes sur l'Histoire de Jeanne d'Arc*, 2nd ser., 13–95. Paris: Librairie Ch. Poussielgue, 1903.

Duparc, Pierre, ed. *Procès en nullité de la condamnation de Jeanne d'Arc*. 5 vols. Paris: C. Klincksieck, 1977–88.

Du Tillet, Jean. *Recueil des roys de France, leurs couronne et maison*. Paris: Jacques du Pays, 1580.

Edgar, Chad. "Felicia Hemans and the Shifting Field of Romanticism." In *Felicia Hemans: Reimagining Poetry in the Nineteenth Century*, edited by Nanora Sweet and Julie Melnyk, 125–34. Basingstoke, U.K.: Palgrave, 2001.

Eggert, Katherine. *Showing Like a Queen: Female Authority and Literary Experiment in Spenser, Shakespeare, and Milton*. Philadelphia: University of Pennsylvania Press, 2000.

Egnatius, Johannis Baptista. *De exemplis illustrium virorum Venete civitatis atque aliarum gentium*. Venice: Nicolaum Tridentinum, 1554.

Elliott, Dyan. *Proving Woman: Female Spirituality and Inquisitional Culture in the Late Middle Ages*. Princeton: Princeton University Press, 2004.

Espinosa, Ruben. *Masculinity and Marian Efficacy in Shakespeare's England*. Farnham, U.K.: Ashgate, 2011.

Evelyn, John. *The Diary of John Evelyn*. Edited by E. S. de Beer. Vol. 2. Oxford: Oxford University Press, 1955.

Fabyan, Robert. *The New Chronicles of England and France*. Edited by Henry Ellis. London: F. C. & J. Rivington, 1811.

Fenton, Geoffrey. *Certaine Tragicall Discourses written out of Frenche and Latin . . . no lesse profitable than pleasaunt*. London: Thomas Marshe, 1567.

Fenton, Kirsten A. *Gender, Nation and Conquest in the Works of William of Malmesbury*. Woodbridge, U.K.: Boydell Press, 2008.

Ferguson, Arthur B. *Clio Unbound: Perception of the Social and Cultural Past in Renaissance England*. Durham, N.C.: Duke University Press, 1979.

Ferguson, John. *English Diplomacy, 1422–1461*. Oxford: Clarendon Press, 1972.

Flower, John. *Joan of Arc: Icon of Modern Culture*. East Sussex: Helm Information, 2008.

Forbes, Thomas R. "A Jury of Matrons." *Medical History* 32, no. 1 (January 1988): 23–33.

Fraioli, Deborah A. *Joan of Arc and the Hundred Years War*. Westport, Conn.: Greenwood Press, 2005.

———. *Joan of Arc: The Early Debate*. Woodbridge, U.K.: Boydell Press, 2000.

Fraser, Antonia. *Mary Queen of Scots*. Reprint, London: Orion Books, 2009.

Fudge, Thomas. *The Trial of Jan Hus: Medieval Heresy and Criminal Procedure*. New York: Oxford University Press, 2013.

Fuller, Thomas. *The Holy State and the Profane State*. Cambridge: Printed by Roger Daniel for John Williams, 1642.

———. *Joseph's Partie-Colored Coat containing, a comment on part of the 11. chapter of the 1. epistle of S. Paul to the Corinthians: together with severall sermons. . . .* London: John Dawson, 1640.

———. *Thomas Fuller's The Holy State and the Profane State*. Edited by Maximilian Graff Walten. 2 vols. 1938. Reprint, New York: AMS Press, 1966.

Gaguin, Robert. *Compendium Roberti Gaguini super Francorum gestis*. Paris: Jean Petit, 1504.

Geddes, Duncan. "An Icon Betrayed: How the Bishop of Winchester Helped Joan of Arc to Her Death." *Hampshire Chronicle*, May 14, 2015. Accessed August 7, 2015. http://www.hampshire chronicle.co.uk/leisure/feature/129 47685.An_icon_betrayed__Behind _Joan_of_Arc_and_the_Bishop_of _Winchester/.

Genest, John. *Some Account of the English Stage from the Restoration in 1660 to 1830 in ten volumes*. Bath: H. E. Carrington, 1832.

Geoffrey of Monmouth. *The History of the Kings of Britain*. Edited and translated by Michael A. Faletra. Peterborough, ON: Broadview Editions, 2008.

Geritz, Albert J., and Amos Lee Laine. *John Rastell*. Boston: Twayne, 1983.

Gérold, Théodore, ed. *Le Manuscrit de Bayeux. Texte et musique d'un recueil de chansons du XV<sup>e</sup> siècle*. Strasbourg, 1921. Reprint, Genève: Minkoff Reprints, 1971.

*Gesta Stephani*. Edited and translated by K. R. Potter. Introduction and notes by R. H. J. C. Davis. Oxford: Clarendon Press, 1976.

Gibson, Marion, ed. *Witchcraft and Society in England and America, 1550–1750*. Ithaca: Cornell University Press, 2003.

Gilles de Roye. *Chronique*. In *Chroniques relatives à l'histoire de la Belgique sous la domination des ducs de Bourgogne*, edited by Joseph Kervyn de Lettenhove, 167–210. Brussels: F. Hayez, 1870.

Gillet, Pierre. *Sermaize et Jeanne d'Arc*. Chalons-sur-Marne: Journal de la Marne, 1959.

Girardot, Alain. "Entre France, Empire et Bourgogne." In *Histoire de Lorraine*, edited by Michel Parisse, 189–226. Toulouse: Edouard Privat, 1977.

Giry-Deloison, Charles. "France and England at Peace, 1475–1513." In *The Contending Kingdoms: France and England, 1420–1700*, edited by Glenn Richardson, 43–60. Aldershot, U.K.: Ashgate, 2008.

Given-Wilson, Chris. *Chronicles: The Writing of History in Medieval England*. London: Hambledon & London, 2004.

Godefroy, Frédéric. *Dictionnaire de l'ancienne langue française et de tous ses dialectes du 9e au 15e siècle*. Paris, 1881–95. https://archive.org/stream /dictionnairedela01godeuoft#page /n7/mode/2up.

Goldring, Elizabeth, Faith Eales, Elizabeth Clarke, and Jayne Elisabeth Archer, eds. *John Nichols's "The Progresses and Public Processions of Queen Elizabeth I": A New Edition of the Early Modern Sources*. Oxford: University Press, 2014.

Goldsmith, Oliver. *The History of England, from the Earliest Times to the Death of George II*. In *Collected Works of Oliver Goldsmith*, edited by Arthur Friedman, vol. 5. Oxford: Clarendon Press, 1966.

Goy-Blanquet, Dominique. "Shakespeare and Voltaire Set Fire to History." In *Joan of Arc, a Saint for All Reasons: Studies in Myth and Politics*, edited by Dominique Goy-Blanquet, 1–38. Aldershot, U.K.: Ashgate, 2003.

Grave, Geo. Ann. *Memoirs of Joan d'Arc, or Du Lys, Commonly Called the Maid of Orleans*. London: Longman, 1812.

Green, David. *The Hundred Years War: A People's History*. New Haven, Conn.: Yale University Press, 2014.

Greg, W. W. *Henslowe's Diary*. Part 1: Text. London: A. H. Bullen, 1904.

Grene, Nicholas. *Shakespeare's Serial History Plays*. Cambridge: Cambridge University Press, 2002.

Griffin, Margaret. *Regulating Religion and Morality in the King's Armies, 1639–1646*. Leiden: Brill, 2004.

Grimeston, Edward, ed. and trans. *A Generall Historie of France written* by John de Serres. . . . Translated out of French into English, by Edward Grimeston, Gentleman. London: George Eld, 1607.

Grummitt, David. *Henry VI*. London: Routledge, 2015.

Guest, Harriet. *Small Change: Women, Learning, Patriotism, 1750–1810*. Chicago: University of Chicago Press, 2000.

Gury, Jacques. "L'Historien et les mythes de Jeanne d'Arc des lumières au romantisme." In *Jeanne d'Arc: Une époque, un rayonnement*. Colloque d'Histoire Médiéval, Orléans, 1979, 267–75. Paris: Éditions du Centre National de la Recherche Scientifique, 1982.

Guthrie, William. *A General History of England: From the Invasion of the Romans Under Julius Cæsar to the Late Revolution In MDCLXXXIII*. . . . 3 vols. London: Printed for D. Browne by T. Waller, 1744.

———. *A General History of Scotland from the Earliest Accounts to the Present Time*. London: A. Hamilton, 1767.

———. *A New Geographical, Historical and Commercial Grammar and Present State of the Several Kingdoms of the World*. . . . London: J. Knox, 1770.

———. *A New Geographical, Historical and Commercial Grammar and Present State of the Several Kingdoms of the World: A new edition, improved and enlarged; the astronomical part by James Ferguson, FRS*. London: Printed for J. Knox, 1776.

Guthrie, William, John Gray et al. *A General History of the World*. Vol. 11. London: Newbery, Baldwin et al., 1764–67.

Gutierrez, Nancy A. "Gender and Value in *1 Henry VI*: The Role of Joan de Pucelle." *Theatre Journal* 42, no. 2 (May 1990): 183–93.

Guyon, Catherine, and Magali Delavenne, eds. *De Domremy . . . à Tokyo: Jeanne d'Arc et la Lorraine*. Nancy: Éditions Universitaires de Lorraine, 2013.

Haberling, Wilhelm. "Army Prostitution and Its Control: An Historical Study." In *Morals in Wartime*, edited by Victor Robinson, 3–90. New York: Publishers Foundation, 1943.

Hacker, Barton. "Women and Military Institutions in Early Modern Europe: A Reconnaissance." *Signs* 6, no. 4 (Summer 1981): 643–71.

Hackett, Helen. *Virgin Mother, Maiden Queen: Elizabeth I and the Cult of the Virgin Mary*. New York: St. Martin's Press, 1995.

Hale, Matthew. *Historia placitorum coronæ. The History of the Pleas of the Crown. . . . Now first published from his Lordship's Original Manuscript . . . by Sollom Emlyn*. Vol. 1. London: E. and R. Nutt and R. Gosling for F. Gyles, 1736.

Hall, Edward. *The Union of the Two Illustrious Famelies of Lancastre and York*. In *Hall's Chronicle Containing the History of England, during the Reign of Henry the Fourth . . .* , edited by Sir Henry Ellis. London: J. Johnson, 1809.

Hammelmann, Hanns. "Shakespeare's First Illustrators." Supplement, *Apollo Magazine* 88 (1968): 1–4.

Hamy, E.-T., ed. *Le Livre de la description des pays de Gilles de Bouvier, dit Berry, premier Roi d'Armes de Charles VII, Roi de France*. Paris: Leroux, 1908.

Hanawalt, Barbara A. "Golden Ages for the History of Medieval English Women." In *Women in Medieval History and Historiography*, vol. 1, edited by Susan Mosher Stuard, 1–24. Philadelphia: University of Pennsylvania Press, 1987.

———. "Women Before the Law: Females as Felons and Prey in Fourteenth-Century England." In *Women and the Criminal Law*, edited by D. Kelly Weisberg, vol. 1 of *Women and the Law: A Social Historical Perspective*, 165–95. Cambridge: Schenkman, 1982.

Hanawalt, Barbara A., and Susan Noakes. "Trial Transcript, Romance, Propaganda: Joan of Arc and the French Body Politic." *Modern Language Quarterly* 57, no. 4 (December 1996): 605-31.

Harashima, Takako. "The Narrative Functions of John Rastell's Printing: *The Pastyme of People* and Early Tudor 'Genealogical' Issues." *Journal of the Early Book Society for the Study of Manuscripts and Printing History* 11 (2008): 43-86.

Hardin, Richard F. "Chronicles and Mythmaking in Shakespeare's Joan of Arc." *Shakespeare Survey* 42 (1990): 25-35.

Harding, Sylvester, and Edward Harding. *Shakespeare Illustrated by an Assemblage of Portraits and Views.* London: S. Harding and E. Harding, 1793.

Harikae, Ryoko. "John Bellenden's *Chronicles of Scotland:* Translation and Circulation." Ph.D. thesis, St. Hilda's College, Oxford University, 2009.

Harriss, Gerald. *Shaping the Nation: England, 1360-1461.* Oxford: Clarendon Press, 2005.

Hay, Denys. *Polydore Vergil: Renaissance Historian and Man of Letters.* Oxford: Clarendon Press, 1952.

Hays, Mary. *Appeal to the Men of Great Britain in Behalf of Women.* Edited by Gina Luria Walker. New York: Garland, 1974.

———. *Female Biography, or, Memoirs of Illustrious and Celebrated Women, of All Ages and Countries, Alphabetically Arranged.* 6 vols. London: Richard Phillips, 1803.

———. "Memoirs of Mary Wollstonecraft." In *The Annual Necrology, for 1797-8,* 411-60. London: R. Phillips, 1800.

Heal, Felicity, and Harry Summerson. "The Genesis of the Two Editions." In Kewes, Archer, and Heal, *Oxford Handbook of Holinshed's Chronicles,* 3-20.

Heilig, Marc. "Les collections archéologiques du Musée de Toul." *Archeographe.* Last updated 2008. Accessed May 21, 2018. https://archeographe.net/node/190.

Heimann, Nora M. *Joan of Arc in French Art and Culture (1700-1855): From Satire to Sanctity.* Aldershot, U.K.: Ashgate, 2005.

Hemans, Felicia. *Felicia Hemans: Selected Poems, Prose, and Letters.* Edited by Gary Kelly. Peterborough, ON: Broadview Press, 2002.

———. *Records of Woman with Other Poems.* Edited by Paula R. Feldman. Lexington: University of Kentucky Press, 1999.

Henry, Archdeacon of Huntingdon. *Historia Anglorum: The History of the English People.* Edited and translated by Diana Greenway. Oxford: Clarendon Press, 1996.

Henzler, Christine Juliane. *Die Frauen Karls VII. und Ludwigs XI.: Rolle und Position der Königinnen und Mätressen am französischen Hof (1422-1483).* Beihefte zum Archiv für Kulturgeschicte 71. Cologne: Böhlau Verlag, 2012.

Herman, Peter C. "Rastell's Pastyme of People: Monarchy and the Law in Early Modern Historiography." *Journal of Medieval and Early Modern Studies* 30, no. 2 (2000): 275-308.

Heylyn, Peter. *Cosmographie, in four bookes.* . . . London: Henry Seile, 1652.

———. *Microcosmos. A little description of the great world.* Oxford: John Lichfield and William Turner, 1625.

———. *A Survey of the Estate of France.* . . . London: Printed by E. Cotes for Henry Seile, 1656.

Heywood, Thomas. *"Gynaikeion": or, Nine Bookes of Various History. Concerninge Women; Inscribed by ye names of ye Nine Muses.* London: Printed by Adam Islip, 1624. Facsimile of copy in Henry E. Huntington Library.

———. *The Life of Merlin . . . being a chronographicall history of all the kings, an memorable passages of this kingdome, from Brute to the reigne of our royall soveraigne King Charles.* London: J. Okes, 1641.

Hicks, Philip. *Neoclassical History and English Culture From Clarendon to Hume.* Basingstoke, U.K.: Macmillan, 1996.

———. "Women Worthies and Feminist Argument in Eighteenth-Century Britain." *Women's History Review* 24, no. 2 (2015): 174–90.

Highfill, Phillip H., Jr., Kalman A. Burnim, and Edward A. Langhans, *A Biographical Dictionary of Actors, Actresses, Musicians, Dancers, Managers, and Other Stage Personnel in London, 1660–1800.* Vol. 7. Carbondale: Southern Illinois University Press, 1982.

Hillman, Richard. "La Pucelle and the *Godons* in the *Mistère du Siège d'Orléans:* Civic Pageantry and Popular Tradition." In *Les Mystères: Studies in Genre, Text and Theatricality,* edited by Peter Happé and Wim Hüsken, 167–88. Ludus: Medieval and Early Renaissance Theatre and Drama 12. Amsterdam: Rodopi, 2012.

Hobbins, Daniel, trans. and introd. *The Trial of Joan of Arc.* Cambridge: Harvard University Press, 2005.

Hoenselaars, Ton. "La Jeanne d'Arc de Shakespeare et l'art du recyclage." In *Jeanne d'Arc entre les nations,* edited by Ton Hoenselaars and Jelle Koopmans, 17–32. Cahiers de recherches des instituts néerlandais de langue et de literature françaises [CRIN] 33. Amsterdam: Rodopi, 1998.

Hogan, Charles Beecher. *The London Stage, 1660–1800.* Part 5, *1776–1800.* Carbondale: Southern Illinois University Press, 1968.

Holinshed, Raphael. *Holinshed's Chronicles of England, Scotland, and Ireland.* Edited by Sir Henry Ellis. 6 vols. London: J. Johnson, 1807–8.

Holmes, P. J. "Mary Stewart in England." *Innes Review* 38, no. 38 (1987): 195–218.

Hopkins, Lisa. "Christopher Marlowe and the Succession to the English Crown." *Yearbook of English Studies* 38, nos. 1–2 (2008): 183–98.

Houghton, Walter E., Jr. *The Formation of Thomas Fuller's Holy and Profane States.* Harvard Studies in English XIX. Cambridge: Harvard University Press, 1938. Reprint, New York: Johnson Rept., 1968.

Howard, Jean E., and Phyllis Rackin, *Engendering a Nation: A Feminist Account of Shakespeare's English Histories.* London: Routledge, 1997.

Howell, James. *Epistolae Ho-Elianae. The Familiar Letters of James Howell, Historiographer Royal to Charles II.* Edited, annotated, and indexed by Joseph Jacobs. London: David Nutt, 1892.

Howell, William. *Medulla historiæ Anglicanæ.* London: Abel Swalle, 1679.

Hughes, Paul L., and James F. Larkin, eds. *Tudor Royal Proclamations.* Vol. 1, *The Early Tudors (1485–1553).* New Haven, Conn.: Yale University Press, 1964.

Hughes-Warrington, Marnie. "Writing on the Margins of the World: Hester Lynch Piozzi's *Retrospection* (1801) as Middlebrow Art?" *Journal of World History* 23, no. 4 (2013): 883–906.

Hume, David. *David Hume: Essays, Literary, Moral, and Political.* Edited with a foreword, notes, and glossary by Eugene F. Miller. Indianapolis: Liberty Classics, 1985.

———. *The History of England, from the Invasion of Julius Caesar to the Revolution in 1688.* London: A. Millar, 1762.

———. *The History of England, from the Invasion of Julius Caesar to the Revolution in 1688. Embellished with engravings on copper and wood, from original designs.* Vol. 3. London: J. Wallis, 1803.

———. *Philosophical Essays Concerning Human Understanding.* London: A. Millar, 1748.

Huston, Nancy. "The Matrix of War: Mothers and Heroes." *Poetics Today* 6, nos. 1–2 (1985): 153–70.

Hutchinson, Francis. *An Historical Essay Concerning Witchcraft.* . . . London: R. Knaplock, 1718.

Hutson, Lorna. "Fictive Acts: Thomas Nashe and the Mid-Tudor Legacy." In *The Oxford Handbook of Tudor Literature, 1485–1603*, edited by Mike Pincombe and Cathy Shrank, 718–32. Oxford: Oxford University Press, 2009.

*Illustrations of Shakespeare; comprised in two hundred and thirty vignette engravings by Thompson, from designs by John Thurston: adapted to all editions.* London: Sherwood, Gilbert, and Piper, 1826.

*Itinerarium peregrinorum et gesta regis Ricardi. Chronicles and Memorials of the Reign of Richard I.* Edited by William Stubbs. Vol. 1. London: Longman, Green, Longman, Roberts, and Green, 1864.

Jackson, Gabriele Bernhard. "Topical Ideology: Witches, Amazons, and Shakespeare's Joan of Arc." *English Literary Renaissance* 18, no. 1 (1988): 40–65.

Jameson, Anna Brownell. *Diary of an Ennuyée.* London: Henry Colburn, 1826.

Jerome, Saint. *Against Jovinianus.* In *A Select Library of Nicene and Post-Nicene Fathers of the Christian Church*, edited by Philip Schaff and Henry Wace, 2nd ser., vol. 6, 346–86. Oxford: James Parker and Company; New York: The Christian Literature Company, 1893.

"Joan of Arc Memorial in Winchester Cathedral." Appeal leaflet. Hampshire Archives and Local Studies, DC/E4/5/2/1.

Johnson, Samuel. *The Plays of William Shakespeare.* 8 vols. London: J. and R. Tonson, 1765.

Jouffroy, Jean. *Ad Pium Papam II, de Philippo Duce Burgundiae oratio.* In *Chroniques relatives à l'histoire de Belgique sous la domination des ducs de Bourgogne (texts Latins)*, edited by J.-M.-B.-C. Kervyn de Lettenhove, 117–206. Brussels: F. Hayez, 1876.

*Journal de Clément de Fauquembergue, greffier du Parlement de Paris, 1417–1435.* Edited by A. Tuetey and H. Lacaille. 3 vols. Paris: H. Laurens, 1903–15.

*Journal du siège d'Orléans 1428–29.* Edited by P. Charpentier and C. Cuissard. Orléans: H. Herluison, 1896.

Joyce, George. "Revelation." *The Catholic Encyclopedia.* Vol. 13. New York: Robert Appleton Company, 1912. http://www.newadvent.org/cathen/13001a.htm.

Kairoff, Claudia Thomas. *Anna Seward and the End of the Eighteenth Century.* Baltimore: Johns Hopkins University Press, 2012.

Keate, George. *The Poetical Works of George Keate.* Vol. 2. London: J. Dodsley, 1781.

Keen, Maurice. *England in the Later Middle Ages: A Political History.* 2nd ed. London: Routledge: 2003.

Kelley, Donald R., and David Harris Sacks, eds. *The Historical Imagination in Early Modern Britain: History, Rhetoric, and Fiction, 1500–1800.* Cambridge: Cambridge University Press, 1997.

Kelly, Gary. "Gender and Memory in Post-Revolutionary Women's Writing." In Campbell, Labbe, and Shuttleworth, *Memory and Memorials*, 119–31.

———. *Women, Writing, and Revolution, 1790–1827.* Oxford: Clarendon Press, 1993.

Kelly, John. "Joan of Arc, or the Maid of Orleans." *Gentleman's Magazine* 7 (May 1737): 287–88.

Kempe, William. *A Dutiful Invective, against the most haynous treasons of Ballard and Babington with other their adherents, latelie executed. . . . Newly compiled and set foorth, in English verses: for a New yeares gifte to all loyall English subjects.* London: Richard Jones, 1587.

Kennedy, Deborah. "Benevolent Historian: Helen Maria Williams and Her British Readers." In *Rebellious Hearts: British Women Writers and the French Revolution*, edited by Adriana Craciun and Kari E. Lokke, 317–36. Albany: SUNY Press, 2001.

———. *Helen Maria Williams and the Age of Revolution.* Lewisburg: Bucknell University Press, 2002.

Kenyon, John. *The Popish Plot.* New York: St. Martin's Press, 1972.

Kewes, Paulina. "History Plays and the Royal Succession." In Kewes, Archer, and Heal, *Oxford Handbook of Holinshed's Chronicles*, 493–510.

Kewes, Paulina, Ian Archer, and Felicity Heal, eds. *The Oxford Handbook of Holinshed's Chronicles.* Oxford: Oxford University Press, 2013.

Keymer, Thomas, and Peter Sabor. *Pamela in the Marketplace: Literary Controversy and Print Culture in Eighteenth-Century Britain and Ireland.* Cambridge: Cambridge University Press, 2005.

Keyser, Lester Joseph. "Joan of Arc in Nineteenth-Century English Literature." Ph.D. diss., Tulane University, 1970.

Kingsford, Charles. *Chronicles of London.* Oxford: Clarendon Press, 1905. Reprint, Totowa, N.J.: Rowman and Littlefield, 1977.

———. *English Historical Literature in the Fifteenth Century.* 1913. Reprint, New York: Burt Franklin, 1962.

Kipling, Rudyard. *Souvenirs of France.* London: Macmillan, 1933.

Kirk, Andrew. *The Mirror of Confusion: The Representation of French History in English Renaissance Drama.* New York: Garland Publishing, 1996.

Knox, John. *The First Blast of the Trumpet against the Monstrous Regiment of Women.* [Geneva: J. Poullain and A. Rebul], M.D.LVIII. [1558].

———. *History of the Reformation in Scotland.* Edited by William Croft Dickinson. Vol. 2. London: Thomas Nelson and Sons, 1949.

Kors, Alan Charles, and Edward Peters, eds. *Witchcraft in Europe, 400–1700: A Documentary History.* 2nd ed. Revised by Edward Peters. Philadelphia: University of Pennsylvania Press, 2001.

Kostick, Conor. "Women and the First Crusade: Prostitutes or Pilgrims?" In Meek and Lawless, *Victims or Viragos?*, 57–68.

Krumeich, Gerd. "La Date de la naissance de Jeanne d'Arc." In Guyon and Delavenne, *De Tokyo . . . à Domrémy*, 21–31.

———. *Jeanne d'Arc à travers l'histoire.* Translated by Josie Mély, Marie-Hélène Pateau, and Lisette Rosenfeld. Paris: Bibliothèque Albin Michel Histoire, 1993. Orig. pub. as *Jeanne d'Arc in der Geschichte.* Sigmaringen: Jan Thorbecke Verlag Gmbh, 1989.

Kucich, Greg. "Romanticism and the Re-Engendering of Historical Memory." In Campbell, Labbe, and Shuttleworth, *Memory and Memorials*, 15–29.

———. "Women's Historiography and the (dis)Embodiment of Law: Ann Yearsley, Mary Hays, Elizabeth Benger." *Wordsworth Circle* 3, no. 1 (Winter 2001): 3–6.

Kyffin, Maurice. *The Blessednes of Brytaine, or A Celebration of the Queenes Holyday.* London: John Windet, 1587.

Labanoff, Alexandre, ed. *Lettres, instructions et mémoires de Marie Stuart, reine d'Écosse. . . .* 7 vols. London: C. Dolman, 1844.

La Fontaine, Jean de. *Contes et nouvelles en vers.* Amsterdam: Henry Desbordes, 1685.

Laine, Amos Lee. "John Rastell and the Norman Conquest." In *The Rusted Haubert: Feudal Ideals of Order and Their Decline*, edited by Liam O. Purdon and Cindy L. Vitto, 299–308. Gainesville: University Press of Florida, 1994.

Laird, Karen. "Adapting the Saints: Romantic Hagiography in Felicia Hemans's *Records of Women.*" *Women's Writing* 20, no. 4 (2013): 496–517.

Lake, Peter. *How Shakespeare Put Politics on the Stage: Power and Succession in the History Plays.* New Haven, Conn.: Yale University Press, 2016.

Lamb, Charles, and Mary Anne Lamb. *The Letters of Charles and Mary Anne Lamb.* Edited by E. V. Lucas. Vol. 2. London: Methuen, 1905.

Lamond, John. *Joan of Arc and England.* London: Rider & Company, 1927.

Lanéry d'Arc, Pierre. *Le Livre d'or de Jeanne d'Arc: Bibliographie raisonnée et analytique des ouvrages relatifs à Jeanne d'Arc.* Paris: Librairie Techener, 1894.

Le Brusque, Georges. "Chronicling the Hundred Years War in Burgundy and France in the Fifteenth Century." In *Writing War: Medieval Literary Responses to Warfare*, edited by Corinne Saunders, Françoise Le Saux, and Neil Thomas, 77–92. Cambridge: D. S. Brewer, 2004.

Le Cacheux, Paul. *Actes de la Chancellerie d'Henri VI concernant la Normandie sous la domination anglaise (1422–35).* Vol. 2. Rouen: A. Lestringant; Paris: A. Picard fils et Cie, 1908.

Lefèvre-Pontalis, Germain. "Episodes de l'invasion anglaise: La guerre de partisans dans la Haute Normandie (1424–1429)." *Bibliothèque de l'École des chartes* 54 (1893): 475–521.

———. *La panique anglaise en mai 1429.* Paris: Emile Bouillon, 1894.

Leicester Cathedral. "Remembering World War I in Leicester Cathedral." http://www.storyofleicester.info/media/1444/leicester-cathedral-memorial-window.pdf.

———. *Saint Martin's Parish Magazine*, 1920. http://leicestercathedral.org/our-life-and-work/world-war-one/st-martins-parish-magazine-1920/.

Le Moyne, Pierre. *The Gallery of Heroick Women.* Written in French by Peter Le Moyne, of the Society of Jesus. Translated into English by the Marquesse of Winchester. London: Printed by R. Norton for Henry Seile, 1652.

Lenglet-Dufresnoy, Nicolas. *Histoire de Jeanne d'Arc dite la Pucelle d'Orléans. . . .* Paris: Coutellier, 1753–54.

Le Roux de Lincy, Antoine. *Recueil de chants historiques français depuis le XII$^e$ jusqu'au XVIII$^e$ siècle.* 1st ser. Vol. 1. Paris: Librairie de Charles Gosselin, 1841.

Leslie, John. *A Defence of the Honour of the Right Highe, Mightye and Noble Princesse Marie Quene of Scotlande and Dowager of France. . . .* Reims: J. Foigy, 1569.

Levin, Carole. "'Murder not then the fruit within my womb': Shakespeare's Joan, Foxe's Guernsey Martyr, and Women Pleading Pregnancy in Early Modern English History and Culture." *Quidditas* 20 (1999): 75–93.

Levin, Carole, and Christine Stewart-Nuñez, eds. *Scholars and Poets Talk About Queens.* New York: Palgrave Macmillan, 2015.

Levine, Nina S. *Women's Matters: Politics, Gender, and Nation in Shakespeare's Early History Plays.* Newark: University of Delaware Press, 1998.

Levy, F. J. *Tudor Historical Thought.* San Marino, Calif.: Huntingdon Library, 1967.

Liébaut, Achille. *La Mothe: Ses Sièges, sa destruction.* Nancy: Louis Kreis, 1896.

Lightbody, Charles. *The Judgements of Joan: A Study in Cultural History.* Cambridge: Harvard University Press, 1961.

Lightfoot, William. *The Complaint of England. . . .* London: John Wolfe, 1587.

Lingard, John. *The History of England, from the First Invasion by the Romans to the Accession of Henry VIII.* Vol. 3. London: J. Mawman, 1819.

*Literary Panorama and National Register.* Unsigned review of *Memoirs of Joan D'Arc, or Du Lys, Commonly Called the Maid of Orleans,* by Geo. Ann Grave. 13 (1813): 67–72.

Lloyd, Lodowick. *Certaine English Verses Presented Unto the Queenes most Excellent Majestie. . . .* London: Henrie Haslop, 1586.

Lockman, John. *A New History of England from Question and Answer.* 8th ed. London: T. Astley, 1752.

Lockwood, Thomas. "John Kelly's 'Lost' Play *The Fall of Bob* (1736)." *English Language Notes* 22, no. 1 (September 1984): 27–32.

Longnon, Auguste. "Les Limites de la France et l'étendue de la domination anglaise à l'époque de Jeanne d'Arc." *Revue des questions historiques* 18 (July–December 1875): 444–546.

Looser, Devoney. *British Women Writers and the Writing of History, 1670–1820.* Baltimore: Johns Hopkins University Press, 2000.

LoPrete, Kimberly A. "Gendering Viragos: Medieval Perceptions of Powerful Women." In Meek and Lawless, *Victims or Viragos?,* 17–38.

Lorenzi de Bradi, Michel. "Jeanne d'Arc dans la littérature anglaise. I. La 'Jeanne d'Arc' de Shakespeare." *Nouvelle Revue,* 4th ser., vol. 31 (October 1, 1917): 193–214.

———. "Jeanne d'Arc dans la littérature anglaise. II. Le Poème de Robert Southey." *Nouvelle Revue,* 4th ser., vol. 31 (October 15, 1917): 327–48.

Luce, Siméon. *Jeanne d'Arc à Domrémy: Recherches critiques sur les origines de la mission de la Pucelle.* 2nd ed. Paris: Librairie Hachette et Cie, 1887.

Lynch, Michael. "The Reassertion of Princely Power in Scotland." In *Princes and Princely Culture, 1450–1650,* edited by M. Gosman, A. Macdonald, and A. Vanderjagt, vol. 1, 198–238. Leiden: Brill, 2002.

Lyndsay, Sir David. *Sir David Lyndesay's Works.* Part 1, *The Monarchie and Other Poems,* edited by F. Hall. London: For the Early English Text Society by N. Trübner, 1865–67.

Lyons, John D. *Exemplum: The Rhetoric of Example in Early Modern France and Italy.* Princeton: Princeton University Press, 1989.

Macaulay, Catharine. *The History of England from the Accession of James I to That of the Brunswick Line.* 8 vols. London: J. Nouse [etc.], 1763–83.

Maccoll, Alan. "The Construction of England as a Protestant 'British' Nation in the Sixteenth Century." *Renaissance Studies* 18, no. 4 (2004): 582–608.

Macleod, John. *Dynasty: The Stuarts 1560–1807.* New York: St. Martin's Press, 2001.

Macleod, Malcolm. *Macleod's History of witches, etc. The majesty of darkness discovered.* London: J. Roach, 1793.

Maguire, Nancy Klein. "Factionary Politics: John Crowne's *Henry VI.*" In *Culture and Society in the Stuart Restoration,* edited by Gerald Maclean, 70–92. Cambridge: Cambridge University Press, 1995.

Maillard, Olivier. *Sermones de adventus, quadragesimales, dominicales, et de peccati.* Lyon: Geynardi, 1503.

*Malleus Maleficarum. Henricus Institoris, O.P. and Jacobus Sprenger, O.P.* Edited and translated by Christopher S. Mackay. 2 vols. Cambridge: Cambridge University Press, 2006.

Marcus, Leah. *Puzzling Shakespeare* Berkeley: University of California Press, 1988.

Margolis, Nadia. *Joan of Arc in History, Literature, and Film.* New York: Garland, 1990.

———. "Rewriting the Right: High Priests, Heroes and Hooligans in the Portrayal of Joan of Arc (1824–1945)." In *Joan of Arc, A Saint for All Reasons: Studies in Myth and Politics*, edited by Dominique Goy-Blanquet, 59–104. Aldershot, U.K.: Ashgate, 2003.

Marlowe, Christopher. *Edward the Second.* Edited by Mathew R. Martin. Peterborough, ON: Broadview Editions, 2010.

Marot, Pierre. *Neufchâteau en Lorraine au Moyen Age.* Nancy: Imprimeries A. Humblot et Cie, 1932.

Marsden, Jean. "Rewritten Women: Shakespearean Heroines in the Restoration." In *The Appropriation of Shakespeare: Post-Renaissance Reconstructions of the Works and the Myth*, edited by Jean I. Marsden, 43–56. New York: St. Martin's Press, 1991.

Martial de Paris. *Les poésies de Martial de Paris, dit d'Auvergne, procureur en Parliament.* Part 1. Paris: Antoine Urbain Coustelier, 1724.

Martin, Hervé. *Le Métier de predicateur à la fin du Moyen Age, 1350–1520.* Paris: Editions du Cerf, 1988.

Martin le Franc. *Le Champion des Dames.* Edited by Robert Deschaux. 5 vols. Paris: Honoré Champion, 1999.

Martyn, William. *The Historie and Lives of Twentie Kings of England.* London: W. Stansby for Henrie Fetherstone, 1615.

Mason, Roger. "Scotland." In Kewes, Archer, and Heal, *Oxford Handbook of Holinshed's Chronicles*, 647–62.

Matheson, Lister M. "Historical Prose." In *Middle English Prose: A Critical Guide to Major Authors and Genres*, edited by A. S. G. Edwards, 209–48. Rutgers: Rutgers University Press, 1984.

———. "Printer and Scribe: Caxton, the *Polychronicon*, and the *Brut.*" *Speculum* 60, no. 3 (July 1985): 593–614.

———. *The Prose Brut: The Development of a Middle English Chronicle.* Tempe, Ariz.: Medieval and Renaissance Texts and Studies 80, 1998.

Maurer, Helen E. *Margaret of Anjou: Queenship and Power in Late Medieval England.* Woodbridge, U.K.: Boydell Press, 2003.

McCabe, Richard A. "The Masks of Duessa: Spenser, Mary Queen of Scots, and James VI." *English Literary Renaissance* 17, no. 2 (Spring 1987): 224–42.

———. "The Poetics of Succession, 1587–1605: The Stuart Claim." In Doran and Kewes, *Doubtful and Dangerous*, 192–211.

McCullough, Peter. "Out of Egypt: Richard Fletcher's Sermon Before Elizabeth After the Execution of Mary Queen of Scots." In *Dissing Elizabeth: Negative Representations of Gloriana*, edited by Julia M. Walker, 118–49. Durham, N.C.; Duke University Press, 1998.

McElroy, Tricia A. "Genres." In Kewes, Archer, and Heal, *Oxford Handbook of Holinshed's Chronicles*, 267–83.

McGavran, James Holt, Jr. "Felicia Hemans's Feminist Poetry of the Mid 1820s." *Women's Writing* 21, no. 4 (2014): 540–58.

McIntosh-Varjabédian, Fiona. "Probability and Persuasion in 18th-Century and 19th-Century Historical Writing." In *Tropes for the Past: Hayden White and the History/Literature Debate*, edited by Kuisma Korhonen, 109–17. Amsterdam: Rodopi, 2006.

McLaren, A. N. *Political Culture in the Reign of Elizabeth I: Queen* and *Commonwealth 1558–1585.* Cambridge: Cambridge University Press, 2006.

McLaren, Mary-Rose. *The London Chronicles of the Fifteenth Century: A Revolution in English Writing.* Cambridge: D. S. Brewer, 2002.

McLaughlin, Megan. "The Woman Warrior: Gender, Warfare and Society in Medieval Europe." *Women's Studies* 17 (1990): 193–209.

McLeod, Glenda. *Virtue and Venom: Catalogs of Women from Antiquity to the Renaissance.* Ann Arbor: University of Michigan Press, 1991.

Meek, Christine, and Catherine Lawless, eds. *Victims or Viragos?* Studies on Medieval and Early Modern Women 4. Dublin: Four Courts Press, 2005.

Meek, Edward. "The Practice of English Diplomacy in France, 1461–71." In *The English Experience in France c.1450–1558: War, Diplomacy, and Cultural Change,* edited by David Grummitt, 63–94. Aldershot, U.K.: Ashgate, 2002.

Merchant, W. Moelwyn. *Shakespeare and the Artist.* London: Oxford University Press, 1959.

Michelet, Jules. *Histoire de France.* Tome cinquième. Paris: Librairie Classique et Élémentaire, 1841.

*Mirouer des femmes vertueuses.* Paris, 1547.

Mitchell, Rosemary. *Picturing the Past: English History in Text and Image, 1830–1870.* Oxford: Clarendon Press, 2000.

Monstrelet, Enguerrand de. *La Chronique d'Enguerrand de Monstrelet en deux livres avec pièces justicatives (1400–44).* Edited by L. Douët d'Arcq. 6 vols. Paris: 1857–62.

Montagu, Elizabeth. *An Essay on the Writings and Genius of Shakespear, compared with the Greek and French Dramatic Poets. With Some Remarks upon the Misrepresentations of Mons. De Voltaire.* London: J. Dodsley, 1769.

Montaiglon, Anatole de, ed. *Recueil des poésies françoise des XV$^e$ et XVI$^e$ siècles: morales, facétieuses, historiques.* Vol. 2. Paris: P. Jannet, 1855.

*Monthly Mirror.* Unsigned review of *Joan of Arc; an Epic Poem,* by Robert Southey. 1 (1795–96): 354–58.

*Monthly Review.* Unsigned review of *Joan of Arc,* 2nd ed., by Robert Southey. N.s., 28 (1799): 58–62.

*Monthly Review.* Unsigned review of *Memoirs of Joan D'Arc or Du Lys, Commonly Called the Maid of Orleans,* by Geo. Ann Grave. 71 (1813): 126–32.

*Monthly Review.* Unsigned review of *The History of the Public Revenue of the British Empire,* Part Third, by John Sinclair. 3 (September 1790): 1–13.

Mossner, Ernest Campbell. "An Apology for David Hume, Historian." *Publications of the Modern Language Association* 56, no. 3 (September 1941): 657–90.

Mottram, Stewart. *Empire and Nation in Early English Renaissance Literature.* Cambridge: D. S. Brewer, 2008.

*Le mystère du siège d'Orléans.* Edited by Gerald Gros. Paris: Librairie Générale Française, 2002.

Nashe, Thomas. *Pierce Penilesse His Supplication to the Divell.* Edited by Ronald B. McKerrow. Vol. 1 of *The Works of Thomas Nashe.* London: A. H. Bullen, 1904. Reprint, edited by F. P. Wilson. New York: Barnes & Noble, 1966.

Neill, Kerby. "Spenser's Acrasia and Mary Queen of Scots." *Publications of the Modern Language Association* 60, no. 3 (September 1945): 682–88.

Neville, C. J. "Gaol Delivery in the Border Counties, 1439–1549." *Northern History* 19 (1983): 45–60.

Newhall, Richard Ager. *Muster and Review: A Problem of English Military Administration, 1420–1440.* Cambridge: Harvard University Press, 1940.

Newman, C. N. "Joan of Arc in English Literature." *Sewanee Review* 34, no. 4 (October–December 1926): 431–39.

Newstead, Christopher. *An Apology for Women or, Womens defence. Pend by C. N. late of Albane Hall in Oxon.* London: Edward Griffin, 1620.

Nicolas, Sir Harris, ed. *Proceedings and Ordinances of the Privy Council of England.* 6 vols. London: The Commissioners on the Public Records of the Kingdom, 1834–37.

Nicolas, Nicholas H., and Edward Tyrrell, eds. *A Chronicle of London, from 1090 to 1483.* London: Longman, Rees, Orme, Brown, and Green, 1827.

Nider, Johannis. *Formicarium Ioannis Nyder.* Douai: Baltazaris Belleri, 1602.

Novack, Brenda E. *A Double-Edged Sword: Jehanne d'Arc and Claims to Divine Sanction in Acts of War.* Eugene, Ore.: Pickwick Publications, 2014.

Nussbaum, Felicity. *Rival Queens: Actresses, Performance, and the Eighteenth-Century British Theater.* Philadelphia: University of Pennsylvania Press, 2010.

O'Brien, Karen. "English Enlightenment Histories, 1750–c.1815." In *The Oxford History of Historical Writing*, vol. 3, *1400–1800*, edited by José Rabasa, Masayuki Sato, Edoardo Tortarolo, and Daniel Woolf, 518–35. Oxford: Oxford University Press, 2012.

———. *Narratives of Enlightenment: Cosmopolitan History from Voltaire to Gibbon.* Cambridge: Cambridge University Press, 1997.

O'Connell, Michael. "Mary Queen of Scots." In *The Spenser Encyclopedia*, edited by Albert Charles Hamilton, 452. Toronto: University of Toronto Press, 1990.

Okie, Laird. *Augustan Historical Writing: Histories of England in the English Enlightenment.* Lanham: University Press of America, 1991.

Oldham, James. "On Pleading the Belly: A History of the Jury of Matrons." *Criminal Justice History* 6 (1985): 1–64.

O'Quinn, Daniel J. "Introduction to Wallace's *The Ton*: 'the sport of a theatrical damnation.'" *British Women Playwrights around 1800.* http://www.etang.umontreal.ca/bwp1800/oquinn_ton_intro.html (site discontinued).

Orgelfinger, Gail. "Joan d'Arc." In Mary Hays, *Female Biography; or Memoirs of Illustrious and Celebrated Women, of All Ages and Countries* (1803), edited by Gina Luria Walker, 172–98. Chawton House Library Series: Women's Memoirs; Memoirs of Women Writers, vol. 8. London: Pickering & Chatto, 2014.

Osherow, Michele. *Biblical Women's Voices in Early Modern England.* Farnham, U.K.: Ashgate, 2009.

Otway-Ruthven, Jocelyn. *The King's Secretary and the Signet Office in the Fifteenth Century.* Cambridge: Cambridge University Press, 1939.

*The Oxford Dictionary of National Biography.* Edited by Sir David Cannadine. Oxford University Press. http://www.oxforddnb.com.

*The Oxford English Dictionary.* Oxford University Press. https://public.oed.com.

Paris, Gaston. "James Darmesteter." *Revue de Paris* 6 (November–December 1894): 483–512.

Paris, Louis. "Écosse: Documents inédits concernant l'histoire de ce pays." *Cabinet historique* 5, no. 2 (1859): 21–32.

Parry, Glyn. *The Arch-Conjurer of England: John Dee.* New Haven, Conn.: Yale University Press, 2013.

Pasquier, Etienne. *Les Oeuvres d'Estienne Pasquier contenant ses Recherches de la France.* Amsterdam: Compagnie des Libraires Associés, 1723.

Paulus Emilius Veronensis. *De rebus gestis Francorum.* Paris: Michel de Vascoson, 1548.

Peccatte, Patrick. "Les Figurations sensuelles et érotiques dans l'imagerie de Jeanne d'Arc." Déjà Vu. Last updated May 15, 2018. Accessed May 20, 2018. https://dejavu.hypotheses.org/2693.

Peele, George. *The Troublesome Reign of John, King of England: George Peele.* Edited by Charles R. Forker. The Revels Plays. Manchester: Manchester University Press 2011.

Pernoud, Régine. *Jeanne d'Arc par elle-même et par ses témoins.* Paris: Editions du Seuil, 1962.

———. *Joan of Arc: By Herself and Her Witnesses.* Translated by Edward Hyams. Lanham, Md.: Scarborough House, 1982.

———. *The Retrial of Joan of Arc: The Evidence for Her Vindication.* Translated by J. M. Cohen. San Francisco: Ignatius Press, 1955. Reprint, 2007.

Pernoud, Régine, and Marie-Dominique Clin. *Joan of Arc: Her Story.* Edited by Bonnie Wheeler. Revised and translated by Jeremy DuQuesnay Adams. New York: St. Martin's Press, 1998.

Perrin, Noel. *Dr. Bowdler's Legacy: A History of Expurgated Books in England and America.* New York: Atheneum, 1969.

Perroy, Edouard. *The Hundred Years War.* 1945. Reprint, Bloomington: Indiana University Press, 1959.

Peters, Christine. *Patterns of Piety: Women, Gender and Religion in Late Medieval and Reformation England.* Cambridge: Cambridge University Press, 2003.

Phillips, Mark Salber. *Society and Sentiment: Genres of Historical Writing in Britain, 1740–1820.* Princeton: Princeton University Press, 2000.

Pilkington, Mary. *A Mirror for the Female Sex: Historical Beauties for Young Ladies. . . .* London: Vernor and Hood, 1798.

Piozzi, Hester Thrale. *Retrospection: or A Review of the Most Striking and Important Events, Characters, Situations, and their Consequences, which the last eighteen hundred years have presented to the view of mankind.* Vol. 1. London: John Stockdale, 1801.

Plummer, Charles, and John Earle, eds. *Two of the Saxon Chronicles Parallel.* Vol. 1. Reprint, Oxford: Clarendon Press, 1965.

Pope, Alexander, ed. *The Works of Mr. William Shakespear. Volume the Fourth: Consisting of Historical Plays.* London: Jacob Tonson, 1723.

Pugh, R. B. *Imprisonment in Medieval England.* Cambridge: Cambridge University Press, 1968.

Purkiss, Diane. *The Witch in History: Early Modern and Twentieth-Century Interpretations.* London: Routledge, 1996.

Quicherat, Jules, ed. *Procès de condamnation et de réhabilitation de Jeanne d'Arc dite la pucelle,* 5 vols. Paris: Renouard, 1841–49.

———. "Récit des tribulations d'un religieux du diocèse de Sens pendant l'invasion Anglaise de 1358." *Bibliothèque de l'école des chartes* 18 (1857): 357–60.

———. "Supplément aux témoignages contemporains sur Jeanne d'Arc." *Révue historique* 19, no. 1 (1882): 60–83.

Rabbe, Félix. *Jeanne d'Arc en Angleterre.* Paris: Albert Savine, 1891.

Raknem, Ingvald. *Joan of Arc in History, Legend and Literature.* Oslo: Universitetsforlaget, 1971.

Rapin de Thoyras, Paul de. *Histoire d'Angleterre.* 2nd ed. The Hague: Alexandre de Rogissart, 1727.

———. *The History of England.* Written originally in French by M. Rapin de Thoyras. Translated into English by John Kelly. London: James Mitchell, 1732.

———. *The History of England.* Written in French by Mr. Rapin de Thoyras. Translated into English with additional notes by N. Tindal. 3rd ed. London: John and Paul Knapton, 1743.

Rapp, Maria. "Jeanne d'Arc in der englischen und amerikanischen Literatur." Tübingen, 1934.

Rastell, John. *"The Pastyme of People" and "A New Boke of Purgatory": With a facsimile of 'The Pastyme'; A Critical Edition*. Edited by Albert J. Geritz. The Renaissance Imagination 14. New York: Garland Publishing, 1985.

Rickard, P. *Britain in Medieval French Literature, 1100–1500*. Cambridge: Cambridge University Press, 1956.

Rissanen, Matti. *Studies in the Style and Narrative Technique of Edward Hall's Chronicle*. Helsinki: Société Néophilologique, 1973.

Ritchie, Fiona. "The Influence of the Female Audience on the Shakespeare Revival of 1736–1738: The Case of the Shakespeare Ladies Club." In *Shakespeare and the Eighteenth Century*, edited by Peter Sabor and Paul Yachnin, 57–69. Aldershot, U.K.: Ashgate, 2008.

———. *Women and Shakespeare in the Eighteenth Century*. Cambridge: Cambridge University Press, 2014.

Ritson, Joseph. *Remarks, Critical and Illustrative, on the Text and Notes of the Last Edition of Shakespeare*. London: J. Johnson, 1783.

Roberts, Gareth. "The Descendants of Circe: Witches and Renaissance Fictions." In *Witchcraft in Early Modern Europe*, edited by Jonathan Barry, Marianne Hester, and Gareth Roberts, 183–206. Cambridge: Cambridge University Press, 1996.

Roger of Hovedon. *Chronica magistri Rogeri de Hovedene*. Edited by William Stubbs. Vol. 2. London: Longmans, Green, 1869.

Rogers, Clifford J. "By Fire and Sword: *Bellum hostile* and 'Civilians' in the Hundred Years' War." In *Civilians in the Path of War*, edited by Mark Grimsley and Clifford J. Rogers, 33–78. Lincoln: University of Nebraska Press, 2002.

Rogers, Katharine M. *Feminism in Eighteenth-Century England*. Urbana: University of Illinois Press, 1982.

Rogers, Pat. "The Breeches Part." In *Sexuality in Eighteenth-Century Britain*, edited by Paul-Gabriel Boucé, 244–58. Manchester: Manchester University Press, 1982.

Rogers, Thomas. *An Historical Dialogue Touching Antichrist and Poperie....* London: John Windet, 1589.

Rollison, David. *A Commonwealth of the People: Popular Politics and England's Long Social Revolution, 1066–1649*. Cambridge: Cambridge University Press, 2010.

Rose, Herbert Jennings. "Circe." In *Oxford Classical Dictionary*, edited by M. Cary et al. Oxford: Clarendon Press, 1964.

———. "Penthesilea." In *Oxford Classical Dictionary*, edited by M. Cary et al. Oxford: Clarendon Press, 1964.

Rowe, J. H. "John Duke of Bedford and the Norman 'Brigands.'" *English Historical Review* 47, no. 188 (October 1932): 583–600.

Rowe, Nicholas, ed. *The Works of Mr. William Shakespear: in Nine Volumes. With his Life*. London: Jacob Tonson, 1714.

———. *The Works of Mr. William Shakespear: in six volumes. Adorn'd with cuts. Revis'd and corrected, with an account of the life and writings of the author*. London: Jacob Tonson, 1709.

Royan, Nicola. "National Martyrdom in Northern Humanist Historiography." *Forum for Modern Language Studies* 38, no. 4 (October 2002): 462–75.

———. "The Relationship Between the *Scotorum Historia* of Hector Boece and John Bellenden's *Chronicles of Scotland*." In *The Rose and the Thistle: Essays on the Culture of Late Medieval and Renaissance Scotland*, edited by Sally Mapstone and Juliette Wood, 136–57. East Linton, Scotland: Tuckwell Press 1998.

Ruggier, Jennifer. "Nation 'belongs exclusively to a particular, and historically recent, period': Counteracting Evidence from the Hundred Years War." *Emergence* 4 (Autumn 2012): 23–26. Proceedings of the 2012 GradNet annual conference, Southampton University, "Interactions and Identity," edited by Peter Girdwood and Sara Shawyer.

Sackville-West, Vita. *Saint Joan of Arc: Born, January 6th, 1412*. New York: The Literary Guild, 1936.

Sainte-Palaye, Jean-Baptiste de la Curne de. *Dictionnaire historique de l'ancien langage françois, ou glossaire de la langue françoise depuis son origine jusqu'au siècle de Louis XIV.* 10 vols. Edited by L. Favre and M. Pajot. Niort: L. Favre; Paris: H. Champion, 1875–92.

Saunders, Clare Broome. *Women Writers and Nineteenth-Century Medievalism.* New York: Palgrave Macmillan, 2009.

Saunders, Corrine. "Women and Warfare in Medieval English Writing." In *Writing War: Medieval Literary Responses to Warfare*, edited by Corrine Saunders, Françoise Le Saux, and Neil Thomas, 187–212. Cambridge: D. S. Brewer, 2004.

Sayles, G. O., ed. *Select Cases in the Court of King's Bench Under Richard II, Henry IV and Henry V.* Vol. 7. Seldon Society Publications 83. London: Bernard Quaritch, 1971.

Schmidt, Claudia M. "Hume as a Philosopher of History." In *David Hume: Historical Thinker, Historical Writer*, edited by Mark G. Spencer, 163–79. University Park: Pennsylvania State University Press, 2013.

Schwarz, Kathryn. *Tough Love: Amazon Encounters in the English Renaissance.* Durham, N.C.: Duke University Press, 2000.

Schwoerer, Lois G. *The Ingenious Mr. Henry Care, Restoration Publicist.* Baltimore: Johns Hopkins University Press, 2001.

Schwyzer, Philip. "Archipelagic History." In Kewes, Archer, and Heal, *Oxford Handbook of Holinshed's Chronicles*, 593–607.

Scot, Reginald. *Discovery of Witchcraft, proving the common opinions of witches contracting with divels, spirits, or familiars . . . to be but imaginary, erronious conceptions and novelties.* London: Printed by R. C., 1584.

Scott, Sir Walter. *The Heart of Midlothian.* Edited by David Hewitt and Alison Lumsden. Edinburgh: Edinburgh University Press, 2004.

———. *Letters on Demonology and Witchcraft.* London: John Murray, 1830.

———. *Tales of a Grandfather. Being Stories Taken from the History of France. Inscribed to Master John Lockhart.* 3 vols. Edinburgh: Robert Cadell, 1831.

Scott, W. S. *Jeanne d'Arc.* London: Harrup, 1974.

Scoufos, Alice-Lyle. *Shakespeare's Typological Satire: A Study of the Falstaff-Oldcastle Problem.* Athens: Ohio University Press, 1979.

Seary, Peter. "The Early Editors of Shakespeare and the Judgments of Johnson." In *Johnson After Two Hundred Years*, edited by Paul J. Korshin, 175–86. Philadelphia: University of Pennsylvania Press, 1986.

Serle, Thomas James. *Joan of Arc: The Maid of Orleans.* London: Henry Colburn, 1841.

Serres, Jean de. *Inventaire général de l'histoire de France.* Saint-Gervais: Pour les Heritiers d'Eustace Vignon, 1603.

Servais, Victor. *Annales historiques du Barrois de 1352 à 1411, ou histoire politique, civile, militaire et ecclésiastique du duché de Barre sous le règne de Robert, duc de Bar.* Vol. 1. Bar-le-Duc: Contant-Laguerre et Cie, 1865.

Sevin, Adolphe. *Jeanne d'Arc dans la littérature anglaise contemporaine.* Lille: Victor Ducolumbier, 1894.

Seward, Anna. "Lines Written by Anna Seward, After Reading Southey's 'Joan of Arc.'" *European Magazine* 33 (August 1797): 118.

Shakespeare, William. *As You Like It*. Edited by Juliet Dusinberre. The Arden Shakespeare. London: Thomson Learning, 2007.

———. *The Comedy of Errors*. Edited by R. A. Foakes. The Arden Shakespeare. London: Methuen, 1962.

———. *Henry VI, Part I*. Edited by Michael Taylor. The Oxford Shakespeare. Oxford: Oxford University Press, 2003.

———. *Henry VI, Parts I, II, and III*. Edited by Lawrence V. Ryan. New York: Signet Classics, 1986.

———. *King Henry VI Part I*. Edited by Edward Burns. The Arden Shakespeare, 3rd ser. London: Thomson Learning, 2000.

———. *King Henry VI Part Three*. Edited by John D. Cox and Eric Rasmussen. The Arden Shakespeare, 3rd ser. London: Thomson Learning, 2001.

———. *King John*. Edited by E. A. J. Honigmann. The Arden Shakespeare. London: Methuen, 1967.

———. *A Midsummer Night's Dream*. Edited by Harold F. Brooks. The Arden Shakespeare, 3rd ser. London: Methuen, 1979.

———. *The Plays of William Shakespeare: accurately printed from the text of the corrected copy left by the late George Steevens: with a series of engravings from original designs of Henry Fuseli . . . in nine volumes*. London: Printed for F. C. and J. Rivington et al., 1805.

———. *Richard III*. Edited by James R. Siemon. The Arden Shakespeare, 3rd ser. London: Methuen, 2009.

———. *The Winter's Tale*. Edited by John Pitcher. The Arden Shakespeare, 3rd ser. London: Methuen, 2010.

Sharpe, James. *Instruments of Darkness: Witchcraft in Early Modern England*. Philadelphia: University of Pennsylvania Press, 1997.

Shaw, George Bernard. *St. Joan: A Chronicle Play in Six Scenes and an Epilogue*. Edited by Dan H. Laurence. London: Penguin Books, 1957.

Sherbo, Arthur. *Samuel Johnson, Editor of Shakespeare, with an essay on "The Adventurer."* Illinois Studies in Language and Literature 42. Urbana: University of Illinois Press, 1956.

Shirley, John. *The Illustrious History of Women, or, a Compendium of the many Virtues that Adorn the Fair Sex*. London: John Harris, 1686.

Shirley, William. *Edward the Black Prince; or, the Battle of Poictiers: An Historical Tragedy*. 2nd ed. London: J. and R. Tonson, 1760.

Shrank, Cathy. *Writing the Nation in Reformation England, 1530–1580*. Oxford: Oxford University Press, 2004.

Siberry, Elizabeth. *Criticism of Crusading, 1095–1274*. Oxford: The Clarendon Press, 1985.

Siebert, Donald T. *The Moral Animus of David Hume*. Newark: University of Delaware Press, 1990.

Sillars, Stuart. *The Illustrated Shakespeare, 1709–1875*. Cambridge: Cambridge University Press, 2008.

Sims, Richard J. "Secondary Offenders? English Women and Crime c.1220–1348." In Meek and Lawless, *Victims or Viragos?*, 69–88.

Slater, Graeme. "Hume's Revisions of the *History of England*." *Studies in Bibliography* 45 (1992): 130–57.

Smith, Bonnie. "The Contribution of Women to Modern Historiography in Great Britain, France, and the United States, 1750–1940." *American Historical Review* 89, no. 3: 709–32.

Smith, G. C. Moore, ed. *Gabriel Harvey's Marginalia*. Stratford-upon-Avon: Shakespeare Head Press, 1913.

Smith, Orianne. *Romantic Women Writers, Revolution and Prophecy: Rebellious*

*Daughters, 1786–1826*. Cambridge: Cambridge University Press, 2013.

Somerset, Anne. *Elizabeth I*. New York: St. Martin's Press, 1991.

Sommer, H. Oskar, ed. *The Kalendar of Shepherdes*. London: Kegan Paul, Trench, Trübner, 1892.

Southey, Robert. *Joan of Arc, An Epic Poem*. Bristol: Bulgin and Rossner for Joseph Cottle, 1796.

———. *Joan of Arc, An Epic Poem*. 2nd ed. Bristol: N. Biggs, 1798.

———. *Joan of Arc: An Epic Poem*. 3rd ed. London: Longman, Hurst, Rees, and Orme, 1806.

———. *Robert Southey: Poetical Works, 1793–1810*. Vol. 1, *Joan of Arc*, edited by Lynda Pratt. London: Pickering & Chatto, 2004.

Sowernam, Ester. *Ester hath hang'd Haman: or An Answer to a lewd Pamphlet, entituled, The Arraignment of Women*. London: Nicholas Bourne, 1617.

Speed, John. *The Historie of Great Britaine under the Conquests of the Romans, Saxons, Danes and Normans . . . from Julius Cæsar, to our most gracious Souveraigne King James*. 2nd edition. London: By John Beale for George Humble, 1623.

Spongberg, Mary. *Writing Women's History Since the Renaissance*. Basingstoke, U.K.: Palgrave Macmillan, 2002.

Stabler, Jane. *Burke to Byron, Barbauld to Baillie, 1790–1830*. Basingstoke, U.K.: Palgrave, 2002.

Stafford, Pauline. "The Portrayal of Royal Women in England, Mid-Tenth to Mid-Twelfth Centuries." In *Medieval Queenship*, edited by John Carmi Parsons, 143–67. Stroud: Sutton Publishing, 1994.

*Statutes at Large, of England and of Great-Britain: From Magna Carta to the Union of the Kingdoms of Great Britain and Ireland*. Vol. 4, *From 1 Mary, A.D. 1553.–To 16 Charles I. A.D. 1640*. Edited by John Raithby. London: George Eyre & Andrew Strahan, 1811.

*Statutes of the Realm. Printed by the Command of His Majesty King George the Third, in Pursuance of an Address to the House of Commons of Great Britain*. Vol. 4, part 1. London: Dawsons of Pall Mall, 1817.

Steevens, George, ed. *The Plays of William Shakespeare in ten volumes*. Vol. 6. London: C. Bathurst et al., 1778.

Stern, Virginia F. "The Bibliotheca of Gabriel Harvey." *Renaissance Quarterly* 25, no. 1 (Spring 1972): 1–62.

Stevens, Anne. "Tales of Other Times: A Survey of British Historical Fiction, 1770–1812." *Cardiff Corvey: Reading the Romantic Text* 7 (December 2001). http://digitalscholarship.unlv.edu/english_fac_articles/23.

Stow, John. *The Annales, or generall chronicle of England, begun first by maister John Stow, and after him continued and augmented with matters forreyne, and domestique, aunciert and moderne, unto the ende of this present yeere 1614. By Edmond Howes*. London: T. Adams, 1615.

Strauss, Paul. "The Virgin Queen as Nurse of the Church: Manipulating an Image of Elizabeth I in Court Sermons." In Levin and Stewart-Nuñez, *Scholars and Poets Talk About Queens*, 185–202.

Strype, John. *Annals of the Reformation and the Establishment of Religion in the Church of England*. Vol. 3. London: Edward Symon, 1728.

Stuard, Susan Mosher. "Fashion's Captives: Women in French Historiography." In *Women in Medieval History and Historiography*, edited by Susan Mosher Stuard, 59–80. Philadelphia: University of Pennsylvania Press, 1987.

Sullivan, Alvin, ed. *British Literary Magazines*. Vols. 1–2. Westport, Conn.: Greenwood Press, 1983.

Sullivan, Karen. *The Interrogation of Joan of Arc*. Medieval Cultures 20. Minneapolis: University of Minnesota Press, 1999.

———. "La Justice magnanime des anglais: Les Biographes brittaniques de Jeanne d'Arc." In *Jeanne d'Arc entre les nations*, edited by Ton Hoenselaars and Jelle Koopmans, 115–32. Cahiers de recherches des instituts néerlandais de langue et de littérature françaises [CRIN] 33. Amsterdam: Rodopi, 1998.

Summerson, Henry. "Holinshed's Sources." The Holinshed Project. Last updated 2018. Accessed May 20, 2018. http://www.cems.ox.ac.uk/holinshed/chronicles.shtml#two2.

———. "Sources: 1587." In Kewes, Archer, and Heal, *Oxford Handbook of Holinshed's Chronicles*, 61–76.

Swetnam, Joseph. *The Arraignment of Lewd, idle, froward, and Unconstant Women. . . .* London: Printed by Edw. Allde for Thomas Archer, 1615.

Taylor, Craig. *Chivalry and the Ideals of Knighthood in France During the Hundred Years War*. Cambridge: Cambridge University Press, 2013.

———. *Joan of Arc: La Pucelle*. Manchester: Manchester University Press, 2006.

Taylor, Gary. *Reinventing Shakespeare: A Cultural History, from the Restoration to the Present*. New York: Weidenfeld & Nicolson, 1989.

Taylor, Gary, and Rory Loughnane. "The Canon and Chronology." In *The New Oxford Shakespeare: Authorship Companion*, edited by Gary Taylor and Gabriel Egan, 417–602. Oxford: Oxford University Press, 2017.

Taylor, Larissa Juliet. *Soldiers of Christ*. Oxford: Oxford University Press, 1992.

———. *The Virgin Warrior: The Life and Death of Joan of Arc*. New Haven, Conn.: Yale University Press, 2009.

Theobald, Lewis, ed. *The Works of Shakespeare*. Vol. 4. London: Printed for A. Bettesworth and C. Hitch, J. Tonson, F. Clay, W. Feales and R. Wellington, 1733.

Thickett, Dorothy. *Bibliographie des oeuvres d'Estienne Pasquier*. Geneva: Librairie E. Droz, 1956.

Thurston, Herbert. "Blessed Joan of Arc in English Opinion." *The Month* 113 (May 1909): 450–64.

———. "A Fleur de Lys and Two Godons." *The Month* 113 (May 1909): 416–20.

———. "Our Popular Devotions. V. The Angelus. 1. The Hail Mary." *The Month* 98 (November 1902): 483–99.

Tisset, Pierre, and Yvonne Lanhers, eds. *Procès de condamnation de Jeanne d'Arc*. 3 vols. Paris: C. Klincksieck, 1960–71.

Trimble, William R. "Early Tudor Historiography, 1485–1548." *Journal of the History of Ideas* 11 (January 1, 1950): 30–41.

Trussell, John. *A Continuation of the Collection of the History of England, beginning where Samuel Daniell esquire ended, with the raigne of Edward the Third, and ending where the honourable Vicount Saint Albones began, with the life of Henry the Seventh, being a compleat history of the beginning and end of the dissention betwixt the two houses of Yorke and Lancaster*. London: Printed by M. D. for Ephraim Dawson, 1636.

Turner, James Grantham. *One Flesh: Paradisal Marriage and Sexual Relations in the Age of Milton*. Oxford: Clarendon Press, 1987.

Tuve, Rosamund. *Allegorical Imagery: Some Mediaeval Books and Their Posterity*. Princeton: Princeton University Press, 1966.

Twain, Mark. *Personal Recollections of Joan of Arc*. New York: Harper & Brothers, 1896.

Utley, Francis. *The Crooked Rib: An Analytical Index to the Argument About Women in English and Scots Literature to the End of the Year 1568*.

Contributions in Languages and Literature 10. Columbus: The Ohio State University, 1944.

Vale, Malcolm. *The Ancient Enemy: England, France, and Europe from the Angevins to the Tudors, 1154–1558*. London: Hambledon Continuum, 2007.

———. *Charles VII*. Berkeley: University of California Press, 1974.

Vaughan, Richard. *John the Fearless: The Growth of Burgundian Power*. London: Longmans, 1966.

Velasco, Sherry Marie. *The Lieutenant Nun: Transgenderism, Lesbian Desire, and Catalina de Erauso*. Austin: University of Texas Press, 2000.

Vergil, Polydore. *The Anglica Historia A.D. 1485–1537*. Edited and translated by Denys Hay. London: Royal Historical Society, 1950.

———. *Three Books of Polydore Vergil's English History*. Edited by Sir Henry Ellis. London: Printed for the Camden Society, 1844.

Vernier, Richard. *The Flower of Chivalry: Bertrand du Guesclin and the Hundred Years War*. Woodbridge, U.K.: D. S. Brewer, 2007.

Vickers, Brian. "Incomplete Shakespeare: Or, Denying Coauthorship in *1 Henry VI*." *Shakespeare Quarterly* 58, no. 3 (Fall 2007): 311–52.

———. "*The Troublesome Raigne*, George Peele, and the Date of *King John*." In *Words That Count: Essays on Modern Authorship in Honor of MacDonald P. Jackson*, edited by Brian Boyd, 78–116. Newark: University of Delaware Press, 2004.

Virgil. *Eclogues, Georgics, Aeneid: Books 1–6*. Translated by H. Rushton Fairclough. Revised by G. P. Goold. Loeb Classical Library 63. Cambridge: Harvard University Press, 1916.

Wagner, John A. *Encyclopedia of the Hundred Years War*. Westport, Conn.: Greenwood Press, 2006.

Wahrman, Dror. *The Making of the Modern Self: Identity and Culture in Eighteenth-Century England*. New Haven, Conn.: Yale University Press, 2004.

———. "Percy's Prologue: From Gender Play to Gender Panic in Eighteenth Century England." *Past and Present* 159 (1998): 113–60.

Wainwright, F. T. "Æthelfled, Lady of the Mercians." In *New Readings on Women in Old English Literature*, edited by Helen Damico and Alexandra Hennessey Olsen, 44–55. Bloomington: Indiana University Press, 1990.

Walker, Gina Luria. *Mary Hays (1759–1843): The Growth of a Woman's Mind*. Aldershot, U.K.: Ashgate, 2006.

Walpole, Horace. *Horace Walpole's Correspondence with the Countess of Upper Ossory*. Vol. 32 of *The Yale Edition of Horace Walpole's Correspondence*, edited by W. S. Lewis and A. Dayle Wallace. New Haven, Conn.: Yale University Press, 1965.

———. *Horace Walpole's Correspondence with Hannah More*. Vol. 31 of *The Yale Edition of Horace Walpole's Correspondence*, edited by W. S. Lewis, Robert Smith, and Charles H. Bennet. New Haven, Conn.: Yale University Press, 1965.

Walsh, Brian. *Shakespeare, The Queen's Men and the Elizabethan Performance of History*. Cambridge: Cambridge University Press, 2009.

Warner, Marina. *Joan of Arc: The Image of Female Heroism*. Berkeley: University of California Press, 2000.

Warren, Nancy Bradley. "Joan of Arc, Margaret of Anjou, and Malory's Guenevere at the Stake." In *Political Allegory in Late Medieval England*, edited by Ann Astell, 138–60. Ithaca: Cornell University Press, 1999.

Warter, John Wood, ed. *Selections from the Letters of Robert Southey*. Vol. 1. London: Longman, Brown, Green, & Longmans, 1856.

Watts, William [attrib.]. *The Second Part of the Swedish Discipline: religious, civile,* and military. London: John Dawson, 1632.

Waugh, W. T. "Joan of Arc in English Sources of the Fifteenth Century." In *Historical Essays in Honour of James Tait*, edited by J. G. Edwards, V. H. Galbraith, and E. F. Jacob, 387–98. Manchester: Printed for the Subscribers, 1933.

Wavrin, Jehan de, Seigneur du Forestel. *Recueil des croniques et anchiennes istories de la Grant Bretaigne, à présent nommé Engleterre*. Edited by William Hardy. Vol. 3. London: Longman, 1879.

*Western News and Mercury*. "Joan of Arc." May 31, 1923, 4.

White, Arthur Franklin. *John Crowne: His Life and Dramatic Works*. Cleveland: Western Reserve University Press, 1922.

Wijsman, Hanno. "History in Transition: Enguerrand de Monstrelet's Chronique in Manuscript and Print (c.1450–c.1600)." In *The Book Triumphant: Print in Transition in the Sixteenth and Seventeenth Centuries*, edited by Malcolm Walsby and Graeme Kemp, 199–252. Leiden: Brill, 2011.

Wikander, Matthew. *The Play of Truth and State: Historical Drama from Shakespeare to Brecht*. Baltimore: Johns Hopkins University Press, 1986.

William of Malmesbury. *Gesta regum Anglorum: The History of the English Kings*. Edited and translated by R. A. B. Mynors. Completed by R. M. Thomson and M. Winterbottom. Vol. 1. Oxford: Clarendon Press, 1998.

———. *Historia novella: The Contemporary History*. Edited by Edmund King. Translated by K. R. Potter. Oxford: Clarendon Press, 1998.

William of Newburgh. *Historia rerum Anglicarum. Chronicles of the Reigns of Stephen, Henry II, and Richard I*. Edited by Richard Howlett. Vol. 1. London: Longman, 1884.

———. *The History of English Affairs*. Book 1, edited and translated by P. G. Walsh and M. J. Kennedy. Warminster: Aris & Phillips, 1988.

Williams, Helen Maria. *Letters from France: Containing Many New Anecdotes Relative to the French Revolution, and the Present State of French Manners*. 3rd ed. London: G. G. and J. Robinson, 1796.

———. *Letters Written in France, in the Summer 1790, to a Friend in England; Containing Various Anecdotes Relative to the French Revolution*. Edited by Neil Fraistat and Susan Lanser. Vol. 2. Peterborough, ON: Broadview Literary Texts, 2001.

*Winchester Cathedral: A Short History for Visitors*. 35th ed. Winchester: Warren and Son, n.d.

Winstanley, William [attrib.]. *Histories and Observations Domestick and Foreign, Or, a Miscellany of Historical Rareties*. London: William Whitwood, 1683.

———. *The New Help to Discourse, or, Wit, Mirth, and Jollity*, London: T. S., 1680.

———. *Poor Robin's Character of France. . . .* London: [s.n.], 1666.

Wiseman, Susan. *Conspiracy and Virtue: Women, Writing, and Politics in Seventeenth-Century England*. Oxford: Oxford University Press, 2006.

Wolffe, Bertram. *Henry VI*. New ed. New Haven, Conn.: Yale University Press, 2001.

Wolfson, Susan. "'Domestic Affections' and 'The Spear of Minerva': Felicia Hemans and the Dilemma of Gender." In *Re-Visioning Romanticism*, edited by Carol Shiner Wilson and Joel Haefner, 128–66. Philadelphia: University of Pennsylvania Press, 1994.

Wollstonecraft, Mary. *Vindication of the Rights of Man*. London: J. Johnson, 1790.

———. *A Vindication of the Rights of Woman*. London: Joseph Johnson, 1792.

Womersley, David. *Divinity and State*. Oxford: Oxford University Press, 2010.

Wood, Jeanne. "'Alphabetically Arranged': Mary Hays's *Female Biography* and the Biographical Dictionary." *Genre* 31, no. 2 (Summer 1998): 117–42.

Wood, Manley, ed. *The Plays of William Shakespeare with Notes of Various Commentators*. London: George Kearsley, 1806.

Woodbridge, Linda. *Women and the English Renaissance: Literature and the Nature of Womankind, 1540–1620*. Urbana: University of Illinois Press, 1984.

Woods, Gillian. *Shakespeare's Unreformed Fictions*. Oxford: Oxford University Press, 2013.

Woolf, D. R. "A Feminine Past? Gender, Genre, and Historical Knowledge in England, 1500–1800." *American Historical Review* 102, no. 3 (June 1997): 645–79.

———. "Genre into Artifact: the Decline of the English Chronicle in the Sixteenth Century." *Sixteenth Century Journal* 19, no. 3 (1988): 321–54.

———. *Reading History in Early Modern England*. Cambridge: Cambridge University Press, 2000.

Wright, Louis B. *Middle-Class Culture in Elizabethan England*. Ithaca: Cornell University Press, 1958.

Wright, Nicholas. *Knights and Peasants: The Hundred Years War in the French Countryside*. Woodbridge, U.K.: Boydell Press, 1998.

Wrightson, Keith. *English Society, 1580–1680*. New Brunswick, N.J.: Rutgers University Press, 1986.

Yates, Frances. *Astraea: The Imperial Theme in the Sixteenth Century* London: Routledge and Kegan Paul, 1975.

# INDEX

Locators in *italics* indicate illustrations.

"Act against Conjurations, Enchantments, and Witchcrafts" (1563), 66
"Act against Conjurations, Witchcrafts, Sorcery, and Enchantments" (1541/2), 66
*Acts of Stephen*, 44
"Act to Restrain Abuses of Players" (1606), 125
Ælfleda of Mercia, 11, 43–44, 78, 174n47
*Against Jovinianus* (Jerome), 74–75
Agrippa, Cornelius. *See also* Clapham, David
  on Joan of Arc, 78–79, 106, 110
  translations of, 77, 78, 80, 87, 105
  witchcraft and, 66
  on women, 77, 82, 87
Aikin, John, 133
Aikin, Lucy, 152
Aimond, Charles, 22
"Alderman" portrait, 119, 135
Alexander, William, 72, 120, 150, 152
Alexander the Great, 110
Amazons
  in David Clapham's translation, 78, 105
  gender and, 106
  in *Gynaikeion* (Heywood), 77, 83
  Hippolyta as, 106
  Joan of Arc and 75, 78–79, 83
  popularity of, 151
  Penthesilea as, 45, 63, 70
  portrayed in literature, 105–6
  Stuart, Mary (queen) as, 112
*Analytical Review*, 133, 142
*Anglica Historia* (Vergil), 55, 177n113
Anslay, Bryan, 75
*Anti-Jacobin Review*, 133, 134

*Apology for Women* (Newstead), 82
*Appeal to the Men of Great Britain in Behalf of Women* (Hays), 152
Armagnacs, 39, 171n122
articles of indictment, 39, 40, 64, 167n4
Aske, James, 106
Astell, Ann, 10, 182n44
Astell, Mary, 130
Astraea, 107–8
Aylmer, Bishop John, 76, 81–82

Babington conspiracy, 95, 96, 99, 101, 107, 109
Bailey, Michael, 64
Baker, Sir Richard, 48–50, 57, 166n40
Ballard, George, 151
Bandello, Matteo, 80
*Barrois mouvant*, 20
Bastard of Orléans. *See* Dunois, Jean (Bastard of Orléans)
Bate, Jonathan, 116
Baudricourt, Robert de
  on Joan of Arc (in Guthrie), 138–40
  relationship with Joan of Arc, 105, 136
  in Vaucouleurs 20, 24, 26
beatification and canonization of Joan of Arc, 8, 161, 162
Beaufort, Cardinal Henry (bishop of Winchester), 1, 5
Bedford, Duchess of (Anne), 31, 139
Bedford, Duke of (John of Lancaster)
  Betham, Matilda on, 153
  death of, 187n38
  de Serres, Jean on, 60
  on Joan of Arc, 5, 11, 32–34
  as regent, 17

Bellenden, John, 47–48
*Bell's Edition of Shakespeare's Plays*, 116, 119, 124
Bernau, Anke, 47, 51
Betham, Matilda, 151, 152, 153-4
*Biographical Dictionary of the Celebrated Woman of Every Age and Country* (Betham), 151, 152, 153
*Biographium Fæmineum* (anonymous), 93, 151–52
Blackstone, William, 46
blasphemy, 31, 32, 88, 171n135. See also *godon*; profanity
"Blessednes of Brytaine, The" (Kyffin), 101
Boccaccio, Giovanni, 75
Boece/Boethius, Hector, 46–48, 52, 56
Boisguillaume, Guillaume, 139, 172n155
Boisteau, Pierre, 80, 179n60
Boitard, François, 116–18, *117*
Booth, Alison, 76
Boulton, Richard, 68
Bovet, Richard, 67–68, 95
Bowdler, Henrietta and Thomas, 125–26
Bowyer, Robert, 145
Boydell, John, 123
Boydell Shakespeare Gallery, 116, 120, 123, 145
Branston, Allen R., 122, *123*
"Break thou in pieces!" (J. Thurston), 123, *124*
breeches. See also cross-dressing; petticoats
    "breeches roles," 119
    Joan of Arc and 3–4, 127, 137
    as metonymy, 131
    Wallace, Lady Eglantine and, 129
Briand, Julien, 23–24
Brown, John, 150
Brownley, Martine, 48–49
*Brut*, 42–43, 45–47, 174n41
Buchanan, George, 111–13
Burden, Emily, 125
Burgundy, Duke of (Philip), 30, 74
Burgundy/Burgundians, 19, 20, 22, 27, 168n49
Burstein, Miriam, 149
Butterfield, Ardis, 7

Cade, Jack, rebellion, 39
Cadiere, Marie-Catherine, 136–37
Caldwell, Ellen, 50–51
Calvary monument in Orléans, 36, 79, 135, 161, 173n2

canonization of Joan of Arc. see beatification and canonization of Joan of Arc
capture and imprisonment of Joan of Arc. See also condemnation trial; execution of Joan of Arc
    assault during, 4, 46, 175n60
    Duke of Burgundy and, 30
    escape from Beaurevoir, 16
    profanity and, 31–32
    reported in London chronicle, 39–40
Care, Henry, 78–79, 179n54
Carte, Thomas, 144–45, 154
Catherine (Katherine), Saint, 4, 19, 84
Catherine of Valois, 17, 41, 174n30
Catholicism. See also Protestantism; Virgin Mary
    Catholic Church as Circean, 101
    censorship and, 96–97
    influence of, 9
    Joan of Arc and, 3, 9, 10, 87
    Joan Puzel and, 96, 99, 101, 103, 124
    in *Letters on Demonology* (Scott), 73
    in *Malleus Maleficarum*, 65
    popery and, 67, 74, 114
    post-Reformation politics and, 51–52, 114
    witchcraft trials and, 65
Cave, Edward, 136
Caxton, William,
    in Bruges, 175n61
    and pregnancy claim, 38, 43, 46–47, 174n41
*Certaine Tragicall Discourses written out of Frenche and Latin* (Fenton), 80
Challet, Vincent, 15
*Champion des dames, Le* (le Franc), 75
Charles VII (king), 17, 33, 41, 176n83. See also Armagnacs
Chartier, Alain, 19
Chastellain, Georges, 42
*Chronicle of the Kings of England* (Baker), 48–49, 166n40
*Chronicles* (Holinshed)
    1587 edition of, 47, 57, 74, 91, 96
    and the Babington conspiracy, 109
    sources for, 48,
    Stuart, Mary (queen) and, 97, 104
chronicle writing/chronicle writers. See also *Chronicle of the Kings of England* (Baker); *Chronicles* (Holinshed);

*Cronycles of England* (Caxton);
*Famous Chronicle of Edward I* (Peele);
London chronicle; *New Chronicles of England* (Fabyan)
Chastellain, Georges, 42
de Venette, Jean, 21
    on Joan of Arc, 38, 62, 173n10
    McLaren, Mary-Rose on, 39
    Monstrelet, Enguerrand de, 15, 30
    tradition of, 48
    witchcraft trials and, 40
    on women in the military, 43–45, 128
Circe, 99–101, 105, 107
*City of Ladies* (Anslay), 75
Clapham, David, 77–79, 80, 87, 105
Clegg, Cyndia, 96
Cloelia/Clalia, 57, 61
clothing. *See* breeches; cross-dressing; petticoats
Coleridge, Samuel Taylor, 130, 189n117
*Collection of the History of England* (S. Daniel), 61
Colley, Linda, 149
*Commonplace Book* (Harvey), 37, 110
*Compendium de origine et gestis Francorum* (Gaguin), 53
*Complaint of England* (Lightfoot), 109
*Compleat History of Magick, Sorcery, and Witchcraft* (Boulton), 68
condemnation trial. *See also* execution of Joan of Arc; nullification trial
    articles of indictment and, 39–40, 64, 167n4
    defense of trial and execution, 32–33
    inquiry into, 13, 41, 176n83
    judges and gender roles, 93, 113
    "witch craze" mindset, 65
*Continuation* (Trussell), 61
*Cosmographie* (Heylyn), 70–71
Coxe, Francis, 12, 66–67
criminal law (English), 47. *See also* pregnancy plea
*Critical Review*, 132, 133
Crompton, Hugh, 79
*Cronycles of England* (Caxton), 38, 43, 46
cross-dressing, 87, 128, 149. *See also* breeches; petticoats
Crowne, John, 114
Curry, Anne, 20–21, 22

Cusquel, Pierre, 14

d'Alençon, duc (Jean), 37, 40, 49–50, 189n88
Daniel, Gabriel, 138–39, 188n50
Daniel, Samuel, 61
Darc, Jacques, 17, 21, 22, 169n61
d'Arc, Lanéry, 5
Darmesteter, James, 3, 5–7
d'Arras, Franquet, 144–45, 176n85
Dash, Irene, 123
d'Auvergne, Martial, 42
David (in Old Testament Judeo-Christian tradition), 110
Davies, Mrs. Christian ("Mother Ross"), 131
de Belleforest, François, 80, 179n60, 186n164
Deborah (in Old Testament Judeo-Christian tradition), 105–7
*Declamation* (Agrippa), 77
de Coutes, Louis, 28
de Erauso, Catalina, 92
d'Estivet, Jean, 14, 31
*De exemplis illustrium virorum* (Egnazio), 110
Defoe, Daniel, 68
de Foug, Geoffroy, 26
de Guernier, Louis, *118*, 119
de la Pierre, Isambart, 14
de l'Averdy, Clement, 155
de Macy, Aimon, 31
de Metz, Jean (de Nouillonpont), 24, 27, 31
demonism, 65
demonologies, 12, 63, 68, 74. *See also* superstition; witches/witchcraft
de Montgeron, Hugo, 21
*De mulieribus claris (On Famous Women)* (Boccaccio), 75
d'Epinal, Gerardin, 19, 168n47
de Quincey, Thomas, 10, 159
de Serres, Jean
    French history and, 177n121, 177n124
    on Joan of Arc, 60
    translation of, 57–58, 80, 82
de Venette, Jean, 21
de Vignolles, Etienne (la Hire), 27, 31
DeVries, Kelly, 28
*Dialog Concerning the Monarchie* (Lindsay), 71
*Diary of an Ennuyée* (Jameson), 158
Dickson, Lisa, 107

*Dictionnaire de l'ancien langue française* (Godefroy), 28
*Dictionnaire historique* (Sainte-Palaye), 32
*Discourse Touching the Pretended Match betwene the Duke of Norfolke and the Queene of Scottes, A*, 96
*Discovery of Witchcraft* (Scot), 67
*XVIII (Dix-huit) Histoires tragiques* (Boisteau and de Belleforest), 80
Dolan, Frances, 47
Domrémy (Lorraine), 16, 23
Downes, Stephanie, 75
Dronsart, Marie, 9
du Bellay de Langey, Guillaume, 8, 166n26, 177n119
du Haillan, Bernard de Girard, 105, 174n56
Dunand, P.-H., 9–10
Dunois, Jean (Bastard of Orléans), 15, 28–29, 150–51, 154
Durand, Laxart, 26
du Tillet, Jean, 57, 177n119, 177n125

Edgar, Chad, 159
*Edward, the Black Prince* (W. Shirley), 115
Egnazio, Giovanni, 110, 184n89
Elizabeth I (queen), 103, 108, 184n84. *See also* Mary Stuart (queen)
England/English
 Civil War, 86
 in France, 169n56, 171n108
 Hundred Years' War and, 16–17, 51
 Joan of Arc's letter to, 29
 politics and religion in, 51–52, 101, 114
 prophesy in, 104
 rebellion/uprising in, 39–40
"Enter Fiends" (Fuseli), 122–23, *123*
Esther (in Old Testament Judeo-Christian tradition), 63, 76, 77
Evelyn, John, 37
execution of Joan of Arc. *See also* capture and imprisonment of Joan of Arc; condemnation trial
 testimony of witnesses to, 14, 38
 letter defending, 11, 18
 miter worn to, 64
 pregnancy claim and, 38, 42–43
exemplum/exemplars, 74–77, 152, 183n66

Fabri, Jean, 15

Fabyan, Robert.
 on Joan of Arc, 53–54, 66–67, 79
 *New Chronicles of England*, 7, 51–53
 sources for, 54, 60
*Family Shakespeare in Ten Volumes* (H. Bowdler and T. Bowdler), 125–26
*Famous Chronicle of Edward I* (Peele), 98
female biography, 93, 149, 152
*Female Biography* (Hays), 129, 152–53
*Female Pre-eminence* (Care), 78–79
femininity, 44, 149, 151
femmes fortes/"female worthies," 63, 93, 150, 151
Fenton, Geoffrey, 80
*First Blast of the Trumpet* (Knox), 76, 81, 105
Fleming, Abraham, 109
Flower, John, 10
Folger Shakespeare Library, 127–28, *128*
Fontaine, Jean de la, 136
*Formicarium/Formicarius (The Ant Hill)* (Nider), 64
Forrest, Ian, 15
Foxe, John, 51
France/French. *See also* Armagnacs
 characterizations of, 181n12
 English and Burgundians in, 18–22
 *Geography of Joan of Arc's Youth* (map), 25
 Hall, Edward on, 51
Fuller, Thomas. *See also Holy State and the Profane State, The* (Fuller)
 Bovet, Richard and, 68
 on Joan of Arc, 3, 86–87, 94, 151, 180n85
 on negative exemplars/vice, 77, 86
 and "sentence"/judgement, 88, 90–91, 92
Fuseli, Henry, 122–23, *123*, 127

Gaguin, Robert, 53–54
Gardiner, William Nelson, 119, *120*
gender/gender roles
 Amazonian confusion of, 106
 aspirations and, 149
 chroniclers in the Middle Ages and, 128
 domestic duty and, 152–53
 in Elizabethan England, 95, 98
 in historiography, 130
 Joan of Arc and, 12, 151
 women in war and, 88–89, 174n43
*General History of England* (Carte), 144

*General History of England* (Guthrie), 7–8, 129, 137, 140
*General History of Scotland* (Guthrie), 140
*General History of the World* (Guthrie), 140
Genest, John, 115
*Gentleman's Magazine, The*, 3–4, 135–38
Gentleman, Francis, 124–25
Gerson, Jean, 75, 180n85
Girardot, Alain, 20
Given-Wilson, Chris, 39
Glasdale, Captain William, 28–29
Gloucester, Duke of (Humphrey), 33–34, 40
Godefroy, Frédéric, 28, 32
*godon*
  connotations of, 172n142
  Joan of Arc and use of, 30–32
  referring to English, 16, 35, 172n145, 172n147, 172n149
Goldsmith, Oliver, 129, 147
Grave, Geo. Ann, 154–55
Grimeston, Edward, 57–58
Guest, Harriet, 151
Gustavus Adolphus (king), 89-90
Guthrie, William
  *General History of England*, 7–8, 129, 137, 140
  *General History of Scotland*, 140
  *General History of the World*, 140
  on Joan of Arc, 138–41, 158
  *New Geographical, Historical, and Commercial Grammar*, 140
  sources for, 188n50
*Gynaikeion* (Heywood), 63, 77, 82–83, 150

Hackett, Helen, 103
Hall, Edward
  on behavior, 5, 61, 85
  on crossdressing, 129
  images/idols and, 79
  on Joan of Arc and manliness, 91, 113
  on Joan of Arc as a monster, 179n66
  on Joan of Arc's physical appearance, 67, 94–95
  sources for, 110
  *Union of the Two Noble and Illustre Famelies of Lancastre & Yorke*, 51, 79–81
Hamilton, William, 120–21, 122, 123
Hammelmann, Hanns, 116

Harding, Sylvester (*Shakespeare Illustrated*, 1790), 119
Harikae, Ryoko, 48
Harvey, Gabriel, 37, 110
Hay, Denis, 52, 56
Hays, Mary, 129, 152–53
*Heart of Midlothian, The* (Scott), 72
Hélary, Xavier, 16
Hemans, Felicia, 151, 155–58
Henry V (king)
  Treaty of Troyes and, 5, 16-17
  and Anglo-Burgundian rule, 22
  Duke of Bedford and, 33, 34
  political legacy of, 41
Henry VI (king)
  on Joan of Arc, 13, 32–33, 174n32
  reign of, 17, 41
*Henry VI, part 1* (Shakespeare). *See also* Joan Puzel in *1 Henry VI*; Shakespeare, William
  censorship of, 125–26
  criticism of, 124–25
  Crowne, John and, 114
  illustrations for, 116–123, *117*, *118*, *121*, *122*, *123*, *124*
  Joan of Arc name in, 181n1
  revival of, 115
  sources for, 96
  Talbot, John in, 99–100, 104, 109–10
*Henry VI, The First Part* (Crowne), 114
Henry VII (king), 41, 51, 56, 113, 174n30
Henry VIII (king), 51, 177n113
Henry of Huntingdon, 44
heresy, 15, 64, 66, 167n4, 178n13
Heylyn, Peter, 69–72
Heywood, Thomas
  *Gynaikeion*, 63, 77, 82–83, 150
  on Joan of Arc, 74, 83–86, 93
  *Life of Merlin*, 12, 74, 85, 86, 150
  on viragos, 5, 12, 83, 85
Hippolyta, 106
*Histoire de France* (G. Daniel), 138–39
*Histoire de France* (Michelet), 10
*Histoire de Jeanne d'Arc dite la Pucelle d'Orléans* (Lenglet-Dufresnoy), 154
*Historia Scotorum* (Buchanan), 112–13
*Historical Essay Concerning Witchcraft* (Hutchinson), 68–69
*Historical Rarities* (Winstanley), 92

INDEX | 225

*Historie and Lives of Twentie Kings of England* (Martyn), 37
*Historie of Great Britaine* (Speed), 37
historiography
    European Renaissance historiography, 51–52
    female historiography, 130, 150
    Joan of Arc and, 129, 134, 155
*History of England* (Goldsmith), 129, 147
*History of England* (Hume), 12, 121–22, 141, 144
*History of England* (Macaulay), 130
*History of Witches* (Macleod), 72
*History of Women* (Alexander), 72, 150
Holinshed, Raphael. *See also Chronicles* (Holinshed)
    Heywood, Thomas and, 84, 85
    on Joan of Arc, 47, 85, 94, 103
    sources for, 48, 105
    Stuart, Mary (queen) and, 97, 111, 112, 113
    Vergil, Polydore and 61, 91
*Holy State and the Profane State, The* (Fuller)
    alternative sentence in 88–90
    Bovet, Richard and, 68
    illustration for, 69
    Joan of Arc in, 7, 11, 87, 90–91
    negative exmplars/vice in, 77, 86
Howell, James, 36
Howell, William, 147
Hughes-Warrington, Marnie, 148
Hume, David
    *History of England*, 12, 121–22, 141, 144
    influence of 153–54
    on Joan of Arc, 141–46
    "On Miracles," 143
    popularity of, 145
    sources and methodology for, 137, 148
    "Of Superstition and Enthusiasm," 141–42
    Williams, Helen Maria on, 135
Hundred Years' War, 16–17, 40–41, 51
Huston, Nancy, 45
Hutchinson, Francis, 68–69

*Illustrious History of Women* (J. Shirley), 93
images/idols, 79–80, 90, 102–3
imposter, Joan of Arc as, 8, 37, 40, 140–41, 177n119, 180n83
Innocent VIII (pope), 65

*Inventaire général de l'histoire de France* (de Serres), 57–58

Jameson, Anna Brownell, 158
Jeannette. *See* Joan of Arc
Jehanne. *See* Joan of Arc
Jerome, Saint, 74–75
Joan de Pucil. *See* Joan of Arc
Joanna (Joan), Queen of Naples, 67–68
Joan of Arc. *See also* capture and imprisonment of Joan of Arc; condemnation trial; execution of Joan of Arc; Joan Puzel in *1 Henry VI*; nullification trial; sexuality; viragos; witches/witchcraft
    age of/birth of, 17, 168n32, 168n33, 185n105
    attitude toward English, 16, 20–21, 30, 35
    banner and sword, 148–49
    on Burgundians, 19, 170n100
    Catholicism and, 3, 9, 10, 87
    clothing and, 3–4, 137, 180n85
    courage of, 110, 132
    de Erauso, Catalina and, 92
    diction of, 18–19, 126
    epithets of, 28, 29, 30, 62, 91
    journeys of, 22–27
    "Letter to the English," 27, 29
    motherhood metaphor and, 108
    as an object of fear, 14–15
    in Orléans, 27–28
    profanity/blasphemies and, 31, 171n135
    prophesy and, 15, 32, 143, 149, 189n88
    Protestant attitude toward, 9, 80, 103
    revelations/voices and, 17, 18–19, 101, 180n73
    as saint, 161–62, 164
    sexual assault of, 175n60
    spirituality of, 15, 33, 39, 87, 182n44
    Stuart, Mary (queen) and, 96
    trial testimony of, 84, 167n31, 169n53, 170n100, 179n63
*Joan of Arc* (Southey), 4, 6, 131–32
"Joan of Arc and the Furies" (Hamilton), 120–21, 122, 123
"Joan of Arc Declaring Her Mission" (Opie), 145, *146*
Joan of Arc in art. *See individual works*

Joan of Arc in literature. *See individual authors and titles*
"Joan of Arc in Prison" (J. Thurston), 146–47, *146*
"Joan of Arc in Rheims" (Hemans), 156
*Joan of Arc; or, The Maid of Orleans* (Cross and Reeve), 131–32
Joan Puzel in *1 Henry VI*. See also *1Henry VI* (Shakespeare); Joan of Arc; Shakespeare, William
   as Amazonian, 105
   Baddeley, Sophia as, 119–20, *121*
   Catholicism and, 96, 99, 101, 103, 124
   characterizations of, 94–95, 181n1
   Circe and, 99
   courage of, 110–12, 134
   promiscuity and, 47, 104–5
   prophesy and, 104
   as saint, 91, 103
   speech and, 107–9, 112, 115
   Stuart, Ann as, 119–20, *121*
   Stuart, Mary (queen) and, 97, 104–5, 113, 182n30
   Talbot, John on, 109–10
   Virgin Mary and, 68, 102–4
   witches/witchcraft and, 85, 100, 183n65
Johnson, Samuel, 126, 186n160
Jouffroy, Jean (Bishop of Arras), 30
*Journal du siège d'Orléans*, 28–29
"Joyfull New-yeares Guift, A" (Kempe), 100
Judith (in Old Testament Judeo-Christian tradition), 57, 63, 71, 77, 106

Keate, George, 115
Kelly, Gary, 155–56
Kelly, John, 136–37
Kempe, William, 100, 107
Kipling, Rudyard, 161
Knox, John
   *First Blast of the Trumpet*, 76, 81, 105
   on Mary Stuart (queen), 103, 112, 113
   on women leaders/rulers, 98, 106–7
Krumeich, Gerd, 10
Kucich, Greg, 130
Kyffin, Maurice, 101

Laine, Amos Lee, 52
Laird, Karen, 156

Lamb, Charles, 124
Lamond, John, 10
Lanéry d'Arc, Pierre, 5, 7–8
laundresses in military life, 88–89, 181n97
Leicester Cathedral (memorial window), 162, *162*, *163*, 164
Lemaistre, Husson, 25–26
Lenglet-Dufresnoy, Nicolas, 154
*Letters from France* (Williams), 129, 134–35
*Letters on Demonology* (Sir Walter Scott), 12, 72–73
Levine, Nina, 95, 99
Levy, F. J., 58
*Life of Merlin* (Heywood), 12, 74, 85, 86, 150
Lightbody, Charles Wayland, 9
Lightfoot, William, 109
Lindsay, Sir David, 71–72
Lingard, John, 9, 181n100
*Livre de la cité des dames, Le* (de Pizan), 75
Lloyd, Lodowick, 99
Lockman, John, 141, 147
London chronicle, 3, 38–40
Looser, Devoney, 147
Lorraine, Duke of (Charles), 20
Luxembourg, Count of (John), 31
Lynch, Michael, 107-108
Lyons, John D., 74

Macaulay, Catharine, 130
Mackay, Christopher, 65
Macleod, John, 96
Macleod, Malcolm, 72
Maid, The/ Maid of Orléans, The. *See* Joan of Arc
*Malleus Maleficarum*, or *The Hammer of Witches*, 65
Manchon, Guillaume, 4, 175n60
Marcus, Leah, 95, 106
Margaret, Saint, 18, 19
Margaret of Anjou (queen), 41, 43, 59, 60, 61, 83, 98
Margolis, Nadia, 159
Marlowe, Christopher, 98-99, 182n33
Marsden, Jean, 119
Martin le Franc, 75
Martin, Hervé, 23
Martyn, William, 37, 40

INDEX | 227

Mary Stuart (queen)
    Circe and, 99–100, *101*
    compared to Joan of Arc/Joan Puzel, 12, 95–97, 104–5, 182n30
    courage of, 111–12
    imprisonment, trial, execution of, 108–9, 113–14, 182n30
    portrayed in literature, 97–98
    speech and, 107
    witches/witchcraft and, 96, 103–4
Massieu, Jean, 4, 14, 31
Matheson, Lister, 42
Maud (empress), 11, 43–44, 174n4
McCullough, Peter, 108
McGavran, James, 158
McIntosh-Varjabédian, Fiona, 142
McLaren, Mary-Rose, 39–40, 167n3, 173n22
McLaughlin, Megan, 45
Meek, Edward, 41
*Memoirs of Celebrated Female Characters* (Pilkington), 152
*Memoirs of Several Ladies of Great Britain* (Ballard), 151
mendicant friars, 23, 24
Michelet, Jules, 10, 159–60
*Microcosmos* (Heylyn), 70
Miget, Pierre, 15
*Miseries of Civil War* (Crowne), 114
Mitchell, Rosemary, 147
Monstrelet, Enguerrand de, 15, 30
Montagu, Elizabeth, 147
Montagu, Robert (Lord Mandeville), 37
*Monthly Mirror*, 133
*Monthly Review*, 130, 133, 155
"Mother Ross," 131
motherhood metaphor, 108

Nashe, Thomas, 110, 117
Neufchâteau, 24–26, 170n100, 170n102
*New Chronicles of England* (Fabyan), 7, 51–53
*New Geographical, Historical, and Commercial Grammar* (Guthrie), 140
*New Help to Discourse, The* (Winstanley), 92
*New History of England* (Lockman), 141
Newstead, Christopher, 82
Nider, Johannes, 64, 178n4
*Novelle* (Bandello), 80
nullification trial, 40–42, 166n21, 176n83.
    *See also* condemnation trial; trial testimonies

Opie, John, 145, *146*
O'Quinn, Daniel J., 129
Orléans, 28–29, 36–37, 171n110
Orléans, Duke of (Charles) 28
Osherow, Michele, 107

*Pandaemonium, or, The devil's cloyster* (Bovet), 67–68
Paris, Gaston, 6
Pasquerel, Jean, 29–30
Pasquier, Etienne, 4, 136, 137, 144
*Pastyme of People* (Rastell), 8, 54–55
Patten, William, 96–97
Peele, George, 98
Penthesilea, 45, 70–71
Perroy, Edouard, 38–39
*Personal Recollections of Joan of Arc* (Twain), 171n105, 186n7
petticoats, 130–31, 188n47. *See also* breeches, cross-dressing
Pilkington, Mary, 152
*pillard*, 28
Piozzi, Hester Thrale, 129, 147–49, 154, 155
Pius II (pope), 42
Pizan, Christine de, 15, 75–76, 108
*Play of King John, The* (Keate), 115
"pleading the belly." *See* pregnancy plea
*Political History of the Devil* (Defoe), 68
*Poor Robin's Character of France* (Winstanley), 91
Pope, Alexander, 125
popery, 67, 74, 114
Poulengy, Bertrand de, 24, 26, 27
Pragmatic Sanctions of 1438, 41
pregnancy plea, 42–43, 46–47, 174n41, 175n70
profanity, 30, 32, 171n135, 171n136, 171n140.
    *See also godon*
propaganda, 23, 34, 107–8, 161
prophesy/prophetic voice, 15, 32, 104, 143, 149, 189n88
Protestantism, 51, 67, 79, 96, 114. *See also* Catholicism; religion
"Pucelle de Dieu." *See* Joan of Arc
*Pucelle d'Orleans, La* (Gardiner), 119, *120*

*Pucelle d'Orleans, La* (Voltaire), 131, 133
Pucelle, La. *See* Joan of Arc
Puckering, John, 97
Purkiss, Diane, 66

querelle des femmes/"woman question," 63, 76, 81–82, 130
Quicherat, Jules-Jacques, 30, 32, 190n124

Rabbe, Félix, 9
Raknem, Ingvald, 10
Ramberg, J. H., 119–20, *121*
Randolph, Thomas, 111–12
Rastell, John, 8, 54–55, 177n108, 177n110
rebellion, political/religious, 39, 40
*Recherches de la France, Les* (Pasquier), 4
*Records of Women* (Hemans), 155
religion. *See also* Catholicism; Protestantism
   historiography and, 51
   Hume, David on, 141, 144
   influence on opinion, 8–9
   Joan of Arc and, 15, 33, 39, 87, 182n44
   Protestant anxieties and, 103
   Reformation-era influences and, 51
   Stuart, Mary (queen) and, 96, 103
*Retrospection* (Piozzi), 129, 147-149
*ribaud*, 28
Rissanen, Matti, 52
Ritson, Joseph, 116
Roberts, Gareth, 101
Roberts, James, 119, *121*
Rogers, Clifford J., 22
Rogers, Thomas, 102
Romée, Isabelle (Vouthon), 17, 22, 41
Rowe, Nicholas, 117, *117*, 118
Royan, Nicola, 48, 51, 52

Sainte-Palaye, Jean-Baptiste de la Curne de, 32
*Saint Joan* (Shaw), 164
Salisbury, Earl of, 33, 34, 173n159
Sancta Joanna de Arc (statue of), 1, 2, 161, 165n1
*Scotorum Historiae/History of Scotland* (Boece), 47
Scot, Reginald, 67
Scott, Sir Walter, 10, 12, 72–74
Scott, W. S., 6
Seward, Anna, 134
sexuality
   cross-dressing and, 128
   Joan of Arc as virgin, 172n155, 175n64
   pregnancy myth in *Brut*, 42–43
   speech and, 107
   viragos and, 45

Shakespeare Ladies Club, 115
Shakespeare, William, 98–99, 106, 124, 183n70.
   See also *Henry VI*, part 1 (Shakespeare); Joan Puzel in *1 Henry VI*
shamefastness, 81
Sharpe, Jack, rebellion, 39, 40
Shaw, George Bernard, 164
Shirley, John, 93
Shirley, William, 115
*Short Treatise declaring the detestable wickednesse of magicall sciences* (Coxe), 12, 66
Sims, Richard J., 47
Slater, Graeme, 144
Smith, Anker, 120
Smith, Bonnie, 150
Southey, Robert
   criticism of *Joan of Arc*, 132–34, 187n22
   *Joan of Arc*, 6, 130–32, 156-57
speech, 115–16
Speed, John
   influence of, 154
   on Joan of Arc, 58–61, 85, 86
   and the magnanimity of the English, 66, 91, 134
   on Margaret of Anjou (queen), 41
   and narrative of English history, 37
   sources for, 8, 11, 57, 177n125
Stafford, Pauline, 45
Steevens, George, 116, 124, 185n124
St. Martin of Tours Church. *See* Leicester Cathedral (memorial window)
Stow, John, 179n67
Stuard, Susan Mosher, 141
Sullivan, Karen, 6
superstition, 13, 73, 90, 141–42. *See also* witches/witchcraft
*Survey of the Estate of France* (Heylyn), 70
Swetnam, Joseph, 76

*Tait's Edinburgh Magazine*, 159
*Tales of a Grandfather* (Scott), 74
Taylor, Craig, 42
Taylor, Larissa, 27
"Then Take My Soul" (Branston), 122, *123*
Theobald, Lewis, 125–26
Thurston, Herbert, 8–9
Thurston, John, 123, *124*, 146–47, *146*
*Times, The* (London), 129, 131, 132

INDEX | 229

Ton, The (Wallace), 129
Treatise of the Nobilitie and Excellence of Woman Kynde, The (1542), 77–78
Treaty of Troyes, 17, 167n27, 169n51
trial. see condemnation trial; nullification trial
trial transcripts, 18, 126, 190n124
"Triumph of Trophes in Saphic verse of Jubiles" (Lloyd), 99
Troublesome Reign and Lamentable Death of Edward the Second (Marlowe), 98
Troublesome Reign of John, King of England (Peele), 98
"trull," 106, 116, 124–25
Trussell, John, 61–62
Tuve, Rosamund, 98
Twain, Mark, 27, 171n105, 186n7

Union of the Two Noble and Illustre Famelies of Lancastre & Yorke (Hall), 51, 80–81

Vale, Malcolm, 6–7, 37, 166n21
Vaucouleurs, 16, 19–20, 24, 26
Vergil, Polydore,
    Anglica Historia (Vergil), 55, 177n113
    Hall, Edward and, 110
    on Joan of Arc, 55–57, 91
    Speed, John and, 60–61
    the Tudors and, 52, 177n113
Verneuil, battle of, 21, 24, 27, 34, 48
"Victorious Joan Pucell," 132
viragos
    Classical examples of, 75
    definition, 173n4
    downgrading, 151–52
    English viragos in Thomas Heywood's writing, 83
    Joan of Arc as, 5, 37, 110
    Mary Stuart (queen) as, 111, 184n91
    Old Testament, 76–77
    sexuality and, 45
virginity, 67, 172n155, 175n64
Virgin Mary. See also Catholicism
    Elizabeth I (queen) and, 103, 184n84
    Joan of Arc and, 101, 182n44
    in "Joan of Arc in Rheims," 156
    Joan Puzel and, 103–4
    theology of, 102
Voltaire, 131, 133

Walker, Gina Luria, 153
Wallace, Lady Eglantine, 129
Walpole, Horace, 128, 129, 130
War of the Roses, 38, 41
Warner, Marina, 7
Warren, Charles Turner, 121, 122
Warren, Nancy Bradley, 46
Waugh, W. T., 38
Whall, Christopher, 162, 164, 190n3
whores, 29, 105, 136, 174n56
Wikander, Matthew, 114
William of Malmesbury, 44–45
William of Newburgh, 44
Williams, Helen Maria, 129, 130, 134–35
Winchester memorial, 3, 164
Winstanley, William, 91–92
Wiseman, Susan, 74, 76
witches/witchcraft. See also Circe; demonologies
    articles of indictment and, 64, 167n4
    Cadiere, Marie-Catherine and, 136–37
    demonologies and, 68
    Joan of Arc and, 4–5, 34, 72, 94, 120
    Joan Puzel and, 85, 100, 183n65
    physical ugliness/deformities and, 67–68
    Scott, Sir Walter on, 72–73
    Stuart, Mary (queen) and, 96
    witchcraft trials, 40, 65–66
    women warriors and, 45
Wolfson, Susan, 158–59
Wollstonecraft, Mary, 131, 152, 187n14
"woman question." See querelle des femmes/"woman question"
women warriors, 41, 43, 45, 128, 149. See also Ælfleda of Mercia; Amazons; Maud (empress)
Womersley, David, 51, 102
Wood, Jeanne, 149
Woolf, D. R., 48
Wright, Nicholas, 22–23

Yates, Frances, 107
Yolande d'Aragon, 27

www.ingramcontent.com/pod-product-compliance
Lightning Source LLC
Chambersburg PA
CBHW021942290426
44108CB00012B/936